FRENCH CLASSICS MADE EASY

FRENCH CLASSICS MADE EASY

RICHARD GRAUSMAN

WORKMAN PUBLISHING ✦ NEW YORK

Library of Congress Cataloging-in-Publication Data
is available.

ISBN 978-0-7611-5854-7 (pb)
ISBN 978-0-7611-6551-4 (hc)

Originally published as *At Home with the French Classics,* now revised and updated.

Cover design: Jean-Marc Troadec
Cover photo: Michael Paul/StockFood Munich
Interior design: Lisa Hollander
Illustrations: Alan Witschonke based on illustrations by Donna Ruff

Workman books are available at special discounts when purchased in bulk for premiums and sales promotions as well as for fund-raising or educational use. Special editions or book excerpts also can be created to specification. For details, contact the Special Sales Director at the address below, or send an e-mail to specialmarkets@workman.com.

Workman Publishing Company, Inc.
225 Varick Street
New York, NY 10014-4381
www.workman.com

First printing April 2011
Printed in the United States of America
10 9 8 7 6 5 4 3 2 1

To Susan, Jennifer, and Deborah,
the three loves of my life.

and

To all the C-CAP graduates . . .
whose achievements have given
my life greater meaning.

ACKNOWLEDGMENTS

There are many people to thank for the creation of this book and for its new life, so I start by offering thanks to Peter Workman for his steadfast support over the years.

In the beginning, there were my loving and nurturing parents, Elizabeth and Roland Grausman, who urged me to find a profession that I would work hard at and enjoy. My passion for cooking was sparked when, while working in the import business, a friend offered me his place at a series of cooking classes with the legendary James Beard, whose praise and encourgement started me thinking in new directions. The spark was ignited and fueled by a two-year stint in Paris at Le Cordon Bleu. The strict, yet gentle and humorous Madame Elisabeth Brassart, who single-handedly resurrected and strengthened the famed school after World War II, supported my interest in teaching and gave me the opportunity of a lifetime. As the school's first and only representative (1969–1985), I was privileged to bring the tastes and techniques of the Paris school to people in cities across the United States and Canada, doing for them what James Beard had done for me. Thank you Jim and thank you Aunt Lizzy.

I am indebted to my loving wife, Susan, without whose encouragement and assistance this book might never have been written; to my agent, Jane Dystel, whose persistent efforts brought this book to print in the able hands of Workman Publishing; to my very talented brother Philip and nephew David, whose love for the food on these pages keeps me happily busy in the kitchen for family gatherings.

My appreciation to all the dedicated teachers in the Careers through Culinary Arts Program (C-CAP) who have used this book over the past 20 years to inspire their students to broaden their palates and their horizons.

I would like to express my deep gratitude to Kate Slate, whose exceptional editorial and organizational skills helped me to shape this book; to Alan Witschonke, for his illuminating drawings, which add so greatly to the pages; to Jean-Marc Troadec and Lisa Hollander, whose cover and interior design and graphics give this book its fresh new look; to those at Workman Publishing responsible for the production of the book; and special thanks go to my editor, Suzanne Rafer, for her enthusiastic support and overall guidance in the production of this volume. Last, but certainly not least, to all my fans who over the years have told me that my recipes have made them better cooks, their children better eaters, and their spouses happier. For this reaffirmation of my work, I am truly grateful.

CONTENTS

INTRODUCTION

For close to four decades I have traveled from coast to coast, teaching and giving demonstrations on classic French cooking for Americans. Although many books have been written on the subject, I have come to realize that just as classical music can be transformed by the individual style and interpretation of the performing artist, so can recipes be "played" differently and thus made to reflect the personality and sensibilities of the individual cook.

The recipes in this book are my interpretations and updates of French classics, based on my years of teaching. No recipe has been put into this book without my first asking: Is it really delicious? Does it deserve to be re-created? If the answer is yes, I then ask: Is it too rich? Too sweet? Too heavy? Too costly? Does it take too long to prepare? If the answer is yes again, which often is the case, I then go about changing it.

"My goal is to provide clear, easy instructions, free of some of the restraints of the classic French kitchen."

The most rewarding part of updating classic recipes is making them more compatible with today's health and calorie concerns. The results are the meals I've enjoyed day after day with my family and friends, both informally and on the most festive occasions. Over the years I have found that the amounts of salt, sugar, butter, egg yolks, and cream called for in most classic French recipes far exceed the dishes' needs. I have, therefore, reduced such ingredients without altering the essential nature of the dishes. Salt, for example, is traditionally called for in all pastry recipes to enhance flavor; I find, however, that if sugar is present, salt is dispensable, and I have adjusted such recipes accordingly.

Most of the techniques used in preparing French classics are handed down from one generation of French chefs to the next by means of a strict apprentice system. Under this system you do as you're told and never ask why. In doing so you learn the "one right way." This system of learning may be one of the reasons that French cooking has remained distinctive through the ages and that many of the original techniques are still in use today.

Although I was taught by chefs who trained under this system, I have learned through my own teaching that there is always more than one way to achieve a desired result.

In updating French recipes, my goal is to provide clear, easy instructions, free of some of the restraints of the classic French kitchen and more appropriate to the time constraints of today's busy home cook. Where a step is not imperative, I have eliminated it. If a shortcut works, I have used it. When something can be done in advance, I do it.

It has also been a concern of mine that Americans are intimidated not only by the lengthy, detailed preparation they feel to be inherent in French cooking, but by the ingredients as well. Since my desire is for the American cook to feel comfortable and at home with the French classics, I have used ingredients in this book that for the most part can readily be found at local supermarkets. Items that may not always be available I have made optional or have given other, more accessible ingredients as substitutes.

Above all, my primary objective has been foolproof recipes that remain unmistakably French even though their proportions and preparation may have changed. It is my hope that this book will bring understanding and enjoyment of fine French cooking to all who read it, and give pleasure to all who feast from it.

Since 1990 this book has served as an inspirational text for the Careers Through Culinary Arts Program (C-CAP). I began this program in the public high schools of New York City in an effort to upgrade Home Economics to the culinary arts and to offer students opportunities for jobs in the food service industry. C-CAP is now a not-for-profit organization, growing nationally and increasingly having a positive effect on a large number of high school students. The development and growth of C-CAP has been extremely gratifying for me. *Pressure Cooker,* a documentary film (2009) produced and codirected by my daughter Jennifer Grausman and Mark Becker, gives you a look into one of the high school classrooms where C-CAP is helping to effect change in the lives of the culinary arts students.

COMING TO TERMS

ONE OF THE MOST IMPORTANT THINGS I try to give my readers, and that I hope my recipes succeed in doing, is the knowledge, and therefore the confidence, to be creative. If you understand what it is that you want to accomplish, you most likely will find several ways of doing it. The techniques used in this book are those that work best for me. You may already know techniques that are more efficient for you than mine. Give my methods a try, but if you find that some of yours work better, continue to use them.

I also believe that there should be considerable flexibility in cooking, with your own palate and senses being the ultimate guides in seasoning a dish or in determining whether or not it is properly cooked. I do encourage you to follow my recipes exactly the first time you try them. Once you have tasted my finished dish, you may agree that it is delicious and no changes are needed. On the other hand if you do want to change it, you will have a frame of reference in which to work. What follows is some information that should help you understand how I cook and why the recipes are written as they are.

THE INGREDIENTS

As mentioned earlier, these recipes were developed using ingredients largely available in supermarkets. If I have called for an exotic ingredient, it is either presented as optional or given a substitute.

Unless otherwise specified, all fruits and vegetables are medium size.

APPLES

In France I often use an apple called the Reinette du Canada, which has a firm flesh that is not too juicy, holds its shape when cooked, and can be browned like potatoes when sautéed. If you can find Russet apples (which are similar), you should try cooking with them, but in all the recipes in this book the widely available Golden Delicious has been used. In the past few years the growth of farmers' markets has been a boon for everyone. The variety of available fruits and vegetables has grown. New varieties of apples—and sometimes the reappearance of heirlooms—always add to my enjoyment of shopping in the fall. Ask the farmer for a taste of any unfamiliar variety. The flavor of one might be better for your tart or applesauce and another for eating out of hand.

BACON

I use slab, or unsliced, bacon in my recipes, preferably the smoked variety. Although smoked slab bacon is sometimes hard to find, most butchers will order it for you. When not available, use thick-sliced smoked bacon to achieve similar flavor results.

BUTTER

Although I use unsalted butter in almost all of my cooking, I realize that many people use only salted butter. If you normally use salted butter, continue to do so. But because my recipes were created with *un*salted butter, you will want to reduce the amount of salt you add to avoid oversalting. I also encourage you to use unsalted butter when making desserts that have a high proportion of butter, like cookies. I strongly believe that we use too much salt in our desserts, and part of that can be corrected by not using salted butter.

CARROTS

While carrots with the tops on are the freshest, and the bagged variety are the most common, I find that the large, loose ones are often the best. In addition to finding them tastier, I also like that I have fewer to peel. However, the carrots called for in the recipes are the average-size plastic bag variety.

CHEESE

The cheese most commonly used in French cooking is Gruyère, but any Swiss-style cheese is fine. Try any of the following: Gruyère, Emmentaler (called Emmental in France), Comté, Beaufort, or other cheeses sold in supermarket delis as "Swiss."

EGGS

All eggs used in this book, unless specifically mentioned, are USDA Grade A Large, weighing 60 to 65 grams or approximately 2 ounces each.

FLOUR

I use unbleached all-purpose flour because it has a better flavor than the bleached, but if you have bleached flour, use it.

HERBS

Fresh herbs will almost always be more satisfying than dried. However, dried herbs are often more readily available. If a fresh herb is specifically called for in a recipe, it is usually because the herb is added at the end of the preparation, not cooked with it; and dried herbs should not be substituted, for they will not impart the fresh taste and color desired.

Although many cookbooks tell you to substitute 1 teaspoon of a dried herb for 1 tablespoon of fresh, there is no easy formula for this, because the strength of an herb varies from plant to plant, season to season, and variety to variety. As a general rule, start by using whichever you have—fresh or dried—in the amount given in the recipe. If you're concerned that you may be adding too much dried, start with a smaller amount. You can always add more.

When buying dried herbs, try to get them in as whole a form as possible. For example, use thyme that is in leaf form, not powdered. A ground herb has a much greater chance of being flavorless when you buy it and will certainly lose its flavor quickly.

MILK

I used whole milk when creating the recipes. However, because of my wife's preference for skim milk, I have been cooking "light" for more than 15 years. Feel free to use whatever milk is on hand.

Many classic French recipes call for milk to be scalded. This practice dates back to the days before pasteurization and was important for health reasons. Today, if I heat milk in a recipe, it is to shorten the overall cooking time.

MUSHROOMS

For general cooking, the mushrooms I use are small white mushrooms—often called button mushrooms because of their size, that of a suit button. They are always left whole in recipes. Some supermarkets package button mushrooms, but many don't. When button mushrooms are not available, larger white mushrooms can be cut in half or quartered to approximate their size. There are a number of other mushrooms now easily found in supermarkets: portobellos, cremini (which are small portobellos), and shiitake. These all have more flavor than white mushrooms and though they are not found in traditional French food, don't let that stop you from trying them.

OIL

I use olive oil or such vegetable oils as soy, sunflower, peanut, and safflower. Many blended oils also work well. Find one that has a good, delicate taste. Generally speaking, and for most recipes, I use a light olive oil as opposed to the heavier, fruitier extra-virgin oils. However, in recipes originating in the south of France (Provence), or in dishes containing olives, a strong, fruity extra-virgin oil is desirable.

ONIONS

Our normal yellow cooking onion is similar to the strong yellow variety commonly used in France and is the one I have used for general cooking in this book. For those recipes that call for pearl onions, if you can't get them, you can substitute small white onions. If they are too large, simply peel off one or two layers.

SALT

Although salt was, and in some cases still is, used as a preservative, it is mainly used as a taste enhancer. I tend to use it sparingly, and you may wish to increase the quantities I specify. You will note that in most recipes, especially where a sauce is used, you will be instructed to taste and adjust the seasoning, if necessary. A French chef will usually taste a dish just before serving it, and if he does not detect any salt, he will add a little. The constant use of salt numbs our taste buds, and over a period of years you may find yourself increasing the amount of salt used. I have often eaten in restaurants where I found the food too salty. More often than not, the chef had been cooking for many years.

I became aware of the effect that salt has on taste buds while teaching. When I started teaching, a good 30 percent of the people attending my classes found the food I prepared too salty, while about 10 percent thought it needed more salt. Over a three-year period, I found this remained constant no matter where I taught. Shortly after the birth of our first daughter, however, I was shocked to find that 90 percent of my classes suggested that I should use more salt. On reflection, I quickly realized what had happened during the six months I'd stopped teaching. For the last three months of my wife's pregnancy and the first three months of my child's life, the doctor had placed my wife on a low-salt diet, and since I was doing most of the cooking, I, too, was on the same diet. This was enough time to rejuvenate my taste buds, and so when I started teaching again, the food I cooked, which tasted fine to me, was undersalted for my students.

Because of the prevalence of heavily salted packaged and prepared foods in this country, I find that many young people today use too much salt when they cook—in both savory and sweet preparations. So if you grew up eating packaged chocolate chip cookies that have salt in the dough, salt in the butter, and salt in the chocolate chips, you will probably find my recipes light on salt. Feel free to adjust the seasoning, but keep in mind the numbing effect that salt has on your taste buds and please stay away from salting fruit desserts, caramels, and ice cream.

SUGAR

Sugar, like salt, can be a very personal taste. What is too sweet for one is not sweet enough for another. I find many classic French desserts too sweet, and have adapted them over the years, removing sugar to suit my taste. In most cases sugar can be added or subtracted, but in some recipes the addition or removal of too much will alter the final product. Sugar, for example, is what gives a cookie its crunch. If the amount is cut down too much, the cookie's texture will be too cakelike.

Once you have made a recipe, feel free to adjust the sugar, a teaspoon or two at a time, until it is perfect for you.

THICKENING AGENTS

In my recipes I usually give a choice of thickeners: arrowroot, potato starch, or cornstarch. I realize that cornstarch is the one most available in the American home, and in fact the one used in certain pastry preparations in France. But for cooking, and especially sauce making, I, along with most French chefs, prefer the use of arrowroot or potato starch. Both produce sauces that are brighter and of better consistency than those made with cornstarch. Arrowroot is found in the spice section of the supermarket, and potato starch is normally found in the kosher or foreign specialty section.

TRUFFLES

French black truffles are most definitely not a supermarket item, and I have therefore made their use optional. Truffles are fungi that grow underground and are prized for their unique flavor. They can range in size from ½ inch in diameter to as large as 2 to 3 inches, and in their fresh form are usually found only in a few high-end specialty stores and expensive restaurants. I call for medium-size truffles, which measure about ¾ inch in diameter, packed in cans or jars.

VINEGAR

When vinegar is called for in a French kitchen, plain white distilled vinegar is used. For salad dressings, wine vinegars are used. The quality of commercial wine vinegars varies widely, and I find in general that white wine vinegars are milder than red ones. I also use balsamic a lot (even though it is Italian) and, from time to time, sherry vinegar and a number of fruit vinegars. One of my favorite vinegars is a homemade tarragon vinegar (using tarragon from my herb garden). I stuff a clean plastic quart container with the leaves and branches cut from the plants and then fill the container with white distilled vinegar. Within a couple of days the vinegar takes on the color and flavor of the tarragon. It always makes a welcome gift when I am invited to a friend's home for dinner.

WINES FOR COOKING

The popularity of wines in the United States has grown dramatically, and you can now find good, reasonably priced wines from countries all around the world. When a white wine is called for, I use light, dry inexpensive white wines from France, California, Spain, Italy, South Africa, Chile, New Zealand, or Australia. Look for a light, delicate, and dry wine that is not too acidic and similar in quality to a Mâcon Blanc. A few dishes are made with red wine. In these cases, I use a full-bodied red, such as Mâcon Rouge or Côtes-du-Rhône.

INGREDIENT PREPARATION

I assume that all vegetables and fruits are washed and trimmed. I emphasize washing only when the vegetable requires extra attention, as for leeks (see "Washing Leeks," page 186) or when my method is perhaps unexpected (see "Washing Mushrooms," page 189).

I assume that all vegetables that are ordinarily peeled you will peel, and I only indicate it when it's important (see "Peeling and Seeding Tomatoes," page 194).

In cutting up ingredients, I use the following terms:

FINELY CHOPPED

I use this term when I want something to be minced, but not so finely minced that it verges on a purée, as can sometimes happen if you use a food processor.

CHOPPED

Cut into pieces about ⅛ to ¼ inch.

DICED

Small square pieces, usually between ¼ and ½ inch. When food is diced finer than ¼ inch it is called a *brunoise.*

JULIENNE

Julienned ingredients are cut into thin strips about 2 inches long. They can be as fine as a hair or as thick as matchsticks and are often used as garnish.

SLICED ON THE DIAGONAL

Mostly used with carrots for greater surface area, better browning, and appearance.

ADJUSTING SEASONING

A good chef will always taste soups and sauces after making them to determine if additional seasoning is necessary. For this reason, I will remind you to taste and adjust seasoning. Many students have asked, "How do I know what to adjust?" Although the knowledge usually comes with experience, here are a few hints for the beginner.

Adjusting the seasoning usually refers to salt and pepper. If you like the way the sauce tastes as it is, then nothing needs to be added. If you think it is missing something, look at the ingredients in the recipe and see if you might need to add a small amount of one of them. For example, the sauce may have called for a small amount of vinegar, lemon juice, port, Madeira, or Cognac. Perhaps a drop or two more is all that is needed to make the sauce perfect. Sometimes a specific herb is used to accent a sauce; if its flavor is not discernible on tasting, an additional pinch is probably necessary.

Everyone has a different sense of taste, so what seems like a perfect blend of flavors to one person may be bland to someone else. All these recipes have been tested for seasoning and I hope you will like them as they are, but please feel free to adjust any seasoning according to your own taste.

MEASUREMENTS

Instead of giving precise cup measurements for many cooking ingredients—such as ½ cup chopped onion or 1 cup diced carrots—I list them as "1 onion, chopped" and "2 carrots, diced." There are two reasons for doing this. One is so that you can more easily visualize the recipe while shopping. Carrots and onions are found whole in the markets, not diced and measured in cups. The second, and perhaps more important, reason is that there should be flexibility in cooking, and no need for many ingredients to be measured precisely. It makes little difference to the end results if one reader uses a medium-small onion while another uses a medium-large one.

The pastry recipes, on the other hand, are more precise than most American recipes, and a quick reading of "The Metric System in Cooking and Pastry Making" (see page 360) will give you an understanding of some of the inaccuracies possible in measuring solids and the importance for accurate measurement in pastry recipes.

Although I encourage the use of a gram/ounce scale for pastry making, following my precise cup measurements should give you the same results time after time. When I measure dry ingredients such as flour and sugar, I use the dip-and-level method: If, for example, a recipe calls for ⅔ cup flour, I dip the cup marked "⅓" (since the average measuring cup set comes only with ¼-, ⅓-, ½-, and 1-cup measures) into the flour and scoop up more than the cup can hold. With the back of a knife I level it off, and then repeat the process to make ⅔ cup. If you usually spoon the flour into your cup before leveling, you will be using less flour than I do.

An observation about measuring spoons: For some reason most inexpensive sets no longer come with the ⅛ teaspoon size. It is my belief that this has caused some recipe writers to use ¼ teaspoon as their smallest measurement. This may be the reason I often find recipes too salty or too heavy on cinnamon or other strong spices. I also have found that many writers no longer use the smaller measurement of a "pinch" (the amount of a substance that you can pick up with your thumb and forefinger). In France, a *point,* the amount of ground spice or pepper that you can lift on the point of a paring knife that is held sideways and dipped and lifted from the spice container, is often used instead of a pinch.

OVEN TEMPERATURE

Oven temperature is very important, especially for baking. The oven temperatures in this book have been checked using a Taylor mercury thermometer. If your recipe takes more or less time than I have indicated it should, the calibration of your oven is probably incorrect. I have known ovens that have been off by 50 to 75 degrees. When I bake, I always use a thermometer to ensure an accurate temperature.

PLACEMENT IN THE OVEN

Understanding how your oven works and where its "hot spots" are will allow you to use it more efficiently. The heat in most American ovens comes from the bottom and reflects off the top, making those two areas the hottest. Most ovens vent from either the front or back, causing one area to be slightly cooler than the other. When placing something in the oven, think of how you want it to cook. For even cooking and browning, the center is the optimal location. To prevent the browning of a baked custard or rice pudding, place it on the bottom rack of the oven. Most tarts should be baked on the bottom rack to ensure a dry crust, and moved to the top if their surface needs browning. Bake only one sheet of pastry or cookies at a time, or else the bottom of one sheet and the top of the other will be unevenly baked.

CONVECTION OVENS

Theoretically convection ovens have no hot spots since they use fans to circulate the heat. This allows you to bake as many trays of pastry as the oven will hold without the uneven results of a conventional oven. Because of the circulating heat, a convection oven cooks and bakes faster than a conventional oven. I often will bake and roast at a temperature 50 degrees lower than what my recipes call for and will check on them several times during the cooking period. If you are not sure, use your oven without the convection option to see the end results using the time and temperatures in the recipe. The next time you make the recipe try the convection and note the time and temperature adjustments necessary to achieve the same results.

MICROWAVE OVENS

A tool I rarely use for cooking since I find the results less satisfying than the more conventional methods. I do use a microwave for making Chocolate Sauce (see page 344) and reheating or defrosting from time to time.

TESTS FOR DONENESS

"Cook until tender" or "cook until done" are terms often used in recipes that confuse many amateur cooks. "What is tender?" "How do you test for it?" and "What is meant by 'done'?" are questions often asked by students.

VEGETABLES

Vegetables are tender when the point of a knife penetrates them without resistance. This technique yields tender, not crunchy, vegetables. In most cases you should support the vegetable with a fork or spoon while inserting your knife. Potatoes tested this way will cling to the blade until fully cooked, at which point they will slide off.

For those who prefer undercooked, crunchy vegetables, biting into one is the best way to check for doneness. Lift a string bean or broccoli stem from the pot, run it under cold water, and taste it. The difference between perfectly cooked and overcooked vegetables may be just a matter of seconds, so pay close attention while cooking them.

Whatever your preference, test for doneness and don't rely solely on the times shown in recipes. Both altitude and freshness can affect timing considerably.

MEAT

The single prong of a roasting fork or skewer is often used for testing the doneness of meat. Tough or raw meat will resist or cling to the prong, but when the meat is tender the prong will easily penetrate and the meat will no longer cling to it. This is precisely the way to test meat in a stew (*ragoût*). Chicken, veal, and pork are pierced to release their inner juices for testing. Clear juices indicate that the meat is done; if the juices run pink, additional cooking is necessary.

Red meat to be served rare or medium-rare is pressed with a finger, not pierced, to ascertain doneness. The more meat is cooked, the firmer it becomes. Rare meat is soft, while medium-rare is springy to the touch.

To ensure that your meat will cook properly, see that it is dry and at room temperature before starting. When sautéing or grilling meat, wait for the first drops of blood or juice to appear on the uncooked surface before turning it. The meat is medium-rare when the interior juices begin to appear again on the surface after the meat has been turned.

PASTRY

In the case of pastry, a variety of indicators are used to determine doneness. Among them are color, aroma, shrinkage, and texture. In this book, I have provided signs to assist you in determining proper cooking time.

COOKING TIMES

The timing given in recipes should be viewed merely as a guide, not an absolute. Keep an eye on what is happening in your pan, not just on the clock. If a recipe instructs you to "sauté onions over medium heat until browned, about 5 minutes," the important words are "until browned." If after 5 minutes your onions are still white, you'll know that my stove was hotter than yours, and that you can use higher heat. If, however, your onions start to burn after 2 minutes, you'll know to reduce your heat the next time.

It has often been said that a good cook needs to use all five senses while cooking, but little is said about our use of common sense. If a cake should be light brown after 30 minutes, but is still white, don't remove it from the oven. If you are frying but it sounds like boiling, turn your heat up. If your nose tells you that something is burning, it probably is, so remove it from the heat.

MAKING RECIPES AHEAD OF TIME

The two main considerations in making food ahead of time are how to store it and how to ready it for serving. Most of the information necessary for preparing dishes ahead is contained in the recipes themselves, but I think it worth calling attention to two important aspects here as well.

COVERING

Many foods, like soups and sauces, form crusts or skins if exposed to air. To prevent this I use plastic wrap placed directly on the surface of the mixture in question. A surface covered this way will not dry out, and the air that is ordinarily trapped and can promote bacterial growth is eliminated.

REHEATING

Reheating does not mean re-cooking. In French cooking, reheating is an art. Food must be brought back to the temperature at which it should be served without allowing any additional cooking. For some foods this can be done quickly, while for others it must be done slowly. You can reheat a soup or sauce over high heat, and serve it as soon as it comes to a boil. A large pot of stew, on the other hand, must reheat slowly, so that by the time the sauce is simmering, everything is just hot, not overcooked. In the same fashion, a rare roast beef must be reheated slowly so it will be warm when served but not cooked any more.

For warming or reheating sauces that are extremely sensitive to heat, such as béarnaise or crème anglaise, it is essential to use a water bath (*bain-marie;* see page 328).

COOKING EQUIPMENT

The variety and quality of cooking equipment on the American market today have vastly improved since I first started teaching 40 years ago. Back then I traveled from city to city with a duffel bag full of equipment, for I never knew what would be waiting for me to use when I arrived. I eventually stripped down the equipment I carried to just my knives, but I gave that up, too, when about ten years ago I lost them to airport security.

With the increased variety of kitchen equipment now available comes the dilemma of knowing what will best suit your needs. You may need a good saucepan, or a new knife, but which one is for you? The range of materials is baffling, and the price of some may astound you. You probably wonder if it really can make a difference to your cooking and if you shouldn't just make do with what you already have. Although a good cook can always figure out a way to make the best of what is available, good equipment can make the work much easier.

KNIVES

A sharp knife, no matter what material it is made from, is a cook's most valuable tool. When shopping for a knife, pick it up and see how it feels in your hand. Some knives will be well balanced, while others will be blade- or handle-heavy. Look for a knife with a thin, sharp blade. It is easier to maintain a sharp edge on a thin blade than on a thicker one. No matter what kind of knife you have, *never allow it to get dull.* Keep it sharp by frequently using a steel or other sharpening tool.

Several knives I use regularly are: a small, inexpensive, 2½-inch razor-sharp paring knife; a well-balanced, 8-inch hand-forged chef's knife for general work and chopping (if you regularly cook for more than eight people, you should consider a 10-inch chef's knife); a 10- or 12-inch carving knife; a 6-inch slicing knife; and a 6- or 8-inch serrated knife for slicing bread, tomatoes, cakes, and other pastry.

POTS AND PANS

Pans that are good conductors heat up quickly, transfer heat quickly, and cool down quickly. Materials that conduct heat well include copper and aluminum. A pan made from a material that conducts poorly (such as cast iron) will heat up and transfer heat slowly, but will retain the heat for a long time. (See "The Materials," page 13.)

Although it makes no difference what pan you choose when you boil water, it does make a difference when you boil milk. A good conductor can be used with any degree of heat, while a poor conductor should be used on low to medium heat, and only with care on higher heat. In a pan made from material that conducts heat well, milk will boil on high heat without burning or scorching, but not in a pan made from a lesser conductor. If you do use a poor conductor, pay closer attention to what you cook. Stir the contents of the pan more often, and adjust your heat carefully.

To find out if your pan conducts heat well, try this simple test. Off the heat, place ½ tablespoon of butter in the bottom of the pan. On the inside upper rim of the pan press an even smaller amount of butter against the wall of the pan so it sticks in place. Now place the pan on high heat. If your pan conducts heat well, you will notice that the butter on the bottom starts to melt immediately, and when it has, the butter on the rim will start sliding down to the bottom. With a poor conductor, you may find that by the time the butter on the rim starts to melt, the butter in the bottom has burned.

Pans are available in copper, aluminum, coated aluminum, cast iron, enameled cast iron, stainless steel, heat-resistant porcelain, and glass, and a variety of combined materials. What follows is a list of some of the pros and cons of utensils made from these materials. Knowing these will help you when you are going to be using a pan for a specific purpose.

SUGGESTED CHECKLIST: Some Basic Cooking Equipment

- ✦ A selection of sharp knives, a sharpening steel, and cutting boards
- ✦ A set of copper-clad or aluminum-bottomed stainless-steel saucepans and stockpots for general use, including 1- , 2- , 3- , and 4-quart saucepans, a 7- or 8-quart soup pot, and a 12- or 16-quart stockpot (look for one that is light in weight when empty)
- ✦ Several heat-conducting heavy saucepans (copper or stainless with an aluminum core), 1- , 2- , and 3-quart
- ✦ 10- and 12-inch coated aluminum, stainless with an aluminum core, or cast-iron sauté pans or skillets, with lids
- ✦ Nonstick omelet and crêpe pans
- ✦ Cast-iron grill pan with raised ridges
- ✦ Dutch ovens, 5- and 8-quart, at least one good for oven-to-table use
- ✦ Gratin or baking dishes and roasting pans
- ✦ 2 nonstick baking sheets and/or nonstick silicone liners for regular baking sheets
- ✦ Wire cooling racks and an oven thermometer
- ✦ Gram/ounce scale, measuring cups (both dry and liquid), and measuring spoons
- ✦ French rolling pin (see page 85), tart pans, cake pans, bread pans, pastry brushes, pastry bags and tubes
- ✦ Mixing bowls of different sizes; some metal and some glass
- ✦ Colanders and strainers, with at least one fine-mesh sieve for sauces
- ✦ 8- and 10-inch sauce whisks; silicone (or rubber) spatulas, French wooden spatula (see page 226), and long metal spatulas
- ✦ Ladles and skimmer
- ✦ Kitchen scissors and fine grater
- ✦ Food processor, immersion blender, blender, and 250-watt handheld mixer

THE MATERIALS

COPPER

Excellent conductivity allows you to cook rapidly over high heat without worrying about sticking and burning. It also allows even cooking over low heat. It is lined with tin, nickel, stainless steel, or silver for general cooking. Unlined copper pots are used for cooking sugar and jam. If you like shiny copper pans, be prepared to polish them frequently. Years ago in French kitchens, copper pans were cleaned with a combination of salt and vinegar. Sometimes sand was added for extra scrubbing power. These days, a variety of copper polishes easily do the job, but the pans should be well washed with soap and water to make sure no polish is left on the cooking surface. However, I still use vinegar and salt when cleaning a copper egg white bowl (see "Beating Egg Whites: The Magic of the Copper Bowl," page 42). And though 30 to 40 years ago I used my copper pans on a daily basis, I find I rarely use them today.

ALUMINUM

Also an excellent conductor of heat. Can be used with high or low heat. It is not recommended for boiling water because certain minerals cause a dark gray oxide to form, making it difficult to clean. However, when cooking with tomatoes, vinegar, and other acidic ingredients, which pit aluminum, use a utensil that is lined with stainless steel or a nonstick coating, or one that is electroplated with aluminum oxide. The latter creates a virtually indestructible dark gray coating with excellent cooking properties.

CAST IRON AND ENAMELED CAST IRON

Iron is a fairly poor conductor of heat, which means that it takes a long time to get hot, and once hot, it takes a long time to cool down. This property makes it an excellent material for casseroles or Dutch ovens used for long, slow oven cooking, for oven-to-table preparations, and for grill pans and griddles. However, when using cast iron for cooking sauces, care should be taken to stir often to prevent sticking and burning. You should avoid using plain cast iron for cooking sauces containing wine or tomatoes, because a metallic taste often results.

STAINLESS STEEL

By itself, a poor conductor of heat. Utensils made from thin sheets of the metal are usually strong and light and are excellent for boiling vegetables and for making stocks and soups. Aluminum-bottomed or copper-clad stainless steel makes excellent all-purpose pans.

OVENPROOF PORCELAIN AND GLASS

These are very poor heat conductors but are excellent for low-temperature oven cooking and for oven-to-table serving.

CHAPTER ONE

FIRST COURSES

IN FRANCE, a first course is called (confusingly to English speakers) the *entrée,* which means "entry." And to begin a French meal properly, there must be one. This is true for the simplest family supper or the most elegant restaurant meal. At home, the first course might be a soup or a crudité or perhaps something from the charcuterie, such as a slice of pâté. At a restaurant, the possibilities are expanded.

In the United States, first courses at home are rare except when entertaining. Americans have a tradition of putting the main part of the meal on the table all at once. The French break the meal into courses, serve smaller portions, and spend more time at the table. To my mind, this is one of the reasons the French do not have the obesity problems that we do. When you eat quickly, you tend to overeat.

The first-course recipes in this chapter were designed to be part of a multicourse meal—just as the main courses in this book are designed to be preceded by a starter course. However, because this is not the way we eat on a daily basis, many of the first-course dishes are also perfectly suited as the main course for a lunch or light supper, and I have given a range of servings to indicate their dual nature.

SOUPS

FORMAL DINING, in years past, always included a soup. It came before the first course, and in general it was a cream soup for lunch and consommé for dinner. This style of dining has all but disappeared (although you can still experience it in some of the fine resort hotels of Europe). I generally use soup as a first course or, when served with bread, salad, and a dessert, as a main course—especially hearty soups such as Mediterranean Fish Soup (page 21) or Split-Pea Soup (page 23).

Although the generic term for soups in French cooking is *potages,* the classic breakdown of types and terms is far more complex. Simply speaking, soups can be divided into two groups: clear soups (or consommés) and thickened soups. Thickened soups are classically further divided into purées, veloutés, and crèmes, and each follows certain rules. Purées are thickened with a purée of a starchy vegetable or grain (such as potato or rice) or a legume (such as lima bean, lentil, or pea). Veloutés are thickened with a light velouté sauce (a white sauce made with stock), while crèmes are thickened with a light béchamel (a white sauce made with milk). Veloutés are enriched, just before serving, with a liaison of egg yolks and butter, and crèmes are finished with heavy cream.

Over the years, these classic distinctions have been blurred. And, in the case of my soups, they have been deliberately altered to make them lighter than the classics that inspired them. I eliminate the egg yolk and butter enrichment and a good deal of the starch, and use heavy cream sparingly.

CHICKEN CONSOMME

[CONSOMMÉ DE VOLAILLE]

ONE OF THE TRUE TESTS of a good chef is his ability to make an excellent consommé. It should be crystal clear, full of flavor, yet not too salty, and it should have a lovely color ranging from light gold to deep amber. The process for making consommés is long and tedious, and it is rare to find them on restaurant menus today. If you do find one, you can be sure the chef is proud of it.

A classic consommé is made with a double-strength veal, beef, or chicken stock. This stock is further strengthened and then clarified (a process necessary for a perfectly clear soup). From beginning to end, making a consommé can take up to two days.

Since most of us rarely are able or willing to devote so much time to making a soup, this version takes some shortcuts without short-changing the taste. By starting with canned stock (see "Using Canned Stocks," page 305), the consommé takes less than an hour.

It can be served cold (it will be lightly jelled) or hot. If you are making a hot consommé and want to serve it in the French fashion, garnish it with finely diced or julienned cooked vegetables, shredded chicken, rice, or vermicelli. **SERVES 6 TO 8**

2 quarts double-strength chicken stock, homemade (see Note), or canned (see chart, page 305)
2 egg whites, well whisked
4 envelopes unflavored gelatin, softened in ¾ cup cold water
1 pound ground skinless, boneless chicken breast
1 carrot, finely chopped
1 onion, chopped
1 leek (white part only), washed and chopped
2 celery ribs, with leaves if possible, chopped
1 large tomato, chopped
10 sprigs parsley, chopped
3 sprigs fresh tarragon or 2 teaspoons dried
20 sprigs fresh chervil or 2 teaspoons dried (optional)
1 teaspoon salt (omit if using canned stock)
⅛ teaspoon freshly ground pepper
2 tablespoons Chicken Glaze (optional; page 310)

1. Clarify and intensify the stock: Place the stock in a 4- to 5-quart saucepan. Add the egg whites, stirring vigorously so they blend with the stock. Add the softened gelatin and all the remaining ingredients.

2. Stir the mixture slowly and constantly with a whisk (to keep the egg whites well distributed in the stock) over high heat until the first sign of boiling, about 12 minutes. Immediately stop stirring; reduce the heat and simmer gently for 20 minutes. As the egg whites cook in the hot stock, they harden and rise to the surface, carrying impurities with them.

3. Using a skimmer, gently remove most of the vegetables, chicken, and egg white from the surface of the stock. Line a strainer with a dampened kitchen towel or several thicknesses of dampened cheesecloth and pour the stock through it. The strained stock or consommé should be perfectly clear. If not, it may require a second straining.

4. Degrease the consommé: If, after straining, there are any remaining droplets of fat on the surface of the consommé, cut a paper towel into quarters. Place one square at a time on the surface of the soup, and immediately draw it across and away. Continue this with as many squares as you need (cutting more paper towels, if necessary) until there is no more visible fat.

5. Serve hot or cold.

NOTE: If you are interested in making your own strong chicken stock, you might consider making the Poule au Pot on page 113. The chicken for this simple and delicious dish is cooked in chicken stock, thus creating a double-strength stock that can be used to make the consommé.

IN ADDITION

The seasoned ground chicken, cooked egg white, and vegetables used to clarify the consommé do not have to be discarded once their job is done. After skimming them from the soup in step 3, set them aside, let cool, and refrigerate, covered. A quick béchamel flavored to taste with tomato paste or curry powder can be mixed with the chicken mixture and served with rice—it goes very nicely with basmati or Texmati—for an easy lunch or dinner. The chicken and sauce can also be used as a filling for crêpes.

CLASSIC CONSOMMES

Consommés can be made from beef, veal, chicken, fish, or game. In classic French cooking, the name of the consommé changes depending on the garnish served with it. In the classic repertoire there are hundreds of different garnish combinations and, therefore, soup names. For example: *Consommé Bretonne* is garnished with julienne of leek, celery, onion, and mushroom and shredded chervil. *Consommé Solange* is garnished with pearl barley, squares of lettuce, and chicken julienne. *Consommé Rossini* is thickened with tapioca, flavored with truffle essence, and garnished with profiteroles stuffed with foie gras and chopped truffles.

VARIATION

BEEF CONSOMME

[CONSOMMÉ DE BOEUF]

A beef consommé is made in principally the same way. Replace the chicken stock with 2 quarts double-strength beef stock, homemade or canned (see chart, page 305). Use 1 pound lean ground beef instead of ground chicken breast. Before serving, stir in ¼ cup Madeira (optional).

ONION SOUP

[SOUPE À L'OIGNON]

ALTHOUGH I normally make this soup with stock, a more delicate version can be made with water. The caramelized onions will provide the necessary flavor. **SERVES 6 TO 8**

3 tablespoons butter
1½ pounds onions (5 to 6 medium), halved and thinly sliced
½ teaspoon salt
¼ teaspoon freshly ground pepper
2 tablespoons all-purpose flour
9 cups beef stock, homemade or canned (see chart, page 305), or water
1 tablespoon Cognac
½ pound Swiss-style cheese, such as Gruyère or Emmentaler, grated (about 2 cups)

1. In a large saucepan or 5-quart Dutch oven, melt the butter. Add the onions and cook over medium-high heat, stirring occasionally, until well browned. They will start to brown in 10 to 12 minutes. After another 20 to 25 minutes the onions should be dark brown, not black. Season with the salt and pepper.

2. Reduce the heat to medium and stir in the flour. Brown lightly, stirring, about 3 minutes.

3. Add the stock, increase the heat to high, and bring to a boil, about 15 minutes. Reduce the heat to medium and simmer for 30 minutes. Skim off any foam or butter that comes to the surface. (The recipe can be prepared ahead to this point. Let cool to room temperature, cover, and refrigerate. Bring to a simmer before proceeding.)

4. Just before serving, add the Cognac. Pass the cheese separately.

IN ADDITION

With the addition of bread and cheese, this simple soup becomes French Onion Soup (page 20), perhaps the most famous of all French soups. Without them, it makes a nice, very light first course.

FRENCH ONION SOUP

[SOUPE À L'OIGNON GRATINÉE]

LISTED ON American menus as French Onion Soup and on French menus often simply as a *gratinée,* this delicious soup is served in restaurants throughout the world. Although there is no classic recipe for this classically French soup, most contain bread and Swiss-style cheese, making it virtually a meal in itself. For this reason I usually serve it for lunch or supper with a mixed green salad, and some fruit or pastry for dessert.

The bread should be stale or toasted so it will float and support the cheese on the surface of the soup, where it can easily be browned or gratinéed. **SERVES 6**

Onion Soup (page 19), but increase the cheese to 1 pound
Slices of stale or toasted French bread (see Note), cut ½ inch thick

1. Preheat the broiler.

2. In a large saucepan, heat the soup to a simmer over medium heat.

3. Place enough bread in each of 6 ovenproof bowls (that will hold at least 1½ cups) so the slices will cover the surface once the bowls are filled with the soup. Ladle the soup into the bowls.

4. Sprinkle the soup with the cheese and place the bowls on a baking sheet. Place under the broiler until the cheese has browned, 5 to 7 minutes, and serve.

NOTE: The number of bread slices you need will depend on the diameter of your soup bowls and the diameter of the loaf of bread. The object is to cover the surface of the soup with the bread, which floats to support the cheese. One or two slices per person is usually adequate.

IN ADDITION

An especially appealing feature of this recipe is that the basic onion soup can be made well in advance, then reheated and placed under the broiler for a superb last-minute meal. Special onion soup bowls, which can withstand the high temperature of a broiler, are used in this preparation. If you don't have onion soup bowls, use any ovenproof bowls with a 1½-cup capacity.

Mediterranean Fish Soup

[SOUPE DE POISSON]

THIS SOUP, served with a green salad, rosé wine, and a fruit tart for dessert, makes a wonderful lunch or light supper. It is also the base for the American Bouillabaisse on page 99. Most traditional recipes for this soup call for fish fillets to be cooked as part of the soup base and discarded. With today's fish prices, I find this wasteful and extravagant. In my *Soupe de Poisson,* I poach the diced fillets in the soup at the last minute and serve them with the soup. For an even heartier version I add scallops and/or shrimp, poaching them at the same time as the fish. **SERVES 6**

5 pounds fish heads and bones (see Note)
¼ cup extra-virgin olive oil
2 onions, halved and sliced
2 leeks, washed and diced
½ fennel bulb, diced
About 15 sprigs parsley
3 pounds tomatoes, diced, or 3 cans (14.5 ounces each) diced tomatoes, drained
5 garlic cloves, smashed
1 bay leaf
¼ teaspoon fresh or dried thyme
¼ teaspoon fresh or dried savory
2 to 3 large pinches of saffron threads, to taste
Zest of 1 orange
2 cups dry white wine
6 cups water
½ teaspoon salt
¼ teaspoon freshly ground pepper
1 pound skinless fish fillets (see Note), diced

1. In a large bowl or saucepan, soak the fish heads and bones in ice water for at least 20 minutes or until ready to use them.

2. In a large stockpot, heat the oil over medium heat. Add the onions, leeks, fennel, and parsley and sauté until the vegetables have softened without coloring, 4 to 5 minutes.

3. Add the tomatoes, garlic, bay leaf, thyme, savory, saffron, and orange zest. Stir well with a wooden spoon.

4. Drain the fish bones and heads and add them to the pot along with the wine and water. Season with the salt and pepper. Bring to a boil over medium-high heat and cook gently for 30 minutes.

5. Strain the soup through a sieve, pressing as much liquid from the solid ingredients as possible. Discard the solids. (The soup can be prepared ahead to this point. Let cool to room temperature, cover, and refrigerate for up to 3 days or freeze for up to 1 month. Bring the soup back to a simmer before proceeding.)

6. Add the fish fillets and bring the soup back to a boil just before serving.

NOTE: This can be just about any fish you like. Just be sure that if you are using a strong-flavored fish, such as mackerel or bluefish, that it is very fresh.

SERVING SUGGESTION

Accompany the soup with toasted slices of French bread, Aioli (page 332), or grated Swiss-style cheese.

WATERCRESS SOUP

[POTAGE AU CRESSON]

THIS LOW-CALORIE variation of the classic watercress soup uses zucchini in place of potatoes. The small amount of cream used to lighten the color and flavor while enriching the soup can be omitted, reducing the calories even further. I rarely use the cream today, but encourage you to try it both ways.

I once made this soup for a well-known restaurant critic, who apologized for eating only half a serving, saying that it was a little too rich for someone on a diet. When I explained that the soup has only 70 calories per serving, I received a request for seconds.

This soup can be served hot or cold. If you are using a homemade chicken stock, the soup may jell when cold, making it too thick. If this happens, thin with water and adjust the seasoning. Try using yogurt instead of cream when serving the soup cold. **SERVES 6**

1 tablespoon butter or olive oil
3 leeks (white part only; see Note), washed and diced
1½ pounds zucchini, peeled (see Note) and diced
4 cups chicken stock, homemade or canned (see chart, page 305)
1 bunch watercress, thick stems trimmed
¼ teaspoon salt
⅛ teaspoon freshly ground pepper
⅓ cup heavy cream

1. In a 4-quart pot, heat the butter or oil over medium-low heat. Add the leeks and gently sauté until softened, about 3 minutes.

2. Add the zucchini and sauté for 2 minutes without browning. Add the stock and simmer until the zucchini is just tender, 3 to 4 minutes.

3. Bring the soup to a boil and add the watercress. Reduce the heat and simmer for 1 minute.

4. In a food processor or blender, blend the soup until smooth. Season with the salt and pepper. (The soup can be prepared ahead to this point. Let cool to room temperature, cover, and refrigerate. If serving the soup hot, bring back to a simmer before proceeding.)

5. Just before serving, stir in the cream.

NOTE: I use only the white part of the leeks and peel the zucchini so the color of the soup will be pale green like the classic version. If I am not so concerned about the color, I use the tender green parts of the leeks as well. However, I always peel the zucchini, for otherwise it might look like a spinach soup.

VARIATIONS

Curried Watercress Soup

[POTAGE AU CRESSON ET AU CURRY]

Reduce the amount of watercress to ½ bunch and add 1 tablespoon curry powder along with the stock in step 2.

Arugula Soup

[POTAGE À LA ROQUETTE]

Replace the watercress with a generous handful of baby arugula.

Split-Pea Soup

[POTAGE DE POIS CASSÉS]

GREEN SPLIT-PEA SOUP is a hearty winter soup that, together with some warm bread, a piece of cheese, and fruit, provides a very satisfying meal. In France, it is most often served with croutons (small cubes of fried bread), but because of their high calorie count, I rarely use them.

The traditional version of this soup was somewhat more time-consuming and arduous, the cook having to use a *tamis* (drum-shaped sieve) to achieve the proper consistency. The blender and food processor make this an easier operation for the contemporary cook.

I also use this recipe for lentil, bean, and other legume-based soups. It can easily be cut in half for fewer servings. **SERVES 8 TO 10**

2 pounds green split peas, washed and picked over
2 leeks, washed and diced
2 onions, each studded with 1 clove
2 large carrots, cut in half
2 celery ribs, with leaves if possible
Bouquet Garni (page 306)
1 ham bone, ½ pound slab bacon (see Note), or ½ pound smoked sausage
1 handful lettuce leaves (optional)
½ teaspoon salt
¼ teaspoon freshly ground pepper
3 quarts water
¼ cup dry sherry (optional)

1. Put all of the ingredients, except the sherry, into a stockpot. Bring the soup to a boil and simmer, partially covered, until the peas are tender, about 1 hour.

2. Remove the meat and set it aside (see Note). Discard the onions, bouquet garni, one of the carrots, and the celery.

3. In a blender or food processor, purée the ingredients remaining in the pot until they are smooth. If the soup is too thick, thin it with a little water or milk.

4. Dice the ham or sausage and add it to the soup. (The soup can be prepared ahead to this point. Let cool to room temperature, cover, and refrigerate. Bring to a simmer before proceeding.)

5. Just before serving, add the sherry (if using).

NOTE: If you are using bacon, after removing it in step 2, rinse and dice it. Then sauté it before returning it to the soup in step 4.

VARIATION

PEASANT-STYLE SPLIT-PEA SOUP

[POTAGE PAYSAN DE POIS CASSÉS]

As with most puréed soups, a coarser, more rustic version can be made. To do this, dice all the vegetables except for one of the onions, which you stud with the cloves. When the peas are soft, discard only the whole onion and the bouquet garni. Remove the ham or sausage after cooking, dice, and return to the soup. If using bacon, rinse, dice, sauté, and return to the soup.

CREAM OF ASPARAGUS SOUP

[CRÈME D'ASPERGES]

CRÈME D'ASPERGES is also known as *crème Argenteuil* in honor of the region (in north central France) where the best asparagus are grown. (In fact, any dish that includes the name *Argenteuil* contains asparagus.) What made this a "cream" soup in the classic kitchen was that it was made with a light béchamel, though the rules were often bent to make it with a thickened stock (velouté) or a combination of the two. I find the flavor better when made with stock alone (and even better if made with veal stock). This recipe produces a very light and delicately creamy soup, but for those who prefer theirs thicker or more creamy, it is an easy matter to add up to another tablespoon of arrowroot or double the cream. The soup can also be thickened by using a small potato instead of the starch. Finely dice the potato and add at the same time as the asparagus. **SERVES 8**

2 tablespoons butter
3 pounds asparagus, well washed, tough ends removed, and cut into 1-inch lengths
¼ teaspoon salt
⅛ teaspoon freshly ground pepper
6 cups chicken stock, homemade or canned (see chart, page 305)
2½ tablespoons arrowroot, potato starch, or cornstarch, dissolved in 2½ tablespoons cold water
¼ cup heavy cream

1. In a large saucepan, melt the butter over medium-high heat. Add the asparagus and gently sauté until bright green, about 5 minutes. Season with the salt and pepper.

2. Add the stock and bring to a boil over high heat, skimming off any foam and impurities that rise to the surface. Boil gently until the asparagus are tender, 4 to 5 minutes. If desired, remove 16 to 24 asparagus tips and reserve for garnish.

3. Place the asparagus and stock in a blender, discarding any sand or grit that may remain at the bottom of the saucepan. Blend until smooth. Return the soup to the saucepan.

4. Bring the soup to a simmer and whisk in the dissolved arrowroot to thicken. Stir in the cream. (The soup can be prepared ahead. Let cool to room temperature, cover, and refrigerate. Bring to a simmer before serving.) Place 2 to 3 of the reserved asparagus tips, if using, in each of 8 soup bowls, ladle in the soup, and serve.

PUREEING SOUPS

The smoothness of a soup will vary with the machine you use to purée it. A blender will make the finest purée (although you will have to blend most soups in batches). There are also a number of hand blenders (see below) that will purée the soup directly in the pot. The result will be somewhat coarser, but cleanup will be easier. The food processor will also make a slightly coarser purée, and the soup must often be processed in batches. The secret to getting a smooth soup in a food processor is to first purée the solids as fine as possible and then thin this purée with the liquid.

VARIATION

CREAM OF BROCCOLI SOUP

[CRÈME DE BROCOLI]

Use 3 pounds of broccoli in place of the asparagus. Peel the stalks; cut the florets and stalks into 1-inch pieces, and cook as for the asparagus.

CREAM OF CORN SOUP

[CRÈME DE MAÏS]

A CLASSIC cream of corn soup is made by puréeing cooked corn with a light béchamel sauce, and serving it with a few kernels of corn in each bowl. My version, with its added aromatic vegetables, is closer in appearance to an American corn chowder. I use half milk and half water to create a light yet creamy-tasting soup. It is important to the appearance of the soup to dice the vegetables no larger than the corn kernels. Should you prefer a completely smooth soup, simply blend to a purée and strain. This soup can be made several days in advance and served hot or cold. **SERVES 6 TO 8**

3 tablespoons butter
1 onion, diced
2 carrots, diced
1 celery rib, diced
2 tablespoons all-purpose flour
4 cups water
4 cups milk
About 4 cups cooked fresh corn (from 5 to 6 ears), or 4 cups canned or frozen corn kernels
1 small potato, diced
½ teaspoon salt (omit if using canned corn)
⅛ teaspoon freshly ground pepper

1. In a large saucepan, melt the butter over medium heat. Add the diced vegetables and gently sauté for 2 to 3 minutes. Add the flour and cook, stirring occasionally, for 4 minutes. Make sure that neither the flour nor the vegetables begin to brown during this time.

2. Add the water, milk, corn, and potato and bring to a boil over high heat, stirring occasionally, about 10 minutes.

3. Season with the salt and pepper. Reduce the heat to medium-low and simmer gently for about 40 minutes. Skim the soup several times to remove the foam and butter that rise to the surface. Stir the soup each time after skimming. When finished, the soup should have a light, creamy texture. If too thick, add water. If too thin, boil to thicken. Taste and adjust the seasoning, if necessary. (The soup can be prepared ahead. Let cool to room temperature, cover, and refrigerate. If serving hot, bring to a simmer before serving.)

4. Serve the soup hot or cold.

IN ADDITION

When cutting the kernels from cooked corn on the cob, be sure to scrape the cobs with your knife, for there is often a lot of flavorful corn left after the kernels have been cut off.

SALADS

TRADITIONALLY, a French salad can be composed of many things—vegetables, meat, poultry, seafood, eggs, cheese, herbs, greens, or combinations thereof—just as long as it's dressed with a vinaigrette or a mayonnaise-based dressing. Salads can range in complexity from the simple raw vegetable salads called crudités to cooked vegetables dressed with vinaigrette or even cooked in a sort of vinaigrette—as are dishes prepared *à la grecque* (see Mushrooms à la Grecque, page 190).

A combination of ingredients artfully arranged in a salad bowl or on a plate is known as a *salade composée*—the most well-known example of which is probably *salade niçoise*. By tradition, the components of a *salade composée* are kept separate, not tossed together.

While most composed salads are served as a first course, and in some cases eaten as a main course, a green salad (*salade verte*) is served after the main course.

Endive and Pink Grapefruit Salad

[SALADE D'ENDIVES ET DE PAMPLEMOUSSE ROSE]

BELGIAN ENDIVE is often used in place of lettuce in a variety of simple French salads. There are a number of special combinations (see Variations), but one of my favorites is the combination of endive and grapefruit, which will surprise you if you have never experienced it. Somehow, magically, each seems to cancel out the bitterness or sourness of the other. This is a unique combination that should not be missed. **SERVES 6**

2 tablespoons white wine vinegar
2 pinches of salt
2 pinches of freshly ground pepper
½ cup light vegetable oil
3 Belgian endives
3 pink grapefruit

1. In a small bowl (or jar), mix the vinegar, salt, and pepper together. Add the oil and mix until well blended.

2. Take off 12 of the larger outside leaves from each of the endives (for a total of 36) and set aside. (Reserve the smaller inside leaves for another use.) Peel and section the grapefruit (see "How to Section an Orange," page 286. The salad can be prepared ahead to this point. Store the endive in a plastic bag in the refrigerator. Refrigerate the grapefruit in a colander so it does not sit in its own juices.)

3. To serve, on each plate, place 6 endive leaves, rounded side down, in a spoke pattern. Fill each leaf with a grapefruit section.

4. Whisk the vinaigrette to reblend and spoon it lightly over the grapefruit sections, just before serving.

VARIATIONS

Endive and Watercress Salad

[SALADE D'ENDIVES ET DE CRESSON]

Belgian endive and watercress are both available in the winter when some other greens may not be at their best, and their flavors combine very well. Use 3 Belgian endives, separated into leaves, and 1 bunch of watercress, thick stems trimmed. Add 1 teaspoon Dijon mustard to the vinaigrette. Arrange the salad with the watercress in the center and the endive leaves radiating out in a flower pattern and drizzle with the vinaigrette. Or, alternatively, cut the endive leaves into 1-inch pieces and toss with the watercress and

SALAD GREENS: Washing and Storing

It is important to wash lettuce well, but most people don't know this easy and efficient method of doing it. Wash each variety separately in a large quantity of cold water. The operative word here is "large," the object being to have enough water so the lettuce can float.

Swirl the leaves around, turning them over and over again in the water. In the process, the dirt and sand will drop to the bottom, while any insects will float to the surface along with the leaves. Remove the leaves, discard the dirty water, and repeat this process until you no longer find dirt and sand at the bottom of your washing water. Two washings are generally sufficient.

After washing, thoroughly spin dry the leaves, using a lettuce or salad spinner, and place each variety of salad green in a plastic bag of its own. Washed, dried, and packaged in this way, the greens will stay fresh in the refrigerator for several days. When it is time to make a salad, you can choose from the variety of prepared greens to compose a salad to suit your taste.

vinaigrette. Another modern version adds walnuts, sliced apples, and blue cheese. Go light on the blue cheese.

ENDIVE AND WALNUT SALAD

[SALADE D'ENDIVES AUX NOIX]

Walnuts and Belgian endive make another traditional winter salad that is often served with game. The flavor created by this unusual combination is exceptional. Use 3 Belgian endives, leaves separated and cut into 1-inch pieces, and 30 walnut halves. Toss with a walnut oil vinaigrette: Replace 2 tablespoons of the vegetable oil with 2 tablespoons of walnut oil.

ENDIVE AND BEET SALAD

[SALADE D'ENDIVES ET DE BETTERAVES]

Bake beets according to instructions in Baked Beets (page 175). Dice the beets, then toss lightly with 4 to 6 tablespoons (to taste) of Vinaigrette (page 336). Mound the beets in the center of 6 individual salad plates or a large salad bowl. Arrange the leaves of 3 Belgian endives so they radiate out from the beets in a floral design. Chop a hard-cooked egg and sprinkle it over the center of the beets. The beets can be tossed with the vinaigrette in advance, but the salad should not be assembled until just before serving (to avoid discoloration).

SHRIMP AND SCALLOPS IN AN HERBED LEMON VINAIGRETTE

[SALADE DE CREVETTES ET DE COQUILLES ST.-JACQUES]

THE REPERTOIRE of classic French recipes abounds in cold lobster presentations, most often made with a mayonnaise-based sauce. This recipe substitutes the much more available shrimp and sea scallops for the lobster and sauces them with a delicately seasoned vinaigrette. Both the seafood and the vinaigrette can be prepared well ahead of time and then tossed together at the last minute for easy entertaining. Serve this with warm French bread and a dry white wine such as Muscadet. **SERVES 6**

¾ pound large shrimp, shelled and deveined (see page 101)
¾ pound sea scallops, tendon removed (at right)
3 tablespoons lemon juice or white wine vinegar
2 teaspoons Dijon mustard
½ cup vegetable oil
3 tablespoons light olive oil
Pinch each of salt and freshly ground pepper, or more to taste
2 tablespoons chopped fresh herbs, such as dill, chives, or basil (see Note)
1 large head Bibb lettuce, separated into leaves

1. Place 3 quarts of water in a large pot over high heat and bring to a boil. Add the shrimp and scallops. When the water just returns to a boil, drain the seafood and refresh under cold running water.

2. Slice the shrimp in half lengthwise, and slice the scallops horizontally into 2 or 3 rounds. (The seafood can be prepared up to 1 day ahead. Cover and refrigerate.)

HOW TO CLEAN A SEA SCALLOP

Although many people do not bother with this, the tough tendon on the side of a sea scallop really ought to be removed, as it gets even tougher when it's cooked. After rinsing the scallops, grab the tendon, as shown below, and gently pull to remove.

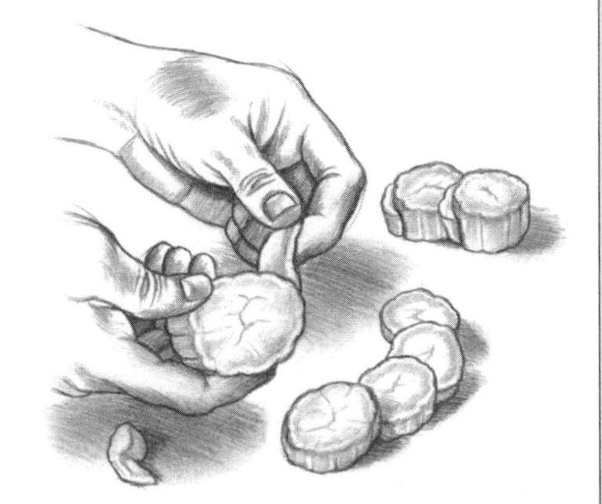

3. In a bowl large enough to hold the seafood, make the vinaigrette. First mix together the lemon juice and mustard. Add the oils and whisk well. Season with the salt and pepper and stir in the chopped herbs. Refrigerate. (This can be done ahead and taken out of the refrigerator when ready to assemble the salad.)

4. To serve, arrange the Bibb lettuce on serving plates. Whisk the vinaigrette until it is smooth, and toss the seafood in it. Either simply mound the seafood in the center of each plate, or arrange each plate by overlapping the shrimp and scallops to form a circular design, and serve.

NOTE: If more than one herb is available, use 1 tablespoon of each, but no more than 3 tablespoons total.

GREEN SALAD: *Salade Verte*

A simple French green salad (*salade verte*) is made with a lettuce similar to our Boston lettuce and tossed with a vinaigrette. The salad can be modified by adding and mixing greens. Most supermarkets offer a variety of salad greens to choose from: Boston, Bibb, red leaf, curly endive (chicory), romaine, watercress, arugula, radicchio, mâche, frisée (baby chicory), and Belgian endive (see Endive and Pink Grapefruit Salad, page 28) are among the most frequently seen. Salad dressings are generally variations of Vinaigrette (page 336). The vinaigrette can be modified by substituting small amounts of nut oil (such as walnut, almond, or hazelnut) for an equal portion of the vegetable oil and olive oil; different types of vinegar, or lemon juice can be used in place of the tarragon vinegar.

Beyond simple Green Salad: There are a large number of ingredients that can be added to greens to change both appearance and flavor. Some of these are:

FRESH HERBS—Chives, chervil, basil, and tarragon. Either chop the herbs and sprinkle over the salad, or use a few small leaves mixed in with the other greens.

EGG—Shred or dice a hard-cooked egg and sprinkle over greens.

TOMATOES—When ripe, tomatoes add wonderful flavor and color to a salad. Use tomatoes that are not too large and cut them into wedges, or use cherry tomatoes cut in half. When available, use the yellow or orange varieties of tomato, as well as the red.

AVOCADO—Diced ripe avocado adds a subtle richness that is often appreciated.

BELL PEPPERS—Diced or julienned, sweet peppers add color, crunch, and flavor.

CUCUMBERS and/or **RADISHES**—Sliced cucumbers add a cool freshness to a salad, and sliced radishes add spicy freshness.

CHEESE—When serving a first-course salad, add a little cheese: grated Parmesan, diced hard cheese (Swiss, St.-Nectaire, Beaumont), blue, or chèvre (goat cheese).

DRIED FRUITS and **NUTS** can also be added.

CHICKEN SALAD WITH FRESH PEACHES IN A CURRY-LIME DRESSING

[SALADE DE VOLAILLE AUX PÊCHES]

THIS DISH is based on the memory of a salad I once had at the then three-star restaurant Lapérouse in Paris. Their salad was made with fragrant white peaches, and it was served the way such composed salads are in France, with the various elements arranged separately on the plate. Instead of this classic presentation, I prefer to toss the salad. By combining the ingredients this way, all the flavors can enter your mouth at the same time, which to me is more enjoyable. This salad serves eight as a first course, but with larger portions (serving six), it makes a good main course for lunch, along with warm French bread and a chilled white or rosé wine. **SERVES 6 OR 8**

3 pounds skinless, boneless chicken half breasts, poached, chilled, and diced
1 avocado, diced
2 white or yellow peaches, peeled and diced
Juice of 1 lime
2 celery ribs, chopped
3 scallions, white and green parts, chopped
2 hard-cooked eggs, chopped
¾ to 1 cup mayonnaise, to taste
¼ teaspoon salt
⅛ teaspoon freshly ground pepper
Pinch of curry powder
1 head lettuce, separated into leaves
Tomato wedges or cherry tomatoes, for garnish

1. In a large bowl, toss the chicken, avocado, and peaches with half of the lime juice. Add the celery, scallions, and hard-cooked eggs.

2. Flavor the mayonnaise with the salt, pepper, curry powder, and remaining lime juice. Gently toss the chicken mixture with the flavored mayonnaise and refrigerate. (The recipe can be prepared up to this point 1 day ahead.)

3. Serve the salad on a bed of lettuce leaves, garnished with tomato wedges or cherry tomatoes.

VARIATIONS

CHICKEN AND MANGO SALAD

[SALADE DE VOLAILLE AUX MANGUES]

Substitute 1 mango for the peaches.

Seafood Salad with Peaches or Mangoes

[SALADE DE FRUITS DE MER AUX PÊCHES OU AUX MANGUES]

Substitute 2 pounds cooked lobster meat or shrimp for the chicken. Crab meat can also be used in the salad.

Chicken Salad with Mangoes and Ginger

[SALADE DE VOLAILLE AUX MANGUES ET AU GINGEMBRE]

Increase the curry powder to 1 to 2 teaspoons (to taste) and add 1 teaspoon chopped fresh ginger.

TOMATO SALAD: *Salade de Tomates*

When tomatoes are in season, I like nothing better than to start an informal meal with a tomato salad. It used to be hard to buy flavorful tomatoes in America, but in the past ten years—with farmers growing a widening variety of heirloom tomatoes—our chances of finding the flavors familiar to the French cook have improved greatly. Slice the tomatoes (one medium-large tomato per person) and place them, in overlapping slices, on individual salad plates. When I have a variety of good tomatoes, I present them on a platter to show the range of colors (for example, red, green, and yellow). Make a vinaigrette of three parts light olive oil, one part lemon juice, and 1 or 2 tablespoons chopped chives or basil. Spoon 1 tablespoon of well-whisked vinaigrette over each portion of tomatoes and serve with warm French bread.

EGGS & OMELETS

ALTHOUGH IN THE PAST 20 YEARS the egg has come under heavy attack for the cholesterol in its yolk, and although I no longer eat them as frequently as I once did, I have not given up the pleasure that this most versatile of foods provides. Besides being an excellent source of protein, eggs are an ingredient in many of the masterpieces of French cooking.

Many a French meal includes an egg dish. Eggs—poached, soft- or hard-boiled, baked, fried, scrambled, or in an omelet or quiche—are offered as first courses, or may be the main attraction of a lunch.

Although something like Caviar-Topped Scrambled Egg Cups (page 36) might be the beginning of an elegant meal, I am more likely to serve these egg dishes with bread, salad, and dessert for a quick, nourishing light meal.

SLOW-SCRAMBLED EGGS WITH TRUFFLES

[OEUFS BROUILLÉS AUX TRUFFES]

THE TERM "scrambled eggs" does not do justice to the French *oeufs brouillés,* a slow-cooked, soft, moist, and creamy dish served as a first course and not for breakfast. When properly made, *oeufs brouillés aux truffes* ranks in my mind as one of the top 20 dishes ever created. Most French recipes call for the eggs to be cooked in a water bath (*bain-marie*) or double boiler, but I have found that a nonstick pan over low heat works just as well, and if you are careful there will be no need for the extra butter or cream, thus saving calories.

The use of truffles here makes the dish, but, unfortunately, it also makes it a luxury. Try it if you are lucky enough to have a truffle, but the eggs by themselves will still impress your guests. Serve the eggs with or on thinly sliced white toast. **SERVES 4**

8 eggs (see Note)
1 medium (¾-inch) black truffle, chopped
2 tablespoons butter (optional)
Pinch each of salt and freshly ground pepper

1. In a bowl, beat the eggs well with a fork or whisk. Stir in the chopped truffle and allow the mixture to stand for 15 to 30 minutes.

2. In a 10-inch nonstick skillet, melt the butter (if using) over medium heat. Add the egg mixture and cook, stirring gently with a wooden spoon or silicone spatula. As the eggs heat up, you will find them thickening. Keep the liquid moving in the pan, and turn the heat to low if the eggs begin to thicken too quickly. Just when you think the eggs will start setting, they will all of a sudden become watery again. Shortly after they thin, you will notice them beginning to set on the bottom of the pan. It is at this point that you should stir and scrape the pan constantly so as not to allow large curds to form. The eggs are done when they are thick, creamy, soft, and shiny, 10 to 15 minutes.

3. Sprinkle the eggs with the salt and pepper and serve immediately.

NOTE: If you can find fresh farm eggs at your local farmers' market, use them for this dish, for plain slow-scrambled eggs, or for any of the variations that follow. Your guests will marvel at the flavor and consistency.

VARIATIONS

EGGS MAGDA

[OEUFS MAGDA]

Replace the truffle with 1 tablespoon chopped parsley, 1 teaspoon Dijon mustard, and 2½ to 3 ounces (¾ to 1 cup) grated cheese, to taste. Classically, Gruyère is used, but I like to use any one of a number of other cheeses, such as St.-Nectaire, Beaumont, or Brie. The softer cheeses cannot be grated, but should simply be diced or cut into small pieces and added to the eggs. Omit the standing period in step 1.

Caviar-Topped Scrambled Egg Cups

[OEUFS BROUILLÉS EN SURPRISE AU CAVIAR]

Because the portions of this variation are smaller, it will serve 8 instead of 4. Replace the truffle with 2 teaspoons chopped chives and eliminate the standing period in step 1. To serve this dish as restaurants do, you must cut the tops off the eggshells, empty the eggs into a bowl, and then wash the shells so you can use them as serving containers. If you can manage this delicate operation (there are soft-boiled egg cutters on the market that work), fill the shells three-quarters full of the scrambled eggs and top each one with 1 teaspoon of sturgeon, whitefish, or salmon caviar. A simpler presentation is to serve the eggs in small ramekins.

Slow-Scrambled Eggs and Chives

[OEUFS BROUILLÉS À LA CIBOULETTE]

Replace the truffle with 3 tablespoons chopped chives and eliminate the standing period in step 1.

OMELET WITH HERBS

[OMELETTE AUX FINES HERBES]

MANY PEOPLE shy away from making omelets, feeling that they involve difficult techniques and a special pan. It is true that until the advent of nonstick surfaces, it was essential to have a well-seasoned omelet pan. Often the mere description of the seasoning process was enough to discourage a prospective omelet maker. But with a nonstick pan and the simple technique used here, omelet making should not be intimidating.

There are numerous approaches to omelet making, but I find that the technique that produces the best texture in the eggs is something I call the "stir-and-shake" method. The object is to keep the eggs moving (if the egg is allowed to sit too long over heat, it becomes hard and tough). When the eggs first hit the hot pan, I rapidly stir them off the bottom of the pan (as you would in making American-style scrambled eggs), at the same time shaking the pan gently. Then when the eggs are nearly set, I stop stirring and let the bottom of the omelet set, shaking the pan once or twice to keep it from sticking.

Everyone seems to have his own "secret" for making a light omelet. Some chefs add water or milk. (I know one who adds Tabasco sauce and swears by it.) I find that water or

HOW TO FOLD AN OMELET: A French Technique

American omelets are folded in half, whereas a French omelet is folded in thirds to encase its filling in a neat package. A professional chef folds an omelet and flips it out of the pan in one seamless motion, and you will, too, once you understand the following simple steps.

1. Stir the eggs until they are nearly set. Stop stirring and let the bottom of the omelet firm slightly.

2. Place the filling, if using, across the center of the omelet.

3. Push the omelet forward so the opposite side rises up.

4. Fold the risen portion to overlap the first fold.

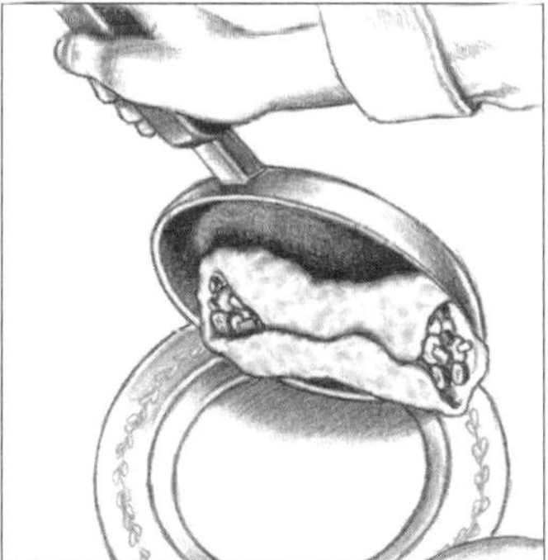

5. With your hand grasping the handle of the pan from underneath, turn the omelet out folded side down onto a serving platter.

OMELET PANS

An omelet pan has sloping sides, and the most popular size is 7 or 8 inches, which will make a 2- to 3-egg omelet. Even better for a 2-egg omelet is a 6-inch omelet pan. You can use larger pans to serve more people, but if you are a beginner, the smaller pan will be easier to work with. If I'm serving more than two people, I almost always use a smaller pan and make several omelets.

milk makes the eggs thinner, which might seem to be lighter, but to me, the only "secret" is working rapidly so the eggs do not toughen.

An *omelette aux fines herbes* is one of the most popular omelets in France and one of the finest omelets I have ever eaten, but only when fresh herbs are used. It serves one as a main course or two as a first course. **SERVES 1 OR 2**

3 eggs
1 teaspoon chopped fresh tarragon
1 teaspoon chopped fresh chives
1 teaspoon chopped fresh chervil or parsley
Pinch each of salt and freshly ground pepper
½ tablespoon butter

1. In a bowl, beat the eggs with the chopped herbs, salt, and pepper until just blended.

2. Melt the butter in a 7- to 8-inch nonstick omelet pan over medium-high heat.

3. Add the egg mixture to the pan and rapidly and constantly stir it with a wooden spoon or silicone spatula. If you can, gently shake the pan at the same time. When the eggs are nearly set but with a little liquid still remaining (you will see the bottom of your pan as you stir), stop stirring and shake the pan for a couple of seconds, making sure that the bottom of the pan is completely covered by the egg. At this point the eggs should be set, yet still moist. Stop shaking the pan and allow the bottom of the omelet to firm slightly, 4 to 5 seconds. (After making several omelets, you will be able to stir and shake the pan simultaneously.)

4. Fold the omelet into thirds by lifting the handle and tilting the pan at a 30-degree angle. With the back of the spoon or spatula, fold the portion of the omelet nearest the handle toward the center of the pan. Gently push the omelet forward in the pan so the unfolded portion rises up the side of the pan. With the pan now flat on your cooking surface, fold this portion back into the pan, overlapping the first fold. Grasping the handle of the pan from underneath, turn the omelet out onto a serving plate so it ends up folded side down (see "How to Fold an Omelet," page 37). Serve immediately.

TURKISH OMELET

[OMELETTE TURQUE]

AN OMELETTE TURQUE is a good example of a filled omelet, in which the flavorings are not mixed with the eggs but folded inside the cooked omelet. If you are lucky enough to have duck, squab, or pheasant livers, use them in place of the chicken livers. It serves one as a main course or two as a first course. **SERVES 1 OR 2**

1½ tablespoons butter
1 shallot, chopped
3 chicken livers, cut into chunks
Pinch of fresh or dried thyme
Salt and freshly ground pepper
2 tablespoons Madeira
2 teaspoons Meat Glaze (optional; page 309)
3 eggs

1. Melt 1 tablespoon of the butter in a 7- to 8-inch nonstick omelet pan over medium-high heat. Add the shallot and sauté until softened but not browned. Add the livers and sauté just until all sides are colored. Season with the thyme and 1 or 2 pinches of salt and pepper, to taste.

2. Add the Madeira and flame, if desired (see "How to Flambé," page 282). Cook to reduce the liquid by half. Add the meat glaze (if using). Toss the livers just to coat with the sauce (the livers should still be pink in the center), and remove from the heat. Using a slotted spoon, separate the livers from the sauce and keep both warm while you make the omelet.

3. In a small bowl, beat the eggs with a pinch of salt and pepper until just blended.

4. Wipe out the omelet pan, add the remaining ½ tablespoon butter and reheat over medium-high heat.

5. Add the egg mixture to the pan and rapidly and constantly stir with a wooden spoon or silicone spatula. When the eggs are nearly set but with a little liquid still remaining, stop stirring and shake the pan for a couple of seconds, making sure that the bottom of the pan is completely covered by the egg. At this point, the eggs should be set, yet still moist. Stop shaking the pan and allow the bottom of the omelet to firm slightly, 4 to 5 seconds. (After making several omelets, you will be able to stir and shake the pan simultaneously.)

6. Before folding the omelet, place the livers across the center. Fold the portion of the omelet nearest to you so it partially covers the livers. Gently push the omelet forward in the pan so the unfilled portion rises up the side of the pan. Using a wooden spoon or silicone spatula, fold this portion over to enclose the filling.

7. Turn the omelet, folded side down, out onto a plate (see "How to Fold an Omelet," page 37) and pour the reserved sauce around it. Serve immediately.

IN ADDITION

Ingredients used to flavor an omelet are sometimes mixed with the eggs before cooking (as in the Omelet with Herbs, page 36), whereas others are folded inside the omelet after it is cooked (as in Turkish Omelet). Although the choice of where to place the ingredients is often a personal one, I like to avoid mixing anything with the eggs that would cause them to discolor, such as tomatoes or sautéed mushrooms.

VARIATIONS

RATATOUILLE OMELET

[OMELETTE À LA RATATOUILLE]

Substitute 2 to 3 rounded tablespoons of Ratatouille (page 193) for the chicken liver filling (steps 1 and 2).

GRUYERE OMELET

[OMELETTE AU FROMAGE]

The classic cheese for an *omelette au fromage* is Gruyère or Emmentaler. If you use another cheese it is no longer *omelette au fromage* but, for example, *omelette au camembert.*

In place of the chicken liver filling (steps 1 and 2), place 2 to 3 rounded tablespoons (about 1 ounce) of grated Swiss-style cheese, such as Gruyère or Emmentaler, across the center of the omelet before folding.

SOUFFLES

THE SOUFFLÉ is perhaps the most famous creation ever to come out of the French kitchen. Light, airy, and delicately flavored, it is most often described in celestial terms. Restaurants rarely offer soufflés on their menus, but many will prepare one if ordered in advance.

I was taught that a soufflé must be made and baked at the last possible moment, and that it can never wait for your guests but rather your guests must wait for it. Over the years I have learned and refined techniques that will allow you to prepare most soufflés in advance (see "Preparing Soufflés for the Oven Ahead of Time," page 264), and to bake them without collars in 10 minutes or less. I cook soufflés in a very hot oven (475°F) so that the surface sets immediately in the high heat, as do the sides as they rise from the mold. The resulting light crust holds the soufflé together as it rises and eliminates the need for the paper collar often used to give extra height and support. (A note of caution, however: This high-temperature method only works with molds no larger than 4 to 5 cups.)

Traditionally, a soufflé is made of a base, a purée or flavoring, and stiffly beaten egg whites. For most classic savory soufflés, the base is essentially a thick béchamel sauce (made with butter, flour, and milk) to which a flavoring (cheese, spinach, ham) and egg yolks are added, before being lightened with stiffly beaten egg whites. Although this base is called for in most soufflé recipes, in my experience even fairly proficient cooks have problems with it. If the base is undercooked, it will be too thin and the soufflé will break off as it rises out of the mold. If overcooked, it will be too thick to easily incorporate with the beaten egg whites, and the results are often heavy or lumpy.

A dessert soufflé, on the other hand, doesn't seem to suffer these problems and it uses a base made without butter. I have therefore adapted this idea for savory soufflés, using what is effectively a sugarless pastry cream as a base.

Should you encounter problems while learning to make soufflés, see the "Soufflé Problem-Solving Chart" on page 45.

HAM SOUFFLE

[SOUFFLÉ AU JAMBON]

A HAM SOUFFLÉ makes a wonderful lunch or light supper when served with a green salad and dessert. The ham used can be baked ham, simple boiled ham, or more flavorful smoked or imported hams. The soufflé serves two for lunch or four as a first course. **SERVES 2 OR 4**

Butter and all-purpose flour, for soufflé mold
1 cup milk
3 egg yolks
1 tablespoon water
3 tablespoons all-purpose flour
⅛ teaspoon freshly ground pepper
1 tablespoon Madeira
1 teaspoon Dijon mustard
¼ pound ham (boiled, baked, or smoked), finely chopped
4 egg whites
⅛ teaspoon cream of tartar

1. Preheat the oven to 475°F with the rack set in the lowest position. Liberally butter a 4-cup soufflé mold and lightly dust with flour, tapping out any excess.

2. In a small saucepan, bring the milk to a boil over medium heat. While the milk is heating, whisk the egg yolks and water together in a small bowl. Add the 3 tablespoons flour to the yolks and blend until smooth and free of lumps.

3. Before the milk boils, stir about ¼ cup of it into the egg yolk mixture to thin it. When the remaining milk boils, add it to the egg yolk mixture and stir well.

4. Return the egg-milk mixture to the saucepan and whisk rapidly over medium-high heat, whisking the bottom and sides of the pan until the mixture thickens and boils, about 30 seconds. (Turning the pan as you whisk helps you easily reach all areas of the pan.) Continue to whisk vigorously for 1 minute while the soufflé base gently boils. It will become shiny and easier to stir.

5. Reduce the heat to medium and allow the soufflé base to simmer while you stir in the pepper, Madeira, mustard, and ham. Remove the pan from the heat and cover.

6. In a large bowl, beat the egg whites with the cream of tartar until stiff peaks form, about 3 minutes.

7. Pour the warm soufflé base into a large bowl. With a whisk, fold in one-third of the beaten egg whites to lighten it. Some egg white will still be visible. With a rubber spatula, fold in the remaining egg whites. Stop folding as soon as the mixture is blended; a little egg white may still be visible.

8. Pour the soufflé mixture into the prepared mold, leveling the surface with your spatula. If any of the batter touches the rim of the mold, run your thumb around the rim to clean it off.

(You can prepare the soufflé ahead to this point; see "Preparing Soufflés for the Oven Ahead of Time," page 264.)

9. Bake for 5 minutes. Lower the temperature to 425°F and bake for another 5 to 7 minutes. The soufflé should rise 1½ to 2 inches above the mold and brown lightly on the top. The top of this soufflé has a tendency to crack slightly. Serve immediately.

VARIATION

Smoked Salmon Souffle

[SOUFFLÉ AU SAUMON FUMÉ]

Substitute ¼ pound finely chopped smoked salmon (or any other smoked fish) for the ham. Omit the Madeira and mustard. Add 2 tablespoons chopped chives or dill with the fish in step 5.

BEATING EGG WHITES: The Magic of the Copper Bowl

A firmly beaten egg white is the "secret" of the success of all soufflés and many desserts; and there is no firmer egg white than the one that has been beaten by hand with a balloon whisk in an unlined copper bowl.

When egg whites are beaten in a copper bowl, the copper combines with the protein to form a polymer. Simply put, this means that the protein molecules and the copper combine to form a strong chemical chain. This allows you to beat the egg whites until they are very stiff without their breaking down.

When egg whites are not beaten in a copper bowl, a little cream of tartar should be added to the egg whites. Cream of tartar is a potassium salt. The potassium reacts with the egg whites as the copper does, although the chemical chain formed is not as strong. Nevertheless, with cream of tartar you can beat egg whites until they are stiff.

There's no reason for you to go out and buy a copper bowl unless you have poor results with the present procedure. If you are planning to buy one, however, I recommend a 10-inch-diameter bowl. With this size bowl you can beat 3 to 9 egg whites.

A balloon whisk is used for beating egg whites. For bowls ranging in size from 10 to 14 inches, I use a 14- to 16-inch balloon whisk. Many people use large sauce whisks or smaller balloon whisks with their large copper bowls, making their task much more difficult.

Before each use, the bowl should be cleaned with a little vinegar and salt, and then rinsed out with cold water and dried.

SPINACH SOUFFLE

[SOUFFLÉ AUX EPINARDS]

THIS IS A VERY LIGHT version of a spinach soufflé; if you make it with frozen spinach, it is also quick and easy. Just be sure to squeeze the spinach as dry as possible. The measurement for nutmeg here is for 2 or 3 pinches, which is difficult to measure accurately, so if in doubt, skimp; although a little nutmeg enhances the flavor of spinach, too much will overpower it. The soufflé serves two for lunch or four as a first course.

SERVES 2 OR 4

Butter and all-purpose flour, for soufflé mold
5 ounces frozen spinach, the washed, stemmed leaves from 1 pound fresh large spinach, or 8 ounces fresh baby spinach
1 cup milk
3 egg yolks
1 tablespoon water
3 tablespoons all-purpose flour
½ teaspoon salt
⅛ teaspoon freshly ground pepper
2 to 3 pinches of freshly grated nutmeg
4 egg whites
⅛ teaspoon cream of tartar

1. Preheat the oven to 475°F with the rack set in the lowest position. Liberally butter a 4-cup soufflé mold and lightly dust with flour, tapping out any excess.

2. If using frozen spinach, cook according to package directions, then drain and refresh under cold running water. If using fresh spinach, drop the leaves into boiling water and cook 1 to 2 minutes. Drain and refresh under cold running water. Squeeze the spinach to extract as much moisture as possible, and finely chop. Set aside.

3. In a small saucepan, bring the milk to a boil over medium heat. While the milk is heating, whisk the egg yolks and water together in a small bowl. Add the 3 tablespoons flour to the yolks and blend until smooth and free of lumps.

4. Before the milk boils, stir about ¼ cup of it into the egg yolk mixture to thin it. When the remaining milk boils, add it to the egg yolk mixture and stir well.

5. Return the egg-milk mixture to the saucepan and whisk rapidly over medium-high heat, whisking the bottom and sides of the pan until the mixture thickens and boils, about 30 seconds. (Turning the pan as you whisk helps you easily reach all areas of the pan.) Continue to whisk vigorously for 1 minute while the soufflé base gently boils. It will become shiny and easier to stir.

6. Reduce the heat to medium and allow the soufflé base to simmer while you season it with the salt, pepper, and nutmeg, then stir in the reserved spinach. Remove the pan from the heat and cover.

7. In a large bowl, beat the egg whites with the cream of tartar until stiff peaks form, about 3 minutes.

8. Pour the warm soufflé base into a large bowl. With a whisk, fold in one-third of the beaten egg whites to lighten it. Some egg white will still be visible. With a rubber spatula, fold in the remaining egg whites. Stop folding as soon as the mixture is blended; a little egg white may still be visible.

9. Pour the soufflé mixture into the prepared mold, leveling the surface with your spatula. If any of the batter touches the rim of the mold, run your thumb around the rim to clean it off. (The soufflé can be prepared ahead to this point; see "Preparing Soufflés for the Oven Ahead of Time," page 264.)

10. Bake for 5 minutes. Lower the temperature to 425°F and bake for another 5 to 7 minutes. The soufflé should rise 1½ to 2 inches above the mold and brown lightly on the top. The top may be slightly cracked, but this is not a problem. Serve immediately.

IN ADDITION

A finished soufflé will be firm and dry around the outside edge and soft and creamy in the center. Since most Americans are used to soufflés that are considerably drier, they often feel they have made a mistake when they find the creamy center. If you prefer a drier center, allow the soufflé to remain in the oven for 3 to 4 minutes longer.

VARIATIONS

You can vary the flavor of this soufflé by adding 1 ounce grated Swiss-style cheese, such as Gruyère or Emmentaler. You might also want to add some crumbled bacon, or a few mushrooms that have been chopped and sautéed. Just remember that the more you add, the heavier the soufflé becomes. If you decide to use all of the above-mentioned ingredients in the soufflé, add one more egg white to provide a little extra lift.

ROQUEFORT SOUFFLE

[SOUFFLÉ AU ROQUEFORT]

SINCE the ingredients for a cheese soufflé are generally at hand, it's easy to prepare an elegant lunch or light supper for unexpected guests. This particular version was inspired by a soufflé I had years ago at the restaurant Taillevent in Paris, but the cheese soufflé most commonly served in France is a *soufflé au fromage* (see Variation) made with Gruyère or Emmentaler. If Roquefort is difficult to find, substitute another blue cheese.

SERVES 2 OR 4

SOUFFLE PROBLEM-SOLVING CHART

PROBLEM	CAUSE	SOLUTION
Heavy uncooked bottom.	Unstable egg whites that break down. Soufflé made too far in advance.	Make sure you use cream of tartar. Make next soufflé just before baking.
Burnt top.	Rack is too high in the oven.	Bake on lowest rack in oven.
Top domed instead of flat.	Sides stuck to the mold as it rose. Mold was insufficiently buttered or insufficiently filled.	Very carefully loosen edge of soufflé with point of a knife and return to oven.
Top is concave, not flat, after the prescribed cooking time.	The center needs more cooking.	Reduce oven heat by 50 degrees and continue cooking for 2 to 5 minutes.
Soufflé rises abnormally high on one side.	Trapped air pocket expanded to push portion of soufflé too high.	When making your next soufflé, take care not to trap air when filling the mold.
Pieces of soufflé break off as it rises.	Soufflé base is too thin or liquidy.	When making soufflé again, add more flour or less liquid to base.

Butter and all-purpose flour, for soufflé mold
1 cup milk
3 egg yolks
1 tablespoon water
3 tablespoons all-purpose flour
1 teaspoon Dijon mustard
⅛ teaspoon freshly ground pepper
Pinch of freshly grated nutmeg
2 ounces Roquefort cheese, crumbled (about ⅔ cup)
4 egg whites
⅛ teaspoon cream of tartar

1. Preheat the oven to 475°F with the rack set in the lowest position. Liberally butter a 4-cup soufflé mold and lightly dust with flour, tapping out any excess.

2. In a small saucepan, bring the milk to a boil over medium heat. While the milk is heating, whisk the egg yolks and water together in a small bowl. Add the 3 tablespoons flour to the yolks and blend until smooth.

3. Before the milk boils, stir about ¼ cup of it into the egg yolk mixture to thin it.

When the remaining milk boils, add it and stir well.

4. Return the egg-milk mixture to the saucepan and whisk rapidly over medium-high heat, whisking the bottom and sides of the pan until the mixture thickens and boils, about 30 seconds. (Turning the pan as you whisk helps you easily reach all areas of the pan.) Continue to whisk vigorously for 1 minute while the soufflé base gently boils. It will become shiny and easier to stir.

5. Reduce the heat to medium and allow the soufflé base to simmer while you stir in the mustard, pepper, and nutmeg. Stir in the cheese and mix well until it melts completely and the mixture comes to a boil. Remove the pan from the heat and cover.

6. In a large bowl, beat the egg whites with the cream of tartar until stiff peaks form, about 3 minutes.

7. Pour the warm soufflé base into a large bowl. With a whisk, fold in one-third of the beaten egg whites to lighten it. Some egg white will still be visible. With a rubber spatula, fold in the remaining egg whites. Stop folding as soon as the mixture is blended; a little egg white may still be visible.

8. Pour the soufflé mixture into the prepared mold, leveling the surface with your spatula. If any of the batter touches the rim of the mold, run your thumb around the rim to clean it off. (You can prepare the soufflé ahead to this point; see "Preparing Soufflés for the Oven Ahead of Time," page 264.)

9. Bake for 5 minutes. Lower the temperature to 425°F and bake for another 5 to 7 minutes. The soufflé should rise 1½ to 2 inches above the mold and brown lightly on the top. Serve immediately.

SOUFFLE SAVOIR-FAIRE

The variety of soufflés that can be made is almost endless. But to be successful in creating your own variations, there are two important rules of thumb to keep in mind:

✦ Any ingredient added to the soufflé base should be fully cooked or ready to eat, because the soufflé cooks so rapidly that there is not enough time for raw ingredients to cook.

✦ Added ingredients should not contain excess moisture, since they will alter the soufflé's consistency.

VARIATION

GRUYERE SOUFFLE

[SOUFFLÉ AU FROMAGE]

Substitute 2 ounces grated (rounded ⅔ cup) Swiss-style cheese, such as Gruyère or Emmentaler, for the Roquefort. In step 5, when you add the cheese, be sure to return the soufflé base to a boil so the cheese loses its stringiness.

FISH MOUSSES

THERE ARE TWO CLASSIC TYPES of fish mousse. One type is made with cooked fish and served cold. If you have ever made a salmon mousse with mayonnaise, heavy cream, and gelatin, you are familiar with this style. Hot fish mousses, *mousselines de poisson,* are made differently.

Classically, a *mousseline de poisson* was made by pounding uncooked fish in a large mortar with a pestle until the strands of muscle fiber were stretched and broken down to form a gummy, springy paste. Egg whites were then pounded into the fish paste. Once smooth, this paste was forced through a fine sieve, leaving any bones, tendons, or fibrous tissue behind. This refined fish paste was then chilled, and cream was added until it became the consistency of creamy mashed potatoes.

Over the years, machines have been used to speed this lengthy process. The food processor's metal blade is usually so efficient that it cuts fish, bones, tendons, and all so small that it is not necessary to put it through a sieve, making the whole process quick and easy.

Although this way of making mousseline is much faster than the original method, the texture of the mousseline is not as smooth. To improve its texture, I use half fish and half shrimp. The shrimp pulverizes into a paste that, when poached, is very smooth. Blended with the fish, it produces a wonderful flavor and texture.

The fish mousseline is technically designed as a hot dish—as in the recipes that follow—but it is also good served cold, although you would then serve it with a cold rather than a hot sauce.

BASIC FISH MOUSSELINE

[MOUSSELINE DE POISSON]

ONE OF THE MOST sublime preparations to come out of the French kitchen is a well-made fish mousseline. Essentially a fish purée bound by egg whites and enriched by heavy cream, it can be poached, steamed, or baked. It can be used as a stuffing, as in Mousseline-Stuffed Trout with Two Sauces (page 52); or baked in a mold and served with a sauce, as for Fish Mousseline with a Hidden Scallop (page 51) or Mousseline Ring with Seafood (facing page); or it can be spoon-molded to make quenelles or small dumplings (see "Spoon-Molding Dumplings," page 71) and served with the Tomato-Flavored Velouté (*sauce aurore,* page 316) or Saffron Sauce with Fresh Tomatoes (page 317). You can use the mousseline plain or change its flavor and appearance by adding chopped truffles and chopped fresh herbs.

Before molding or using the mousseline, you should test its consistency by poaching a teaspoonful in a saucepan of simmering water. It should hold its shape, yet not be too firm or springy when eaten. **SERVES 8 TO 10**

1 pound skinless, boneless firm-fleshed white fish (such as flounder, cod, or tilapia), cut into 2-inch chunks
1 pound large shrimp, shelled and deveined (see Note)
4 egg whites
1 teaspoon salt
¼ teaspoon freshly ground pepper
⅛ teaspoon freshly grated nutmeg
2½ cups heavy cream

1. Place the fish and shrimp in a food processor fitted with the metal blade. Process the fish until it becomes a gummy paste.

2. Add the egg whites, one by one, and process until the mixture is very smooth. Blend in the salt, pepper, and nutmeg. With the machine running, add 2 cups of cream quickly in a steady stream. Turn off the processor as soon as the cream is incorporated. Too much processing at this point can cause the cream to turn to butter.

3. Place the fish mixture in a bowl and place the bowl in a larger bowl containing ice and a little water. Stirring occasionally, let the mixture sit until cold (about 5 minutes); once cold it will stiffen and hold more cream. Stir in the remaining cream a little at a time. Poach a spoonful of the mixture to determine if it needs more seasoning, egg white, or cream. If it's too firm and springy, it needs more cream; if it's soft, add a little more egg white. (The mousseline can be made up to one day in advance. Cover, and refrigerate until ready to use.)

NOTE: You can omit the shrimp if you want and use 2 pounds of fish. The mousseline will have a somewhat grainer texture.

IN ADDITION

Unless you have tasted a hand-pounded mousseline, you would not notice that one made with a processor is a little grainy instead of being silky smooth. To improve the texture of mousseline made in a processor, I occasionally use the plastic blade instead of the metal one. In effect, the duller plastic blade pounds the fish instead of cutting it. However, a mousseline made this way must then be forced through a food mill to eliminate any bones or tendons. To me, the end results are noticeably smoother; however, I go to this extra effort only for very special occasions.

When choosing a fish to use for a mousseline, look for the freshest possible. The fresher the fish, the better the mousseline will be. Look for thick fillets from large fish, which hold their freshness longer than thin ones.

VARIATION

Fish Terrine

[TERRINE DE POISSON]

Follow the instructions for constructing the Home-Style Terrine with Prunes (page 54), using the uncooked fish mousseline in place of the ground meats. Use lightly poached salmon, lobster, or sea scallops in place of the strips of ham and chicken. Bake like the terrine in a 400°F oven until springy to the touch, about 1 hour.

Mousseline Ring with Seafood in a Saffron-Tomato Sauce

[TURBAN DE FRUITS DE MER]

A SPECTACULAR presentation can be created by molding a fish mousseline in a ring mold. When baked and unmolded, the ring, or "turban," is filled with seafood and topped with one of several highly refined sauces. A classic turban is made by first lining the mold with fillets of sole. I find that this adds neither contrast of texture and color nor a smoother surface to the dish. And because it is time consuming and expensive, I have eliminated that aspect of the dish.

Although I have specified the use of small shrimp and bay scallops, if sea scallops are fresher, use them along with medium-size shrimp. Oysters can be used in place of or in addition to the mussels, and Poached Mushrooms (page 95) can be added if desired.

If saffron is not available or not appreciated, serve the turban with Tomato-Flavored Velouté (*sauce aurore,* page 316). The mousseline and the sauce can be prepared a day before serving. **SERVES 8 TO 10**

Butter, for ring mold
Basic Fish Mousseline (page 48)
2 pounds mussels, scrubbed and debearded
2 shallots, finely chopped
½ cup dry white wine
½ pound small shrimp, shelled and deveined
½ pound bay scallops
Saffron Sauce with Fresh Tomatoes (page 317)

1. Preheat the oven to 350°F with the rack set in the lowest position. Butter a 1½-quart ring mold.

2. Fill the mold with the mousseline and smooth the surface. Place the mold in a baking pan. Pour in enough boiling water to reach halfway up the mold and bake until the top is springy to the touch and a cake tester inserted into the center comes out clean, 30 to 40 minutes.

3. Meanwhile, place the mussels, shallots, and wine in a large saucepan. Cover and steam over high heat, shaking the pan several times to toss the mussels. The mussels will open and be cooked after about 5 minutes of steaming. Remove the mussels from their shells and set aside. Discard any that have not opened.

4. Strain the mussel liquid through a fine-mesh sieve into a small saucepan, discarding any sand or grit that may remain at the bottom of the pan. Boil over high heat until reduced to ¼ cup, about 5 minutes. Set aside.

5. Bring a large saucepan of water to a boil over high heat and drop in the shrimp and scallops. When the water returns to the boil, drain the shrimp and scallops immediately and refresh under cold running water. Set aside.

6. In a large saucepan, reheat the saffron sauce over medium heat. Add the shrimp, scallops, mussels, and reduced mussel cooking liquid to the sauce. Heat, stirring occasionally, until the sauce begins to simmer; do not boil.

7. To assemble, unmold the mousseline onto a large, warmed serving platter and use paper towels to absorb any excess moisture. With a slotted spoon, transfer the shellfish to the center of the ring. Spoon the sauce over the shellfish and around the sides of the mousseline ring just before serving.

How to Clean Mussels

Pull the beard out from between the mussel shells with paring knife and thumb as below. Rub the mussels vigorously against each other to remove any debris and at the same time cause the mussels to open slightly, releasing grit. Rinse the mussels in a large bowl of water. Remove the mussels and pour off the dirt and water. Repeat until the water is clean.

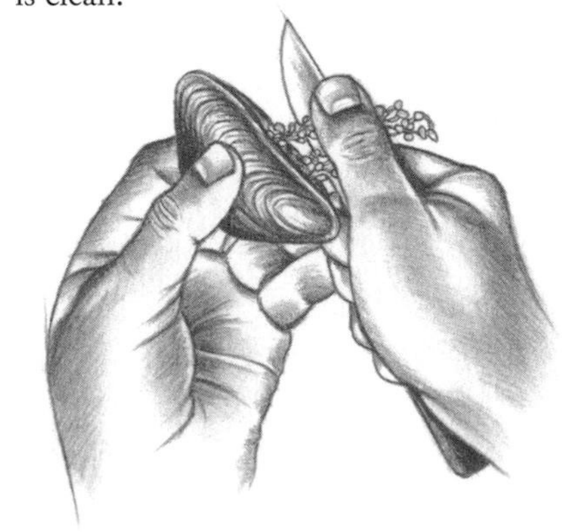

FISH MOUSSELINE WITH A HIDDEN SCALLOP

[COQUILLES ST.-JACQUES EN SURPRISE]

A SCALLOP buried in each ramekin-molded mousseline is the *surprise* in the French title.

The fish mousseline can be made and assembled with the poached scallops in the ramekins up to one day in advance of serving. The ramekins cook rapidly on top of the stove in a covered skillet partially filled with simmering water. **SERVES 10**

Butter, for ramekins
10 sea scallops, tendons removed (see page 30)
Basic Fish Mousseline (page 48)
Beurre Blanc (page 329), Hollandaise Sauce (page 326), Tomato-Flavored Velouté (page 316), or Saffron Sauce with Fresh Tomatoes (page 317)

1. Butter ten ¾-cup ramekins.

2. In a medium-size saucepan of simmering water, poach the scallops for 15 seconds. Drain immediately and set aside.

3. Divide the mousseline equally among the prepared ramekins. Bury a scallop in the center of each portion. (The recipe can be prepared a day ahead to this point. Cover and refrigerate.)

4. Place the ramekins in a large skillet with a cover. Add boiling water to come ½ inch up the sides of the ramekins. Cover and simmer over medium-high heat until the mousseline puffs and is springy to the touch at the center of each ramekin, about 10 minutes.

5. To serve: Unmold the mousselines onto paper towels to drain off the excess moisture and place them on individual serving plates. Serve with your choice of sauce.

IN ADDITION

If you add 2 medium (¾-inch) truffles, chopped, or ¼ cup chopped chives to the mousseline, the color contrast with the hidden scallop is even more dramatic.

MOUSSELINE-STUFFED TROUT WITH TWO SAUCES

[TRUITE FARCIE AUX DEUX SAUCES]

A FISH MOUSSELINE can be used to stuff any size fish. I once sailed on the *S.S. France* and was served one of their specialties, a turbot stuffed with a lobster mousseline. Because there were 12 of us at table, they served an 18-pound turbot.

A more manageable-size fish is a brook trout. Often sold boned, the fish can be easily stuffed and poached. Wrap the fish in plastic wrap to hold it and the stuffing together while poaching. **SERVES 4**

2 small (about 1 pound each) brook trout, boned, with head and tail on
½ recipe Basic Fish Mousseline (page 48)
½ recipe Beurre Blanc (page 329)
½ recipe Watercress Beurre Blanc (page 330)

1. Fill the cavity of each fish with the mousseline, smoothing with a spatula.

2. Wrap each fish in plastic wrap or aluminum foil and place in a single layer in a large skillet, fish poacher, or shallow roasting pan. Pour in enough boiling water to reach halfway up the fish. Cover and simmer over medium heat until the mousseline is firm, 10 to 15 minutes.

3. Unwrap and drain the fish on paper towels. Place the fish on a warmed platter. Carefully peel the skin from the exposed side of the body. For presentation, spoon the plain beurre blanc around the fish on half of the platter. Spoon the watercress beurre blanc around the other half. To serve, divide each trout crosswise in half (two people get heads, and two, the tails).

HOW TO SKIN A COOKED FISH FOR PRESENTATION

Make sure you place the fish on a clean flat surface before beginning

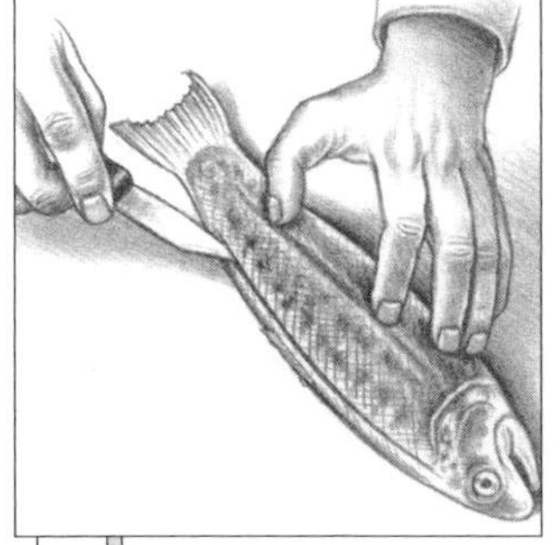

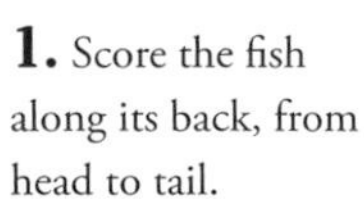

1. Score the fish along its back, from head to tail.

2. Peel the skin down to the belly and remove. Leave the skin on the head intact. Carefully turn the fish and repeat on the second side.

PATES & TERRINES

I REMEMBER EATING PÂTÉ often as a child. It was served on crackers or small rounds of toast as an hors d'oeuvre. It was always smooth and livery tasting. Years later, after my interest in French cooking had taken hold and I was living in France, I learned that the majority of pâtés were more of a coarse, chunky variety—sort of like meat loaf—and only those made from liver (goose, duck, chicken, and pork) were smooth.

Even though the full range of pâtés has been discovered on this side of the Atlantic, there is still a tendency to lump them all under the heading of pâté, whereas there are distinct differences. Literally speaking, the word *pâté* means baked in a crust—which was designed to be a strong, edible, decorative container for the meat mixture. A terrine, on the other hand, is baked in a ceramic mold (called a terrine). In fact, the mold is often designed to look like a pâté's crust. Then there are the galantines and ballotines—the aristocrats of the pâté world. Instead of a crust or a mold, the pâté mixture is usually poached or baked wrapped inside the skin of a chicken or duck and coated in aspic.

Although the container changes, the components and techniques for making a pâté, terrine, galantine, or ballotine are pretty much the same. They all contain a seasoned ground meat called a forcemeat, or *farce,* and strips of meat or poultry to add both a contrasting texture and a pattern to the sliced pâté. Most are served cold, with or without an aspic coating.

For this book, I have omitted pâtés baked in a crust (*en croûte*), because I don't think the crust is worth the effort and even properly made is so thick that it's close to inedible. And I've omitted galantines and ballotines, because they are really quite a time-consuming (though rewarding) production.

In the following recipes, I have removed a great deal of the fat called for in their classic counterparts, using just enough to give the pâtés the proper texture and taste.

HOME-STYLE TERRINE WITH PRUNES

[TERRINE MAISON AUX PRUNEAUX]

THIS TERRINE is a good all-purpose recipe that can serve as a guide for numerous variations. You can use different meats or different flavoring and decorative ingredients (see "Terrines Variées," facing page). Note that terrines need to be made at least a day in advance of serving, and optimally two to three days ahead.

Although this is a typical terrine, it differs from most in its fat content. Most recipes call for the baking mold to be lined with thin sheets of pork fat, and the meat itself covered with the same fat. This method originated in the days before refrigeration, to protect the terrine from airborne bacteria by completely sealing it with fat. I have omitted this fat from the recipe, as well as the strips of pork fat traditionally used to make a mosaic pattern in the sliced pâté.

Although the terrine is usually baked in a loaf shape and served cold, you can also shape the seasoned ground meat into patties, pan-fry like sausage, and serve with eggs for breakfast or with vegetables for dinner. Mixed with some cooked rice or bread crumbs, it can also be used to stuff cabbage or green peppers. **SERVES 8**

4 shallots, trimmed and peeled
5 large sprigs parsley, tough stems removed
¼-inch slice (about ¼ pound) ham (boiled, baked, or smoked), cut into ¼-inch-wide strips
½ pound skinless, boneless chicken breast, cut into ¼-inch-wide strips
1 teaspoon salt
¾ teaspoon freshly ground pepper
½ teaspoon fresh or dried thyme leaves
¼ cup plus 2 tablespoons dry white wine
2 tablespoons Cognac
3 tablespoons Madeira
5 ounces fresh pork fat, cut into chunks
12 pitted prunes, marinated in Madeira (see page 299)
¾ pound lean pork, ground
¾ pound veal (shoulder), ground
⅛ teaspoon ground allspice
1 egg
1 tablespoon potato starch or cornstarch

1. In a food processor, finely chop the shallots and parsley.

2. Lay the strips of ham and chicken in a shallow dish and sprinkle with half of the shallot mixture, ¼ teaspoon of the salt, ¼ teaspoon of the pepper, and ¼ teaspoon of the thyme. Moisten with the 2 tablespoons white wine, 1 tablespoon of the Cognac, and 1 tablespoon of the Madeira.

3. Add the pork fat and 4 of the prunes to the remaining shallot mixture in the processor and process to grind the fat, about 10 seconds.

4. Add the ground lean pork and veal to the

TERRINES VARIEES

✦ Use duck, pheasant, rabbit, or hare in place of the chicken, and the name changes to *terrine de canard, faisan, lapin,* or *lièvre aux pruneaux.*

✦ Use chicken livers (soaked in Armagnac or Cognac) in place of the prunes. Use about the same number of livers as prunes. Substitute strips of beef tongue for the ham.

✦ Add about 2 tablespoons green peppercorns or 1 medium (¾-inch) truffle, chopped, to the ground meat to change both flavor and appearance.

✦ Instead of cutting them into strips, cut the chicken and ham into dice and stir into the seasoned ground meats. This will save time and produce a more typical, though less sophisticated, looking terrine.

processor and season with the allspice and the remaining salt, pepper, and thyme. Moisten with the remaining wine, Cognac, and Madeira. Add the egg and potato starch and process to combine, about 15 seconds.

5. Divide the seasoned ground meat into four even portions. Spread one portion evenly over the bottom of a terrine or 4- to 5-quart loaf pan, using your fingers to make sure the corners are filled in.

6. Completely cover the ground meat with alternating strips of chicken and ham, placing them lengthwise. You may have to cut the strips to fit the terrine. Cover the strips with another layer of ground meat, again using your fingers if necessary to spread the mixture evenly.

7. Make a tight, compact row of prunes down the center, pressing them halfway into the layer of ground meat (you may need all the prunes). Cover with the third layer of ground meat.

8. Cover the ground meat with the remaining chicken and ham strips. Cover with the final portion of ground meat, pressing it down with your hands to fit the terrine. Cover with the terrine lid or aluminum foil. (If time permits, let the terrine stand in the refrigerator overnight before baking to allow the flavors to fully develop.)

9. Preheat the oven to 400°F with the rack set in the lowest position.

10. Place the terrine in a larger baking pan and place on the pulled-out oven rack. Add boiling water to come 1½ inches up the sides of the terrine. Bake for 1 hour.

11. Lower the oven temperature to 350°F and bake an additional 30 minutes. When done, the melted fat and juices should be clear and not cloudy. The meat will have shrunk away from the sides of the terrine, a cake tester inserted into the center of the terrine will come out hot to the touch, and an instant-read thermometer should read about 160°F.

12. Remove the terrine from the oven, but keep it covered in the pan of water. Evenly weight the surface of the terrine with a 4- to 5-pound weight (e.g., 2 large cans of tomatoes) and allow to cool. If your terrine has a lid, remove it and replace it with aluminum foil before weighting.

13. When cool, after about 1½ hours, remove the weight, cover the surface with plastic wrap, and refrigerate. The terrine is best eaten several days after it has been cooked, or it can be frozen for later use. To serve, cut the terrine into ½-inch slices.

IN ADDITION

There are a number of attractive white porcelain terrines that can be used for pâté. Those with ducks or rabbits on their lids can also be used, although technically they should have the meat of those animals in them. Most people, however, will use a ceramic or glass loaf pan and instead of bringing the terrine to the table, will present slices of the pâté on a platter or individual plates.

SERVING SUGGESTION

Slices of the terrine can be served as a first course, or with a mixed green salad, warm baguette, and dessert for lunch or a light supper. Serve the terrine with cornichons (small French pickles) or on a bed of lettuce.

WINE

Both white and red wines are suitable for serving with terrines.

VARIATION

RUSTIC COUNTRY-STYLE PATE

[PÂTÉ DE CAMPAGNE]

For a country-style pâté, simply omit the ham and chicken strips and the prunes and grind up ½ pound of pork liver with the meat and pork fat.

CHICKEN LIVER MOUSSE

[MOUSSE DE FOIE DE VOLAILLE]

THIS IS A QUICK and easy recipe for chicken liver mousse. Traditionally, an equal amount of butter is mixed with the livers to make the mousse. I have used what I consider to be the minimum amount for a successful mousse. When available, use duck, goose, pheasant, or pigeon livers. **SERVES 12**

2 sticks (8 ounces) plus 3 tablespoons butter
3 shallots, chopped
1 pound chicken livers
½ teaspoon fresh or dried thyme leaves
½ teaspoon salt (omit if using salted butter)
⅛ to ¼ teaspoon freshly ground pepper, to taste
¼ cup Madeira
2 teaspoons Meat Glaze (optional; page 309)
2 teaspoons Cognac

1. In a 10-inch skillet, melt 3 tablespoons of the butter over medium heat. Sauté the shallots quickly until they are softened but not browned, 2 to 3 minutes.

How to Easily and Simply Decorate a Mousse

For an impressive finishing touch that's worth the effort, you can layer the top of your molded *mousse de foie de volaille* with aspic. To make an aspic, add 4 packages of unflavored gelatin to either the Chicken Consommé (page 17) or Beef Consommé (page 18). Cool the aspic to room temperature and pour a thin layer over the mousse. Place the mousse in the refrigerator to set the aspic. The unused portion of the aspic can either be reheated and served as a hot consommé or poured into a shallow baking dish or roasting pan, chilled until set, and then chopped and served with the mousse. If you would like to decorate the mousse further (see below), save some of the aspic for the final decorations.

Move the moistened decoration to the chilled mousse with the point of a knife.

For simple decorations, use tomato skin, hard-cooked egg white, and leek, scallion, parsley, or tarragon leaves. (The leaves should be blanched in boiling water for 5 to 10 seconds and refreshed under cold running water to set their color.) Plan the design and cut everything into the desired shapes before placing on the mousse.

When you are ready to decorate, moisten the decoration by spooning some liquid aspic over it. With the point of a knife, move the decoration to the chilled aspic-coated surface (the decorations can also be placed directly on top of a mousse that hasn't yet been coated with aspic). Refrigerate the mousse until the aspic on the decorations has set, about 15 minutes. Cover with another thin layer of liquid aspic and chill for at least 1 hour.

A decorated mousse.

2. Add the livers, increase the heat, and sauté just until all sides have been colored lightly, 2 to 3 minutes. Season with the thyme, salt, and pepper. Transfer the livers to a food processor or blender.

3. Add the Madeira and meat glaze (if using) to the skillet and reduce by half over high heat, about 45 seconds. Set aside.

4. Purée the livers and the remaining 2 sticks butter until smooth. Mix in the reduced pan liquid and Cognac. Taste and adjust the seasoning, if necessary.

5. Pour the mousse into a porcelain mold or individual molds for serving and cover the surface with plastic wrap. Refrigerate for a minimum of 2 hours. Serve with toast or crackers.

CREPES

Crêpes are one of those specialties that go in and out of fashion. At one time there were American restaurants that served nothing but crêpes, but these days they are often overlooked. If they appear at all, they are probably served as dessert.

In France, crêpes can be served throughout the meal, beginning with the first course—folded around a savory filling, coated with a sauce, and baked.

Crêpes freeze exceptionally well, and if you prepare some to have on hand, making stuffed crêpes can be easy. When I make crêpes to freeze for future use, I do not put waxed paper between each crêpe as most cookbooks instruct. I generally freeze the crêpes in a stack, in the quantity that I am most likely to need (assuming two to three crêpes per person). When I'm ready to use them, I put the whole stack to warm in the oven, making them pliable and easy to use.

SAVORY CREPES

[CRÊPES SALÉES]

THE BATTER for these basic crêpes can be used for all savory crêpes. In addition to the salt and pepper, you can add seasoning to the batter based on what the filling will be. A touch of freshly grated nutmeg for a spinach filling, or a little curry powder for creamed chicken or seafood, are just two examples of spices that can be added. I often add chopped chives or a few thinly sliced scallions, which add both color and flavor to the crêpe.

The number of crêpes that you can make from this recipe will depend on how thin the batter is and how thin you make the crêpes. If you let the batter rest after making it, the flour swells, making the batter smoother and thicker. If you find your first crêpe too thick, add a little more milk to the batter. When cooking the crêpes, once the pan is coated with the batter, any excess should be poured out to keep the crêpes thin.

I use a nonstick crêpe pan or a nonstick omelet pan with a 6- to 7-inch surface instead of the classic steel pans, and recommend that you do also. Even with a nonstick pan, you should lubricate it with a touch of oil or butter for the first few crêpes, or whenever needed, if you want to be able to flip the crêpes (which is especially fun for children) as instructed in step 4. Otherwise, the crêpe batter will stick to the pan as it cooks, and you won't be able to shake the crêpe loose to flip it. It is, however, an easy matter to loosen and turn the crêpe with a silicone spatula.

Once made, the stacked crêpes can be set aside to cool, then tightly wrapped in plastic wrap and stored in the refrigerator for up to 2 days, or frozen for several months. To use them, simply reheat in a 250°F oven until warm, about 15 to 20 minutes. When warm, the crêpes will be pliable and will separate easily. **MAKES 16 TO 24 SIX-INCH CRÊPES**

1 cup plus 1 tablespoon (150g) all-purpose flour (see Note)
3 eggs
1½ cups milk
¼ teaspoon salt
⅛ teaspoon freshly ground pepper
3 tablespoons melted butter or vegetable oil, plus extra for the pan

1. In a bowl, stir the flour, eggs, ½ cup of the milk, and the salt and pepper with a whisk until you have a smooth batter. Add the remaining 1 cup milk and stir well. If time permits, allow the batter to rest for 30 minutes. (As the batter rests, the granules of flour absorb the milk and swell, creating a smoother batter and a slightly stronger crêpe than if used right away.)

2. Just before using, whisk in the melted butter.

3. Heat a 6-inch crêpe pan over medium-high heat. The pan is ready when a drop of water dances on the hot surface of the pan. (Lightly coat the pan with butter or oil if needed.) Hold the pan in one hand, tilting it slightly. Using a small ladle or coffee measurer, pour about

2 tablespoons of batter into the pan where the sides and bottom meet. Now turn the pan in a circular motion to spread the batter evenly. The amount of batter used should just coat the bottom of the pan. Any excess should be poured back into the batter bowl.

4. Cook the crêpe until the edge begins to brown. Turn the crêpe, carefully lifting it with a spatula, or flip it. To flip, first make sure that the crêpe can slide in the pan by shaking it vigorously if necessary. Flip with a forward and upward motion of your hand, keeping your eye on the crêpe. Although your first few may land on the floor, you will soon be catching them as they turn over. Cook the second side for only 10 to 15 seconds and slide the crêpe onto a plate.

5. Repeat until all the crêpes are made, stacking them one on top of the other and allowing them to cool. The top surface of the crêpe should be medium brown in color, and the underneath pale yellow. If after making two crêpes you find the color either too dark or too light, adjust your heat accordingly. At the same point, if you find the crêpe is too thick, add a little more milk to thin the batter.

NOTE: I've included gram measurements here, because this is in effect a pastry recipe. See Appendix A (page 360) for more on the metric system in pastry making.

IN ADDITION

The batter can also be made in a blender. Place all ingredients in the container of the blender, cover, and turn the blender on and then off again. Scrape down the flour that has stuck to the sides of the blender and blend again until smooth.

HAM AND MUSHROOM CREPES WITH MORNAY SAUCE

[CRÊPES AU JAMBON SAUCE MORNAY]

I FIND IT DIFFICULT to give set recipes for stuffed crêpes, because to me they are perfectly designed for using leftovers and are an inspiration of the moment, not something for which you should go shopping. Easy to make and elegant to serve, they are ideal for the leftover lamb, turkey, or ham in your refrigerator. They can be eaten on the spot, of course, but you can also stuff, sauce, and store them for up to 2 days in the

STUFFED CREPES: *Crêpes Farcies*

A *crêpe farcie* can be a wonderfully elegant creation, with the crêpe batter, filling, and sauce all designed to go with one another and seasoned accordingly. Or crêpes can dress up leftovers for a simple family meal. The possible combinations of ingredients for stuffing crêpes is limited only by your imagination, but there are some guidelines for a stuffing mixture that to me has the proper consistency and will hold together, and there are some combinations of stuffings and sauces that are also typically French.

BASIC STUFFING FORMULA: For each 6-inch crêpe, use 3 tablespoons of diced or chopped cooked ingredients (such as meat, fish, shellfish, poultry, vegetables, cheese, or combinations) bound together with 1 tablespoon or so of the sauce you will be using to cover the crêpes.

SUGGESTED COMBINATIONS:

✦ Diced chicken and mushrooms with a velouté flavored with tarragon.

✦ Shrimp, crab, lobster, or scallops with a curry-flavored béchamel.

✦ Fill with the four-cheese mixture from Four-Cheese Ravioli (page 84) and serve with a tomato sauce sprinkled with grated Parmesan.

refrigerator or for a month, well wrapped, in the freezer.

But if you are seeking a recipe, this is one of my favorites. It can be made totally in advance and reheated just before serving. Using a processor to chop all the ingredients makes this very easy. **SERVES 8**

Butter, for serving dish
16 Savory Crêpes (page 59)
¼ pound ham (boiled, baked, or smoked), finely chopped
5 sprigs parsley, chopped
Duxelles (page 187)
Mornay Sauce (page 314)
1 or 2 tablespoons milk
1 ounce Swiss-style cheese, such as Gruyère or Emmentaler, grated (about ⅓ cup)

1. Preheat the broiler.

2. Butter 8 individual oval gratin dishes or 1 large baking dish. Place a stack of crêpes, light side facing up, on a plate.

3. Stir the chopped ham and parsley into the duxelles. In a saucepan, bring the mornay sauce to a simmer. Add enough sauce to the ham and parsley to bind it, about ¼ cup. Taste and adjust the seasoning if necessary.

4. Place about 3 tablespoons of filling down the center of the first crêpe. Lift up one edge of the crêpe to cover the filling. Do the same with the other edge, totally enclosing the filling. Place your palms over the crêpe, and with your fingertips facing each other, roll the crêpe onto your hands and transfer it to the baking dish. The fold of the crêpe should be on the bottom. Repeat with the remaining crêpes. If you are using the individual gratin dishes, place 2 crêpes in each.

5. Reheat the remaining sauce. Thin with the milk and bring to a boil, whisking well. Spoon the sauce over the crêpes to completely cover. Sprinkle the grated cheese over all the crêpes. (The crêpes can be prepared in advance up to this point. Cover and refrigerate for up to 1 day or wrap tightly and freeze for up to 1 week.)

6. Place the crêpes under the broiler until the sauce browns lightly, about 5 minutes. Warn your guests that the dishes are *très chaud* (very hot) and serve. (If the crêpes have been made ahead and refrigerated or frozen, bring them back to room temperature before broiling. If time is an issue, you can bake the crêpes straight from the refrigerator or freezer. Reheat them in the upper third of a 475°F oven until the sauce is bubbling and the surface has browned lightly, 10 to 15 minutes. Add a few extra minutes if the crêpes were frozen.)

SOUFFLE-FILLED CREPES: *Crêpes Soufflés*

You can also stuff a crêpe with soufflé batter and then bake it to cook and puff the soufflé. Use any of the first-course soufflés in the book (pages 40–46), and follow the instructions for the dessert version of this soufflé-filled crêpe in "Dessert Crêpe Variations," page 280.

QUICHES

ORIGINALLY A QUICHE was a rich cheese custard tart from Alsace and Lorraine. Sometimes it would be made with the addition of ham or bacon.

In France, if you order quiche, you will probably be served a classic quiche Lorraine. A more contemporary and eclectic approach to cooking, however, has made this simple classic a blueprint that can be used with a multitude of added ingredients. Perhaps the most surprising and delicious quiche I've tasted in this country was made with jalapeño peppers and Monterey Jack cheese. Another of my favorites is one made with crab and a curry-flavored custard in a puff pastry shell (see Curried Crab Quiche, page 67).

The classic custard used for a quiche combines eggs and heavy cream to make a very rich filling. I prefer a lighter custard, using milk instead of cream and fewer eggs to bind it. By using a shallow tart pan with a removable bottom instead of a deep quiche mold or pie dish, the resulting crust will not be soggy and the thinner portions will be more suitable for a first course.

If you'd like to come up with your own combinations of ingredients for a quiche, just keep in mind that you'll need enough diced ingredients to cover the bottom of the tart shell (about 2 cups).

QUICHE LORRAINE

QUICHE LORRAINE is the best known of all quiches. It is traditionally made in a deep crust, and one slice can serve as a light meal. I prefer it made with a light and delicate custard in a shallower tart shell and served as a first course. Recipes for this classic quiche vary in a number of ways. Half an onion can be chopped, sautéed, and added to the filling; crumbled bacon can be used instead of ham; and the custard can be made with more eggs and heavy cream. **SERVES 6 TO 8**

Tart Pastry (page 213)
1 tablespoon Dijon mustard
2 eggs plus 1 egg yolk
1½ cups milk
¼ teaspoon salt
⅛ teaspoon freshly ground pepper
Pinch of freshly grated nutmeg
¼ pound ham (boiled, baked, or smoked), diced, or 8 strips of cooked bacon, crumbled
¼ pound Swiss-style cheese, such as Gruyère or Emmentaler, diced, sliced, or grated (about 1⅓ cups)

1. Preheat the oven to 475°F with the rack set in the middle position.

2. Line a 9½- or 10-inch tart pan with removable bottom with the pastry (see "How to Line a Tart Pan," facing page).

3. Prick the pastry (see Note), line it with aluminum foil, and weight it with 1 pound of dried beans, rice, or aluminum pie weights. Bake until the edges of the pastry begin to color, about 20 minutes. Remove the pan from the oven and remove the foil and beans from the pan. Spread the mustard over the bottom of the pastry. Lower the oven temperature to 425°F.

4. In a bowl, beat the eggs and yolk lightly. Blend in the milk, salt, pepper, and nutmeg.

5. Spread the ham and cheese evenly over the bottom of the tart shell. Pour the custard into the tart shell to within ⅛ inch of the top of the crust. Holding the tart pan by the outer rim (so as not to dislodge the bottom), place the pan in the oven.

6. Bake until the custard puffs, 25 to 30 minutes.

7. Unmold as soon as possible (see "Unmolding a Tart or Quiche," page 218). Allow to cool for at least 10 minutes before cutting into wedges and serving. The quiche is delicious served at any temperature. (The quiche can be made in advance. It will keep well in the refrigerator for several days. Reheat in a 350°F oven for 10 to 15 minutes before serving.)

NOTE: To help prevent the pastry from bubbling up during baking, prick the bottom all over with the sharp point of a paring knife. Do not use a fork for this purpose, for the holes created may be too large and allow liquids to leak out. (At this point the pastry can be covered with plastic wrap and refrigerated or frozen along with any unused pastry.)

How to Line a Tart Pan

1. Lightly butter your tart pan. You need only a very small amount of butter for this purpose, just enough to hold the pastry in the pan.

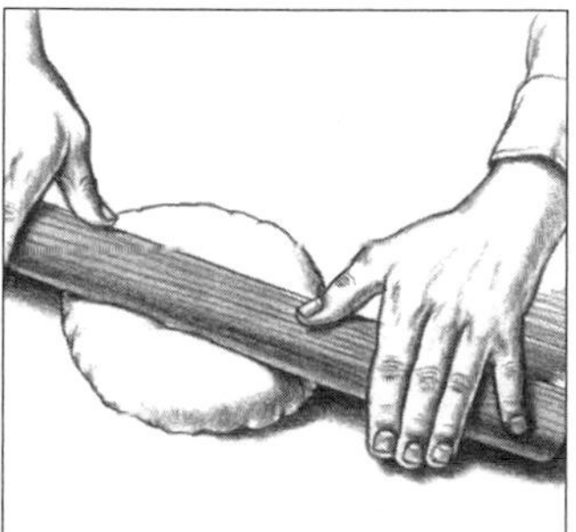

2. Dust the pastry and work the surface lightly. Roll out the pastry (keeping it round), lifting and rotating it one quarter turn after each roll. Dust between each roll. Continue rolling in this fashion until the pastry is about ¼ inch thick.

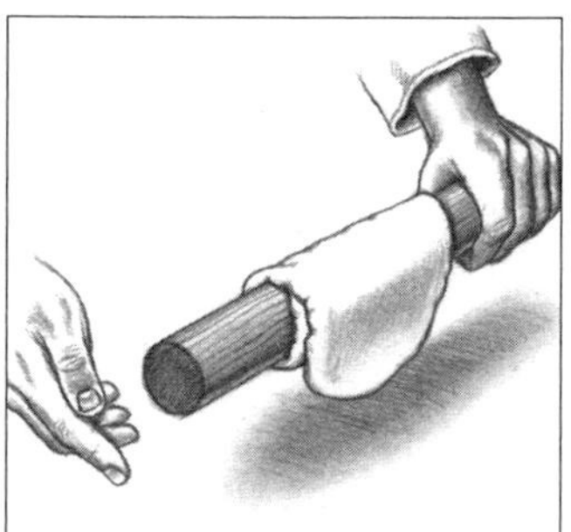

3. Roll the pastry onto the rolling pin, turn it 90 degrees, and unroll it onto your lightly floured work surface. Continue this rolling, lifting, and turning process until the pastry is about ⅛ inch thick. Your pastry should be about 14 inches in diameter. Although, by habit I use this method to roll out tart pastry, I sometimes roll it out between two pieces of plastic wrap. This leaves less flour to clean up.

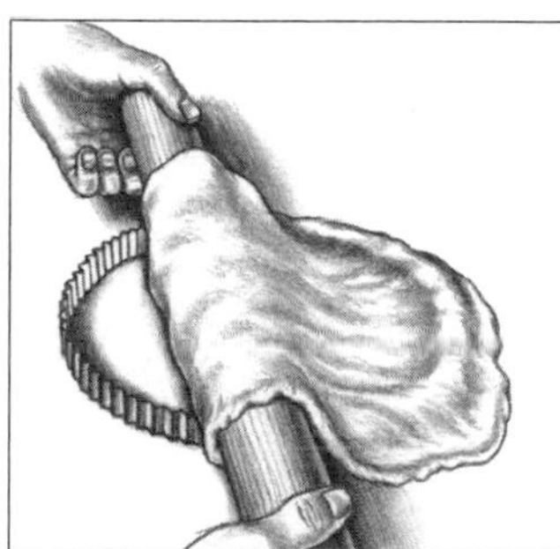

4. Roll the pastry onto the pin, and unroll it into the tart pan. The pastry will overlap the pan an inch or more.

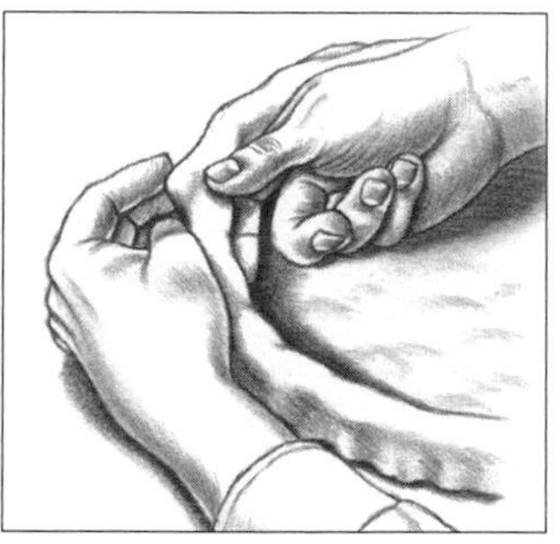

5. After placing the pastry in the tart pan, place your bent index finger at the upper inside edge of the mold. Push about ½ inch of the overlapping pastry in over your finger and press gently with your thumb. Continue around the pan to form a rim.

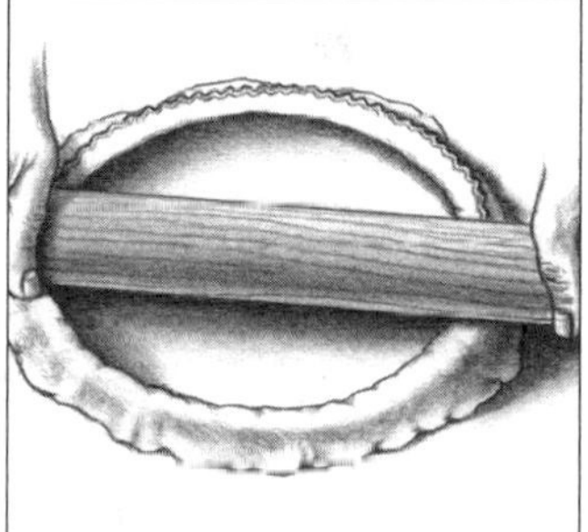

6. Cut off the excess pastry by rolling the pin across the top of the pan. Remove the cutoff pastry from the outer edge of the pan.

7. Lift the rim of dough (see step 5) up at a 45-degree angle and press between the thumb and forefinger to make a raised rim. Note that without a rim, you will have a shallower tart shell that may not hold all the custard in your recipe. To decorate the rim, see "Making a Decorative Rim" (page 68).

ONION TART

[TARTE À L'OIGNON]

THIS SIMPLE onion tart, a member of the quiche family, reminds me of many wonderful meals I have had at inexpensive restaurants in rural France.

In the traditional recipe, the onions are cooked slowly until soft and then mixed with a thick béchamel sauce into which several eggs have been beaten. The finished tart makes a hearty first course.

My recipe is made with the light custard mixture I use for most of my quiches, to make it less filling and easier to fit into a contemporary dinner menu. **SERVES 6 TO 8**

Tart Pastry (page 213)
1 tablespoon butter
3 onions, halved and thinly sliced
2 eggs plus 1 egg yolk
1½ cups milk
¼ teaspoon salt
⅛ teaspoon freshly ground pepper
2 pinches of freshly grated nutmeg

1. Preheat the oven to 475°F with the rack set in the middle position.

2. Line a 9½- or 10-inch tart pan with removable bottom with the pastry (see "How to Line a Tart Pan," page 65).

3. Prick the pastry (see Note, page 64) and line the pastry with aluminum foil and weight with 1 pound dried beans, rice, or aluminum pie weights. Bake until the edges of the pastry begin to color, 20 minutes. Remove the pan from the oven, but leave the oven on. Remove the foil and beans from the pan.

4. Meanwhile, in a large, heavy-bottomed saucepan, melt the butter over medium heat. Add the onions and cover with a tight-fitting lid. Gently steam the onions in their own moisture until soft, uncovering to stir occasionally, about 20 minutes. Lower the heat, if necessary, to keep the onions from browning.

5. In a bowl, beat the eggs and yolk lightly. Blend in the milk, salt, pepper, and nutmeg.

6. Spread the cooked onions evenly over the bottom of the tart shell. Pour the custard into the pan to within ⅛ inch of the top of the crust. Holding the tart pan by the outer rim (so you do not dislodge the bottom), place the pan on the middle rack of the oven.

7. Bake until the custard puffs, about 20 minutes.

8. Unmold as soon as possible (see "Unmolding a Tart or Quiche," page 218). Allow to cool for at least 10 minutes before cutting into wedges and serving. The tart is delicious served at any temperature. (The onion tart can be made in advance. It will keep well in the refrigerator for several days. Reheat in a 350°F oven for 10 to 15 minutes before serving.)

CURRIED CRAB QUICHE

[QUICHE AU CRABE À L'ORIENTALE]

WHILE PLANNING a series of classes on the French island of Martinique in the Caribbean, I was inspired to take the classic quiche of the island's motherland and combine it with the wonderful local seafood. Although I originally made this with langouste (rock lobster), which is plentiful in the Caribbean, I ultimately substituted crab, which is far more easily available elsewhere. Shrimp, scallops, lobster, or mussels can also be used with excellent results (see Note).

The custard for the quiche is delicately flavored with curry powder, Cognac, and Madeira and is made with milk instead of cream. The tart shell is made with puff pastry, which bakes quickly and doesn't need prebaking. Feel free, however, to use *pâte brisée* (Tart Pastry, page 213). **SERVES 6 TO 8**

½ recipe Rough Puff Pastry (page 230), or 1 pound store-bought puff pastry, or Tart Pastry (page 213)
2 eggs plus 1 egg yolk
1½ cups milk
2 tablespoons Madeira
2 tablespoons Cognac
½ teaspoon curry powder
¼ teaspoon salt
⅛ teaspoon freshly ground pepper
¾ pound crabmeat (pasteurized or canned), picked over to remove any shell or cartilage

1. Preheat the oven to 475°F with the rack set in the lowest position.

2. Roll out the pastry: 1/16 inch for the puff pastry and ⅛ inch for the tart pastry. Line a 9½- or 10-inch tart pan with a removable bottom with the pastry (see "How to Line a Tart Pan," page 65) and prick the pastry well all over with the point of a sharp knife. Freeze the lined tart pan until you are ready to bake your quiche. (If you are using tart pastry, prebake the shell as in step 3 of Quiche Lorraine, page 64.)

3. In a bowl, combine the eggs, egg yolk, milk, Madeira, Cognac, curry powder, salt, and pepper and mix well with a whisk without vigorously beating.

4. Cover the bottom of the tart shell with the crabmeat and fill three-quarters full with the custard mixture.

5. Holding the tart pan by the outer rim (so as not to dislodge the bottom), place it in the oven. (If using a prebaked tart shell, do not put it in the oven until the temperature is reduced to 425°F.) After 5 minutes, reduce the temperature to 425°F and bake until the pastry is golden brown and the custard begins to puff and brown lightly, 25 to 30 minutes more.

6. Unmold as soon as possible (see "Unmolding a Tart or Quiche," page 218). Allow it to cool for at least 10 minutes before serving. The quiche is delicious served at any temperature. (The quiche can be made up to a day in advance. It will keep well in the refrigerator for several days. Reheat in a 350°F oven for 10 to 15 minutes before serving.)

NOTE: If you do substitute another kind of shellfish for the crab, be sure to cook it first. (Crabmeat is already cooked when purchased.) Also, be sure to cut the seafood into bite-size pieces.

SERVING SUGGESTION

If you serve the quiche as a first course, you might follow it with grilled lamb chops and vegetables, or a sautéed chicken or veal dish. Since such a meal starts with pastry, fruit or sorbet makes a good dessert.

Making a Decorative Rim

Here's how to make a decorative rim like those typically found in pastry shops. Follow the instructions in "How to Line a Tart Pan" (page 65) through step 7, then proceed with the steps shown below.

1. Supporting the inner wall of the rim with the forefinger of one hand, use a fork or pastry pinch (a tweezerlike instrument used to give a decorative edge to both tarts and quiches) to decorate the top edge.

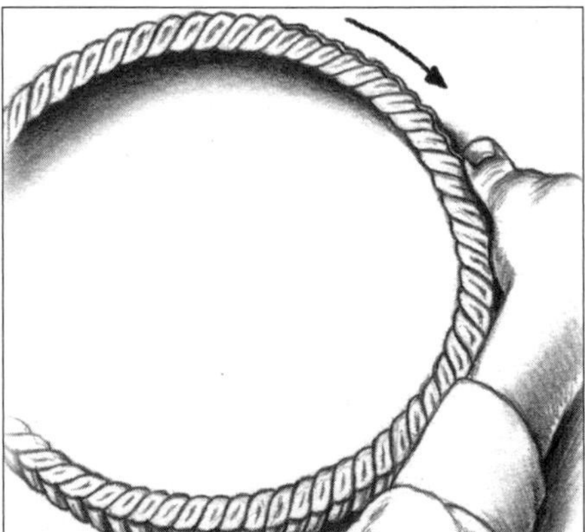

2. Gently run your thumb along the outer top edge of the pan to ensure that the pastry remains on the inside of the pan when baked. This will prevent problems when unmolding.

SAVORY CREAM-PUFF PASTRIES

Most people know *pâte à choux* or cream-puff pastry in its dessert form—such as cream puffs or éclairs—but the dough is also used for savory dishes.

Savory cream-puff pastries can be filled with numerous mixtures. For a hot presentation, the fillings can be similar to those used in the puff-pastry cases (see Puff-Pastry Shells Filled with Seafood in White Wine Sauce, page 76). Served cold, the pastry can be filled with shrimp or chicken salad.

The recipes that follow are for two uses of cream-puff pastry that are a little more unusual. For Parisian-Style Gnocchi (page 70), small pieces of the pastry are poached like dumplings and served with a sauce. For the Gruyère Pastry Ring Filled with Cheese Soufflé (page 72), a cheese-flavored cream-puff pastry is baked in the form of a ring, filled with a cheese soufflé mixture, and baked again.

PARISIAN-STYLE GNOCCHI

[GNOCCHI À LA PARISIENNE]

GNOCCHI are Italian dumplings usually made from potatoes. If you've ever had them, you probably remembered them long after the meal was over as they often tend to be heavy and, in the hands of an inexperienced cook, leaden.

FORMING PARISIAN GNOCCHI

Fill a pastry bag fitted with a ½-inch (#6) plain tube with the cream-puff pastry dough and rest it on the edge of a pan of simmering water. Gently squeeze out about 1 inch of pastry and cut it off with the tip of a paring knife, letting the pastry fall into the simmering water.

Although these Parisian-style dumplings are called gnocchi and have the same shape, the similarity to the Italian dish ends there. French gnocchi are made from cream-puff pastry piped from a pastry bag into simmering water and poached. The resulting dumplings are light and delicately flavored.

Traditionally, these dumplings are served with a Mornay sauce, which I find much too heavy. Instead I serve them with a sauce of cream and fresh tomatoes, which makes this a much lighter, fresher dish. You can of course serve them, as with Italian gnocchi, with a tomato sauce. **SERVES 6**

Double recipe Savory Cream-Puff Pastry (page 221)
2 ounces Swiss-style cheese, such as Gruyère or Emmentaler, grated (about ⅔ cup)

CREAM SAUCE WITH FRESH TOMATOES

1 cup heavy cream
⅛ teaspoon salt
⅛ teaspoon freshly ground pepper
2 tomatoes, peeled, seeded, chopped, and well drained
1 ounce Parmesan cheese, grated (about ¼ cup)
2 tablespoons chopped fresh chives or 1 tablespoon chopped fresh basil, tarragon, or parsley

1. Make the cream-puff pastry and stir the grated Swiss-style cheese into the dough in step 3, after you've beaten in the eggs. Fill a pastry bag fitted with a ½-inch (#6) plain tube with the mixture.

2. Fill a 5-quart saucepan three-quarters full of water and bring to a simmer. Resting the tube on the edge of the pan, gently squeeze the pastry to approximately 1 inch in length and cut off the gnocchi with the point of a knife. (If the pastry clings to your knife, dip the knife into the hot water.)

3. As the gnocchi simmer, they will rise to the surface of the water and become springy to the touch when fully cooked, about 10 minutes.

4. Drain the gnocchi on paper towels. (The gnocchi can be made 1 day in advance. Cover and refrigerate until you are ready to serve them.)

5. Make the Cream Sauce with Fresh Tomatoes: In a large saucepan, bring the cream to a boil and season with the salt and pepper. Add the gnocchi to the cream to reheat.

6. When the cream has thickened slightly, gently stir in the tomatoes and half the Parmesan. Taste and adjust the seasoning if necessary.

7. Pour into a warm serving dish; sprinkle with the chopped herbs and serve immediately. Pass the remaining Parmesan separately.

IN ADDITION

The gnocchi can also be formed into small spoon-shaped dumplings; see "Spoon-Molding Dumplings," this page.

SPOON-MOLDING DUMPLINGS

This spoon-molding method of making Parisian gnocchi can also be used with the Basic Fish Mousseline (page 48) to make quenelles.

1. Dip two spoons into hot water and scoop the pastry with one spoon.

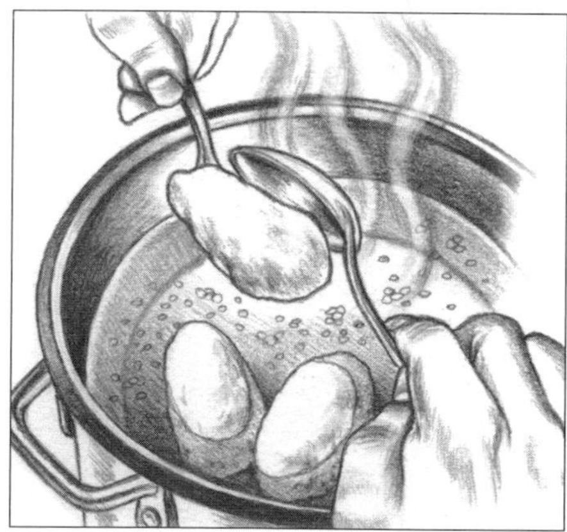

2. Use the second spoon to scoop and mold the pastry as it drops into simmering water.

VARIATIONS

GREEN GNOCCHI

[GNOCCHI VERTS]

I often make green gnocchi by coloring the dough with a dried purée of watercress or spinach as I do when making Fresh Green Pasta (page 81). Try coloring half the recipe green and serving a combination of green and white *gnocchi à la parisienne.*

HERBED GNOCCHI

[GNOCCHI AUX HERBES]

In step 1, stir 2 tablespoons minced fresh herbs, such as chives or tarragon, into the dough.

GRUYERE PASTRY RING FILLED WITH CHEESE SOUFFLE

[GOUGÈRE SOUFFLÉE]

A GOUGÈRE is simply baked cream-puff pastry to which Gruyère (Swiss) cheese has been added. It is a traditional dish from the Burgundy region of France. The pastry, with cheese stirred in, is spooned out onto a pastry sheet in a ring or baked as small cream puffs and served with cocktails.

I have taken the somewhat rustic *gougère* and transformed it into an elegant first course. Based on a cream-puff pastry dessert called Paris-Brest (page 228), the *gougère* is baked in its traditional ring form, but filled with an airy cheese soufflé and placed in a hot oven just before serving. **SERVES 6 TO 8**

Butter and all-purpose flour, for baking sheet (optional)
Savory Cream-Puff Pastry (page 221)
2 ounces Gruyère or other Swiss-style cheese, grated (about ⅔ cup)
1 egg, beaten
Gruyère Soufflé (page 46), prepared through step 7

1. Preheat the oven to 475°F with the rack set in the lower third of the oven. Butter and flour a regular or nonstick baking sheet, or line it with parchment paper. Use a pot lid to draw the outline of a 7-inch circle.

GOUGERES

The cheese-flavored cream-puff dough used to make the pastry ring (facing page) is more commonly baked as individual puffs—called *gougères*—that are served with cocktails or a glass of wine.

Using a pastry bag fitted with a ½-inch (#6) tube, shape the *gougères* by piping the dough into quarter-size puffs about 1 inch in diameter. Or simply drop the dough by the teaspoon onto a baking sheet that has been buttered and floured or lined with a silicone liner. Bake in a preheated 400°F oven. Remember, as with any cream puff, the pastry should puff, turn golden, and bake dry, 20 to 25 minutes.

In addition to the traditional Gruyère cheese used to flavor *gougères,* you can add chopped fresh herbs like parsley, chives, or rosemary. I even had one served to me with chopped seaweed and lots of black pepper, which I enjoyed a lot. Or try a little finely chopped ham to make ham-and-cheese *gougères*.

For a wonderful crispy hors d'oeuvre, deep-fry the puffs: Heat the oil to a depth of 4 inches in a deep fryer to 365°F and drop the dough by the teaspoon or half-teaspoon into the oil. The puffs will be done in 4 to 5 minutes, depending on their size.

2. Make the cream-puff pastry and stir three-fourths of the grated cheese into the dough in step 3, after you've beaten in the eggs. Fill a pastry bag fitted with an 11⁄16-inch (#9) plain tube with the mixture. Following the outline of the circle, squeeze a ring of pastry about 1 inch wide onto the baking sheet. (You can spoon out the pastry to make the ring, although it will have a rougher look.) Brush the ring lightly with the beaten egg and sprinkle with the remaining cheese.

3. Place in the oven for 5 minutes. Lower the temperature to 400°F and bake until light brown all over, 25 to 30 minutes more.

4. While the pastry is still warm, cut off the top one-third with a serrated knife and reserve. Allow both portions of the pastry to cool on a pastry rack. (The pastry shell can be made 1 day in advance and stored in a plastic bag, unrefrigerated.)

5. When you are ready to serve, preheat the oven to 475°F with the rack set in the lowest position. Place the bottom of the pastry ring on a baking sheet and top the ring with the Gruyère soufflé mixture so that it is rounded on top. Gently replace the top of the ring and bake for 3 to 4 minutes, or until the soufflé just begins to rise.

6. Using two metal spatulas, gently transfer the filled pastry ring to a serving platter. Use a serrated knife to cut into individual portions and serve warm.

SAVORY PUFF PASTRIES

The secret to puff pastry's wonderful flakiness and glorious flavor is in the butter. Because it is so rich, I reserve it for special occasions.

Although making puff pastry is certainly not quick and easy, using what's called rough puff pastry instead of the classic puff pastry, as I do, greatly simplifies the procedure, shortening the process by about 2½ hours. I would suggest to anyone approaching puff pastry for the first time that you try the following recipes with store-bought puff pastry first, to get a feel for the dough. Then I recommend that you try it with homemade Rough Puff Pastry (page 230). I think you will be surprised not only by the difference in taste, but also by the relative ease with which you can make a truly impressive pastry.

What makes puff pastry so perfect for entertaining—in addition to its special-occasion richness—is that in most cases the pastry can be cut, filled, or formed on baking sheets and frozen until ready to bake. Or it can be fully baked in advance and then reheated just before serving.

PUFF PASTRY WITH ANCHOVY BUTTER

[FEUILLETÉS D'ANCHOIS]

THIS DELICIOUS puff-pastry hors d'oeuvre is excellent with cocktails. The warm strips of flaky pastry filled with the delicately flavored anchovy butter are a pleasant surprise. **SERVES 10 TO 12**

Butter, for baking sheet
½ recipe Rough Puff Pastry (page 230) or 1 pound store-bought puff pastry
1 egg, beaten

ANCHOVY BUTTER

10 tablespoons (1 stick; 4 ounces) butter, softened to room temperature
10 anchovy fillets, finely chopped
Juice of ½ lemon
1 teaspoon Dijon mustard
⅛ teaspoon freshly ground pepper

1. Preheat the oven to 400°F with the rack set in the lower third of the oven. Lightly butter a 17 x 14-inch baking sheet.

2. Roll the pastry into a rectangle ⅛ inch or less thick, and large enough to cover the baking sheet. Sprinkle the baking sheet with water. Lift the pastry onto a rolling pin and unroll it onto the baking sheet, pressing down gently. Trim the edges of the pastry even with the edges of the baking sheet. Brush the pastry with the beaten egg and place in the refrigerator for 15 minutes.

3. Cut the chilled pastry into strips 3½ inches long and 1 inch wide, for a total of 64. The pastry can be made ahead to this point. Refrigerate or freeze on the baking sheet. Bake without defrosting, adding 1 minute to the cooking time.

4. Bake the pastry strips for 20 to 25 minutes, or until the pastry has risen and browned evenly. Transfer to a rack, but while still warm, split the strips in half horizontally. (The strips can be baked in advance and reheated in a 350°F oven for 3 minutes before serving.)

5. Make the Anchovy Butter: Cream the butter with a whisk. Add the minced anchovy fillets, lemon juice, mustard, and pepper and blend well.

6. Spread the bottoms of the pastry strips evenly with the anchovy butter, replace the tops, and serve lukewarm.

VARIATION

PUFF PASTRY WITH GRUYERE

[FEUILLETÉS AU FROMAGE]

Omit the Anchovy Butter. In step 2, after brushing with the egg, sprinkle the top of the pastry with an even layer of grated Gruyère cheese (about ½ cup). Cut into strips, bake as directed, and serve warm.

PUFF-PASTRY SHELLS
FILLED WITH SEAFOOD IN WHITE WINE SAUCE

[BOUCHÉES DE FRUITS DE MER]

BOUCHÉES are puff-pastry shells that can be filled with seafood, chicken, or sweetbreads along with a sauce and served as a first or main course. The shells can also be filled with fruit and served as dessert: For example, use the bouchées in place of the square-cut puff-pastry case in Strawberry-Topped Puff Pastry Tartlets (page 232).

Seafood tossed in a rich white wine sauce and served in warm, flaky puff-pastry shells makes a delicious and elegant first course, especially if served with Champagne. (The seafood sauce served over rice also makes a great main course.) **SERVES 8**

Butter, for baking sheet and skillet
½ recipe Rough Puff Pastry (page 230) or 1 pound store-bought puff pastry
1 egg, beaten, plus 3 egg yolks
3 medium shallots, finely chopped
½ pound mushrooms, sliced
1 pound sea scallops, tendons removed
1 pound medium shrimp, shelled and deveined
About 1 cup dry white wine
2 tablespoons butter, softened to room temperature
¼ teaspoon salt
⅛ teaspoon freshly ground pepper

1. Preheat the oven to 400°F with the rack set in the middle position. Lightly butter a large baking sheet.

2. Roll out the pastry about ⅛ inch thick. Cut out 16 rounds and cut out the centers of 8 of the rounds (see "Making Bouchées," facing page).

3. Sprinkle the baking sheet with water. Place the solid rounds on the baking sheet. Brush the tops lightly with the beaten egg. Place a pastry ring on the top of each round and press together gently. Brush the surface lightly with the beaten egg. Prick the center several times with the point of a knife. (The bouchées can be made ahead up to this point. Refrigerate or freeze. Bake without defrosting, adding about 1 minute to the baking time.)

4. Bake until the pastry has risen and colored evenly to a golden brown, 20 to 25 minutes. Allow to cool on a wire rack. With a sharp paring knife, following the inside edge of the rim, cut out the pastry in the center, going down about ½ inch. Gently lift this piece out with the tip of the knife and set aside to use as a lid. With your fingers, pull out the remaining excess pastry in the center, leaving a well to be filled. (These pastry shells can be baked in advance and reheated in a 350°F oven for 3 minutes before serving.)

5. Lightly butter a 12-inch skillet and sprinkle with the chopped shallots. Add the mushrooms, scallops, and shrimp to the pan in that order. Pour in enough white wine to cover the seafood halfway. Cut a piece of waxed paper to fit over the surface of the seafood, and cover the pan with a lid.

6. Place the pan over low heat and bring slowly to a simmer, 10 to 15 minutes. When the seafood begins to simmer, it should be done. Check to make sure the seafood has turned opaque. If not, simmer an additional minute, but do not overcook.

7. With a slotted spoon, transfer the seafood and mushrooms to a bowl and keep warm. Reduce the liquid over high heat until about ½ cup remains, and pour it into a small saucepan.

8. Add the egg yolks to the reduced poaching liquid in the saucepan and whisk over medium-high heat until thick and fluffy, 2 to 3 minutes. Reduce the heat to low and immediately beat in 1 tablespoon of the butter. Remove from the heat and add the second tablespoon of butter. Season with the salt and pepper.

9. Pour off and discard any liquid that may have accumulated in the bowl with the seafood. Toss the seafood with the sauce and fill the warm pastry shells, allowing some of the seafood and sauce to overflow onto the plates. Serve immediately.

MAKING BOUCHEES

To make pastry shells (bouchées), you will need two round pastry cutters: one 3½ or 4 inches in diameter, fluted if possible; the other 2 to 2½ inches in diameter and plain. Cut out rounds of pastry with the larger (fluted) cutter, and then use the smaller (plain) cutter to cut out the centers of half of the rounds to form rings. (Use the centers for another purpose.) The rings are placed on top of the solid rounds to form a border.

VARIATION

Puff Pastry Shells a la Normande

[BOUCHÉES À LA NORMANDE]

Omit the scallops. In a large saucepan steam 16 scrubbed oysters and 16 scrubbed and debearded mussels in the cup of dry white wine over high heat until the shells open, about 5 minutes. Strain the cooking liquid and use in step 5 to poach the mushrooms and shrimp. Remove the cooked mussels and oysters from their shells (discarding any that have not opened) and toss with the white wine sauce, shrimp, and mushrooms in step 9.

PASTA

MAKING PASTA AND BREAD is very much alike. Each uses flour and water to make an inexpensive food that is enjoyed by all. In developing a pasta recipe for my classes, I wanted to create one that would be easy to roll out by hand (since many people do not have pasta machines) and delicious enough for people to want to make on special occasions.

A good noodle exhibits a slightly chewy or springy texture when eaten. The elastic texture is developed by kneading and rolling the dough. The same elasticity makes noodles difficult to roll out. Over the years, chefs have added butter, cream, oil, or extra egg yolks to help relax the dough, making it easier to roll.

I add about three times as much oil as others do, making the dough relatively easy to roll and stretch. You can vary the type of oil used to change the flavor of the dough.

FRESH PASTA

[PÂTES FRAÎCHES]

FOR ME, the difficult part of making pasta is the kneading process. Although there are those who will insist on kneading by hand and rolling by machine, I find the opposite easier. What normally takes many minutes of strenuous hand labor requires only seconds to accomplish with a food processor.

In addition to the sauces in the recipes following, I also like to serve homemade noodles simply with butter, or Cream Sauce with Fresh Tomatoes (page 70), or Tomato Sauce (page 325). **MAKES ABOUT 1 POUND/ SERVES 4 TO 6**

2 cups (300g) all-purpose flour
3 eggs
3 tablespoons vegetable oil
1 tablespoon water
1½ teaspoons salt
Butter or your favorite sauce, for serving

1. Place all the ingredients in a food processor and process until a smooth, soft dough forms, about 1 minute. If the dough is too sticky, add more flour, 1 teaspoon at a time. If the dough is too firm, add more water, ½ teaspoon at a time.

2. Remove the dough from the machine and divide in half. Shape each half into a rough square or rectangle. Wrap in plastic wrap and refrigerate for 30 minutes or more. (If the dough is not to be used within 24 hours, freeze it and bring back to room temperature before proceeding.)

3. Dust the work surface and the dough lightly with flour and roll one of the squares of dough into a sheet as thin as possible, between 1⁄16 and 1⁄32 of an inch and about 16 x 18 inches, dusting and turning the dough so it does not stick to the surface. If the dough becomes too elastic to flatten or roll out, allow it to rest, covered with plastic wrap to prevent drying, for 3 to 5 minutes before continuing. (If you have the space, roll out both pieces of dough at the same time, alternating from one to the other as they build up tension.)

4. Cut into noodles: Lightly dust the surface of the dough to prevent sticking and fold the fully rolled-out dough in half, then in half again, always folding in the same direction. Using a large chef's knife, cut crosswise to form noodles of a desired width (for extremely thin, delicate noodles, see "Stretching Noodles," page 82). The noodles can be cooked at this point if desired; see step 5. (You can make the noodles ahead to this point. Allow the noodles to dry on a flat surface or draped over a drying rack for 15 to 30 minutes. They will still be flexible, but may begin to crack when folded. Place the noodles in plastic bags and freeze if not using within 24 hours. Frozen pasta does not have to be thawed before cooking.)

5. To cook the noodles, bring a large pot of water to a boil over high heat. Drop the noodles into the pot and cook until tender yet a bit chewy, 3 to 5 minutes. The drier the noodles are, the longer they will take to cook.

6. Drain the noodles and toss them with butter or one of your favorite sauces. Serve immediately.

IN ADDITION

If you have a pasta-rolling machine and are accustomed to using it, by all means do. I also encourage you to roll it by hand to see which method is easier for you.

FRESH PASTA WITH CREAM, PEAS, AND PARMESAN

[PÂTES FRAÎCHES AUX PETITS POIS]

ALTHOUGH SPECTACULAR when made with fresh noodles and fresh, sweet peas, this recipe is so good that I often make it with refrigerated store-bought pasta and frozen baby peas. The peas can be taken from the freezer and heated in the cream while it thickens in step 2. (Increase your cooking time by 1 to 2 minutes.)

Pasta of all shapes and sizes can be cooked, according to the package directions, and mixed with the cream, peas, ham, and cheese.

SERVES 6

Fresh Pasta (page 79) or 1 pound refrigerated fettuccine
1 cup heavy cream
⅛ teaspoon salt
⅛ teaspoon freshly ground pepper
1 cup fresh or frozen baby peas, cooked
1 slice ham, cut ¼-inch-thick (boiled, baked, or smoked), diced
2 ounces Parmesan cheese, grated (about ½ cup)

1. If making your own pasta, follow the Fresh Pasta recipe through step 3. In step 4, cut the noodles into ¼-inch widths. Continue with the recipe through step 5.

2. While the noodles are cooking, bring the cream to a boil in a small saucepan over medium-high heat. Season with the salt and pepper and allow to boil gently until the cream thickens enough to coat a spoon, about 30 seconds. Gently stir in the peas, ham, and half the Parmesan. Heat for several seconds.

3. When the noodles have finished cooking, drain them in a colander. Transfer them to a warm serving bowl and pour the sauce over.

4. Serve immediately, with the remaining Parmesan on the side.

FRESH GREEN PASTA

[PÂTES FRAÎCHES VERTES]

I USE WATERCRESS to make green pasta because it produces a lovely color and a fresh taste, but you can use spinach, basil, arugula, or combinations such as watercress, tarragon, chives, and a touch of parsley and basil.

In addition to adding color and flavor, the purée makes the dough less elastic and easier to roll out.

Serve this with Tomato Sauce (page 325), or substitute it for the dumplings in the recipe for Parisian-Style Gnocchi (page 70), or for the plain pasta in Fresh Pasta with Cream, Peas, and Parmesan (facing page).

MAKES ABOUT 1 POUND/SERVES 4 TO 6

2 bunches watercress, thick stems trimmed
2 cups (300g) all-purpose flour
3 eggs
3 tablespoons vegetable oil
2 teaspoons water
1½ teaspoons salt
Butter or your favorite sauce, for serving

1. Place a large saucepan filled with water over high heat and bring to a boil. Plunge the watercress into the boiling water and blanch for about 45 seconds. Drain and refresh under cold running water.

2. Place the watercress in a food processor and process until puréed, 1 to 2 minutes. Transfer the purée to a sieve lined with a double thickness of paper towel and set over a bowl. Gently press out as much moisture as possible; set aside the watercress liquid. Press the watercress purée dry between two thicknesses of paper towel, changing the towels frequently. The purée should be as dry as possible. It will end up as a thin sheet of pressed purée.

3. Place the purée, 2 teaspoons of the reserved watercress liquid, and the remaining ingredients in a food processor and process until a smooth, soft dough forms, about 1 minute. If the dough is too sticky, add more flour, 1 teaspoon at a time. If the dough is too firm, add more water, ½ teaspoon at a time.

4. Proceed as for Fresh Pasta (page 79) from step 2 through step 5.

5. To serve, drain the noodles and toss them in butter or one of your favorite sauces. Serve immediately.

IN ADDITION

As with any pasta, if I'm not cooking it right away, I dry or partially dry the finished pasta before placing it in plastic bags. (If the pasta is not partially dried first, it may stick together.) It can be refrigerated for a few days, but I prefer freezing it. Like all fresh pasta, it can be frozen for several months. In certain areas of the country where humidity may be extremely high, stickiness may cause drying to be a problem. In such cases, dusting the noodles with cornmeal will prevent this.

EGG NOODLES WITH MORELS

[NOUILLES AUX MORILLES]

MORELS ARE ONE of nature's treasures. Fresh morels are available in season in parts of the country, but I use dried ones in this recipe. While both dark brown and white morels are available, I recommend using only the more robust-flavored brown ones for this recipe. Dried morels can be easily found in specialty shops and on the Internet, but when you find fresh ones, use them! Try preparing this recipe with dried shiitake or dried chanterelle mushrooms as well. This cream sauce with mushrooms is delicious when served with sautéed chicken and veal. The noodles serve four as a main course or six as a first course. **SERVES 4 TO 6**

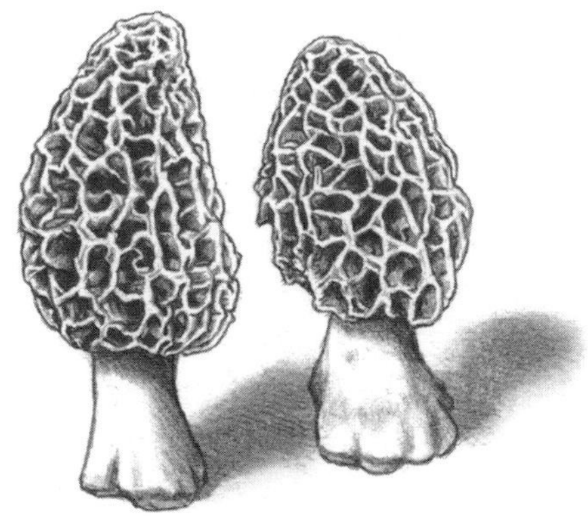

STRETCHING NOODLES

Instead of rolling the dough paper thin before cutting it into noodles, I find it easier and more fun to stop rolling when the dough is about 1⁄16 inch thick, and after cutting into noodles, to stretch them the rest of the way to increase their length and thinness.

It is extremely important to allow the noodles to rest, covered with plastic wrap, before attempting to stretch them. A 2-foot cut noodle that has not rested will snap or break before being stretched to 4 feet. But if you let the noodles rest for 1½ hours, they can easily be stretched up to 8 feet.

Finding a place to hang the stretched noodles to dry can be a problem. Cut in half, they hang nicely over the backs of kitchen chairs or on a clothes-drying rack; or you can spread them out on your countertop. Many years ago, while driving through Naples, I saw women hanging pasta up to dry on their outdoor clotheslines. For those who wish to try this method, be warned that I also saw the neighbors' dogs nibbling on the ends.

Fresh Pasta (page 79) or 1 pound refrigerated fettuccine
1 ounce dried morel mushrooms or ⅓ to ½ pound fresh morels
1 cup heavy cream
½ teaspoon salt
⅛ teaspoon freshly ground pepper, plus more for serving
2 ounces Parmesan cheese, grated (about ½ cup)

1. If making your own pasta, follow the Fresh Pasta recipe through step 3. In step 4, cut the noodles into ¼-inch widths.

2. Meanwhile, soak the dried mushrooms in a small bowl of cold water. Stir the mushrooms in the water as they soak, making sure that there is sufficient water in the bowl for them to float, and allow any dirt or sand to fall to the bottom of the bowl. As the mushrooms swell in size and soften, the water will become brown and it will acquire the strong flavor of the mushroom. This will take 10 to 15 minutes.

3. When the mushrooms are soft, gently squeeze them over the bowl and then place them in a small saucepan. When the dirt has fallen to the bottom of the bowl and the water in the bowl is clear, very carefully pour it into the saucepan with the mushrooms and discard the dirt at the bottom.

4. Bring the mushrooms and liquid to a boil and gently boil until only 1 teaspoon of liquid remains, about 4 minutes. Add the cream, season with the salt and pepper, and set aside.

5. In a stockpot, bring 4 quarts of water to a boil. Add the noodles and boil until tender yet a bit chewy, 3 to 5 minutes. Stir the noodles several times to prevent them from sticking together.

6. While the noodles are cooking, bring the cream and mushrooms to a boil. When the noodles have finished cooking, drain them in a colander. Transfer them to a warm serving bowl and cover with the sauce. Toss with half of the grated Parmesan cheese.

7. Serve immediately, with the remaining cheese and additional pepper on the side.

FOUR-CHEESE RAVIOLI

[RAVIOLI AUX QUATRE FROMAGES]

RAVIOLI, ALTHOUGH ITALIAN in origin, have been used quite imaginatively by French chefs for hundreds of years. If you enjoy making pasta, you will find making ravioli a very creative experience. You can make miniature ravioli to serve in soups and ragouts, or extra-large ones that can serve as individual portions for a first course. The ravioli for this recipe will serve 6 as a main course and 12 as a first course.

If you are not up to making your own pasta, try making ravioli with wonton skins, which can be found in most supermarkets. Two wonton skins will make four standard-size ravioli or one giant one.

The options for making ravioli ahead of time are many. You can freeze the ravioli before cooking them and cook them later without thawing (they'll take a little longer to cook). Or you can cook the ravioli, refrigerate them, and reheat in the sauce later. Or you can combine the cooked ravioli and sauce before refrigerating or freezing and then reheat the whole dish later. **SERVES 6 OR 12**

Fresh Pasta (page 79)
2 ounces Swiss-style cheese, such as Gruyère or Emmentaler
1 ounce Parmesan cheese, grated (about ¼ cup)
8 ounces cream cheese
4 ounces ricotta cheese
12 fresh basil leaves
1 egg, beaten with a pinch of salt
Tomato Sauce (page 325)

1. Make the fresh pasta through step 3 of the recipe, rolling each rectangle of dough as thin as possible into a sheet about 16 x 19 inches, dusting and turning the dough so it does

RAVIOLI GUIDELINES

The types of ravioli fillings are endless, and—with just a few guidelines—I leave them to your imagination. Fillings used should not require additional cooking. Fillings should be relatively dry. If necessary, use bread crumbs to absorb excess liquid. Try fillings of cooked meat, poultry, seafood, sweetbreads, tongue, mushrooms, spinach, vegetable purées, cheese, or combinations thereof. If you do use cheese, just keep in mind that dry cheeses (such as Parmesan) and low-fat cheeses do not generally soften when boiled and the resulting filling will be dry or coarse.

Although traditional sauces are based on cheese, cream, or tomato, any sauce that complements your filling can be used.

If you are not interested in making ravioli, make the cheese filling to spread on crackers or to fill cherry tomatoes to serve as an hors d'oeuvre.

not stick to the work surface. If the dough becomes too elastic to roll, cover it with plastic wrap to prevent drying and allow it to rest for 2 or 3 minutes before continuing. If you have the space, roll out both pieces of dough at the same time, alternating from one to the other as they build up tension. Cover the pasta with plastic wrap while you make the cheese filling.

2. In a food processor, finely chop the Swiss-style and Parmesan cheeses. Add the cream cheese, ricotta, and basil leaves and process well.

3. Brush a light coat of beaten egg on one of the sheets of pasta. With a pastry bag fitted with a ½-inch (#6) plain tube, or with a spoon, drop the cheese filling onto the sheets of pasta in ½-teaspoon mounds spaced about ¾ inch apart.

4. Roll up the second sheet of pasta onto your rolling pin and unroll it to cover the filling. Press the dough together firmly around the filling to seal. Using a knife or ravioli-cutting wheel, cut between the rows of filling to form little square ravioli. At this point, let the ravioli rest 15 to 20 minutes: If the egg sealant is not allowed to dry, the filling will escape during cooking. (If the ravioli will not be used within a few hours, freeze them in layers separated by sheets of plastic wrap. Do not thaw before cooking.)

5. To cook the ravioli, bring a large pot of water to a boil. Add the ravioli and cook until tender, 8 to 10 minutes (1 minute or so longer for frozen). Drain in a colander or remove from the pot and place on paper towels. (The ravioli can be cooked in advance, cooled, covered, and refrigerated until ready to use. For reheating information, see Note.)

6. Serve with the tomato sauce. The ravioli can be topped with the sauce, tossed with it, or presented on *top* of it.

NOTE: To reheat cooked ravioli, place them in an ovenproof serving dish and cover with the sauce. Place the dish in a 400°F oven until the sauce bubbles, 10 to 15 minutes. You can also combine the ravioli and sauce in the serving dish and refrigerate or freeze. Reheat as above, but allow a few more minutes.

FRENCH ROLLING PINS

A French rolling pin, made from a single piece of wood, is about 19 to 20 inches long and 1½ to 2 inches in diameter. (An American-style pin is usually shorter and has handles with ball bearings, which help in the rolling.) Because a French pin has greater surface area, it is especially helpful when rolling large pieces of dough (as for pasta) or when transferring dough from work surface to baking sheet or tart pan. A French pin is rolled with an open hand. As the fingertips and palm run over the top of the pin, a downward pressure is exerted to flatten the dough.

CHAPTER TWO

MAIN COURSES

THE MAIN COURSE, the focal point of a French meal, is the course around which the balance of the menu is planned. It can be as simple as a grilled steak or a roast duck, as hearty as a robust *ragoût,* or as elegant as a rack of lamb or a poached fish served with a rich sauce. Once chosen, it should be complemented by an appropriate first course and dessert.

The repertoire of French main courses is so large that it could easily take up a book on its own. I have therefore chosen a sampling of classic recipes that you will both enjoy and learn from. The recipes that follow are my timeless favorites.

SEAFOOD

IN FRANCE, fish dishes are the aristocrats of the culinary repertoire. Fish are accorded a respect and admiration that is born of several things. First, fish has always been expensive, making it a rarity and a delicacy. Second, because of the delicate taste of most fish, it has always been served with highly refined sauces. If you go to a restaurant that is known for its fish dishes in France, be assured the sauces will be well prepared.

In this country, it has been for only about 25 years that we have had a reliable source of fresh fish and seafood outside of coastal cities. As soon as we started appreciating sushi and all the different ways fish is prepared in other countries, we started eating more fresh fish—and expecting the market to provide it.

On the downside, with the world demand for seafood climbing every year, our oceans are being depleted of the fish we love. Much of what we now find in the market is not wild-caught, but rather raised in pens.

When shopping for fish, there are some things to know in order to judge its freshness. Whole fish fresh from the sea have a smell of the ocean water. They have shiny, slippery skins, and a flesh that is firm to the touch. Their eyes are clear and their gills are crimson in color. Fish that is past its prime will have an unpleasant odor, dull, dry skin, and flesh that yields to the press of a finger, retaining its imprint. The eyes will be cloudy and the gills will be gray. Fresh fillets of fish will be firm to the touch and glistening in appearance. Fillets not worth purchasing will be soft, dull, and dry looking.

If you have bought fish and won't be home for several hours, ask the market to surround your package of fish in a bag of crushed ice. This is especially important in the summer.

With the expanding number of fish varieties now appearing in our markets, you shouldn't be limited by the types of fish in this chapter. If the fish looks fresh, try it. Some of the following recipes are quick and easy, others are a little more complex. If you try them all, you will learn a great deal about cooking seafood.

GRILLED SALMON FILLETS

[FILETS DE SAUMON GRILLÉS]

MOST FRENCH recipes call for grilling salmon steaks (*darnes de saumon*), but I prefer to use fillets. I like the texture of the fillets better than that of steaks and also find the fillets make a more attractive presentation.

It was actually by accident that I came upon my technique of grilling fish fillets. For years I tried to find a way to grill fillets on both sides without having them either stick to the grill or fall apart in the turning process. One day when in a hurry, I just threw them, skin side down, onto a hot, unoiled grill. Unable to turn them, I covered them with a lid. When cooked, I found that because the skin was firmly stuck to the grill, I was easily able to slide a metal spatula between the skin and the fish and lift the fish to a waiting plate. In doing so, all I had left behind was a piece of (often strong-tasting) skin. The end results were succulent and delicious, and I have grilled fish fillets this way ever since. This recipe works for any fish fillet. If I am using wild salmon, which is drier than farmed salmon, I am particularly careful not to overcook the fish. **SERVES 6**

6 salmon fillets (see Note), unskinned (4 to 6 ounces each)
2 to 3 tablespoons soy sauce, or lemon or lime juice (optional)
4 tablespoons (½ stick) butter, melted
2 tablespoons chopped fresh chives, tarragon, or basil

1. Rinse the fillets under cold water and pat dry with paper towels. If not extremely fresh, or if desired, sprinkle them with soy sauce or lemon or lime juice. (This can be done several hours in advance of cooking. The fish should be kept refrigerated until shortly before grilling.)

2. Preheat your grill to high. If you do not have a lid, make one by loosely covering the grill with heavy-duty aluminum foil or use a large domed pot lid to cover the fish while it is cooking.

3. Combine the melted butter and the herbs in a small dish.

4. Place the fillets on the grill and cover. Grill until the fish is fairly firm yet springy to the touch, 4 to 8 minutes. Moisture or juices from the fish will pool on the surface of the fish and look opaque.

5. Slide a metal spatula between the skin and the fish. Lift the fish onto a plate, leaving the skin on the grill to be scraped off later. Pour a little of the herb butter over the fish and serve immediately.

NOTE: When ordering fillets, I try to get them cut so that each fillet is of even thickness. The top part of the fish is generally thicker than is the bottom, or belly. A 4-ounce piece from the belly may be larger yet thinner than a 6-ounce piece cut from the back. If your fish market is obliging, they will cut the fish to meet your needs. If not, you will need to cut them when you get home.

GRILLING FISH

If you find yourself fortunate enough to be near a source of fresh fish, you will want to grill it often, for it is healthy, quick, and delicious.

Cooking a whole fish, fillets, or steaks on a grill can be difficult. The flesh of most fish is delicate and tends to stick. Coat the metal grates with a vegetable oil spray to help prevent major sticking.

For large whole fish that are hard to turn, use aluminum foil strips to form a sling. This makes it easier to support the fish when lifting it. Should you have one of the special hinged fish grills that encloses the fish and allows you to turn it easily, so much the better.

Boneless steaks, such as swordfish and tuna, which have firm flesh, are ideal for grilling. Have the fish cut into 1¼- to 1½-inch steaks, and remove all the skin and fat. Steaks like salmon and halibut that do have a bone are grilled and served with the skin on. Grill fish steaks as you would grill a rib steak (see page 145). Some people like their fish well done while others like theirs rare or medium. I like most fish cooked medium to medium-well, but when it comes to tuna I like it very rare. Serve with melted butter and chopped fresh herbs, or with a Beurre Blanc (page 329).

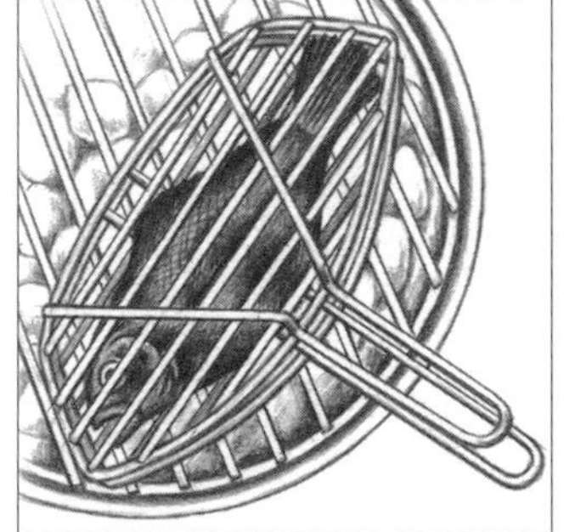

Fillets and whole sides of fish should be prepared as for Grilled Salmon Fillets.

Baked Red Snapper in a Mediterranean Tomato Sauce

[ROUGET À LA SUZANNE]

THIS LOW-CALORIE baked fish dish (named for my wife, Susan) is actually a combination of two classic Mediterranean presentations: *rouget à l'algéroise,* made with a tomato sauce containing fennel and saffron, and *rouget à la portugaise,* which uses a fresh tomato sauce made with shallots, garlic, and parsley. Both use considerably more olive oil than I have used here.

Since *rouget* is hard to come by—and expensive—my version uses red snapper. When snapper is not available, try another similar-size fish, such as bluefish or black sea bass. **SERVES 6**

½ tablespoon extra-virgin olive oil
4 pounds tomatoes, peeled (see page 194), seeded, and diced, or 2 cans (28 ounces each) diced tomatoes, drained
3 shallots, finely chopped
2 cloves garlic, finely chopped
1 small bulb fennel, finely diced (see Note)
1 pinch of saffron
½ teaspoon salt
¼ teaspoon freshly ground pepper
10 sprigs parsley, chopped, plus 8 whole sprigs, for garnish
1 whole red snapper (4 to 5 pounds)

1. Preheat the oven to 350°F.

2. In a large skillet, heat the oil over high heat. Add the tomatoes, shallots, garlic, and fennel and cook, stirring occasionally, until the tomatoes soften but still have some shape, about 5 minutes. The tomatoes' excess moisture should have evaporated, but if not, strain and reserve the tomatoes and return the excess liquid to the pan. Cook the liquid over high heat until it is reduced to a syrup. Return the tomatoes to the pan and season with the saffron, salt, and pepper. Stir in the chopped parsley. (The sauce can be made ahead of time. Let cool to room temperature, cover, and refrigerate.)

3. Place a layer of the sauce on a large, deep ovenproof serving platter. Place the fish on the platter and cover all but the head and tail with the remaining sauce. Bake 50 to 60 minutes, until a knife penetrates easily to the bone.

4. Decorate the platter with parsley sprigs and serve.

NOTE: If fennel is not available, either leave it out or use ¼ teaspoon anise seed or fennel seed for a similar flavor.

IN ADDITION

In French cooking, a *point* is the amount of powdered spice that can be lifted on the tip (*point*) of a paring knife and is basically equal to a pinch. The technique is used with strong spices, such as cayenne, which you might not want to get on your fingers.

SERVING SUGGESTION

Start with Zucchini Stuffed with Mushrooms and Ham (page 195). Rice Pilaf (page 207), made with a touch of saffron and 1 teaspoon of chopped fresh tarragon, makes an excellent accompaniment for the fish. Follow with a mixed green salad made with an olive oil and lemon juice vinaigrette. For dessert, serve fruit sorbet and cookies.

WINE

I like a chilled rosé or Beaujolais with this dish.

POACHED SALMON WITH BEURRE BLANC

[FILET DE SAUMON POCHÉ SAUCE BEURRE BLANC]

POACHING SMALL FISH or fish fillets is a quick technique used in French restaurants. Although classically such a dish would be made by poaching the fish in a court bouillon (light vegetable stock), I find the use of court bouillon advantageous only when poaching fish to be served cold (see Cold Poached Salmon with Green Mayonnaise, facing page). So I just poach fish fillets (salmon as here, or another thick fish such as sea bass or striped bass) in water, sometimes adding an acid such as vinegar, wine, or lemon juice if the fish is not extremely fresh.

The traditional sauce for poached fish is Hollandaise Sauce (page 326), but I prefer to serve it with beurre blanc. You should have everything you want to serve ready before starting to poach the fish since it cooks in just a few minutes. **SERVES 6**

3 pounds salmon fillet, skinned, cut into individual serving pieces, and rinsed well in cold water
⅓ cup white (distilled) vinegar, juice of 1 lemon, or 1 cup dry white wine (optional)
Beurre Blanc (page 329)

1. Place the salmon fillets in a large nonaluminum skillet or Dutch oven and add water to cover the fillets by an inch or more. Remove the fillets and set aside. Bring the water to a boil. If the fish is not extremely fresh, add the vinegar, lemon juice, or white wine.

2. Immerse the fish in the boiling water and adjust the heat so that the water barely simmers; do not let it boil. Cooking time is approximately 8 to 10 minutes per inch of thickness of the fish. When done, the fish will be firm yet springy to the touch.

3. Remove the fish from the water using a skimmer or slotted spoon and drain on paper towels.

4. To serve: Place the fish on warm plates or a platter and cover with the beurre blanc before serving.

IN ADDITION

When poaching large pieces or whole fish, it is important to start with a cool or cold stock (with small fish or fillets you start with boiling stock). Fish does not need much heat to cook and is therefore poached at a simmer. If you place the fish in hot stock, or if you bring the cold stock to a simmer too rapidly, it will usually overcook the outside while undercooking the center of the fish.

SERVING SUGGESTION

The fish is usually served only with rice or steamed potatoes. The delicate flavor of the fish and sauce go well with the relatively bland flavor of the starches, while a more assertive vegetable would upset the balance of flavors. In such cases I will often serve a vegetable first course or start with a mixed green salad.

WINE

Muscadet, Pouilly-Fuissé, and Chardonnay all go well with poached salmon.

COLD POACHED SALMON WITH GREEN MAYONNAISE

[SAUMON POCHÉ SAUCE VERTE]

HERE IS A CLASSIC French summer buffet dish. Poaching a whole salmon is an elegant way to serve this majestic fish, provided you have a fish poacher the size of your salmon. The fish is cooked in a light vegetable stock (court bouillon) in which it is then allowed to partially cool, thus keeping the fish moist and flavorful. **SERVES 6 TO 8**

2 quarts water
2 carrots, sliced
1 onion, sliced
1 shallot, sliced
Bouquet Garni (page 306)
½ cup white (distilled) vinegar
3- to 4-pound center cut piece of fresh salmon or 5-pound whole salmon
3 lemons, sliced
1 bunch parsley
Green Mayonnaise (page 334)

1. Make the court bouillon: In a 4-quart saucepan, combine the water, carrots, onion, shallot, bouquet garni, and vinegar and simmer for

PRESENTATION OF THE SALMON

Cold Poached Salmon is a wonderful dish for entertaining, since it is done well ahead of time and is as simple as it is impressive. For a more decorative presentation, you can coat the salmon with the green mayonnaise and use very thin, overlapping cucumber slices to create a scale pattern on top of the fish.

20 minutes. Strain, discarding the solids, and let cool to room temperature.

2. Place the salmon in a fish poacher, or in a pan large enough to hold it, and cover it with the court bouillon. Slowly bring to a simmer over medium to medium-high heat, about 20 minutes.

3. Allow the fish to simmer, but not boil, for 10 minutes. Remove from the heat and let stand 15 to 20 minutes.

4. Remove the fish from the poaching liquid and transfer it to a serving platter lined with a white cloth napkin or paper towel to absorb the excess moisture and keep the fish from sliding on the platter. Cover with plastic wrap and refrigerate (up to 24 hours ahead).

5. To serve: Remove the skin from the top side of the fish and decorate both the fish and platter with lemon slices and sprigs of parsley. Serve the green mayonnaise on the side, or coat the fish with the sauce.

VARIATION

The salmon can also be served hot. If the salmon is extremely fresh, you can simply poach it in lightly salted water, otherwise poach it in the same court bouillon as for the cold salmon (steps 1 and 2). In step 3, let the salmon stand in the hot poaching liquid for only 5 minutes. Transfer the fish to a serving platter and prepare for presentation as described in step 5, serving Hollandaise Sauce (page 326) in place of the green mayonnaise.

SOLE FILLETS
WITH POACHED MUSHROOMS AND SHRIMP SAUCE

[FILET DE SOLE GRANVILLE]

THIS IS AN EXAMPLE of just how good a classic recipe can be. Traditional Sole Granville was made with a whole fish that was surrounded by shrimp and mushrooms and decorated with truffles. I use sole fillets in place of the whole fish, and often leave out the truffle. I have also cut back considerably on the egg yolks, cream, and butter normally used in the recipe.

In France this would be made with Dover sole—a firm and delicious fish, which you can at times get in this country, although it is extremely expensive. If your market has Dover sole, I recommend trying it here, but failing that, you can use any of the many varieties of flatfish native to American waters: The most common are grey, lemon, Rex, and petrale sole; flounder; fluke; and dab. The two varieties I find closest in texture to Dover sole are grey sole and petrale sole. **SERVES 6**

POACHED MUSHROOMS

¾ pound button mushrooms, washed
Juice of ½ lemon
Pinch of salt and freshly ground pepper

SAUCE PARISIENNE

3 tablespoons butter
3 tablespoons all-purpose flour
2 cups Fish Stock (page 306)
¼ teaspoon salt
⅛ teaspoon freshly ground pepper
2 egg yolks
⅓ cup heavy cream
¾ pound medium shrimp, shelled, deveined (see page 101), and cooked
1 medium (¾-inch) black truffle, diced (optional)

FISH AND FINISHING

2 tablespoons butter
3 shallots, chopped
2 pounds grey sole fillets, folded in half (see "Folding a Fillet," page 97)
½ cup Fish Stock (page 306)
½ cup dry white wine
1 medium (¾-inch) black truffle, sliced (optional)

1. Poach the mushrooms: Place the mushrooms in a saucepan and add enough water to come halfway up their sides. Add the lemon juice, salt, and pepper. Cover the pan and bring to a boil over high heat. Reduce the heat and simmer gently for 2 to 3 minutes. (The mushrooms can be poached ahead. Store in the poaching liquid.)

2. Drain the mushrooms, reserving the poaching liquid. Place the poaching liquid in a small saucepan and reduce over high heat to ¼ cup, about 3 minutes.

3. Make the sauce: In a medium-size saucepan, melt the butter over medium-high heat. Stir in the flour and cook until pale yellow, 30 to 45 seconds.

4. Add the fish stock and the reserved reduced mushroom liquid. Bring to a boil while whisking. Reduce the heat and simmer for 5 to 10 minutes, skimming off the butter and impurities as they rise to the surface. Season with the salt and pepper and whisk well.

5. In a small bowl, blend the egg yolks and cream together. Remove the sauce from the heat and whisk in the egg yolk–cream mixture. Return to medium heat and whisk the sauce until it returns to a simmer. Remove from the heat and gently stir in the mushrooms, shrimp, and diced truffle (if using). Cover the surface of the sauce with plastic wrap. (The sauce can be made 1 day ahead to this point and refrigerated. Reheat gently.)

6. Prepare the fish: Butter a 12-inch skillet with 1 tablespoon of the butter and sprinkle with the chopped shallots. Place the folded fillets in the pan and add the fish stock and wine. Cut a piece of wax paper to fit over the surface of the fish. Place it on the fish and cover with the pan lid. (The fish can be prepared up to 1 hour in advance and kept at room temperature.) Reheat the sauce in a water bath (*bain-marie*).

7. Bring the skillet to a simmer over medium heat and cook until the fish is white and opaque throughout, about 10 minutes.

SKINNING FISH FILLETS

Two ways to make not perfectly fresh fish taste fresher are skinning and soaking the fish in ice water for 10 to 15 minutes before cooking. Cooking the skin heightens any fishy flavors that exist in the fish itself.

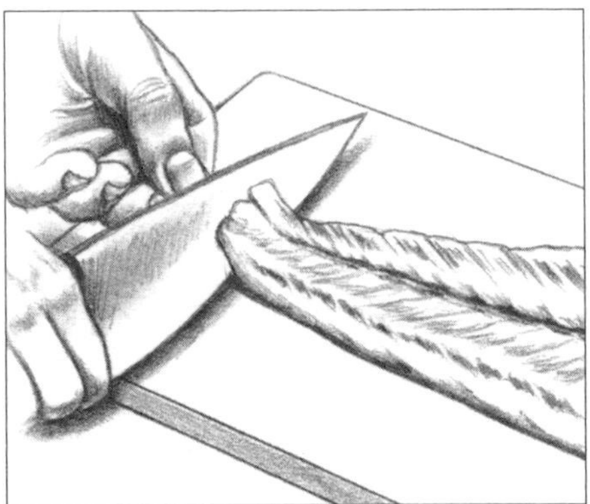

1. Place the fillet skin side down. Start at the tail and cut a little of the fish away from the skin so you can grab the skin with your fingers.

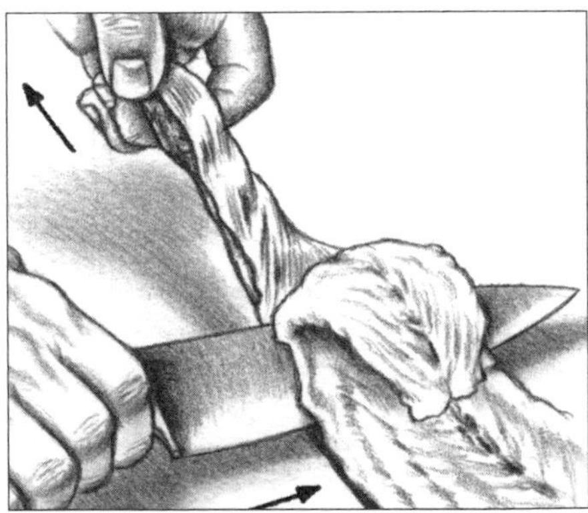

2. With your knife held at about a 30-degree angle to the work surface, slice back and forth between skin and fish while at the same time pulling the skin in the opposite direction.

8. With a skimmer or slotted spoon, transfer the fish to a hot platter, overlapping the fillets around the outside of the platter. Cover loosely with foil to keep warm. Blot up any excess liquid from the platter with paper towels. Reduce the fish-poaching liquid over high heat until only 2 tablespoons remain, 4 to 5 minutes.

FOLDING A FILLET

In France, sole fillets are cut in half, down the middle, into two long, thin fillets (each fish thus yields four fillets).

To make a sole fillet easier to remove from the poaching liquid, and to create an attractive package for presentation, it is customarily folded in half (or sometimes rolled up to form something called a *paupiette*) before being placed in the liquid. When folding a fillet, the smooth outside of the fillet (where the skin was) should be on the inside, and the inside (where the bones were) should be on the outside. If you don't want to have to remember any of this, just try folding in both directions; the one in which the fish folds flatter is the correct one.

9. With a slotted spoon or skimmer, remove the shrimp, mushrooms, and diced truffle from the sauce and place in the center of the platter.

10. Strain the reduced fish-poaching liquid into the sauce. Taste and adjust the seasoning, if necessary, and whisk well over high heat until the sauce just begins to boil. Remove the sauce from the heat, beat in the remaining 1 tablespoon of butter, and spoon or pour the sauce over the sole. Use the sliced truffle to decorate the fish, if desired, and serve immediately.

IN ADDITION

When working with fish, keep a bowl of water containing several tablespoons of vinegar nearby, and use this acidulated water to rinse your hands and to wipe knives and countertops to help prevent fish odors from developing.

SERVING SUGGESTION

Start with Chicken Consommé (page 17) or Cream of Asparagus Soup (page 24). Serve the fish with steamed rice and follow with a green salad. For dessert, serve Oranges in Champagne (page 285).

WINE

This dish goes nicely with a top-quality white Burgundy or Champagne.

DEEP-FRIED FISH FINGERS WITH PARSLEY AND ONION RINGS

[GOUJONNETTES DE SOLE]

A GOUJON is a small, 2- to 3-inch minnowlike fish that is caught in the rivers of France. *Goujons* are usually deep fried and served as an hors d'oeuvre with lemon and fried parsley. These crunchy, tender fish are eaten head and all, for their bones are hardly noticeable. Some restaurants in towns bordering rivers will serve them while you sip an aperitif and contemplate the menu.

Goujonnettes de sole, or *filets de sole en goujon,* is fillet of sole that is cut to resemble *goujons* and then served in the same way. If you've never tasted fried parsley, you will be pleasantly surprised. **SERVES 6**

1½ pounds sole fillets
2 cups milk
½ teaspoon salt
¼ teaspoon freshly ground pepper
3 onions, cut into rings
About 1 cup all-purpose flour, for dredging
2 to 2½ quarts vegetable oil, for deep-frying
1 bunch curly parsley, stems removed
3 lemons, cut in half
Remoulade Sauce (page 335)

1. Preheat the oven to 250°F.

2. Cut the fillets in half lengthwise (follow the "seam" down the middle of the fillet). Cut the fillet halves on the diagonal to form strips about 2½ to 3 inches long and ½ inch wide.

3. Place 1 cup of the milk in a bowl large enough to hold the *goujons* and add the salt and pepper. Soak the fish in the seasoned milk for 10 minutes.

4. In a deep-fryer, heat the oil to very hot (just smoking).

5. Place the onion rings in a bowl with the remaining 1 cup milk to moisten. Drain and toss in the flour to coat. Fry the onion rings in the hot oil until golden brown, 1 to 2 minutes. Drain on paper towels and keep warm in the oven.

6. Drain the fish and toss in the flour to coat each piece just before frying.

7. Let the oil get very hot again and fry the fish, in 3 batches, until golden brown and crunchy, 2 to 3 minutes per batch. Drain on paper towels, and keep warm.

8. Fry the parsley for about 5 seconds. Drain on paper towels.

9. Serve the fish with the parsley, fried onion rings, lemon halves, and remoulade sauce.

WINE

Serve the fish with a dry white wine, such as Muscadet or Pouilly-Fuissé.

AMERICAN BOUILLABAISSE

[BOUILLABAISSE AMÉRICAINE]

FOR ANYONE who has spent any time on the French Riviera, the name *bouillabaisse* can bring back fond memories. In essence, a bouillabaisse is simply a "fish boil" with lots of good flavors. The local fish traditionally used were small; they were the ones left behind in the fisherman's nets. But instead of being thrown back, the fish were thrown into a pot with local flavoring ingredients and boiled. The result was a platter of fish and a very flavorful broth.

The recipe that follows uses only seafood easily available in this country (which is why I called it American Bouillabaisse) and is really just an elaboration of my Mediterranean Fish Soup (page 21), which you can make well ahead of time (and even have stored in the freezer).

The only ingredients the least bit difficult to find are fresh fennel, saffron, and savory. For the fennel, you can substitute 1 teaspoon of aniseed or fennel seed or 1 tablespoon of an anise-flavored aperitif such as Pernod or Ricard. Unfortunately, there is no substitute for saffron if you want this to be a bouillabaisse instead of just a fish stew, although it will still be very good. If you do not have savory, omit it.

To serve the bouillabaisse, place a basket of toasted slices of French bread on the table with dishes of aioli and rouille. Each diner spreads one of the two flavorful mayonnaises on the toast rounds before adding them to the bowl with the soup and fish. **SERVES 6 TO 8**

2 tablespoons extra-virgin olive oil
1 onion, halved and sliced
1 leek, washed and diced
½ fennel bulb, diced
2 cloves garlic, smashed
5 sprigs parsley, chopped
1 tomato, peeled (see page 194), seeded, and diced
½ bay leaf
1 sprig fresh or 1 pinch of dried savory (optional)
1 sprig fresh or 1 pinch of dried thyme
1 pinch of saffron
½ teaspoon salt
⅛ teaspoon freshly ground pepper
2 pounds live lobster (see "Cooking with Live Lobsters," page 100), cut into serving pieces
2 pounds mussels (optional), scrubbed and debearded (see page 50)
2 pounds fish fillets (see Note), cut into chunks
Mediterranean Fish Soup (page 21), prepared through step 5; omit the fish fillet
2 pounds medium shrimp, shelled and deveined (see page 101)
1 pound sea scallops, tendon removed (see page 30)
1 baguette, sliced and toasted
½ recipe Aioli (page 332)
½ recipe Rouille (page 333)

Cooking with Live Lobsters

Lobster is best kept alive until just before you are ready to cook it. A lobster that has been killed ahead of time can spoil and/or the meat will be tough. For most, the idea of killing anything is unpleasant. I try to cause the lobster the least amount of trauma. Because the lobster is a cold-blooded animal, its body temperature (as I learned in my ninth-grade biology class), adjusts to that of its surroundings. Having observed that a lobster is less active when cold than when warm, I find that if I place a lobster in the freezer 30 to 60 minutes before I am ready to cook it, the lobster becomes very relaxed and sleepy. In this state, the lobster doesn't react to the boiling water, steam, or knife blade as much as when at room temperature. I don't know if this is more humane, but it makes me feel better.

If I am cutting the lobster up before cooking (as with American Bouillabaisse), once the lobster is well chilled I kill it by putting the point of my chef's knife through the shell about an inch behind the eyes and bringing the knife down firmly between the eyes. If I am boiling the lobster whole, I tuck the tail under the body and holding the tail and body in one hand, I plunge the head into the boiling water before releasing the lobster into the pot. (If you don't tuck the tail underneath, the lobster will flap its tail and the splashing boiling water can cause burns.) If I am steaming lobster, I place them live into the steam (some people have trouble with the method, since the lobsters do move around a bit once the steam wakes them up and before it cooks them).

1. In a large stockpot, heat the oil over medium heat. Add the onion, leek, and fennel and cook until tender, about 5 minutes. Stir in the garlic, parsley, tomato, bay leaf, savory (if using), thyme, saffron, salt, and pepper and cook for 1 minute.

2. Place the lobster, mussels (if using), and fish fillets in the pot and cover with the cold Mediterranean fish soup. Bring to a boil over medium heat, about 20 minutes, and boil gently for 1 minute.

3. Add the shrimp and scallops. When the soup returns to a boil, the shellfish and fish should all be done. If not, simmer an additional minute.

4. Remove the fish and shellfish and place on a large serving platter. (Discard any mussels that did not open during cooking.)

5. Bring the soup back to a boil, taste, and adjust the seasonings, if necessary. Strain, if desired, into a large soup tureen and bring to the table.

6. Divide the fish and seafood among large individual soup bowls and ladle the hot soup over it. Serve with the toasted baguette and bowls of the aioli and rouille on the side.

NOTE: Use any fish that appeals to you, the freshest possible and preferably thick over thin pieces. Try for 1 pound each of two types. And avoid strongly flavored fish such as mackerel and bluefish unless they are extremely fresh.

SERVING SUGGESTION

Serve this hearty soup with a green salad and a fruit tart for dessert and you will have a wonderful meal.

WINE

Accompany the meal with a chilled rosé from Provence and the flavors will make you feel as though you were on the Côte d'Azur.

Shelling and Deveining Shrimp

There are two schools of thought on the subject of shelling and deveining shrimp. Those who believe it is either unhealthy or undesirable to eat the intestinal tract of the shrimp remove the shell and "vein" before cooking. Those who feel it is important to cook shrimp in their shells, for the added flavor, eat the cooked shrimp, intestine and all.

I like the increased flavor offered by the shells, and do not object to the occasional grittiness of the vein. However, since I find that the ease of eating unshelled shrimp generally outweighs the added flavor, I usually remove the shell and veins before cooking.

The system I use for shelling and deveining shrimp was taught to me many years ago by the wife of a fisherman in East Hampton, Long Island.

Be sure to save the shrimp shells, though. They can be used to make a flavorful liquid for a sauce, or to make a rice pilaf. Once the shells are removed, rinse them well and place them in a saucepan. Cover them with cold water, bring to a boil, and simmer them for 15 minutes to extract their flavor. The liquid can be stored, covered, in the refrigerator for several days and in the freezer for several months.

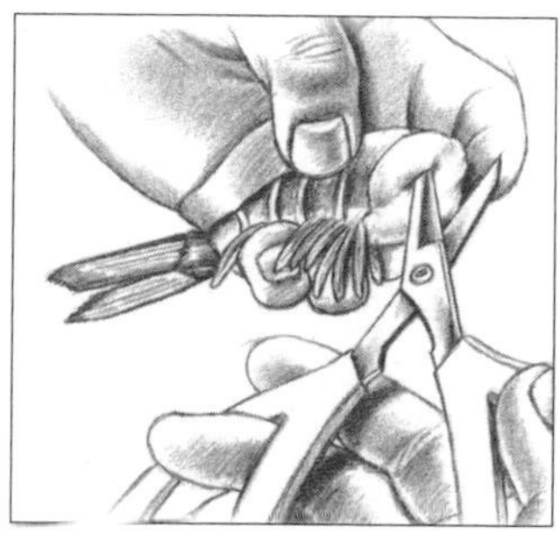

1. Place the blade of a small kitchen scissors into the intestinal tract.

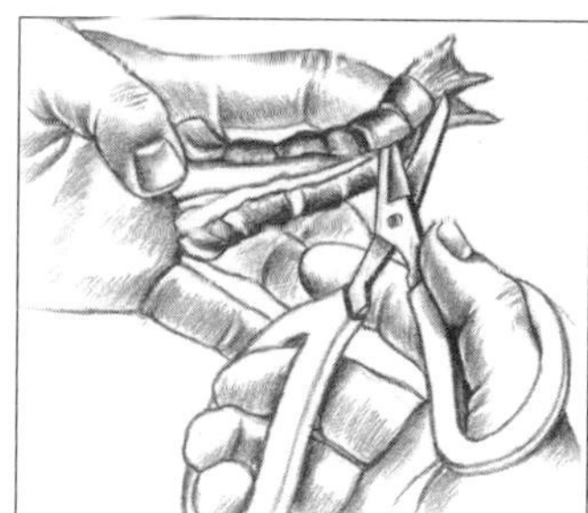

2. Cut through the shell down the back of the shrimp to the tail.

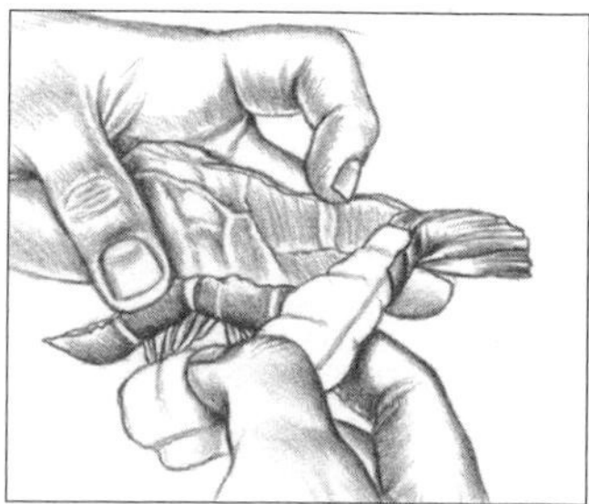

3. Peel off the shell, remove the vein, and rinse.

SHRIMP A LA PROVENCALE

[CREVETTES À LA PROVENÇALE]

THIS FLAVORFUL RECIPE is fast and easy. You sauté shrimp and then add them to a Provence-style sauce made with ingredients typical of the south of France: tomatoes, garlic, and olive oil. Traditionally this sauce is covered and cooked slowly. I use high heat instead to cook it rapidly, and have also reduced the quantity of olive oil used to about half. The recipe serves four as a main course with rice pilaf or six as a first course.

SERVES 4 OR 6

4 tablespoons extra-virgin olive oil
2 pounds tomatoes, peeled, seeded, and diced, or 1 can (28 ounces) diced tomatoes, drained
3 cloves garlic, finely chopped
¼ teaspoon salt
⅛ teaspoon freshly ground pepper
6 sprigs parsley, chopped
1½ pounds large shrimp, shelled and deveined (see page 101)

1. Make the sauce: In a skillet, heat 2 tablespoons of the oil over high heat until it is smoking. Add the tomatoes. (Be careful; the hot oil may spatter.) Toss or stir quickly. Add the garlic and cook until most of the liquid has evaporated, 3 to 5 minutes. Season with the salt and pepper, remove from the heat and stir in three-fourths of the chopped parsley. Pour the sauce into a bowl and set aside. (The sauce can be made 1 day in advance. Cover and refrigerate.)

2. In a skillet, heat the remaining 2 tablespoons of oil over medium-high heat. Add the shrimp and sauté until they change color and begin to curl, 2 to 3 minutes.

3. Add the sauce to the cooked shrimp and bring to a boil. Transfer the shrimp and sauce to a hot serving platter and sprinkle with the remaining chopped parsley before serving.

IN ADDITION

The Provençale sauce in this recipe is extremely simple and, therefore, quite versatile. It can also be used with fish, chicken, veal, pasta, and omelets. Using the proportions here you can make larger quantities, but do not try to make any more than a double recipe. You need a great amount of heat to evaporate the liquid from the tomatoes rapidly without cooking them to a purée (and most home stoves don't get hot enough). The sauce as I have designed it should, if possible, retain the texture of the diced tomatoes. You can vary the sauce by adding ¼ pound of sautéed sliced mushrooms.

SERVING SUGGESTION

Serve with a salad and Rice Pilaf (page 207). For dessert, serve a fruit tart.

WINE

I enjoy a red Côtes-du-Rhône with this flavorful sauce, but it also goes well with chilled white or rosé from Provence.

SHRIMP WITH CURRY, GINGER, AND TOMATO

[CREVETTES À L'ORIENTALE]

IF A CLASSIC French dish has the word *orientale* or *indienne* in its name, it generally signifies that a curried sauce is a part of the presentation. In most cases, curry powder is used to flavor a flour-based sauce, such as béchamel or velouté. In this lightened version of a French curry dish, I use cream and fresh tomatoes for the sauce and add two Asian and Indian ingredients: cilantro and fresh ginger. Cilantro has a flavor that our taste buds either like or hate. If you don't like it, use parsley. **SERVES 6**

1 tablespoon vegetable oil
1 onion, chopped
3 cloves garlic, chopped
1 piece (1 to 1½ inches) fresh ginger, peeled and chopped
2 to 3 teaspoons curry powder, to taste
2 to 3 pinches of cayenne pepper, to taste
¼ cup dry white wine
1 cup heavy cream
¼ teaspoon salt
⅛ teaspoon freshly ground pepper
2 pounds large shrimp, shelled and deveined (see page 101)
2 pounds tomatoes, peeled (see page 194), seeded, chopped, and drained, or 1 can (28 ounces) diced tomatoes, drained
12 sprigs cilantro, chopped

1. In a 12-inch skillet, heat the oil over medium-low heat. Add the onion and gently cook until softened, about 5 minutes. Add the garlic, ginger, curry powder, and cayenne pepper and stir with a wooden spoon. Add the wine and boil over high heat until reduced by half, 10 to 15 seconds. Stir in the cream and season with the salt and pepper. (This sauce can be made up to 2 hours in advance and held at room temperature.)

2. About 5 minutes before serving, bring the sauce to a boil, add the shrimp, and cook rapidly, turning the shrimp occasionally, until they change color and begin to curl, 2 to 3 minutes. Stir in the tomatoes and two-thirds of the cilantro and cook just long enough to heat the tomatoes through. (Do not boil the sauce after the tomatoes have been added or it will become watery.) Transfer to a warm serving platter and sprinkle with the remaining cilantro before serving.

SERVING SUGGESTION

Watercress Soup (page 22) or another light vegetable soup makes a good first course. Serve the curry with Boiled White Rice (page 206) or Rice Pilaf (page 207) and your favorite chutney. Follow with a mixed green salad and a soufflé or a fruit sorbet for dessert.

WINE

Try a dry white wine or rosé with the shrimp.

GRILLED LOBSTER

[HOMARD GRILLÉ]

THE FIRST TIME I had grilled lobster was in France in a small town on the Brittany coast, a region renowned for its lobsters. The small half-lobster that was served was very delicious and very expensive, but the flavor was superior to any steamed lobster I had ever eaten, although its claws and legs were dry.

Over the years I have re-created the delicious flavors of a grilled lobster and solved the problem of dry claws and legs. I cook the body of the lobster on the grill, to develop its flavor, and steam the claws and legs separately, to keep them moist and sweet. **SERVES 6**

3 lobsters (3 to 4 pounds each; see Note), split lengthwise, claws and legs removed (see "Preparing a Lobster for Grilling," right)
2 tablespoons chopped fresh herbs, such as tarragon, chives, dill, or basil
8 tablespoons (1 stick; 4 ounces) butter, melted

FOR SERVING (OPTIONAL)
2 lemons, cut into wedges
2 sticks (8 ounces) melted butter, for dipping

1. Preheat a grill to high.

2. Place the lobsters on a large tray or baking sheet. Cut off the antennae, and if the two halves have not been completely separated, use a pair of scissors to do so. Reserve the claws and legs. Place a large pot with 1 inch of water over high heat and bring to a boil.

PREPARING A LOBSTER FOR GRILLING

Lobsters are generally split in half lengthwise for grilling to gain flavor from the grill.

After you split the lobster, remove the stomach (which is found in the head area) and the intestine (a small clear or black tube running the length of the lobster), if you find it. Twist the claws and legs from the body and keep separate for steaming. The claw shell, which is softer before being cooked, can be cut on one side with a large knife. This will alleviate the need to crack them at the table.

Because lobster meat breaks down or spoils rapidly once the lobster is dead, they are most often split just before grilling. If you are unable to kill and split the lobsters yourself, have the market do it for you no more than 4 to 6 hours in advance and keep the lobsters well iced until you are ready to cook them.

3. Add the chopped herbs to the 1 stick of melted butter and use a pastry brush to coat all the interior parts of the lobster bodies.

4. Place the lobster bodies, shell side down, on a very hot grill and cover. If your grill does not have a cover, make one with aluminum foil. Put the legs and claws into the pot of boiling water, cover, and cook until the bodies on the grill are done, 10 to 15 minutes. When done, the juices in the shell will be sizzling, the meat will be opaque and firm to the touch, and (if female) the roe, which is dark green when raw, will be red.

5. To serve: Lift or slide the bodies onto individual serving plates and serve. Bring the drained legs and claws to the table in a large bowl and serve with lemon wedges and melted butter, if desired.

NOTE: These large-size lobsters can be hard to find, so you will most likely have to order them in advance.

SERVING SUGGESTION

I usually grill lobster during the summer months when there is a great selection of fresh vegetables. A simple string bean salad can be made by cooking and chilling the beans and tossing them with some Vinaigrette (page 336) made with some finely chopped shallot and parsley. The same vinaigrette can be used to dress ripe sliced tomatoes. Make sure to have warm baguettes on hand to wipe up the juice left on the plate. A summer Blueberry Tart (page 214) is a perfect ending for this meal.

LOBSTER IN A SPICY TOMATO SAUCE

[HOMARD À L'AMÉRICAINE/HOMARD À L'ARMORICAINE]

THIS WONDERFUL lobster dish could be found for years on restaurant menus as either *homard à l'américaine* or *homard à l'armoricaine.* One possible explanation for the name of the dish is that the Brittany region of France, famous for its lobsters, is also known as Armorica, thus *homard à l'armoricaine.* Another explanation is that a chef from the south of France working in a Parisian restaurant made this dish for an American couple that wanted lobster in a hurry. This makes some sense since the flavors in the dish—olive oil, garlic, tomatoes, and herbs—are typical of the southern region of Provence. Either way, the dish has pleased diners ever since. Although the traditional recipe calls for fresh live lobsters, this recipe uses lobster tails, which are easier to deal with.

SERVES 6

3 tablespoons extra-virgin olive oil
6 lobster tails (5 to 6 ounces each), cut into 1- to 1½-inch pieces
1 onion, chopped
3 shallots, chopped
5 cloves garlic, chopped
¼ cup Cognac
½ cup dry white wine
3 pounds tomatoes, peeled, seeded, and diced, or 3 cans (14.5 ounces each) diced tomatoes, drained
1 tablepoon chopped fresh or dried tarragon (see Note)
¼ teaspoon salt
⅛ teaspoon freshly ground black pepper
2 to 4 pinches of cayenne pepper, to taste (see Note)
1 tablespoon tomato paste
2 tablespoons butter
Chopped parsley, for garnish

1. In a 12-inch skillet, heat 2 tablespoons of the olive oil over high heat until it is very hot (smoking). Add the lobster pieces and quickly cook until the shells turn red, about 2 minutes. With a slotted spoon, transfer the lobster to a bowl.

2. Reduce the heat, add the remaining 1 tablespoon olive oil and the onion, and sauté until softened but not browned, about 3 minutes. Add the shallots and garlic and cook, stirring, for 15 seconds. Return the lobster to the pan, remove from the heat, add the Cognac, and flame. (See "How to Flambé," page 282.)

3. Add the wine, tomatoes, tarragon, salt, black pepper, and 2 pinches of the cayenne pepper. Boil gently, uncovered, until the lobster is thoroughly cooked, 10 to 15 minutes.

4. With a slotted spoon, transfer the lobster to a warm serving dish. Add the tomato paste to the sauce in the skillet and boil rapidly to thicken, about 5 minutes. Taste and adjust the seasoning, if necessary. Stir in the butter. Pour the sauce over the lobster and sprinkle with parsley.

NOTE: If you are not a tarragon lover, you can reduce the amount in the recipe. If you want to opt for the greater amount of cayenne, add the second 2 pinches of cayenne, but not until the lobster has cooked and the sauce is ready to serve.

SERVING SUGGESTION

Start with an artichoke vinaigrette. Serve the lobster with Rice Pilaf (page 207). For dessert, try Strawberries with Sabayon (page 283).

WINE

Serve a chilled white or rosé with the lobster.

POULTRY

In France, it is not at all uncommon for a home cook to prepare recipes for guinea hen, goose, pheasant, squab, quail, and partridge in addition to chicken, duck, and turkey. Chicken, however, is the clear favorite. There are more French recipes for chicken than any other bird—in fact, more than for any other food. Its delicate flavor lends itself to a host of sauces as well as numerous cooking methods. Chicken can be grilled, sautéed, oven-roasted, spit-roasted, fried, poached, and braised.

Duck, whose popularity in this country seems to go up and down, is a less versatile yet delicious dark-meat bird that stands up well to more assertively flavored sauces. In America, where the predominant breed of duck available (the White Pekin) has a layer of fat under its skin, roasting is really the best method of cooking.

When roasting duck, or indeed any poultry (under 7 pounds), I use the high-temperature method that is used in France to produce wonderful flavors in a short time. I also roast all birds on their sides instead of breast up. This places the joints, which take longer to cook, in the path of the most direct heat, and prevents overcooking the breast. I am less concerned about roasting the birds on their sides when using a convection oven.

The recipes in this chapter include light-meat fowl (chicken and pheasant) and dark-meat fowl (duck and squab). Among the white-meat poultry recipes is a recipe for rabbit, which is treated in much the same way as chicken and for which chicken can easily be substituted.

TRUFFLED ROAST CHICKEN

[POULARDE TRUFFÉE ET FARCIE]

TRUFFLED TURKEY, *dindonneau truffé,* is a specialty in France for Christmas and New Year's. When I was living in Paris in the late '60s, I would see stacks of truffled turkeys in the windows of charcuterie shops a week to ten days before the holidays. (The shops, which were never heated, were as good as refrigerators in the winter.) Each turkey had slices of truffles placed under the skin, where they developed flavor while the turkeys gently aged. The flavor that the truffle adds to the roast bird is heady and earthy, and incomparable. Trying to describe a truffle to someone who hasn't had one is impossible, like trying to describe the taste of a mushroom.

Sliced truffles are a superb flavoring for any and all roast poultry, but there is something particularly satisfying in using them to flavor chicken—it changes the ordinary into something extraordinary.

I roast chicken in a manner that most Americans will find unusual. First, I roast at 475°F. A bird of the same size cooked at the more usual, lower temperature of 350°F to 375°F could take up to 2 hours; my 4-pound chicken is done in 1 hour. I also roast the chicken on its side to expose the thickest parts of the bird, the joints, to the hottest part of the oven so they will cook in the same time the breast does. Cooking the chicken breast side up results in overcooked breast meat and undercooked joints.

The stuffing used in this recipe is my favorite. It is a good basic stuffing recipe (which can have other ingredients, such as dried fruit or chopped cooked chestnuts, added to it) and, like all the stuffings I use in roasted fowl, is fully cooked. Using a cooked stuffing eliminates the need for extra time in the oven. If you can't get truffles, eliminate them. You will still have a delicious, stuffed roast chicken. If you like the stuffing, double or triple the recipe for your next turkey. **SERVES 6**

1 chicken (4 to 5 pounds); neck, gizzard, and wing tips reserved
1 medium-large (1-inch) black truffle, cut into 10 thin slices
½ pound slab smoked bacon or ½ pound thick-sliced smoked bacon, diced
2 onions (see Note)
3 chicken livers, coarsely chopped
1 cup unseasoned dried bread crumbs
½ teaspoon salt
¼ teaspoon freshly ground pepper
1 teaspoon fresh or dried thyme leaves, or 4 fresh or dried sage leaves, chopped
½ cup Madeira
1 carrot, sliced ½ inch thick (see Note)
3 tablespoons butter, softened to room temperature
1 cup water

TRUFFLING A CHICKEN

In preparing the chicken for truffling, it is necessary to separate the skin from the meat. This is done quite easily once the thin membrane connecting the two is broken. Pull the neck skin back over the breast and you will find the membrane. Holding the skin up, puncture the membrane with your fingernail and spread it apart with your fingers. Once under the skin, you will find that you can easily slide your hand along the surface of the meat. As you reach down toward the leg and second joint, you will find your way impeded by another membrane. Break this one and your hand will slide over the leg.

The truffles, which are very thinly sliced, are fragile and need to be protected as you move them to their resting place under the skin. I use my first two fingers like chopsticks to hold the truffle between the nail of one and the flesh of the other. Once I reach the spot where I want to deposit the truffle, I simply slide it off my nail and onto the meat with the upper finger.

Although the chicken will not develop the same flavor, other ingredients can be placed under the skin of the bird in a similar way. Some suggestions include wild mushrooms, prosciutto, or smoked ham.

1. Starting at the neck, separate the skin from the body of the chicken by inserting your fingers underneath the skin and loosening any membranes you encounter (see "Truffling a Chicken," this page). Place 3 truffle slices on each side of the breast and 2 on each leg. (This can be done 1 to 2 days in advance, and the chicken should be covered with plastic wrap and refrigerated. Bring back to room temperature before proceeding.)

2. Preheat the oven to 475°F.

3. In a large skillet, sauté the bacon over medium-high heat until it is half cooked. Finely chop 1 onion, add it to the pan, and cook, with the bacon, over medium-high heat until the onion is softened, but not browned, 2 to 3 minutes.

4. Add the livers and brown them quickly over high heat, about 30 seconds. Remove the mixture from the heat and add the bread crumbs, which will absorb the fat. Season with the salt, pepper, and thyme. If the stuffing is too dry, moisten it with 1 tablespoon of the Madeira. Taste and adjust the seasoning with salt and pepper. (The stuffing can be made several hours in advance of roasting, but should not be refrigerated.)

5. Stuff and truss the chicken just before roasting (see "How to Truss a Bird," page 133).

6. Place the chicken on its side in a nonstick roasting pan or on a rack in a roasting pan. Quarter the remaining onion and arrange it, the carrot, and the reserved wing tips, neck, and gizzard around the chicken. Spread the butter over the chicken and sprinkle with salt and pepper.

7. Roast the chicken for 30 minutes. Turn it onto its other side and roast another 30 minutes. Baste every 15 minutes. Turn the chicken breast up for the last 5 to 10 minutes, if necessary, for even browning. The chicken is done when, if poked at the leg joint with a fork, the juices run clear; or when an instant-read thermometer inserted into the thickest part of the thigh reads 160°F to 165°F. Remove the chicken from the pan and allow it to stand 10 to 15 minutes before carving.

8. To make a simple pan juice, deglaze the pan and its contents by adding the remaining Madeira and the water to the pan and stirring to loosen the caramelized bits from the pan, vegetables, and chicken parts. Over high heat, reduce by about half. Taste and adjust the seasoning, if necessary. Strain and remove the fat. Carve the chicken and serve with the pan juices.

NOTE: The quartered onion and carrot slices are added to the roasting pan to add flavor and color to the pan and ultimately to the sauce. But they are also there to keep the chicken fat that is rendered out during the roasting from burning. To do this, they must cover a good part of the pan bottom (without being so close together that they won't cook). Therefore, if you have a very large roasting pan, and the quantity of onion and carrot called for here does not seem like enough, add more.

SERVING SUGGESTION

Start with a green salad. Serve Waterless Cooked Carrots (page 178) and Broccoli Purée (page 180) alongside this delicious chicken. End a memorable meal with Tarte Tatin (page 219).

WINE

A fine red Bordeaux from Médoc or Graves is equal to the elegance of this dish.

MAIGRE-GRAS AND FAT SEPARATOR

A *maigre-gras,* a sauceboat used in France, has two spouts. One spout pours off the fat, the other the *jus*. One version of a fat separator looks like a small watering can. The *jus* or clear liquid can be poured out, leaving the fat in the separator.

POACHED CHICKEN WITH CREAMY TARRAGON SAUCE

[POULARDE POCHÉE À L'ESTRAGON]

A SUMPTUOUS and elegant dish, *poularde pochée à l'estragon* begins with a whole chicken poached in a veal or chicken stock with a few aromatic vegetables. The resulting fortified stock is turned into a creamy white tarragon sauce. In restaurants, the dish would be offered only if two or more people were sharing it. At the three-star restaurant Oustaù de Baumanière in Les-Baux-de-Provence (in the south of France), however, I was allowed to order *poularde à l'estragon* just for myself. The entire chicken was brought to the table in a huge white tureen, my piece carved off and the rest returned to the kitchen. (The staff ate well that day.)

FRENCH CHICKEN TERMS

Americans are often confused by all the different names used in French chicken recipes: *poussin, poulet, poularde, poule,* and *coq* being only some of them. These terms correspond to the terms we use to indicate size (and often age) of a chicken. A *poussin* is a baby chicken. A *poulet* is a broiler or a fryer, depending on its size. A *poularde* is a roaster. A *poule* is a stewing hen. And a *coq* is a rooster.

In updating this recipe, I use chicken parts or boneless breasts in place of the whole chicken. This shortens the cooking time and allows me to easily prepare this dish for a large dinner party. To make things simple, I prepare the chicken and sauce (a tarragon-flavored velouté) in advance. The chicken is then reheated in barely simmering stock and served with the reheated sauce. **SERVES 6**

3½ pounds chicken parts or 6 boneless, skinless half breasts (about 2 pounds)
1 carrot, sliced
1 onion, quartered
Bouquet Garni (page 306)
1 tablespoon plus 2 teaspoons chopped fresh tarragon
2 quarts chicken stock, homemade or canned (see chart, page 305)
½ teaspoon salt (¼ teaspoon if using canned stock)
⅛ teaspoon freshly ground pepper
2½ tablespoons butter
3 tablespoons all-purpose flour
½ cup heavy cream

1. In a 4-quart Dutch oven or saucepan, combine the chicken, vegetables, bouquet garni, 1 tablespoon of tarragon, and the stock (it is not necessary for the stock to cover the chicken completely). Bring to a boil over high heat and season with the salt and pepper. Reduce the heat, cover, and simmer until the juices run clear when the chicken is pierced with a fork, 25 minutes for chicken parts, 15 minutes for breasts.

2. Remove the poached chicken pieces and skin them. Strain the stock. Measure out 3 cups of the stock, skim to remove any fat, and set aside. Return the remaining stock and the chicken to the Dutch oven and keep warm. (If you are preparing the chicken in advance—up to 2 days—refrigerate it in the poaching liquid. Before proceeding, bring the stock and chicken to a bare simmer. When ready to serve, remove the chicken to a heated platter and keep warm. Reserve the poaching liquid for another use.)

3. Place 1 cup of the skimmed stock in a small saucepan. Reduce over high heat until only 2 or 3 tablespoons remain, about 7 minutes.

4. In another small saucepan, melt the butter over medium heat. Add the flour and whisk until the mixture becomes pale yellow and frothy, 30 to 45 seconds. Add the remaining 2 cups skimmed stock and stir with a whisk until the sauce comes to a boil, 2 to 3 minutes. When it comes to a boil, whisk vigorously for about 10 seconds, then reduce the heat and simmer gently, whisking the velouté sauce well from time to time until it is the consistency of heavy cream, 2 to 3 minutes. Skim the surface, removing the butter and impurities several times during the cooking, and follow by whisking the velouté well each time.

5. Add the reduced stock, cream, and the remaining tarragon. Bring the velouté back to a boil, reduce the heat, and simmer until it is the consistency of heavy cream, about 10 minutes. Taste and adjust the seasoning, if necessary. (The velouté can be prepared up to 2 days in advance. Cover the surface with plastic wrap, let cool, and refrigerate. Before serving, bring to a boil and whisk well.)

6. To serve: If you have not already done so, remove the chicken from the poaching liquid (reserve for another use) and drain on paper towels. Place the chicken in a deep serving dish and pour the sauce over it. You can strain the hot velouté sauce over the chicken, removing the tarragon as it is done in the classic style, or omit the straining if you prefer. Serve immediately.

SERVING SUGGESTION

Start with a first course of asparagus. Serve the chicken with Boiled White Rice (page 206) or Rice Pilaf (page 207). For dessert, serve a sorbet and Almond Tuiles (page 252) or Oranges in Champagne (page 285).

WINE

Champagne or chilled Chardonnay goes well with poached chicken.

CHICKEN IN A POT

[POULE AU POT]

WHEN YOU'RE NOT feeling your best or you are in the mood for a light meal, this dish of tender chicken and vegetables simmered in stock is just right.

Ordinarily, the soup and the chicken would be served as separate courses, but I prefer to skin the chicken and take the meat off the bone, making the dish both easier to eat and easier to make ahead of time. You can also simplify things by using canned chicken stock if you don't have homemade.

SERVES 4 TO 6

1 chicken (about 4 pounds), cut into 8 serving pieces, or equivalent parts
3 quarts chicken stock, homemade or canned (see chart, page 305)
1 leek (white part only), washed and cut into 2-inch pieces
2 onions, quartered (see Note)
2 small white turnips, peeled and quartered (optional)
3 carrots, cut into 2-inch pieces
2 celery ribs, cut into 2-inch pieces
Bouquet Garni (page 306)
½ teaspoon salt (¼ teaspoon if using canned stock)
⅛ teaspoon freshly ground pepper
½ cup rice, cooked; or ¼ pound cooked thin egg noodles; or 6 new potatoes, diced and cooked

1. In a large stockpot or flameproof casserole, combine the chicken and stock. Bring to a boil, uncovered, over high heat, about 20 minutes. Skim the foam, fat, and impurities that rise to the surface.

2. Add all the remaining ingredients except the cooked rice, noodles, or potatoes. Bring back

CUTTING POULTRY INTO SERVING PIECES

To halve (for 1-pound bird): Cut out the back and remove the breastbone.

To quarter (for 2-pound bird): Above steps, plus separate the breasts from the legs.

To cut into 8 serving pieces (for 3- to 4-pound bird): Remove legs (thigh and drumstick). Remove the back and then the remaining backbone. Cut through the white cartilage covering the sternum from the inside—do not cut through the breastbone. Pry the breasts back to reveal the breastbone and remove it with your fingers. Halve the breast and cut each half in two with poultry shears or a cleaver. Turn the legs skin side down; you will see a line of fat on the inside of the joint between the drumstick and thigh. Where that line ends is the proper place to separate the thigh and drumstick.

to a boil, reduce the heat, and simmer, partially covered, until the chicken is cooked and the vegetables are tender, about 30 minutes. If necessary, cook an additional 5 to 10 minutes. Skim occasionally to remove fat, foam, and impurities that rise to the surface.

3. Remove the pot from the heat and uncover. Transfer the chicken and vegetables to a large bowl. Discard the bouquet garni. Skim the surface of the soup to remove all fat. Strain, if necessary.

4. When the chicken is cool enough to handle,

To Cut a Cooked Bird into Serving Pieces

Carving a chicken or other bird into serving pieces is not hard, as long as you have a sturdy, sharp knife. Remember that the knife will cut easily through joints, but not through bone. If you run into a bone, move a little to the left or right to find the joint and then cut through it.

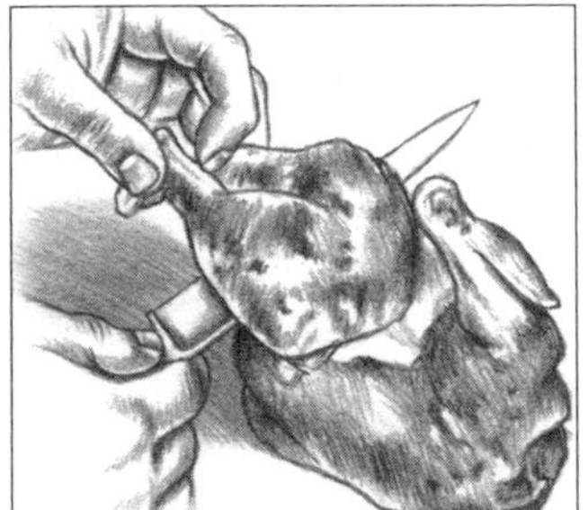

1. Turn the bird on its side. Slice down the body to remove the leg (thigh and drumstick).

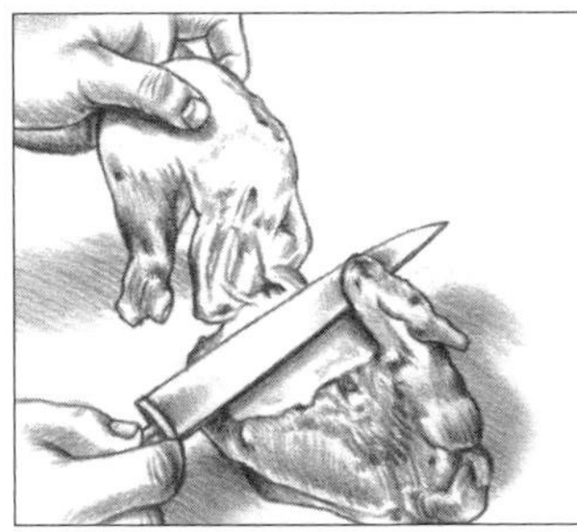

2. Pull the leg away.

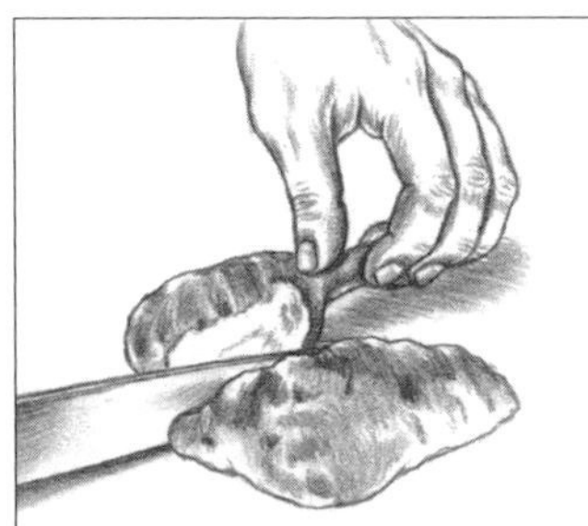

3. Separate the leg into drumstick and thigh.

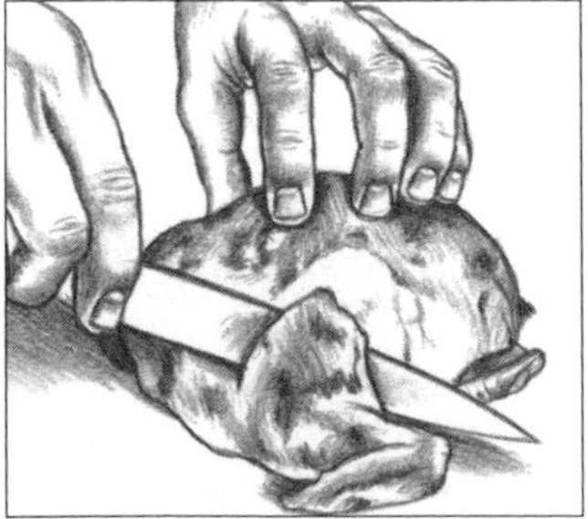

4. Slice along the breast to remove the wing and a small piece of the breast.

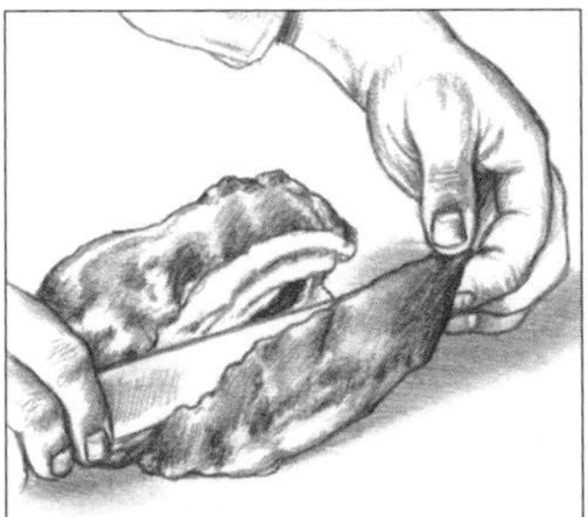

5. Run your knife down between the breast and the carcass and lift the breast away.

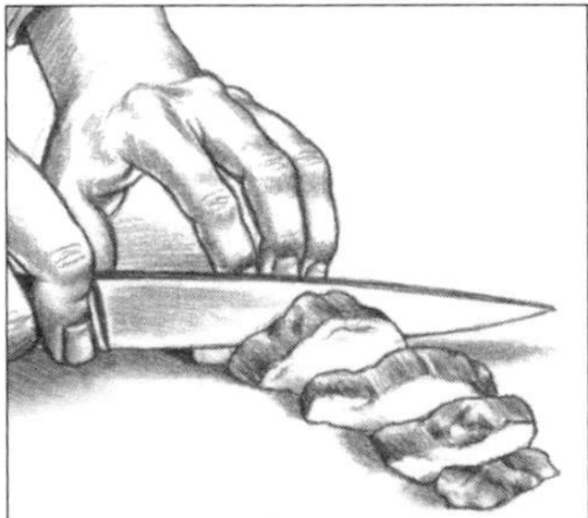

6. Diagonally slice the breast into pieces.

skin it and pull the meat off the bones. Return the chicken to the pot along with the vegetables.

5. To serve: Bring the soup to a simmer. Place the rice, noodles, or potatoes in a strainer or colander and dip into the soup to heat them. Place some of the vegetables, chicken, and rice (or noodles or potatoes) in each of four deep soup bowls. Ladle some of the soup over all and serve.

NOTE: Trim but do not remove the root ends of the onions before quartering in order to keep the onion layers together.

IN ADDITION

Besides producing a lovely and tender chicken dish, what *poule au pot* does, in essence, is make a double-strength chicken stock. The same basic ingredients that go into regular-strength chicken stock are here cooked in stock instead of water. In France, the resulting soup would be served as a separate course (followed by the chicken and vegetables). But you can also save it and use it as the basis for Chicken Consommé (page 17), and serve the chicken and vegetables simply, with mustard and cornichons (small French gherkin pickles).

VARIATION

Creamy Poule au Pot

[POULE AU POT SAUCE SUPRÊME]

Prepare a Velouté (page 315) with the stock. Add ½ cup heavy cream to the sauce and simmer until the sauce thickens enough to coat a spoon, 10 to 15 minutes. Serve the chicken (skinned, but not pulled from the bones) and vegetables on a platter accompanied by Boiled White Rice (page 206) and the sauce.

Coq au Vin

THERE ARE GOOD coq au vin recipes and many that are mediocre. This is one that you and your guests will remember. Taking the extra time to cook the bacon, mushrooms, and onion separately from the main dish keeps the flavors vibrant. It makes all the difference.

Coq au vin was originally designed to make a tough rooster (*coq*) tender enough to eat. The earliest versions came from the Loire Valley, where the French kings lived, and the wines used in the dish were Bourgueil and Chinon, which come from the same area. These wines are available to us today, and using a plump, tender chicken in place of the firmer-fleshed rooster produces a succulent masterpiece.

When this dish was made with a rooster, its blood was saved, diluted with a little vinegar to prevent coagulation, and used to thicken the sauce. For everyone's convenience, I, along with most cooks, use flour to thicken the sauce in this more contemporary version.

Classic coq au vin recipes call for the chicken to be flamed with Cognac. I have omitted this step from the recipe, finding it adds little to the final flavor of this dish. In France, rendered pork fat or lard (called *saindoux*) is often used in place of the light vegetable oil that I use. If you have it handy, use it.

Chicken, veal, and fish are normally cooked in white wine (when wine is called for), but coq au vin requires a full-bodied red wine to produce its rich sauce. Sometimes a red wine of unusual quality and character is used; in these cases the dish takes on the name of the wine. *Coq au Chambertin* is an example of this. I have made this recipe with many red wines. French reds from the Loire, Mâcon, and Rhone regions have all produced memorable meals. Some California Zinfandels work extremely well with this recipe, as do many of the red wines of Spain, Argentina, and Australia.

This dish can be fully prepared one to two days in advance and reheated on top of the stove or in a 350°F oven for about 45 minutes before serving. **SERVES 4 TO 6**

3 tablespoons light vegetable oil
1 chicken (3½ to 4 pounds), cut into 8 serving pieces
1 onion, diced
3 tablespoons all-purpose flour
3 shallots, sliced
4 cloves garlic, sliced
2 cups full-bodied dry red wine, such as Pinot Noir, Côtes-du-Rhône, or Zinfandel
1½ cups beef stock, homemade or canned (see chart, page 305)
1 teaspoon tomato paste
1 teaspoon Meat Glaze (optional; page 309)
Bouquet Garni (page 306)
¼ teaspoon salt
⅛ teaspoon freshly ground pepper
20 pearl onions, peeled, root ends trimmed but left intact to hold the onions together
½ pound smoked slab bacon, cut into ½-inch rectangles
½ pound mushrooms, washed, dried, and halved or quartered, to match size of the onions
Salt and pepper, to taste
5 sprigs parsley, chopped, for garnish

1. In a large flameproof casserole, heat the oil over high heat. Add the chicken and brown well on one side, about 3 to 4 minutes; turn and partially brown the other side, about 1 minute.

2. Add the diced onion and reduce the heat slightly. Sauté the onion until it begins to brown, 2 to 3 minutes.

3. Sprinkle the chicken with the flour. Shake the casserole and turn the chicken so the flour mixes with the hot oil. Reduce the heat to medium and cook, stirring occasionally, until the flour browns, about 3 minutes.

4. Add the shallots, garlic, wine, stock, tomato paste, meat glaze, and bouquet garni. Stir well and season with the salt and pepper. Reduce the heat to medium-low, cover, and simmer for 30 minutes. Skim to remove fat. (The recipe can be prepared to this point several days in advance. Let cool to room temperature, cover, and refrigerate or freeze. Bring back to a simmer before continuing in step 9.)

5. Bring a large saucepan of water to a boil and drop the pearl onions into it. Cook until tender, 10 to 15 minutes. Drain.

6. Place the bacon in a medium-size saucepan, cover with cold water, and bring to a boil over medium-high heat. Drain, rinse with cold water, and repeat this blanching process to extract the bacon's excess saltiness. Drain on paper towels.

7. In a 10- to 12-inch skillet, sauté the bacon over medium-high heat until crisp on the outside, yet still soft on the inside, 3 to 5 minutes. Drain on paper towels.

8. Remove all but 2 tablespoons of the bacon fat from the pan, add the mushrooms, and sauté over high heat until browned, 2 to 3 minutes. Season to taste with salt and pepper and remove the mushrooms to a bowl. Add the pearl onions to the pan and brown, stirring, 2 to 3 minutes, then add to the mushrooms.

9. When the chicken is tender, remove it from the casserole and place it in an ovenproof serving dish or clean flameproof casserole. Discard the bouquet garni. Strain the sauce through a fine-mesh sieve and remove any fat remaining on the surface. The sauce should have the consistency of heavy cream. If it is too thick, add a little water; if too thin, boil it to thicken.

10. Add the bacon, mushrooms, and onions to the chicken, and pour the sauce over all evenly. Before serving, heat to a simmer and cook until warm, about 5 minutes. This can be done on top of the stove or in a 400°F oven, depending on the serving dish used. Sprinkle with the parsley and serve.

GRADATIONS OF GARLIC

The strength of garlic flavor varies with the way it is prepared and when it is added to a dish. The subtlest way of using it is to add it to a liquid, without sautéing it first, so that it blends with the other flavors and does not stand out, as in Coq au Vin (page 115) or for Glazed Garlic (page 181). For a more distinct garlic flavor, the garlic should be sautéed first before adding it to a liquid, as in Ratatouille (page 193). For the strongest flavor, garlic is added either raw (as in Aioli, page 332) or close to the end of the cooking (as in the sauce made for Shrimp à la Provençale, page 102).

SERVING SUGGESTION

As a first course I often serve artichokes, asparagus, or a vegetable soup. I usually serve warm French bread with the meal and a mixed green salad before serving dessert, my favorite being Tarte Tatin (page 219).

WINE

When selecting a wine to drink with a coq au vin, choose an excellent red from the same region as the wine you used in the dish.

SAUTEED CHICKEN A LA PORTUGAISE

[POULET SAUTÉ À LA PORTUGAISE]

THE CLASSIC RECIPE for *poulet sauté à la portugaise* presents the chicken in a sauce with tomatoes and sliced mushrooms. The rendition that I have taught for many years adds both black and green olives. Also, the mushrooms are quartered (or left whole if small) so they are about the same size as the olives. Although I usually serve this colorful dish during the summer when tomatoes are best, I also prepare it in the winter using good-quality canned tomatoes.

To make things easier, I often cook the chicken in the sauce a day or two before I am going to serve it. I cook the mushroom, tomato, and olive accompaniment on the day of serving, add it to the chicken, and reheat everything together in a 300°F to 350°F oven for about 45 minutes. The thick sauce will thin to its proper consistency after the tomatoes are added. **SERVES 4 TO 6**

4 tablespoons (½ stick) butter
1 chicken (3½ to 4 pounds), cut into 8 serving pieces
2 onions, diced
⅓ cup all-purpose flour
2 cloves garlic, finely chopped
2 shallots, finely chopped
2 cups beef stock, homemade or canned (see chart, page 305)
1 cup dry white wine
Bouquet Garni (page 306)
1 tablespoon tomato paste
¼ teaspoon salt
⅛ teaspoon freshly ground pepper
3 ounces (about ¾ cup) pitted green olives (see Note)
3 ounces (about ¾ cup) pitted black olives (see Note)
1½ tablespoons vegetable oil
¾ pound mushrooms, washed, dried, and quartered
2 pounds tomatoes, peeled, seeded, and quartered, or 1 can (28 ounces) peeled whole tomatoes, drained and quartered
3 sprigs fresh parsley, chopped, for garnish

1. In a flameproof casserole, melt the butter over high heat. Add the chicken and brown well on one side, about 3 to 4 minutes; turn and brown the other side, about 3 minutes. Add the onions, reduce the heat to medium-high, and cook until golden, about 3 minutes.

2. Stir the flour into the butter with a wooden spoon. Reduce the heat to medium and cook, stirring or shaking the casserole occasionally, until the flour is light brown, 3 to 5 minutes.

3. Add the garlic, shallots, stock, wine, bouquet garni, tomato paste, salt, and pepper. Stir gently.

4. Cover, reduce the heat to medium-low, and simmer until the chicken is tender, 25 to

35 minutes, skimming the fat from the surface several times. Discard the bouquet garni. (The dish can be made to this point 1 or 2 days in advance. Let cool to room temperature, cover, and refrigerate. To reheat, continue with the recipe through step 7 and reheat the entire dish in a 300°F to 350°F oven for about 45 minutes.)

5. Taste both types of olives to see if they are about the same level of saltiness. If they are, blanch them together. Otherwise, blanch them separately. To blanch: Place the olives in a saucepan, cover with cold water, and bring to a boil over high heat. Drain and rinse with cold water. Taste and repeat, if necessary, until they are just slightly salty to the taste.

6. In a 12-inch skillet, heat the oil over high heat. Add the mushrooms and sauté, tossing, shaking, or stirring them occasionally, until they are browned, about 3 minutes. Season to taste with salt and pepper.

7. Add the olives, mushrooms, and tomatoes to the chicken. Simmer for 5 minutes.

8. To serve: If not already in an attractive casserole, transfer to a hot serving dish and sprinkle the chicken with the parsley just before serving.

NOTE: I use pitted olives in this dish, because it's easier on the cook (no tedious pitting) as well as on the guests, who otherwise would have to be on the lookout for pits. Even if the pitted olives you find might not be your first choice as an eating olive, they will be fine in this dish.

SERVING SUGGESTION

Serve Rice Pilaf (page 207) with the chicken. Salad, French bread, and dessert—fruit sorbet and cookies—are all you need to accompany this dish.

WINE

I would serve either a Portuguese red or a chilled Beaujolais with this summer *ragoût.*

CHICKEN WITH RIESLING

[POULET AU RIESLING]

THIS ALSATIAN specialty is quick and easy to prepare. Classically, *poulet au Riesling* was made by simmering the chicken in a combination of wine and water. The resulting stock was thickened to make a velouté sauce, which was further enriched with egg yolks and cream. Mushrooms were poached separately and their liquid reduced and added to the sauce. In this recipe, the mushrooms are cooked with the chicken, eliminating two steps, and only cream is used in the sauce. Omitting the butter, flour, and egg yolks yields a smaller quantity of sauce with a greater intensity of flavor. **SERVES 4**

CREAM SAUCE:
Sauce Crème

A Béchamel (page 313) with the addition of 1 cup of heavy cream becomes a classic *sauce crème*. Once the cream is added, the sauce is boiled to reduce it to the desired consistency. Contemporary cream sauces are made just with heavy cream and reduced cooking liquids, or Meat Glaze (page 309) or other glazes.

Examples of contemporary cream sauces can be seen in the Steak au Poivre (page 141) and in the Chicken with Riesling (page 119).

3 tablespoons butter
1 chicken (2 to 2½ pounds), quartered, or 4 skinless, boneless half breasts (about 1½ pounds)
¼ teaspoon salt
⅛ teaspoon freshly ground pepper
1 onion, halved
2 shallots, finely chopped
¼ pound mushrooms, washed, dried, and sliced
¾ cup plus 1 teaspoon Riesling wine
¾ cup heavy cream

1. In a large skillet, melt the butter over medium heat. Add the chicken and brown it lightly, about 3 minutes on each side.

2. Pour off any excess cooking fat. Season the chicken with the salt and pepper. Add the onion to the pan, cover, and cook gently over low heat for 15 minutes (10 minutes if using only breasts).

3. Add the shallots, mushrooms, and the ¾ cup wine to the chicken. Cover and simmer until the chicken is tender and juices run clear when the chicken is pierced with a roasting fork, about 10 minutes.

4. Transfer the chicken and mushrooms to a serving platter and keep warm. Discard the onion and reduce the liquid over high heat to about ⅓ cup, about 2 minutes.

5. Add the cream and boil to thicken, stirring gently, about 1 minute. Taste and adjust the seasoning, if necessary, and stir in the 1 teaspoon wine.

6. Spoon or pour the sauce over the chicken and serve.

SERVING SUGGESTION

This recipe, as with a number of others, was designed to have a subtle blend of beige and cream colors. No touch of green is necessary on the plate, but you can start your meal with a vegetable or a mixed green salad. Serve the chicken with buttered noodles. For dessert, serve an Alsatian Fruit Tart (page 216).

WINE

A bottle of well-chilled Riesling is the obvious—and perfect—choice.

VARIATIONS

CHICKEN OR VEAL IN CREAM SAUCE

[POULET OU CÔTE DE VEAU À LA CRÈME]

In place of the ¾ cup Riesling use any dry white wine. In step 5, add 1 teaspoon Cognac to the sauce in place of the Riesling. For the veal version, use four 1¼-inch-thick veal chops in place of the chicken. Serve with rice instead of noodles.

Chicken with Champagne

[POULET AU CHAMPAGNE]

Use champagne in place of the ¾ cup Riesling and 1 teaspoon Cognac in place of the Riesling in step 5. Serve with rice instead of noodles.

Apple Cider Chicken

[POULET VALLÉE D'AUGE]

This dish is named for the valley of the Auge River, which passes through Normandy, where most of France's apples grow. Use a hard apple cider, sparkling and lightly alcoholic (French cider, if you can find it), in place of the ¾ cup Riesling; and 1 teaspoon Calvados (applejack) in place of the Riesling in step 5. Serve with sautéed apples instead of noodles.

Chicken with Sherry Vinegar

[POULET AU VINAIGRE DE XÉRÈS]

THIS IS A VARIATION of legendary chef Fernand Point's famous recipe, *poulet au vinaigre.* When I first tasted this dish, I was surprised to find that it did not exhibit the sharpness of the vinegar. Later, when I made the dish I realized that reducing the vinegar until only a small amount remained cut the sharpness.

In this recipe, the unique flavor created by the sherry vinegar will be a pleasing surprise. Sherry vinegar, having a rich sherry taste, is available in many gourmet stores, but if you have difficulty finding it, try the recipe with a good balsamic or red wine vinegar. **SERVES 4**

4 tablespoons (½ stick) butter
1 chicken (2 to 2½ pounds), quartered, or 4 skinless, boneless half breasts (about 1½ pounds)
¼ teaspoon salt
⅛ teaspoon freshly ground pepper
1 onion, cut in half
¼ cup sherry vinegar
2 shallots, finely chopped
3 cloves garlic, finely chopped
1 cup dry white wine
1 tablespoon tomato paste
2 teaspoons Meat Glaze (optional; page 309)
4 sprigs fresh parsley, chopped

1. In a 12-inch skillet, melt 2 tablespoons of the butter over medium-high heat. Add the chicken and brown well on both sides, about 3 to 4 minutes per side. Season with the salt and pepper.

2. Pour off any excess cooking fat. Add the onion to the pan, cover, and cook gently over

FERNAND POINT

A master chef, responsible for many of France's modern classic recipes, Fernand Point was the acknowledged king of French cooking and the teacher of many of France's most acclaimed chefs, including Paul Bocuse and the Troisgros brothers. Until his death in 1955, Point was the chef/owner of the famous restaurant called La Pyramide in Vienne, south of Lyons in the Rhône Valley.

low heat for 15 minutes (10 minutes if using only breasts).

3. Remove the chicken from the skillet, leaving the onion, and pour off and reserve any pan juices. Add the vinegar to the skillet and reduce until almost all of the liquid is evaporated, about 1 minute. Add the shallots, garlic, wine, and reserved pan juices. Return the chicken to the pan, cover, and simmer until the chicken is tender and juices run clear when the chicken is pierced with a roasting fork, about 10 minutes.

4. Remove the chicken, place it on a serving platter, and keep it warm. Discard the onion.

5. Stir in the tomato paste and meat glaze (if using). Taste and adjust the seasoning with salt and pepper, if necessary. The sauce should have the consistency of light cream; if it does not, boil to thicken. Remove the pan from the heat and stir in the remaining 2 tablespoons of butter and the parsley. Pour the sauce over the chicken.

SERVING SUGGESTION

Start with a mixed green salad. Serve the chicken with Madeira-Glazed Carrots (page 179) and Garlic Mashed Potatoes (page 205). For dessert, serve Pears Poached in Port Wine (page 284) and Macaroons (page 257).

WINE

Serve a moderately priced Spanish red with the chicken.

BROILED POUSSINS WITH HERBS AND MUSTARD

[POUSSINS AUX HERBES ET À LA MOUTARDE]

A POULET GRILLÉ À LA DIABLE is a grilled chicken coated with mustard and bread crumbs. I have always found the result too dry, and, in fact, classically this dish is served with a sauce (called *sauce diable*), which compensates for the dryness.

Instead of coating the chicken with bread crumbs, I use only mustard and a number of herbs normally found in a sauce diable, retaining much of the dish's original character. The resulting moist and tender chicken needs no sauce other than the simple pan juices.

A *poussin* is a tender and juicy baby chicken weighing about one pound. If not available, use a Cornish hen or a small broiling chicken.

Changing the herbs used or adding a touch of curry powder will lead to many variations, as will the use of Madeira or sherry in place of the white wine. **SERVES 4 TO 6**

3 poussins or Cornish hens
(about 1 pound each), split in half
3 tablespoons Dijon mustard
1 tablespoon dried tarragon
2 teaspoons dried basil
2 teaspoons dried thyme leaves
⅛ teaspoon salt
⅛ teaspoon freshly ground pepper
¾ cup dry white wine

1. Place the chicken halves skin side up in a roasting pan and spread half of the mustard over them. Sprinkle with half of the herbs and season with half the salt and pepper. Turn the chicken skin side down and repeat the seasoning process. (This can be done up to 12 hours in advance of cooking. Cover well and refrigerate.)

2. Preheat the broiler.

3. Place the chicken halves 3 to 4 inches below the broiler, skin side down. When they have browned well on one side, 8 to 10 minutes, turn and broil on the other side, until well browned, about 7 minutes.

4. Deglaze the pan by adding the wine, tilting the pan, and stirring to loosen the caramelized bits on the bottom of the pan. Baste the chicken with the liquid and broil for an additional 1 to 2 minutes; the juices of the chicken should run clear when it is pierced with a fork. The alcohol in the wine will evaporate and may ignite, but the flames will cease in seconds.

5. Serve the chicken with some of the pan juices.

SERVING SUGGESTION

I normally serve the chicken with buttered noodles, rice, or baked potatoes, and accompany it with peas, green beans, or another green vegetable. Sometimes I serve a vegetable as a first course, such as buttered broccoli or an artichoke vinaigrette.

WINE

Serve this with a dry red wine.

VARIATION

Grilled or Roasted Poussins

[POUSSINS GRILLÉS OU RÔTIS]

If you have a grill or grill pan, you might want to grill the *poussins*. Or roast them as for squab (see page 129). Simply grilled or roasted, they are good served with Wild Rice with Mushrooms (page 208).

Basque-Style Sauteed Chicken Breasts

[SUPRÊMES DE VOLAILLE BASQUAISE]

THE ROBUST FLAVORS of ham, peppers, and tomatoes are typical of the Basque region in the Pyrenees Mountains of southwestern France. Anything served with this combination is labeled *basquaise.* The area is renowned for its pork, and especially the cured hams produced in and around the city of Bayonne. Bayonne ham is either sliced thin and eaten with fruit, like prosciutto, or diced and used to add flavor to dishes. If Bayonne ham is hard to find, use prosciutto.

Instead of making a flour-thickened sauce for this dish, as is customary, I deglaze the pan in which the chicken is cooked with the juices from the tomato, pepper, and ham mixture and reduce them to form a sauce. **SERVES 4 TO 6**

2 tablespoons vegetable oil or rendered pork fat (see Note)
2 onions, halved and sliced
3 cloves garlic, chopped
2 green bell peppers, stemmed, seeded, and cut into julienne
2 red bell peppers, stemmed, seeded, and cut into julienne
¼-inch slice Bayonne ham or prosciutto (about ¼ pound), diced
¼ teaspoon salt
⅛ teaspoon freshly ground pepper
1½ pounds tomatoes, peeled, seeded, and diced, or 2½ cups drained canned diced tomatoes (from a 28-ounce can)
3 tablespoons butter or rendered pork fat (see Note)
6 skinless, boneless chicken half breasts (about 2 pounds)

1. In a medium-size saucepan, heat the vegetable oil over medium-low heat. Add the onions, cover, and cook gently until they are softened but not browned, 4 to 5 minutes.

2. Stir in the garlic, green and red peppers, and ham. Season with the salt and pepper. Cover and cook gently until the vegetables are almost tender, about 5 minutes.

3. Add the tomatoes and cook an additional 3 to 4 minutes. The tomatoes should be soft but still hold their shape. Drain the vegetables, reserving the liquid, and set aside. (The recipe can be prepared in advance to this point. Cover, let cool, and refrigerate. Reheat the ham and vegetables in a small amount of the reserved liquid before proceeding.)

4. In a large skillet, melt the butter over medium-high heat. Add the chicken breasts and cook until the juices run clear when the chicken is pierced with a fork and it is just slightly springy to the touch, 4 to 5 minutes per side. Season to taste with salt and pepper. Remove to a serving platter and keep warm.

5. Pour off any remaining fat and deglaze the pan by adding the reserved vegetable liquid and stirring to loosen the caramelized bits on the bottom and sides of the pan. Reduce the liquid until it has the consistency of light cream. To serve, arrange the vegetables and chicken on a warm platter and pour the sauce over the chicken.

NOTE: Pork fat (lard) is the fat typical of *basquaise* dishes. To render pork fat, dice about ¼ pound fresh pork fat and melt over medium heat. Measure out the quantity called for and save the remainder for another use or discard.

IN ADDITION

A *suprême* of chicken is technically a boned breast of chicken with the skin and the wing's first joint attached. When sautéed and presented on a plate or platter, it has a more attractive shape and has better color than the boned and skinless breasts or cutlets we find in our markets.

SERVING SUGGESTION

Start with Home-Style Terrine with Prunes (page 54). Serve the chicken with Rice Pilaf (page 207) and a green salad, if you'd like. For dessert, try peach Melba (see headnote on page 345) and Biarritz cookies (page 255).

WINE

I enjoy Spanish Riojas or red Bordeaux with this dish.

VARIATION

Basque-Style Roast Chicken

[POULET RÔTI BASQUAISE]

You can also roast a chicken and serve it surrounded by the ham and vegetable mixture (steps 1 through 3).

Sauteed Pheasant Breasts with Juniper

[SUPRÊMES DE FAISAN AU GENIÈVRE]

THE COMBINATION of juniper berries and game birds is classic. The birds are usually roasted, and the juniper berries are used to flavor an accompanying sauce or stuffing.

The following recipe finds its inspiration in the traditional use of juniper with game birds, but gets its innovation from serendipity. About 25 years ago, a student presented me with several pheasants. Unfortunately, they had already been skinned, making them unsuitable for roasting. So I improvised. I took a handful of juniper berries, crushed them, and coated the pheasant breasts as I would for a steak au poivre. I then sautéed them and flamed them with gin (which is flavored with juniper), added meat glaze, and finished the sauce with some cream.

The result so pleased me that I later decided to re-create the recipe with chicken breasts. Although chicken is more delicate in taste, it is similar in size, cooking properties, and texture. The dish was delicious. Try it with chicken, but if you can get pheasant—commercially raised pheasant is available—try the recipe in its original form. **SERVES 4 TO 6**

6 individual skinless, boneless pheasant or chicken half breasts (about 2 pounds)
½ cup juniper berries, crushed
1 tablespoon butter
¼ teaspoon salt
⅛ teaspoon freshly ground pepper
¼ cup plus 1 teaspoon gin
1 tablespoon Chicken Glaze (optional; page 310)
1 cup heavy cream

1. Lightly coat the pheasant breasts with the juniper berries and wrap in plastic wrap. Let stand at room temperature for 2 hours. (If you are preparing this more than 2 hours in advance, wrap well and refrigerate.)

2. In a 10- to 12-inch skillet, melt the butter over medium-high heat. Add the pheasant breasts and sauté until lightly browned, about 3 minutes. Turn the breasts, season with the salt and pepper, cover, reduce the heat to medium-low, and continue cooking until done, 5 to 7 minutes. The breasts should be slightly springy to the touch. If soft or very springy, they need longer cooking; if firm to the touch, they are overcooked.

3. Remove the pan from the heat, add the ¼ cup of gin, and flame (see "How to Flambé," page 282). When the flames die, transfer the breasts to a warm platter or serving plates. Most of the juniper berries will have fallen from the breasts during cooking and should be left in the pan. Add the chicken glaze (if using) and stir until dissolved. Add the cream, increase the heat to high, and bring to a boil. Taste and adjust the seasoning, if necessary. At this point the sauce should be thick enough to lightly coat a spoon. Add the teaspoon of gin to the sauce.

FRESH JUNIPER BERRIES

I have made pheasant with juniper using dried store-bought berries instead of fresh ones, and although my guests always enjoy it, I am always disappointed. For this reason I like to use fresh berries whenever possible. Juniper berries, which can be found on juniper trees and bushes, are green on the tree (or bush), but turn dark blue or black a week or so after picking (this is how you find them in the store). Fresh berries have a stronger taste of resin and are more bitter than the riper dark berries.

Caution: This is important. There are a number of decorative trees and shrubs that look like juniper and bear similar-looking berries, but that are extremely toxic. Before picking or cooking with any berries you assume to be juniper, make absolutely certain that you know the tree or bush is a true juniper. If you are not sure, do *not* pick them!

4. To serve: Pour the sauce over the breasts. Serve only a few berries with the sauce, to indicate where the flavor comes from, and tell your guests that they need not eat them, for most will find them too bitter. Serve immediately.

SERVING SUGGESTION

To start, I would serve a pâté or a consommé made with the rest of the pheasant. Serve the pheasant breasts on a bed of buttered noodles or with wild rice. A green salad rounds out the meal, followed by a Grand Marnier Soufflé (page 265).

WINE

Both white and red Burgundies will go well with this deliciously different pheasant dish.

SAUTEED RABBIT WITH MUSTARD AND ROSEMARY

[LAPIN SAUTÉ À LA MOUTARDE ET AU ROMARIN]

IN CASE YOU THINK I've taken leave of my senses for including rabbit in a chapter called Poultry, in France rabbit is treated much like chicken. Small young rabbits are tender like chicken, but have a more robust flavor.

I know many people who refuse to eat rabbit for a variety of reasons, most of which stem from childhood memories of their Easter bunnies. The following recipe, which combines the flavors of mustard, rosemary, and Cognac, has convinced many skeptics that rabbit is worthy of serious consideration. For those already convinced, who would like more rabbit recipes, substitute rabbit for chicken in recipes such as Chicken with Sherry Vinegar (page 121) and Chicken or Veal in Cream Sauce (page 120).

SERVES 6

3 tablespoons vegetable oil
2 rabbits (2½ pounds each), cut into serving pieces (ask the butcher to do this)
¼ teaspoon salt
⅛ teaspoon freshly ground pepper
1 onion, finely chopped
2 cloves garlic, finely chopped
3 shallots, finely chopped
¼ cup plus 1 teaspoon Cognac
½ cup dry white wine
1 cup chicken stock, homemade or canned (see chart, page 305)
3 teaspoons chopped fresh rosemary, plus a sprig for garnish
1 tablespoon Dijon mustard
1 teaspoon Meat Glaze (optional; page 309)
1 cup heavy cream
6 sprigs parsley, chopped

1. In a large skillet, heat the oil over high heat. Add the rabbit pieces and brown lightly, 3 to 4 minutes on each side. Season with the salt and pepper.

2. Pour off the excess oil and add the onion, garlic, and shallots to the pan. Reduce the heat to medium and cook until softened without browning, about 2 minutes.

3. Remove the pan from the heat, add the ¼ cup Cognac, and flame (see "How to Flambé," page 282). When the flames die, add the wine, stock, and 2 teaspoons of the rosemary. Cover and simmer until the rabbit is tender, 30 to 40 minutes, turning the pieces halfway through the cooking.

4. Remove the rabbit pieces to a serving platter and keep warm. Reduce the liquid in the skillet over high heat to about ¾ cup, about 10 minutes.

5. Whisk in the mustard and the meat glaze (if using). Add the cream and the remaining 1 teaspoon rosemary, and boil the sauce until it thickens enough to lightly coat a spoon. (The dish can be prepared ahead to this point. Return the rabbit to the sauce, cover, and refrigerate. Before serving, slowly return to a simmer, then remove the meat to a serving platter and proceed.)

6. To serve: Strain the sauce, stir in the 1 teaspoon Cognac and three-quarters of the chopped parsley. Pour the sauce over the rabbit. Sprinkle with the remaining parsley. If available, use a sprig of rosemary to decorate the platter.

SERVING SUGGESTION

Start with chilled melon. Steamed rice or buttered noodles are the ideal accompaniment for this cream-sauced dish. Follow with a mixed green salad and a fruit tart or sorbet for dessert.

WINE

Serve the rabbit with a dry white wine.

VARIATION

Sauteed Chicken with Mustard and Rosemary

[POULET SAUTÉ À LA MOUTARDE ET AU ROMARIN]

Substitute a 3½-pound chicken cut into serving pieces. Reduce the mustard and rosemary to 2 teaspoons each.

ROAST SQUABS WITH OLIVE SAUCE

[PIGEONNEAUX AUX OLIVES]

GREEN OLIVES and dark-meat birds such as squab (and duck) are traditional companions in France. The olives are used not only to flavor the sauce but are treated as an accompaniment to the squab. Blanching them several times to extract salt makes the olives a lovely and delicately flavored vegetable.

Whereas classic recipes for squab with olives cook the birds in the sauce, I have designed this recipe so the sauce can be prepared several days in advance, if desired, and simply reheated for serving. Making the sauce ahead of time also gives the birds time to age, something I do to improve their taste. Many people complain that squab has a gamey or livery taste. I have noticed this taste whenever the birds are very fresh, but by allowing them to age for a few days, the strong taste disappears and is replaced by a uniquely delicious flavor. If the birds you have are frozen, defrost them in the refrigerator and let them age 2 to 3 days before roasting. If they are freshly killed, allow them to age 4 days in the refrigerator. **SERVES 6**

BLANCHING

Food is blanched either by adding it to already boiling water, or starting it off in cold water and bringing it to a boil. The latter, cold-water blanching, is used to extract excess salt, as in blanching olives or bacon. Blanching in boiling water is used to retain flavor, color, and nutrients for such things as herbs or green vegetables. Blanching is also used to loosen the skin of tomatoes, peaches, and almonds, making them easier to peel.

6 squabs (about 1 pound each)
¼ cup extra-virgin olive oil
1 onion, diced
1 small carrot, diced
⅓ cup all-purpose flour
2 cups dry white wine
4 cups beef stock, homemade or canned (see chart, page 305)
3 shallots, sliced
3 cloves garlic, sliced
1 tablespoon tomato paste
Bouquet Garni (page 306)
1 tablespoon Meat Glaze (optional; page 309)
¼ teaspoon freshly ground pepper
¾ pound pitted green olives
6 tablespoons (¾ stick) butter
¼ teaspoon salt

1. Remove the squabs' hearts, necks, wing tips, and gizzards and set aside. Truss the birds (see "How to Truss a Bird," page 133).

Serving Small Birds

When serving a small whole bird with a sauce, it is necessary to carve it partway to let out the excess juices. If this is not done, the plate will fill with these juices and dilute your sauce. (On the other hand, when you serve the birds without a sauce, then these juices are desirable.) To partially carve a squab, place the bird on its side. Place the blade of your knife flat on the body, with the sharp edge facing the bird's hip joint (where the thigh joins the body). Move the knife toward the hip, passing the blade under the drumstick. At the joint, cut through the skin (but not through the joint). Repeat on the other side. Then make one or two slices into each breast. Although I prefer serving small birds whole in this fashion, I realize that some guests will have difficulty in cutting them. So for easier serving, the birds can be cut in half.

2. In a medium-size saucepan, heat the oil over medium-high heat. Add the hearts, necks, wings, and gizzards and brown, 5 to 7 minutes. Add the onion and carrot and brown them lightly, 3 to 4 minutes.

3. Reduce the heat to medium, sprinkle the flour into the pan, and brown well, stirring occasionally, about 4 minutes. By the time the flour is browned, the carrot and onion will be dark brown.

4. Add the wine, stock, shallots, garlic, tomato paste, bouquet garni, meat glaze (if using), and pepper. Simmer the sauce for 1 to 1½ hours, stirring from time to time and skimming off any fat or foam that comes to the surface.

5. Meanwhile, blanch the olives by placing them in a saucepan and covering with cold water. Bring to a boil, drain, and rinse with cold water. Taste and repeat, if necessary, until they are just slightly salty to the taste.

6. When the sauce is done, it will have a rich brown color and be the consistency of light cream. Strain the sauce through a fine-mesh sieve. Add the olives and simmer, covered, for 10 to 15 minutes. Taste and adjust the seasoning, if necessary. (The sauce can be made several days in advance. Let cool to room temperature, cover, and refrigerate. Just before serving, bring to a boil.)

7. Preheat the oven to 475°F.

8. Place the birds on their sides in a roasting pan, dot with the butter, and season with the salt and additional pepper to taste. Roast until tender and the juices run clear when the birds are pricked with a roasting fork, about 15 minutes on each side, basting two or three times. Turn the squabs breast side up for an additional 5 to 10 minutes. (I generally roast squabs until thoroughly cooked, yet still moist and tender. Many people enjoy these birds medium-rare, and if this is your preference, reduce the cooking time by 10 minutes.)

9. Using a large fork, lift the squabs to allow the interior juices to drain. Then partially carve them to let more juices out (see "Serving Small Birds," this page). Place the squabs on individual serving plates, surround with olives and sauce, and serve.

SERVING SUGGESTION

Begin with an Endive and Pink Grapefruit Salad (page 28). Steamed potatoes or rice go well with the distinctive olive sauce. For dessert, serve Almond Cake with a Raspberry Purée (page 244).

WINE

Both Châteauneuf-du-Pape and Hermitage wines will complement the olive sauce.

VARIATIONS

GRILLED SQUABS WITH OLIVE SAUCE

[PIGEONNEAUX GRILLÉS AUX OLIVES]

Make the olive sauce (steps 2 through 6). Cut the squabs in half and grill them for 5 to 7 minutes on each side. Serve each half on a plate covered with the olives and sauce. Serve the other half as a second serving.

SAUTEED SQUABS WITH OLIVE SAUCE

[PIGEONNEAUX SAUTÉS AUX OLIVES]

Make the olive sauce (steps 2 through 6). Cut the squabs in half and brown in butter or oil, 3 to 4 minutes on each side. When browned, reduce the heat to low and cook, covered, for 15 minutes longer. Serve with the olives and sauce.

ROAST DUCK WITH OLIVE SAUCE

[CANARD AUX OLIVES]

Make the olive sauce (steps 2 through 6) using the duck heart, neck, wings, and gizzards. Roast a 5-pound duck at 425°F for 30 minutes on each side and 10 minutes breast up. Omit the butter and the basting. Serve a quarter of the duck per person, covered with the sauce.

DUCK A L'ORANGE

[CANARD À L'ORANGE]

A CLASSICALLY prepared *canard à l'orange* is one of the most satisfying and delicious dishes in the French culinary repertoire, yet no one—including most restaurants—seems to have the patience for it anymore.

Admittedly still a fairly time-consuming affair, my version does manage to make things easier. To begin with, I make the sauce a day or more in advance (which has the beneficial side effect of allowing the ducks to age and improve in flavor), and I prepare the sectioned oranges for the accompaniment the night before. I have also shortened the time in the oven by using a high-temperature roasting method, a technique that works well to remove excess fat yet leaves the meat succulent and tender. Finally, to avoid any last-minute scramble, I carve the duck before the guests arrive, and then reheat it briefly in a hot oven just before serving. **SERVES 6 TO 8**

2 ducks (about 5 pounds each)
2 tablespoons rendered duck fat (see step 3) or vegetable oil
1 onion, diced
1 small carrot, diced (optional)
3 tablespoons all-purpose flour
¾ cup dry white wine
2 cups beef stock, homemade or canned (see chart, page 305)
2 shallots, sliced
2 cloves garlic, sliced
Zest of 1 orange (see Note)
Bouquet Garni (page 306)
2 teaspoons tomato paste
1 teaspoon Meat Glaze (optional; page 309)
¼ teaspoon salt
⅛ teaspoon freshly ground pepper
2 tablespoons sugar
1 tablespoon water
¼ cup white (distilled) vinegar
2 tablespoons Madeira
1 tablespoon plus a dash of Cognac
5 large oranges

1. Prepare the ducks for roasting: Cut off the first two joints of the wings (leaving the third portion of the wing attached to the body). Set the wings aside with the necks, hearts, and gizzards. Chop the liver and set aside if you would like to use it in the sauce (see step 6). Remove the fat from the inner cavity at the tail section and set aside. Truss the ducks (see "How to Truss a Bird," facing page). If you are making the sauce ahead of time, wrap the ducks in plastic wrap and refrigerate.

2. Cut the necks, hearts, and gizzards into small pieces. If you do not have a nonstick roasting pan, save the wings to use as a makeshift roasting rack (see step 11); otherwise, cut up and add to the giblets.

3. In a medium-size saucepan, heat some of the reserved duck fat over medium heat. Pour out all but about 2 tablespoons of the rendered fat. Add the cut up parts and giblets and cook over medium-high heat until browned, about 5 minutes. Add the onion and carrot (if using) and cook until lightly browned, about 3 minutes. Reduce the heat to medium, sprinkle with the flour, and brown well, being careful not to burn the onion, 3 to 4 minutes.

4. Add the wine and stock and bring to a boil, stirring. Reduce the heat to medium-low and add the shallots, garlic, orange zest, bouquet garni, tomato paste, meat glaze (if using), salt, and pepper. Simmer until the sauce is thick enough to coat a spoon, 45 minutes to 1 hour, skimming frequently to remove all fat and impurities.

5. Meanwhile, in a small, heavy saucepan, moisten the sugar with the water. Bring to a boil over high heat and cook, without stirring, until a deep amber color—dark, but not burned. Quickly pour in the vinegar—it will spatter violently for a second—and allow the mixture to boil for a moment. Remove from the heat. (This sweet-and-sour flavoring is called a *gastrique*.)

6. When the orange sauce has finished simmering, remove from the heat and stir in the chopped liver, if using. Strain the sauce through a fine-mesh sieve. Taste and adjust the seasoning, if necessary.

HOW TO TRUSS A BIRD: All You Need Is String

Trussing a bird for roasting means to tie it in a neat bundle, which helps with the roasting, presentation, and carving. There are many methods and devices used for trussing, but for me, the simplest is the best. All you need is a length of good, strong, undyed cotton kitchen string.

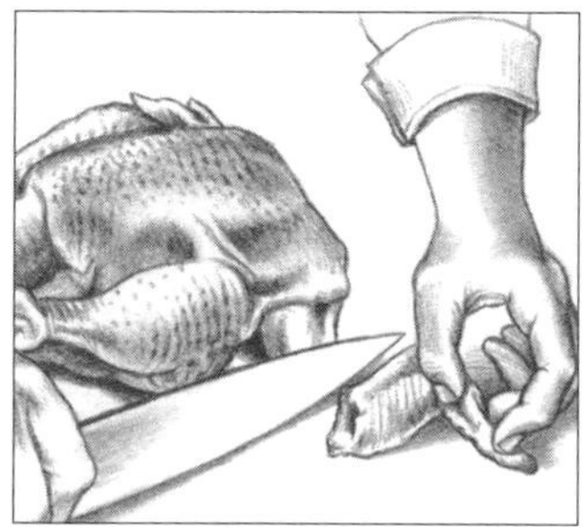

1. Cut off the first two joints of the wing.

2. Push the tail of the bird into the body cavity.

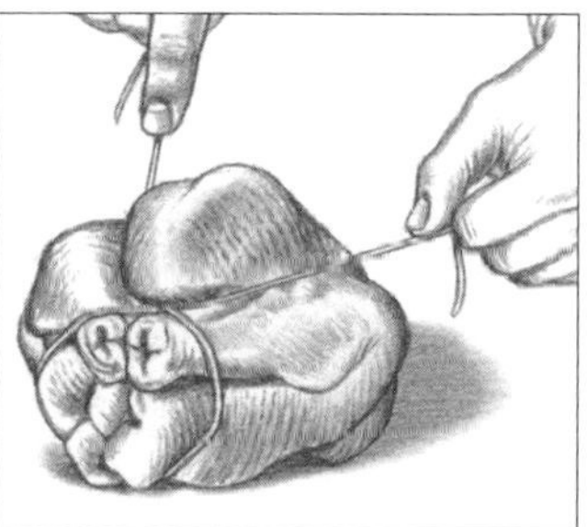

3. Wrap a length of string around the legs and tail sections and cross over as shown. Bring the string between the drumsticks and breast to the front of the bird.

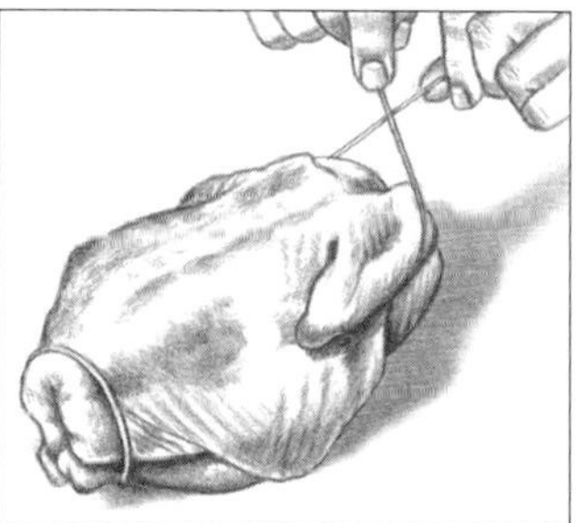

4. Turn the bird breast side down and tie the string securely across the back, in front of the wings.

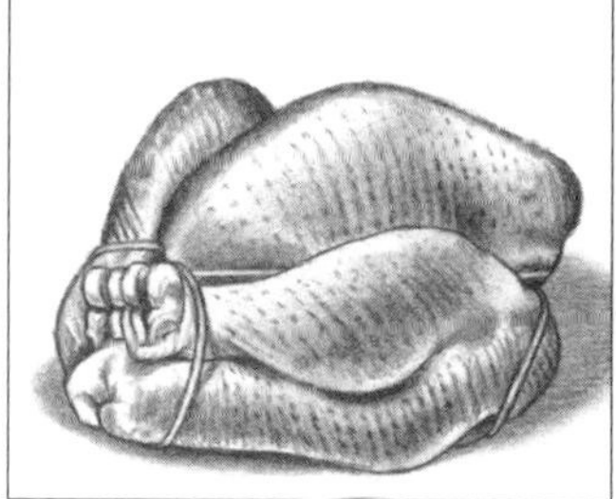

5. A fully trussed bird.

7. Add about half of the *gastrique* to the orange sauce. Taste and add more, if necessary, to offset the bitterness of the orange zest. Stir in the Madeira and the 1 tablespoon Cognac. (The sauce can be made up to 3 days ahead. Cover with plastic wrap to prevent a skin from forming, and refrigerate. If the sauce was made with the liver, it should not boil again. Reheat in a water bath (*bain-marie*). If liver was not used, simply bring to a simmer before serving.

8. With a vegetable peeler, remove the zest from 2 of the oranges and cut into very fine julienne. In a small saucepan, cover the julienned zest with water and bring to a boil. Drain and reserve the julienne.

GASTRIQUE

In French cooking, savory dishes that are made with fruit often include a sweet-tart flavoring called a *gastrique.* A *gastrique* is a combination of sugar and vinegar that gets cooked until it's reduced to a syrup. In some cases, the sugar is first caramelized for an extra depth of flavor (as in Duck à l'Orange).

9. Peel and section all 5 of the oranges, making sure they are completely free of all membranes (see "How to Section an Orange," page 286). Pour off any juice that collects. (The oranges can be prepared ahead of time. Cover and refrigerate.)

10. Preheat the oven to 475°F with the rack placed in the middle position.

11. Prick the ducks all over with a fork to allow the fat to drain during cooking. Place the ducks on their sides in a large roasting pan, preferably nonstick (or rest the duck on the reserved wings; see "If You Don't Have a Nonstick Roasting Pan," facing page). Season lightly with salt and pepper. Place the roasting pan in the oven and roast for 15 minutes.

12. Reduce the heat to 425°F and roast for another 15 minutes, then turn the ducks onto their other sides and with a bulb baster remove as much fat from the pan as possible.

13. Continue roasting for another 30 minutes or so (roasting time is about 15 minutes per pound). For the last 5 to 10 minutes of cooking, turn the ducks breast side up for even color. The ducks are done when their cavity juices run clear; or when an instant-read thermometer inserted into the thickest part of the thigh reads 160°F to 165°F. Let the ducks sit for 10 minutes before carving.

14. Carve the ducks into individual serving pieces: Remove the legs and separate into drumstick and thigh. Carve the breast meat into several vertical slices (the outermost slices will have the remaining wing joints attached). Arrange the breast slices in the center of a serving platter and surround with the thighs and drumsticks. Let the platter of duck sit until about 5 minutes before serving time.

15. Preheat the oven to 500°F with the rack placed in the upper third of the oven.

16. Add the reserved julienned zest to the sauce and bring to a simmer. If the liver was used, reheat in a water bath (*bain-marie*).

17. When ready to serve, place the duck platter in the oven for 3 to 5 minutes to reheat. Meanwhile, sprinkle the orange sections with the dash of Cognac and warm them in a covered skillet over low heat, 3 to 4 minutes (save any juices that collect to thin the sauce, if necessary).

18. To serve: Surround the duck with the orange sections and serve. Pass the sauce separately.

NOTE: Remove the zest in strips with a vegetable peeler. Save the orange for sectioning in step 9.

ROAST DUCK

[CANARD RÔTI]

ALTHOUGH *canard à l'orange* is probably the best known treatment of duck, the bird's rich, full flavor combines well with the tart-sweetness of many fruits. This is a basic recipe for a simple roast duck—delicious in its own right—to which you can add one of three fruit sauces in the recipes that follow. As with Duck à l'Orange, the roasted duck can be carved ahead of time, and then reheated before serving (follow steps 14, 15, and 17 on the facing page). **SERVES 6 TO 8**

2 ducks (about 5 pounds each)
2 onions, quartered
1 carrot, thickly sliced
1 celery rib, cut into 4 pieces
2 shallots, halved
4 sprigs parsley
1 bay leaf
¼ teaspoon fresh or dried thyme leaves
½ teaspoon salt
¼ teaspoon freshly ground pepper
2 cups water or chicken stock

1. Preheat the oven to 475°F with the rack placed in the middle position.

2. Prepare the ducks for roasting: Cut off the first two joints of the wings (leaving the third portion of the wing attached to the body). Set the wings aside with the necks, hearts, and gizzards. Truss the ducks (see "How to Truss a Bird," page 133). Prick the ducks all over with a fork to allow the fat to drain during cooking. Place the ducks on their sides in a large nonstick roasting pan, or rest them on the reserved wings (see "If You Don't Have a Nonstick Roasting Pan," below).

3. Place the necks, giblets, wings (if not already under the duck), vegetables, and herbs around the duck. Sprinkle all with the salt and pepper. Place the roasting pan in the oven and roast for 15 minutes.

4. Reduce the heat to 425°F and roast for another 15 minutes, then turn the ducks onto their other sides and with a bulb baster remove as much fat from the pan as possible.

5. Continue cooking for another 30 minutes or so (roasting time is about 15 minutes per pound), and for the last 5 to 10 minutes of

IF YOU DON'T HAVE A NONSTICK ROASTING PAN

If you don't have a nonstick roasting pan, cut off the first two joints of the wings. Separate the resulting portions at the joint, yielding four 3-inch pieces. Place the pieces down the middle of the roasting pan, about 2 inches apart, to form a rack for the duck to rest on.

cooking, turn the ducks breast side up for even color. The ducks are done when their cavity juices run clear; or when an instant-read thermometer inserted into the thickest part of the thigh reads 160°F to 165°F.

6. Remove the ducks from the pan and let them sit for 10 to 20 minutes before carving while you make a simple pan juice. Pour the fat from the roasting pan, retaining the vegetables and duck parts in the pan. Place the pan over high heat, add 2 cups of water or stock, and bring to a boil, then reduce the heat and simmer for 10 minutes, stirring the vegetables from time to time.

7. Strain the liquid into a small saucepan, discarding the solids. Over high heat, cook until reduced to 1 cup, about 10 minutes. Skim off any remaining fat.

8. Carve the ducks into serving pieces: Remove the legs and separate into drumstick and thigh. Carve the breast meat into several vertical slices (the outermost slices will have the remaining wing joints attached). Arrange the breast slices in the center of a serving platter and surround with the thighs and drumsticks. Spoon some of the sauce over the breast slices and serve the remaining sauce on the side.

SERVING SUGGESTION

To start, serve a mixed green salad. With the duck, serve a potato and a green vegetable. For dessert, serve Chocolate Mousse (page 275).

WINE

I enjoy a wide variety of dry red wines with duck: Pinot Noir, Cabernet Sauvignon, Malbec, Zinfandel, and Syrah/Shiraz.

ROAST DUCK WITH GLAZED APPLES AND CIDER CREAM SAUCE

[CANARD AU CIDRE]

ONE OF MY favorite recipes was inspired by a similar presentation I had years ago at the famous restaurant Taillevent in Paris. This duck is accented by apples in numerous forms, from a garnish of apples flamed with Calvados (applejack) to the French apple cider used in the sauce. Unlike American cider, French apple cider—which along with Calvados comes from Normandy—is sparkling and mildly alcoholic and comes both sweet (*doux*) and dry (*sec*). For cooking, use the dry variety. There are more and more American apple growers who are now making fermented apple cider and bottling it like a sparkling wine. Try these when you find them and compare to the French variety. If you find one that you like, buy some to serve with the duck. **SERVES 6 TO 8**

Roast Duck (page 135)
6 large Golden Delicious apples
1 cup dry white wine
2 cups dry French or American hard apple cider
1 teaspoon Meat Glaze (optional; page 309)
¾ cup heavy cream
4 to 5 drops of white (distilled) vinegar (optional)
2 tablespoons butter
1 tablespoon sugar
¼ cup Calvados (applejack) or Cognac

1. Roast the ducks through step 5 of the recipe.

2. While the ducks are roasting, peel, core, and slice the apples ¼ inch thick (the cores can be added to the roasting pan). As you work, place the apples in a large skillet and moisten them with the wine to prevent discoloration. Add any remaining wine to the apples once they are all sliced and in the skillet.

3. Cover the pan and poach the apples over medium heat until tender but not soft, 5 to 7 minutes. Drain the apples, reserving the poaching liquid. Set both aside.

4. When the ducks are done, place them on a carving board. (If the ducks are cooked several hours in advance of serving, allow them to cool completely before carving.) Pour the fat from the roasting pan, retaining the vegetables and duck parts in the pan. Place the pan over high heat, add the cider, the reserved apple poaching liquid, and the meat glaze (if using). Bring to a boil, reduce the heat, and simmer for 10 minutes, stirring the vegetables from time to time.

Professional Test for Doneness

The professional way of judging the doneness of poultry is to collect cavity juices on a white plate to see if they are running clear. To do this, you have to use a roasting fork to lift the duck out of the pan and tilt it over the plate. The best tool to use, if you have one, is a French roasting fork because its tines are very long and straight (it looks like a giant tuning fork). If you place the fork just above the leg and point it toward the backbone of the duck, you can pierce the backbone and easily lift the duck out of the pan. Tilt the duck to let the cavity juices run out, and when the last few drops are clear and not pink, the duck is done.

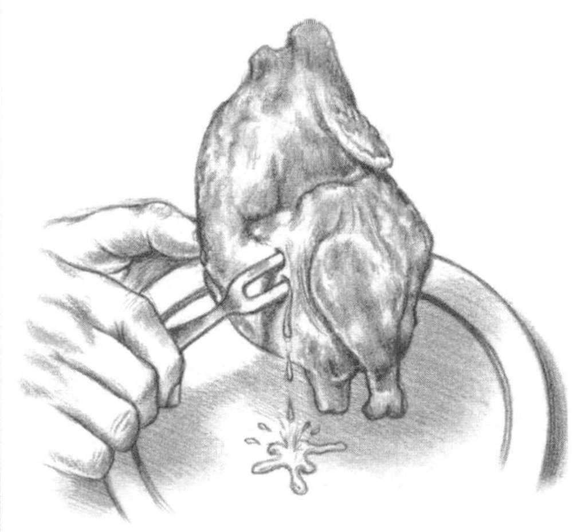

5. Strain the liquid through a fine-mesh sieve into a small saucepan, discarding the solids. Over high heat, cook until reduced to 1 cup, about 10 minutes. Skim off any fat. Add the cream and boil to thicken enough to lightly coat a spoon. Taste the sauce; if it is too sweet, add the vinegar (if using), a drop at a time, to taste. (The sauce can be made several hours ahead. Cover with plastic wrap to prevent a skin from forming. Gently reheat before proceeding.)

6. Preheat the oven to 500°F with the rack set in the upper third of the oven.

7. Carve the ducks into individual serving pieces and place in a roasting pan or on an ovenproof platter. Place the platter in the oven for 3 to 5 minutes to reheat the duck.

8. To serve: In a skillet, reheat the apples with the butter and sugar. Remove the pan from the heat, add the Calvados, and flame (see "How to Flambé," page 282). Place the apples on the platter with the duck and serve. Pass the sauce separately.

SERVING SUGGESTION

As with most duck presentations, I serve wild rice or a combination of wild rice and mushrooms (see page 208) followed by a green salad. For dessert, serve Chocolate Génoise with Grand Marnier Ganache (page 240).

WINE

If in Normandy, I might order an excellent dry cider to drink, but at home I serve either Champagne or a fine red Bordeaux.

ROAST DUCK WITH GLAZED PEACHES

[CANARD AUX PÊCHES]

FRESH FRUIT in season is really the only choice here. If you're inspired to roast a duck in early summer, make it with cherries (see Variation, facing page). If it's mid to late summer, make the duck with peaches; white peaches would be especially nice. Because I find the combination of fruit and duck so wonderful, I like to use quite a bit of fruit—very likely more than you would expect if you've had similar dishes in a restaurant. But the fruit is so good with the duck that I want you and your guests to eat some with each bite. Should any fruit be left over, I am sure your guests will help you finish it. **SERVES 6 TO 8**

Roast Duck (page 135)
6 peaches
1 cup dry white wine
2 cups beef stock, homemade or canned (see chart, page 305)
2 teaspoons Meat Glaze (optional; page 309)
2 teaspoons arrowroot, potato starch, or cornstarch, dissolved in 2 teaspoons cold water
2 tablespoons butter
1 to 2 tablespoons sugar, to taste
¼ cup Cognac

1. Roast the ducks through step 5 of the recipe. While the ducks are roasting, peel, pit, and slice the peaches and place them in a skillet (nonreactive if possible). Moisten them with the wine to prevent discoloration. Add the remaining wine once the peaches are all in the skillet.

2. Cover and poach the peaches over medium heat until tender, 3 to 5 minutes. Immediately drain the peaches, reserving the poaching liquid. Set both aside.

3. When the ducks are done, place them on a carving board. (If the ducks are cooked several hours in advance of serving, allow them to cool completely before carving.) Pour the fat from the roasting pan, retaining the vegetables and duck parts in the pan. Place the pan over high heat and add the reserved poaching liquid, the stock, and meat glaze (if using). Bring to a boil and reduce the heat. Simmer 10 minutes, stirring the vegetables from time to time.

4. Strain the liquid through a fine-mesh sieve into a small saucepan, discarding the solids. Over high heat, cook until reduced to 1½ cups, 8 to 10 minutes. Skim off any fat that comes to the surface. Reduce the heat, stir the dissolved arrowroot into the gently boiling sauce, and whisk until thickened. The sauce should lightly coat a spoon. If too thick, add 1 to 2 tablespoons water to thin.

5. Preheat the oven to 500°F with the rack placed in the upper third of the oven.

6. Carve the ducks into serving pieces and place in a roasting pan or on an ovenproof platter. Place the platter in the oven for 3 to 5 minutes to reheat the duck.

7. To serve: In a skillet (nonreactive if possible), reheat the peaches with the butter and sugar. Remove the pan from the heat, add the Cognac, and flame (see "How to Flambé," page 282). Place the peaches on the platter with the duck and serve. Pass the sauce separately.

SERVING SUGGESTION

Start with Shrimp and Scallops in an Herbed Lemon Vinaigrette (page 30). Accompany the duck with wild rice or fried potatoes. Finish with sorbet and Almond Tuiles (page 252).

WINE

Serve either red Burgundy or Bordeaux.

VARIATION

Roast Duck with Cherries

[CANARD AUX CERISES]

Substitute 1½ pounds cherries, pitted, for the peaches. Omit the sugar. Use ¼ cup kirsch in place of the Cognac. Do not poach the cherries, but add the white wine to the roasting pan in step 4. In step 5, add the cherries and kirsch to the finished sauce and simmer for 3 minutes. To serve, spoon the cherries and the sauce over the duck.

FINE-MESH SIEVE

Whenever a sauce requires straining, a very fine sieve is used to obtain as smooth a sauce as possible. Classically a conical strainer known as a *chinois,* or China cap, is used. There are many fine-mesh sieves available in stores or online, and I have several different sizes in my kitchen.

MEAT

TRADITIONALLY, meat that is prepared for roasting and braising in France is wrapped in a thin sheet of pork fat that is intended to keep it moist while cooking. Lean roasts were often larded (strips of pork fat are woven into the roast) to add interior fat for moisture and flavor. Although the exterior fat is often removed before serving, the interior fat remains to be eaten. For me, the fat, although flavorful in itself, adds little to the flavor of the meat. I find that a combination of the animal's diet, proper aging, and the interior fat, in combination with the final cooking, is what determines its flavor.

Therefore, for most cuts of meat, I remove as much exterior fat as possible before cooking. If I want to take advantage of any flavor the fat might have, I will use some of it together with, or in place of, butter or oil to baste or sauté the meat.

STEAK AU POIVRE

A STEAK AU POIVRE is a thick slice of beef coated with cracked or crushed pepper, pan-fried, and flamed with Cognac. It is classically served rare to medium-rare, with a cream sauce, fried potatoes, and watercress. Although there are many variations on this classic preparation, most of which include the use of a brown sauce and various other ingredients, none equal the flavor created by the combination of just steak, pepper, Cognac, and cream.

The only updating necessary for this French bistro classic is the careful removal of all exterior fat. If the butcher has not already done so, make sure that, when you trim the fat, your knife passes under the fat as well as the membrane lying next to the muscle, so that only red meat is visible when finished. By doing this, you avoid eating unnecessary fat.

Any good individual beefsteak can be used for this recipe, but I prefer boneless shell or strip steak, and my second choice is boneless sirloin. Both cuts have excellent flavor and texture. Allow the meat to come to room temperature, 1 to 2 hours, before sautéing.

When cooking the steaks, it is important to have enough oil in your pan to fry the pepper as well as the meat. If not fried, the amount of pepper used will be too hot for many to eat. Start with just enough oil to coat the bottom of your pan (this is sufficient for sautéing the steak) and then add another tablespoon of oil (this is for frying the pepper). **SERVES 4**

¼ cup black peppercorns (see Note)
4 boneless shell, strip, or sirloin steaks (8 to 12 ounces each), 1¼ inches thick, completely trimmed
2 to 3 tablespoons vegetable oil
¼ teaspoon salt
¼ cup plus 1 teaspoon Cognac
¾ cup heavy cream
1 bunch watercress, thick stems removed

1. Crush the peppercorns, a few at a time, using the bottom of a heavy saucepan (see "Cracking Pepper," below).

2. Place the steaks on the crushed pepper to coat both sides.

CRACKING PEPPER

Cracking pepper is easy if you use a heavy-bottomed saucepan as a lever. Crush 8 to 10 peppercorns at a time, placing them under the portion of the pan nearest the handle. Holding the pan down at the opposite end, use the handle to press down on the peppercorns to crush them. A coffee grinder also works well, but if you are not careful you will have a very "hot" cup of coffee in the morning. Most other machines (such as food processors and blenders) create partially crushed and partially powdered pepper.

3. Cover the bottom of a 10- to 12-inch skillet with a thin layer of oil (1 to 2 tablespoons, depending on the size of the pan), then add 1 more tablespoon. Heat over medium-high heat. Add the steaks and sauté them until rare or medium-rare, 4 to 5 minutes on each side. Season the steaks with the salt and remove them from the pan. Discard the oil.

4. Return the steaks to the pan and remove the pan from the heat. Add the ¼ cup Cognac, and flame (see "How to Flambé," page 282). When the flames die, remove the steaks to a serving platter or individual plates and keep warm.

5. Add the cream to the pan and bring to a boil over high heat, stirring until the cream has thickened enough to coat a spoon. Stir in the teaspoon of Cognac and salt to taste. Spoon the sauce over the steaks and serve with watercress.

NOTE: If it is your first time eating a pepper steak, you may want to use commercially cracked pepper, or scrape some of the pepper off before serving it. Once you have become a steak au poivre lover, you will find yourself going to spice stores to buy specialty peppers, such as tellicherry or Malabar, in search of the ultimate aroma.

SERVING SUGGESTION

In France this steak is served with fried potatoes, but since I do very little deep-frying, I serve this with baked or roasted potatoes, which also go well with any sauce remaining on the plate. Watercress is also an integral part of the presentation. Considered by many a peppery green, watercress becomes a refreshing interlude when eaten with the spicy steak. I often start such a meal with Onion Soup (page 19) or green salad, and I like to serve Crêpes Suzette (page 280) for dessert.

WINE

Zinfandel is one of my recent favorites with this dish, but any full-bodied red goes well with the pepper steak. Notice that while you are eating, your palate is refreshed by the potatoes and the watercress (which is normally a peppery green) following each bite of steak. Then a sip of wine will reignite the flames, sending the aroma of the pepper throughout your mouth—a sensation any pepper lover will cherish.

FILLET STEAKS CHARLEMAGNE

[TOURNEDOS CHARLEMAGNE]

THE COMBINATION of beef, mushrooms, and béarnaise sauce is a treat for any steak lover. This is based on the classic *filet de boeuf Charlemagne,* in which the fillet of beef is roasted, then sliced and reconstructed with a layer of cooked shallots and mushrooms (duxelles) between the slices. Just before serving, the roast is reheated and coated with the béarnaise. This classic presentation is only for experienced cooks, while my adaptation is for everyone. With the addition of two more steaks, it can easily serve six. All accompaniments should be ready to serve before cooking the fillet steaks. **SERVES 4**

2 tablespoons butter
4 large shallots or 1 onion, finely chopped
¾ pound mushrooms, washed, dried, and finely chopped
Salt and freshly ground pepper, to taste
1 teaspoon tomato paste
Béarnaise Sauce (page 327)
1 tablespoon vegetable oil
4 fillet steaks, cut 1 to 1¼ inches thick
1 bunch watercress, thick stems trimmed, for garnish

1. In a skillet, melt the butter over medium heat. Add the shallots and sauté until softened, 3 to 4 minutes. Add the mushrooms and sauté over high heat, stirring occasionally, until most of the moisture has evaporated, about 5 minutes. Season with salt and pepper. Remove from the heat and stir in the tomato paste.

2. Make the béarnaise and keep warm in a water bath (*bain-marie*) while you sauté the steaks.

3. In a 10-inch skillet, heat the oil over medium-high heat. Add the fillet steaks and sauté until rare or medium-rare, 2 to 3 minutes each side. Season with salt and pepper. Place the steaks on a serving platter or plates.

4. To serve: Cover each fillet with a layer of the warm mushroom mixture and coat with béarnaise. Garnish with the watercress and serve immediately.

SERVING SUGGESTION

Sautéed or roasted potatoes together with green beans or sautéed spinach are excellent with the steaks. Follow with a mixed green salad.

WINE

A good red Bordeaux will complement these steaks well.

GRILLED RIB STEAKS

[CÔTE DE BOEUF GRILLÉE]

THE AMERICAN or English rib roast does not exist in France. Instead of roasting three or more ribs together, the French cut them into individual ribs and sauté or grill them. Each serves two people.

There is no better way to cook a steak than on a grill. I can remember when I started grilling 40 years ago that a steak charred black on the outside and pink on the inside was considered perfection. I also remember pouring water onto a fire to douse the flames that were engulfing the steak. To prevent this from happening, I now remove all the exterior fat before cooking. By eliminating it, you prevent flare-ups and avoid the consumption of unnecessary fat.

There is a considerable amount of fat on the rib, and it is always a challenge to remove as much as possible without losing the shape of the steak. It is equally important that the bone be trimmed of fat. **SERVES 6**

3 rib steaks with bone (1¼ to 1½ pounds each), each 1½ inches thick
Salt and freshly ground pepper, to taste
1 bunch watercress, thick stems trimmed, for garnish

1. Trim as much of the fat from the steaks as possible and let them come to room temperature, 1 to 2 hours, before cooking.

2. Preheat a grill to high.

3. Place the steaks in the center of the hot grill (or close to the coals). Cover and cook the steaks 4 to 5 minutes per side. Halfway through the cooking on each side, lift and rotate the meat 90 degrees, to enhance the appearance; the extra grill marks also add flavor by caramelizing more of the steaks' surface. Once

CAST-IRON GRILL PAN

If you do not have access to a grill, do not despair. Most foods (including grilled steak) can be just as easily prepared on the stovetop using a cast-iron grill pan. These pans are either round or square and can be flat like a griddle or have sides like a skillet. What they all have in common are the ridges on the bottom that resemble a grill top.

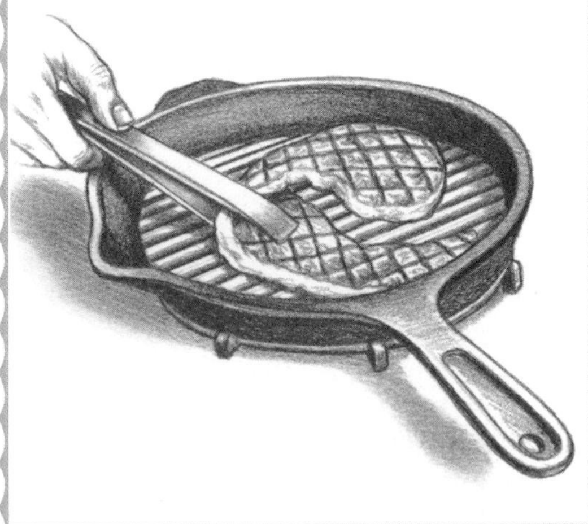

Grilling Beef

Although most cuts of well-aged beef are good on the grill, my favorites are strip or shell steaks, whole fillets of beef, and rib steaks. I watch for sales of these cuts. When I find a good price on a shell or strip roast, I have the "tail" ground for hamburger and the rest completely trimmed of fat and cut into steaks. When buying a fillet I have the long, wide tendon or "silverskin" removed as well as all the fat. It should then be tied to form an evenly cylindrical roast, which will cook in 15 to 20 minutes on a very hot grill. A standing two- or three-rib roast of beef can be cut into two or three individual steaks, each one enough to serve two or three people.

A good piece of beef should be cooked rare or medium-rare for you to enjoy its flavor and tenderness. The most difficult part of grilling a steak is to cook the meat evenly. Often the meat is well done on the outside and raw at the center. To avoid this, grill steaks that are not too thick and always have the meat at room temperature before grilling. Thickness is more important than weight. The ideal thickness, I have found, is 1¼ to 1½ inches.

the meat has been turned, salt and pepper the first side. Check the firmness of the meat from time to time, noticing the changes that occur. Medium-rare is springy to the touch and well done is firm. If after the meat has been turned you see juices beginning to pool or come to the surface, you have reached medium-rare and are approaching medium. Remove from the heat immediately. For me, a good piece of beef or lamb should not be cooked beyond medium-rare. What is tender and juicy at rare or medium-rare, becomes tough and dry if cooked past medium.

4. Bring the steaks to the table on a large carving board surrounded by the watercress. At the table, bone the steak, slice it thinly across its width on the diagonal to form broad slices, and serve.

SERVING SUGGESTION

With grilled beef, I generally serve Ratatouille (page 193) and small red potatoes or Yukon Golds steamed in their skins and tossed in a little chive butter. I often accompany the meat with a Béarnaise Sauce (page 327). A mixed green salad is a nice start, and cut-up fresh fruit and cookies are a great ending to a summer meal.

WINE

A full-bodied red is always enjoyable with this cut of beef.

ROASTED FILLET OF BEEF

[FILET DE BOEUF RÔTI]

THIS VERY ELEGANT cut of meat is perfect for entertaining: It cooks quickly, slices easily, goes well with a variety of sauces, but is also excellent by itself. Because it is relatively thin and cooks quickly, however, it can be difficult to brown (unless cooked on a grill). In my method I put the roasting pan in the oven for 10 minutes before putting the roast in. This way, the roast enters a hot pan and starts to cook immediately.

In France, a *filet de boeuf* would be wrapped in a sheet of pork fat (called a bard), but I omit it. I also trim off all the fat from the fillet.

Fillets are tender and are served rare or medium-rare to retain their juices. Although a sauce is not necessary, the Béarnaise (page 327), Bordelaise (page 320), and Madeira (page 319) sauces all complement the beef and create an elegant presentation. **SERVES 8 TO 10**

1 beef fillet (7 to 8 pounds untrimmed, 4 to 5 pounds well trimmed), tied every 2 inches for roasting (ask the butcher to do this)
2 tablespoons vegetable oil or melted butter
1 carrot, cut into ¼-inch slices
1 onion, halved and cut into ¼-inch slices
2 cups beef stock, homemade or canned (see chart, page 305)
⅛ teaspoon salt
⅛ teaspoon freshly ground pepper
Sauce of choice (see above; optional)

1. Preheat the oven to 475°F.

2. Lightly coat the meat and a roasting pan with the oil. Place the sliced vegetables in the pan and heat in the preheated oven for 10 minutes, or until the vegetables start to sizzle.

3. Place the fillet over the vegetables and roast for a total of 25 to 30 minutes for medium-rare. Turn the roast every 6 to 7 minutes to brown it evenly. The roast should be springy to the touch when done.

4. Transfer the roast to a carving board and deglaze the pan and vegetables by adding the stock and stirring to loosen the caramelized bits on the bottom and sides of the pan. Boil to reduce by half and strain; discard the vegetables. Season the roast with the salt and pepper.

5. To serve: Cut the fillet into slices about ¼ inch thick and serve on plates with a little of the pan juices or your favorite sauce.

SERVING SUGGESTION

Start with a seafood salad. With the fillet, serve Waterless Cooked Carrots (page 178), Cauliflower Purée (page 179), and buttered peas. For dessert, serve Chocolate Génoise with Grand Marnier Ganache (page 240) or a Gâteau Moka (page 241). Roasted beef fillet is also delicious served cold with a Cold Horseradish Sauce (page 335).

WINE

Serve this with a red Bordeaux.

BRAISED BRISKET WITH GINGER AND CORIANDER

[POITRINE DE BOEUF BRAISÉE AU GINGEMBRE ET CORIANDRE]

THIS RECIPE is a wonderful example of how ingredients not normally associated with classic French cooking can be used to bring new life to a traditional dish.

I really should call this recipe Boeuf Braisé Deborah, for it was created on the evening my wife gave birth to our second daughter, Deborah. One of the nurses who attended to my wife was from the British West Indies and a food enthusiast. When she found out my profession, she asked me for my chocolate mousse recipe. In return she gave me her favorite recipe, chicken cooked with fresh ginger, garlic, tomatoes, cilantro, and hot pepper.

When I returned home, I took out the brisket of beef I had in the refrigerator and started to prepare a classic braised beef. Finding a piece of ginger in the vegetable drawer, I thought of the nurse's chicken recipe. Although I did not have cilantro (fresh coriander), I did have ground coriander (the seeds of the coriander plant) and dried hot peppers. My older daughter, Jennifer, and my gourmet mother-in-law were both so pleased with the results that I have been cooking this recipe ever since. As it turned out Deborah was born a "super taster" like her mother, so both find this dish too spicy. Jennifer and I still love it.

SERVES 6 TO 8

3 tablespoons vegetable oil
3 to 4 pounds breast of beef (first-cut brisket)
2 onions, halved and thickly sliced
4 large carrots, thickly sliced on the diagonal
3 tablespoons all-purpose flour
2 cloves garlic, chopped
2 shallots, chopped
1 inch fresh ginger, sliced, or more to taste
2 cups dry red wine
1½ cups beef stock, homemade or canned (see chart, page 305)
2 teaspoons ground coriander
2 teaspoons tomato paste
1 to 2 dried red chili peppers (optional), to taste
Bouquet Garni (page 306)
⅛ teaspoon salt
⅛ teaspoon freshly ground pepper
12 to 16 small Yukon Gold potatoes, peeled

1. In a flameproof casserole or large Dutch oven, heat the oil over high heat. Add the meat when the oil is hot and brown it, about 3 minutes on each side. Remove the meat.

2. Add the onions and carrots and cook over high heat until they are lightly browned, about 10 minutes.

3. Sprinkle on the flour and cook, stirring occasionally, over medium heat until browned, 3 to 5 minutes.

4. Add the garlic, shallots, and ginger, and stir for 10 seconds before adding all of the remaining ingredients except the potatoes.

5. Return the meat to the casserole, cover, and simmer over medium-low heat until tender, 2½ to 3 hours. This can be done on top of the stove or in a 300°F to 350°F oven.

6. Add the potatoes during the last hour of cooking. If your casserole is too small to hold them, boil or steam them separately.

7. When the meat is tender, discard the bouquet garni. Reserving all of the cooked vegetables, strain the cooking liquid, which will have thickened to form a sauce, through a fine-mesh sieve. Skim to remove all fat. (This recipe can be prepared to this point in advance. Reheat the meat and vegetables before serving.)

8. Slice the brisket and serve it with the potatoes and vegetables. Spoon some of the sauce over all and serve the remaining sauce separately.

FIRST-CUT BRISKET

A brisket of beef is cut from the chest or breast of the cow, and although a tough piece of meat, it is excellent and tender after braising or slow cooking.

At one end of the brisket is a thin, flat, lean piece called the first cut. This is the cut that I have called for in this book. At the other end of the brisket is the thicker and fattier end called the second cut. This fattier cut of brisket is best when slow-roasted or smoked on the grill.

Both first and second cuts of brisket are used to make corned beef and pastrami.

SERVING SUGGESTION

Start with an Endive and Pink Grapefruit Salad (page 28) or a green vegetable as a first course. For dessert, serve a Crème Caramel (page 268).

WINE

Serve with a dry red.

VARIATIONS

BRAISED BEEF

[BOEUF BRAISÉ]

Omit the ginger, coriander, and chili peppers and you have my basic braised beef recipe.

BRAISED BEEF A L'HONGROISE

[BOEUF BRAISÉ À L'HONGROISE]

Use the basic Braised Beef (above) and omit the carrot, add another onion and 1 tablespoon of paprika.

ALSATIAN-STYLE BRAISED BEEF

[BOEUF BRAISÉ À L'ALSACIENNE]

Omit the coriander and chili pepper. In place of the ginger, use 15 juniper berries. Add a whole head of cabbage cut into wedges at the same time as the potatoes in step 6.

BEEF BURGUNDY

[BOEUF BOURGUIGNON]

ON A WINTER NIGHT, or after a full day of skiing, nothing is quite as satisfying as a hearty *boeuf bourguignon.* In France this *ragoût* is made with fresh unsmoked bacon, which is not stocked in most American markets. I use smoked bacon and remove the excess salt and smoky flavor by blanching it twice. The delicate smoky taste that is left creates additional character not found in the original recipe, giving this version a sauce that is fuller and more robust.

Traditionally, *boeuf bourguignon* is made with a local, full-bodied Burgundy made from the Pinot Noir grape. Use any similar imported or domestic wine. **SERVES 6**

¼ cup vegetable oil
3 pounds beef chuck (see Note), trimmed, cut into 1½- to 2-inch cubes, and patted dry with paper towels
1 onion, diced
1 small carrot, diced
⅓ cup all-purpose flour
¼ cup Cognac (optional)
3 cups dry red wine
1½ cups beef stock, homemade or canned (see chart, page 305)
2 shallots, sliced
4 cloves garlic, sliced
1 tablespoon tomato paste
1 teaspoon Meat Glaze (optional; page 309)
Bouquet Garni (page 306)
¼ teaspoon salt
⅛ teaspoon freshly ground pepper
24 pearl onions, peeled, root ends trimmed but left intact to hold the onions together
12 to 18 small Yukon Gold potatoes, peeled
1 pound smoked slab bacon, cut into ½-inch rectangles
¾ pound mushrooms, washed, dried, and halved or quartered to match the size of the pearl onions
6 sprigs parsley, chopped, for garnish

1. In a large flameproof casserole, heat the oil over high heat. When the oil begins to smoke, add the beef cubes and brown well on all sides, turning the pieces only after they have browned, about 7 minutes. This can be done in two batches if your casserole cannot hold the meat in one layer. Add the onion and carrot to the casserole, reduce the heat to medium-high, and brown the vegetables lightly, about 3 minutes.

2. Sprinkle the flour over the meat and vegetables and cook over medium heat, stirring occasionally, until evenly browned, about 5 minutes.

3. Remove the casserole from the heat, add the Cognac (if using), and flame (see "How to Flambé," page 282). When the flames die down, add the wine, stock, shallots, garlic, tomato paste, meat glaze (if using), bouquet garni, salt, and pepper. Cover, reduce the heat to medium-low, and simmer, occasionally skimming off the fat or foam that rises to the top, until the beef is tender, about 1½ hours. The cooking time will vary depending on the cut and aging of the meat. It might take as long as 2½ to 3 hours. To test for doneness, stick one prong of a roasting fork into a piece of the meat and lift it from the casserole. If the meat clings to the fork, it needs more cooking. If it drops from the fork, it is tender and ready to serve. (The recipe can be prepared to this point in advance. Let cool to room temperature, cover, and refrigerate or freeze.)

4. Meanwhile, fill two large saucepans with water and bring to a boil over high heat. Add the pearl onions to one and cook until tender, about 10 minutes; drain well. Add the potatoes to the other and cook until tender, about 20 minutes; drain well.

5. Place the bacon in a small saucepan and cover with cold water. Bring to a boil, drain, and rinse under cold running water. Repeat this process one more time and drain well.

6. In a 12-inch skillet, sauté the bacon over medium heat until it is crisp on the outside, yet soft on the inside, about 5 minutes. Drain on paper towels.

7. Remove all but about 2 tablespoons of fat from the skillet, add the mushrooms, and sauté over high heat until browned, 3 to 5 minutes. Season with salt and pepper to taste and remove the mushrooms and place in a bowl.

8. Add the boiled pearl onions to the pan and sauté until browned, about 5 minutes.

9. When the beef is tender, remove it with a skimmer or slotted spoon and place it in an attractive oven-to-table casserole. Add the pearl onions, potatoes, mushrooms, and bacon.

10. Remove any fat from the surface of the cooking liquid. If the sauce is too thick, add a little water; if too thin, boil it to reduce and thicken. The sauce should be the consistency of heavy cream. Adjust the seasoning of the sauce and strain it over the meat and vegetables. (The stew can be prepared up to 2 days in advance. As with all stews, the flavor actually improves if made at least 1 day in advance. Let cool, cover, and refrigerate. Before serving, reheat the stew and simmer for 5 minutes.) Sprinkle with chopped parsley and serve.

NOTE: Although in most of my cooking, and in nearly every meat dish, I seek ways of reducing or omitting unnecessary fat, this is a place where the fat in the meat is absolutely necessary. Chuck, which is the meat called for here, is marbled with fat, which essentially bastes the meat from the inside as it cooks. Many people make the mistake of substituting beef round for the chuck because it contains less fat. I advise against doing so.

SERVING SUGGESTION

Start with an artichoke vinaigrette and serve Lime Mousse (page 276) for dessert. Don't forget French bread to mop up the sauce.

WINE

Serve a Pinot Noir or red Burgundy.

VEAL MEDALLIONS WITH SAUTEED ROOT VEGETABLES

[MÉDAILLONS DE VEAU À LA BRUNOISE]

IN FRENCH COOKING a *brunoise* is a combination of finely diced aromatic vegetables—usually carrots, onions, celery (both root and rib), white turnips, and leeks—used to give flavor to soups and sauces. (It is similar to a *mirepoix*; see Artichokes Barigoule, page 173.) Ordinarily, a *brunoise* is used in relatively small quantities. But the effort involved in preparing a *brunoise* has always seemed out of proportion to me, so in this dish I use the *brunoise* not only to enhance the flavor of the sauce, but as the accompanying vegetables as well. **SERVES 6**

2 tablespoons butter
3 large carrots, diced
3 onions, diced
3 ribs celery, diced
1 white turnip, peeled and diced (optional; see Note)
1 leek (white part only), washed and diced (optional; see Note)
⅛ teaspoon salt
⅛ teaspoon freshly ground pepper
Pinch of thyme leaves
6 veal medallions (boned rib chops), 1 to 1¼ inches thick
2 medium (¾-inch) black truffles (optional; see step 5), 1 diced and 1 sliced
¼ teaspoon arrowroot, potato starch, or cornstarch dissolved in 1 teaspoon cold water
1 teaspoon Meat Glaze (optional; page 309)
2 tablespoons Madeira
1 tablespoon Cognac
3 sprigs parsley, chopped, for garnish (optional; see step 5)

1. In a large skillet, melt 1 tablespoon of the butter over medium heat. Add the diced vegetables and cook until just tender and lightly colored, 10 to 15 minutes. Season with the salt, pepper, and thyme. Remove the vegetables from the pan and set aside.

2. Melt the remaining 1 tablespoon butter in the pan. Add the veal and cook over medium-high heat until brown on both sides, 2 to 3 minutes. Season with salt and pepper to taste. Pour off any excess butter.

3. Spread the cooked vegetables and diced truffle (if using) over the veal, cover, and cook over low heat until the veal is firm to the touch, 12 to 15 minutes. Using a skimmer or slotted spoon, remove the veal and vegetables and arrange on a serving platter (see Serving Suggestion, page 152). Keep warm in a 250°F oven.

4. Add the dissolved arrowroot to the pan to lightly thicken the pan juices. Stir in the meat glaze (if using), Madeira, and Cognac. Taste and adjust the seasoning, if necessary.

5. To serve: Spoon the light sauce over the veal and top each medallion with a slice of truffle, if using. If not using a truffle, sprinkle the chopped parsley over the vegetables and serve.

NOTE: Although the turnip and leek are technically part of a *brunoise,* they can be left out with no ill effect. A classic *brunoise* also includes celery root (celeriac). If you can find it in your market, use a chunk of celery root about the size of a white turnip and dice as for the other vegetables.

SERVING SUGGESTION

I normally present the vegetables mounded in the center of a large, round platter with the medallions set around them in a circle. If a round platter is not available, I place the medallions down the center of an oval platter, and spoon the vegetables on either side of them. Serve the veal with buttered noodles or sautéed potatoes. Begin the meal with asparagus or a green salad and end with Floating Island with Raspberry Sauce (page 274).

WINE

Serve this with a red Bordeaux.

VARIATIONS

Veal Chops with Sauteed Root Vegetables

[CÔTES DE VEAU À LA BRUNOISE]

Substitute 1¼-inch-thick veal chops for the medallions and cook about 15 minutes in step 3.

PROFESSIONAL-STYLE RANGES

The use of professional-style ranges in homes has become popular and I am often asked for my opinion on their use. If you are regularly cooking for 12 or more, a professional-style range will definitely make your task easier, and even though it takes more time to clean than a normal home range does, it will be worth it. However, if you regularly cook for fewer than eight, you will find the burners of a professional-style range too large for your pots, the heat produced too much for your kitchen, and the added cleaning not worth the effort.

Pork Medallions with Sauteed Root Vegetables

[MÉDAILLONS DE PORC À LA BRUNOISE]

Substitute medallions of pork (boneless center-cut rib chops) and omit the truffles.

Chicken Breasts with Sauteed Root Vegetables

[SUPRÊMES DE VOLAILLE À LA BRUNOISE]

Substitute 6 boneless chicken half breasts (about 2 pounds), and cook 10 to 20 minutes in step 3.

VEAL SCALLOPS WITH MUSHROOMS AND TOMATO SAUCE

[ESCALOPES DE VEAU CHASSEUR]

When you see a dish called *chasseur* (which means "hunter") in France, you know right away that it will contain mushrooms. For this *chasseur*, I use wild mushrooms in place of the usual white mushrooms. Normally, the veal would be floured before being sautéed in a preparation like this one. Unless browned quickly, however, the flour becomes pasty and unappetizing, so it has been omitted. **SERVES 4**

3 tablespoons butter
1 pound veal scallops
¼ teaspoon salt
⅛ teaspoon freshly ground pepper
½ pound fresh shiitake (see Note) or porcini mushrooms, washed, dried, and sliced
2 shallots, finely chopped
¼ cup dry white wine
½ cup beef stock, homemade or canned (see chart, page 305)
1 teaspoon Meat Glaze (optional; page 309)
1 tablespoon tomato paste
1 teaspoon Cognac
3 sprigs parsley, chopped, for garnish

1. In a large skillet, melt the butter over medium-high to high heat. Add the veal and cook until lightly browned, about 2 minutes on each side. Season with the salt and pepper. Transfer the veal to a platter and keep warm.

2. Add the mushrooms to the pan and brown lightly, about 2 minutes. Add the shallots and cook for 20 to 30 seconds.

3. Add the wine and cook until the liquid is reduced by half, about 1 minute. Stir in the stock, meat glaze (if using), and tomato paste, and bring the mixture to a boil. Taste and adjust the seasoning, if necessary. Add the Cognac. To serve: Pour the sauce over the veal. Sprinkle with the chopped parsley and serve.

NOTE: The stems of shiitake mushrooms are not edible. Discard them (or save them for broth) before slicing the caps.

SERVING SUGGESTION

Begin with a green vegetable or salad and accompany the veal with Rice Pilaf (page 207) or buttered noodles. Serve fresh fruit for dessert.

WINE

Serve this with a dry red.

CREAMY VEAL STEW
WITH MORELS

[BLANQUETTE DE VEAU AUX MORILLES]

A BLANQUETTE is a *ragoût* made in a white sauce enriched with heavy cream and egg yolks. (Although it is usually made with veal, recipes exist for *blanquettes* made with chicken, lamb, or fish.) A *blanquette de veau* normally contains small white mushrooms, but I make mine with dried *morilles* (morels). These wild mushrooms, prized in France for their unique robust and earthy flavor, transform the *blanquette* of the bistro into one for the palace. **SERVES 6**

1 ounce dried or 1/3 to 1/2 pound fresh morel mushrooms (see Note)
8 cups cold water
3 pounds veal shoulder, cut into 1½-inch cubes
1 onion, studded with 2 cloves
1 large carrot
2 leeks, washed
1 turnip, peeled
2 celery ribs, with leaves if possible
Bouquet Garni (page 306)
24 pearl onions, peeled, root ends trimmed but left intact to hold the onions together
2½ tablespoons butter
3 tablespoons all-purpose flour
1/4 teaspoon salt
1/8 teaspoon freshly ground pepper
2 egg yolks
1/3 cup heavy cream

1. Place the dried morels in a small bowl, cover with 2 cups of the cold water, and let stand until softened, about 30 minutes. Remove the morels and squeeze gently to remove as much liquid as possible. Strain the soaking liquid through a fine-mesh sieve lined with a double thickness of cheesecloth or paper towel to separate any dirt or sand from the liquid; set aside.

2. Place the veal in a stockpot and add cold water to cover (about 6 cups). Bring to a boil over high heat, skimming the foam from the surface frequently.

3. Add the reserved morel soaking liquid, the clove-studded onion, the carrot, leeks, turnip, celery, and bouquet garni. Reduce the heat to medium and simmer for 30 minutes.

4. Add the pearl onions and simmer for 35 minutes more.

5. Add the morels; continue to cook until the veal is tender, 10 to 15 minutes more.

6. Drain the meat and vegetables, reserving the stock. Put the veal, pearl onions, and morels in a large saucepan. Discard the other vegetables and bouquet garni.

7. Strain the reserved veal stock into a medium-size saucepan and boil over high heat until reduced to 3 cups, about 10 minutes.

8. In a small saucepan, melt the butter over medium-high heat. Add the flour and cook, stirring frequently, until the roux is pale yellow and frothy, 30 to 40 seconds. Add 2½ cups of the reduced veal stock and stir well with a whisk until the sauce thickens and comes to a boil, 2 to 3 minutes. Reduce the heat to maintain a gentle simmer and season the sauce with the salt and pepper. Whisk vigorously for about 10 seconds. Simmer gently, whisking the sauce from time to time, until the sauce is the consistency of heavy cream, about 5 minutes. Skim off any butter that comes to the surface.

9. Reduce the remaining ½ cup of reserved veal stock over high heat until only a few teaspoons remain and whisk into the sauce. Remove the sauce from the heat.

10. In a small bowl, mix the egg yolks and cream together and gradually whisk in ½ cup of the hot sauce. Whisk the warmed egg yolk mixture into the sauce. Return the sauce to the heat and bring just to a simmer, whisking constantly. Remove the sauce from the heat and pour it over the veal, onions, and morels. (The recipe can be prepared to this point several days in advance. Cover the surface with plastic wrap, let cool, and refrigerate.)

11. Before serving, reheat the veal and vegetables in a water bath (*bain-marie*), gently stirring occasionally, until the sauce and veal are hot, 15 to 20 minutes.

NOTE: If you don't have dried or fresh morels when you want to make this recipe, you can always make the more usual version of this dish by using ¾ pound fresh button mushrooms. Wash them and add in step 5.

IN ADDITION

If you can't find morels in a local store, look for them online, where you'll find both domestic and imported morels. Morels come in both dark brown and white varieties, but I recommend using only the more robust-flavored brown ones for this recipe.

SERVING SUGGESTION

Start with a salad. Serve the *blanquette* with Boiled White Rice (page 206). For dessert, serve a sorbet and Almond Tuiles (page 252).

WINE

I like a dry white wine with this dish.

VARIATION

CREAMY CHICKEN STEW WITH MORELS

[BLANQUETTE DE VOLAILLE AUX MORILLES]

Substitute 2½ pounds skinless, boneless chicken breasts, cut in large chunks, for the veal. In step 3, add the pearl onions along with the other ingredients and simmer for 35 minutes, or until the pearl onions are tender. Omit step 4 and then proceed with the recipe.

RACK OF LAMB ON A BED OF WATERCRESS

[CARRÉ D'AGNEAU VERT PRÉ]

THE FRENCH name of this superb dish comes from its presentation. The lamb is surrounded by watercress as if it were in a green (*vert*) meadow (*pré*).

Rack of lamb is not only one of the most delectable cuts of lamb, it is also an expensive and, to some, intimidating one. Even though they have probably cooked lamb rib chops (which before they are cut apart comprise a rack), most people will rarely make a rack of lamb at home, thinking of it as a restaurant specialty. However, not only is it not hard to make, it is a good deal less expensive at home.

Since the racks cook quickly, have your vegetable dishes ready to reheat, and roast the racks while eating your first course. Note: In the summer I use my covered grill for this wonderful cut of meat. **SERVES 4 TO 6**

2 racks of lamb (8 chops each), completely trimmed (see facing page)
1 teaspoon fresh or dried thyme leaves
½ teaspoon chopped fresh or dried rosemary
¼ teaspoon salt
⅛ teaspoon freshly ground pepper
1 bunch watercress, thick stems trimmed

1. Preheat the oven to 475°F.

2. Season both sides of the racks with the herbs, salt, and pepper, and place in a roasting pan bone side down. (If seasoning in advance, do not salt until just before roasting.)

3. Place in the oven and lower the temperature to 400°F. Depending on their size, the racks will take 20 to 30 minutes to cook to medium-rare. When done, they will be springy to the touch.

4. To serve: Transfer the lamb to a serving platter or carving board and surround with watercress. Slice into individual chops by cutting between the bones, and serve 2 to 3 chops per person.

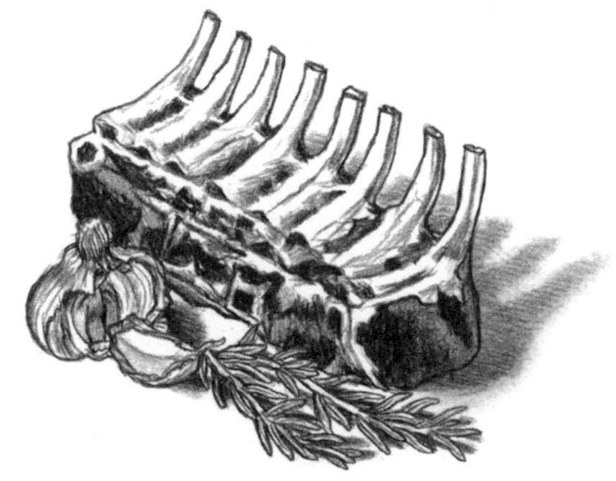

Completely Trimmed Rack of Lamb

A rack of lamb contains 6 to 8 chops, and when found in a supermarket, will have bones ranging from 3 to 4 inches in length. It is usually covered by a thick layer of fat. Although the backbone or chine bone of the chops will have been cut through with a band saw to facilitate carving, they will still be attached. When roasted as is, the rack will leave large, unattractive bones and quantities of fat on the diners' plates.

To make the cooking easy and to improve the presentation, I ask the butcher to cut the rib bones 2 inches from the eye, and to remove the chine and feather bones. I also have all visible fat removed, leaving only the eye of the chop. If there is still fat on the rack when you get it home (butchers are often reluctant to trim all the fat off, because it makes it look like you're not getting enough for your money), you can remove the rest yourself by peeling away the fat covering the meat. Once you have uncovered the eye of the rack, use a knife to slice the fat away from the bones. You will find that you have removed a small piece of meat that is embedded in the fat, and you can trim this and reserve it for later use in a lamb stew.

SERVING SUGGESTION

This wonderful cut of meat can be the centerpiece of a grand dinner. You can serve a simple green salad or an elegant fish mousseline (see pages 47–52) to start. Almost any green vegetable and potato preparation goes well with the lamb; I particularly enjoy buttered or Creamed Spinach (page 191) along with Potatoes à la Boulangère (page 202). Sorbet and cookies are a good ending.

VARIATION

Rack of Lamb with Bearnaise or Choron Sauce

[CARRÉ D'AGNEAU VERT PRÉ SAUCE BÉARNAISE OU CHORON]

Omit the herbs and serve with Béarnaise Sauce (page 327) or Béarnaise with Tomatoes (page 329).

ROAST LEG OF LAMB

[GIGOT D'AGNEAU RÔTI]

A LEG OF LAMB is a luxury in France, and most families reserve it for special gatherings and Sunday lunches. Simply roasted with garlic and herbs, it is most often served with fresh green beans in spring and summer, and one of a variety of dried beans, such as flageolets (pale green kidney beans), in the winter. Potatoes are often roasted in the pan with the lamb.

If you roast leg of lamb in the usual American manner, you will discover that I do a number of things differently. First, I have the butcher cut out the "H" (also known as the "aitch") or hip bone (see "French-Style Leg of Lamb," page 161), which makes the leg easier to carve. Second, as with most meat, I remove as much fat as possible. In this recipe, as in many leg of lamb recipes, garlic is imbedded in the meat before roasting. Most cooks will make random slits in the meat and insert the garlic slices. When eating the lamb, a diner often gets a bite that is more garlic than lamb. To avoid this, I place the slices of garlic near the bone along its length and at both ends of the leg. In this way the leg is lightly scented with garlic without being objectionably strong. **SERVES 6**

1 leg of lamb, 6 to 7½ pounds untrimmed, or 4 to 5 pounds trimmed
2 cloves garlic, sliced
1 tablespoon light olive oil
2 teaspoons fresh or dried thyme leaves
1 teaspoon chopped fresh or dried rosemary
⅛ teaspoon salt
⅛ teaspoon freshly ground pepper

1. Preheat the oven to 475°F.

2. Make several small, deep incisions into the leg of lamb along the length of the bone. Insert the garlic slices, placing them as close to the bone as possible. Rub the leg with the oil and sprinkle all over with the herbs. Season with the salt and pepper.

3. Place the lamb in a roasting pan rounded side up and roast for 15 minutes. Lower the oven temperature to 400°F and roast for another 15 minutes.

4. Turn the leg and roast until springy to the touch, another 20 minutes.

5. Remove the roast when done and allow the leg to stand, covered, for 10 to 15 minutes before carving. To carve the lamb: Place the lamb, rounded side up, on a large meat cutting board. Holding the leg by the bone to steady it, slice the meat with the knife held horizontally, and parallel to the cutting board. When you reach the bone, turn the leg about 45 degrees, and take off more slices from this side of the leg. Continue turning and slicing until you've taken off enough slices for your guests. Transfer the sliced lamb to a platter or serve directly from the cutting board.

GRILLING LAMB: Tips for Legs and Racks

To prepare a leg for grilling, I have the leg butterflied (boned and cut to lie flat). However, some parts are thicker than others, making even cooking a little difficult, and when carving you find yourself cutting several different muscles, some with and some against the grain. To avoid this, after the leg is butterflied, I trim it of *all* its fat, leaving one with individual muscles, which I then grill like steaks.

At least 1 hour before grilling, I sprinkle or rub the leg with seasonings. Unlike other cuts of lamb whose flavors are relatively delicate, the leg is stronger in flavor and can support fairly robust seasonings, such as mustard or rosemary, garlic, ginger, or even crushed juniper berries.

When grilling a rack of lamb, the cooking time on a hot covered grill is generally 13 to 14 minutes. I often season the lamb several hours in advance of cooking, though I am careful not to salt the meat until just before grilling so as not to extract the natural moisture. In general, I do not season any grilled meat with salt until after it has been browned.

SERVING SUGGESTION

Serve with Glazed Garlic (page 181) and Green Beans (page 182) or White Beans à la Bretonne (page 184). Ratatouille (page 193) and Gratin Dauphinois (page 200) are also excellent choices. End the meal with a Fallen Chocolate Soufflé (page 267).

WINE

I enjoy a wide variety of red wines with lamb: Pinot Noir, Cabernet Sauvignon, Malbec, Zinfandel, and Syrah/Shiraz.

VARIATIONS

ROAST LEG OF LAMB WITH CHORON SAUCE

[GIGOT D'AGNEAU SAUCE CHORON]

Omit the garlic and rosemary and serve with Béarnaise with Tomatoes (page 329).

MUSTARD-ROASTED LEG OF LAMB

[GIGOT D'AGNEAU À LA MOUTARDE]

Substitute 2 to 3 tablespoons of Dijon mustard for the olive oil.

VENISON-STYLE LEG OF LAMB

[GIGOT EN CHEVREUIL]

MARINATING LAMB in a marinade frequently used for venison is the basis for this classic recipe. If you have never prepared game, making this recipe will give you the experience you need to do so. Some of my readers are hunters, and this recipe can be used for deer, elk, or antelope.

I recommend serving the lamb with three different sauces that go well with game. On page 322, you will find the basic recipe for a peppery sauce called *poivrade*. It is followed by two variations, Grand Veneur and Chevreuil. It is really easy to make all three sauces, because they are just minor variations of one another. Follow the instructions in "A Trio of Game Sauces" (page 324). **SERVES 8**

1 leg of lamb (see "French-Style Leg of Lamb," facing page), 6 to 7½ pounds untrimmed or 4 to 5 pounds trimmed
Game Marinade (page 324)
1 tablespoon light olive oil
2 teaspoons fresh or dried thyme leaves
1 teaspoon chopped fresh or dried rosemary
⅛ teaspoon salt
⅛ teaspoon freshly ground pepper
Poivrade, Chevreuil, and Grand Veneur sauces (pages 322 to 324)

1. Two to four days before you want to serve the lamb, start to marinate it (see instructions in the marinade recipe).

2. Preheat the oven to 475°F.

3. Remove the lamb from the marinade and dry it well. Strain the marinade and reserve it and the vegetables for the sauces. Rub the lamb with the oil and sprinkle all over with the thyme and rosemary. Season with the salt and pepper.

4. Place the lamb in a roasting pan and roast for 15 minutes. Lower the temperature to 400°F, roast for another 15 minutes, and turn the leg.

5. Meanwhile, make the sauces.

6. Roast the lamb until it is springy to the touch, another 20 minutes, or until an instant-read thermometer registers 125°F for rare or 130°F for medium-rare.

7. Remove the roast when done and allow the leg to stand, covered, for 10 to 15 minutes before carving. Serve on plates with the sauces on the side.

FRENCH-STYLE LEG OF LAMB: A Different Kind of Cut

A leg of lamb is cut differently in France than in America. A French leg ends at the hip, whereas the American leg contains a part of the hip or sirloin. The shank bone on a French leg is left intact and serves as a handle, which you use to turn the leg while cooking and to hold while carving. Some American butchers crack or break this shank bone and fold it back against the leg, or cut it off.

To get a French-style leg, ask your butcher to leave the shank bone intact and uncut. Have him remove the "H" or hip bone. Once removed, you will see the ball joint of the leg. The meat will now extend beyond the ball joint and should be cut off to form a well-shaped leg. Freeze the cutoff portion for future use.

SERVING SUGGESTION

Because this is a winter dish, I often use baked beets in a green salad to start. I like to accompany the roast with Cauliflower Purée (page 179) and Green Beans Almondine (page 183) or sautéed mushrooms. An Apricot Soufflé (page 263) is a great way to end the meal.

FRENCH LAMB STEW

[NAVARIN D'AGNEAU]

AN IRISH STEW is perhaps the best-known lamb stew in the world, but a *navarin d'agneau* is the best-tasting one.

Over the years I've taught this *ragoût* in many cities throughout the country, and I've often had students tell me that at least one member of their family wouldn't eat lamb. They checked the recipe further and found the turnips. Now matters were much worse, for no one in their family ate turnips! Can the turnips be left out? Not if the stew is to be a *navarin.*

Luckily, my students went home, followed

the recipe, and re-created what they had tasted in class. The reports that came back were not only that the *navarin* was a success, but that "they even wanted more turnips." If you are among those who do not like lamb or turnips, be encouraged, you are in for a tasty surprise.

As with any stew, this not only can be made ahead of time, but it improves with age. **SERVES 6**

4 tablespoons vegetable oil
2½ pounds boned shoulder of lamb (see Note), trimmed and cut into 1½-inch cubes
¼ cup all-purpose flour
3 cups beef stock, homemade or canned (see chart, page 305)
1 cup dry white wine
1 tablespoon tomato paste
3 cloves garlic, finely chopped
Bouquet Garni (page 306)
¼ teaspoon salt
⅛ teaspoon freshly ground pepper
4 large carrots, cut into 1-inch pieces
18 pearl onions, peeled, root ends trimmed but left intact to hold the onions together
3 small to medium white turnips, peeled and quartered
18 small Yukon Gold potatoes, peeled
Chopped parsley, for garnish

1. In a large flameproof casserole, heat 3 tablespoons of the oil over high heat until it begins to smoke. Add the cubes of lamb and brown well on all sides, turning the pieces only after they have browned. If your casserole is not large enough to hold the lamb in one layer, this can be done in two batches.

2. Sprinkle the flour over the meat and brown over medium heat, 3 to 5 minutes.

3. Add the stock, wine, tomato paste, garlic, and bouquet garni. Stir with a wooden spoon. Season with the salt and pepper. Bring to a boil, then reduce the heat to medium-low, cover, and simmer.

4. Meanwhile, in a 10- to 12-inch skillet, heat the remaining 1 tablespoon oil over high heat. Add the carrots and brown, shaking the skillet frequently, 3 to 4 minutes. Remove the carrots and set aside. Next, brown the pearl onions and turnips in the same skillet, 3 to 4 minutes.

5. After the lamb has been simmering for 30 minutes, add the browned carrots. After another 15 minutes, add the onions and turnips. Check both meat and vegetables for tenderness from time to time, and if one of the vegetables is fully cooked before the rest, remove it to prevent overcooking. While everything is gently cooking, skim off all the fat and impurities that come to the surface. Total cooking time will be about 1½ hours. (The stew can be made several days ahead to this point. Remove the bouquet

TURNING VEGETABLES

In many classic dishes, vegetables are "turned" (pared into uniform football or olive shapes) to add to the attractiveness of a dish. In France the vegetables in a *navarin d'agneau* or other *ragoûts* would be turned, but it's not worth doing unless you think your guests will appreciate it. To turn large root vegetables (potatoes, turnips, carrots), first cut them into chunks, then trim them to an olive shape with a paring knife. This takes practice.

garni. Let cool to room temperature, cover, and refrigerate or freeze. Bring slowly back to a simmer while you cook the potatoes; see next step.)

6. Bring a large saucepan of water to a boil. Add the potatoes and cook until tender, about 20 minutes; drain well. Add them to the casserole when all the ingredients are tender, and cook for 5 minutes longer.

7. Skim any remaining fat from the sauce, adjust the seasoning if necessary, and remove the bouquet garni. Transfer the stew to a hot serving dish and sprinkle with the chopped parsley just before serving.

NOTE: As in *boeuf bourguignon,* this is one place where using a leaner cut of meat will detract from the dish. The lamb shoulder's fat content will produce moist and tender meat. Your butcher may suggest boned leg of lamb instead, but you should insist on the shoulder.

SERVING SUGGESTION

When serving *navarin d'agneau,* I often start with a green salad and finish with a pastry like Cream Puffs Filled with Chocolate Soufflé (page 226). Or for a simpler dessert, I like Pears Poached in Port Wine (page 284).

WINE

Serve this with a red Bordeaux.

VARIATION

French Lamb Stew with Spring Vegetables

[NAVARIN PRINTANIER]

This version of a *navarin* takes its name from the springtime (*printanier*) vegetables that are added to it. In step 6, along with the cooked potatoes, add about ½ pound cooked peas and ¼ pound cooked green beans.

Pork Rib Roast with Wine-Poached Prunes

[RÔTI DE PORC AUX PRUNEAUX]

In the Loire Valley, the flavorful combination of pork and prunes is often seen in local restaurants, especially in and around the city of Tours. Usually served as a *ragoût* (stew), chunks of pork are cooked with the prunes in a sauce made with white wine and finished with a little heavy cream.

I have taken the components of a simple pork *ragoût* and rearranged them in an elegant main course for a dinner party. Instead of chunks of pork, prunes, and sauce all cooked together, I serve a pork roast accompanied with prunes and golden raisins poached in a full-bodied red wine. The poaching liquid is then used to make a light but intensely flavored sauce. While making the sauce, taste the wine before poaching the prunes and raisins. Then taste it after each addition of the remaining ingredients. You will begin to understand how a sauce is built.

I encourage anyone who has not enjoyed prunes and meat, or those who think poorly of the prune, to try this dish. **SERVES 6 TO 8**

2½ pounds boned pork rib roast (center-cut rib section, 8 ribs; see Notes)
¼ teaspoon salt
⅛ teaspoon freshly ground pepper
½ teaspoon fresh or dried thyme leaves
1 bay leaf, crumbled
2 onions, quartered
3 large carrots, thickly sliced
6 tablespoons (¾ stick) butter
1½ pounds pitted prunes
½ cup golden raisins
1 bottle (750 ml) dry red wine, such as a Côtes-du-Rhône
1 cup beef stock, homemade or canned (see chart, page 305)
1½ teaspoons arrowroot, potato starch, or cornstarch, dissolved in 1½ teaspoons cold water
2 tablespoons port (see Notes)

1. Preheat the oven to 475°F.

2. Season the roast with the salt, pepper, thyme, and bay leaf. Place in a roasting pan with the vegetables. In a small saucepan, melt 4 tablespoons of the butter and pour over the roast. Place in the oven and reduce the temperature to 425°F. Roast until the juices run clear, about 1 hour and 10 minutes.

3. While the pork is roasting, combine the prunes, raisins, wine, and stock in a medium-size saucepan. Cover and simmer over medium heat until the prunes are tender, about 30 minutes. Drain the fruit, reserving the poaching liquid. Return about ¼ cup of the poaching liquid to the fruit. Set the fruit and the remaining poaching liquid aside.

4. When the roast is done, remove it from the pan and allow it to stand 10 to 15 minutes

FRENCH PRUNES:
Les Pruneaux d'Agen

Agen, a town in the southwest of France, is famous for its moist, semidried prunes. Succulent, sweet, and rich tasting, they are treasured by the French, who hold them in high esteem and use them in a variety of ways.

California prunes, or dried plums as they are now being marketed, are nearly as good, although they are not praised in the United States for their culinary value, as they are in France.

I have created several recipes for this very healthy dried fruit that I hope will turn you into a prune lover. The Pork Rib Roast with Wine-Poached Prunes (page 163) is one of my favorites. Other recipes you shouldn't miss are the Chocolate-Dipped Fruit (page 297), Armagnac-Soaked Prunes (page 298), and the Armagnac-Prune Ice Cream (page 292).

before carving. Drain the fat from the roasting pan. Deglaze the pan and vegetables (and bones if used; see Notes) by adding the reserved poaching liquid and stirring over high heat to loosen the caramelized bits. Strain through a fine-mesh sieve into a saucepan. (Reserve the carrots and onions if you wish to serve them.)

5. Bring the sauce to a boil and add the dissolved arrowroot to thicken it slightly. If the sauce is too thick, add a little water to thin it; if too thin, boil to reduce and thicken it. Season with salt and pepper to taste and stir in the port. Just before serving, beat in the remaining 2 tablespoons butter, 1 tablespoon at a time. Do not allow the sauce to boil once the butter has been added.

6. To serve: Slice the roast and arrange it on a platter. (When slicing the roast, I always leave a small piece—2 to 3 inches—unsliced. Placed at one end of the platter and followed by the overlapping slices, this makes an attractive presentation.) Surround it with the prunes and raisins. The carrots and onions from the roasting pan may be mixed with the fruit. Spoon some sauce over the meat and fruit and serve the remaining sauce separately.

NOTES: The roast should be tied like a fillet of beef in one long roast. When you order the pork roast, make sure that the butcher gives you the rib bones with the backbone removed so they can be cut up and scattered in the roasting pan. They will add flavor to your sauce and will be delicious to nibble on before your guests arrive. You can use an unboned roast, but add 20 minutes to the roasting time.

You can use whatever port you have on hand. If you cook with port frequently, buy an inexpensive bottle of tawny port and save your best for drinking.

IN ADDITION

To make entertaining easy, I generally have the roast, sauce, and prunes cooked in advance of my guests' arrival and only need to reheat, carve, and serve. Once roasted, I wrap the meat in aluminum foil. If the meat has cooled by the time I am ready to serve, I reheat it in a 350°F oven for 10 to 15 minutes.

SERVING SUGGESTION

Begin with a soup, Cream of Asparagus (page 24) or Cream of Broccoli (page 25). With the pork roast, serve Garlic Mashed Potatoes (page 205) and Carrots with Ginger (page 179). For dessert, serve Paris-Brest (page 228).

WINE

Try a full-bodied red from the Rhône valley, such as Châteauneuf-du-Pape or St-Joseph.

VARIATIONS

Old-Fashioned Roast Pork with Carrots and Onions

[RÔTI DE PORC GRAND-MÈRE]

Omit the prunes, raisins, red wine, beef stock, arrowroot, and port. Serve the roast with the carrots and onions from the roasting pan and mashed potatoes.

Roast Pork with Sauce Robert

[RÔTI DE PORC SAUCE ROBERT]

Omit the prunes, raisins, red wine, beef stock, arrowroot, and port. Serve the roast with Sauce Robert (page 321).

PORK MEDALLIONS WITH SAUCE ROBERT

[MÉDAILLONS DE PORC SAUCE ROBERT]

PORK SERVED with a classic mustard-based brown sauce called *sauce Robert* is a bit of an undertaking. I make mine with a Thickened Beef Stock (page 318) instead of a demi-glace, which cuts out 2 hours of preparation. In another slight twist on the original sauce, I deglaze the sauté pan with Cognac and add the flavorful juices to the sauce. Since the *sauce Robert* is made in advance, final preparation of this dish is very easy. **SERVES 6**

1½ tablespoons butter
6 boneless center-cut pork loin chops, 1 to 1¼ inches thick
Pinch of salt
Pinch of freshly ground pepper
¼ cup Cognac
Sauce Robert (page 321)
3 sprigs parsley, chopped

1. In a 12-inch skillet, melt the butter over high heat. Add the pork and brown quickly on one side, about 1 minute. Turn and season with the salt and pepper.

2. Cover the pan, reduce the heat to medium-low, and cook gently until the meat is well done, firm or just slightly springy to the touch, 10 to 12 minutes.

3. Transfer the meat to a warm platter and keep warm. Over high heat, reduce the pan juices to a glaze, until no liquid remains. Discard any butter remaining in the pan.

4. Remove the pan from the heat, add the Cognac, and flame (see "How to Flambé," page 282). When the flames die, return the pan to the heat and stir to loosen the glaze in the pan. Add the *sauce Robert,* bring to a simmer, and stir in the parsley. Pour the sauce over the pork and serve.

SERVING SUGGESTION

Start with Watercress Soup (page 22). Serve the pork medallions on a large round platter with a mound of Waterless Cooked Carrots (page 178) in the center. Not only is this an attractive presentation, but it is a delicious combination as well. Finish with an apple Alsatian Fruit Tart (page 216).

VARIATION

PORK CHOPS WITH SAUCE ROBERT

[CÔTES DE PORC SAUCE ROBERT]

Although the medallions make a very elegant presentation, there is no reason why you can't serve the *sauce Robert* with bone-in pork chops. Increase the cooking time by about 3 minutes.

Light Cassoulet

[CASSOULET MAIGRE]

What baked beans are to Boston, cassoulet is to the southwest of France. Toulouse, Carcassonne, and Castelnaudary have competed for generations for the top honors as the city with the best cassoulet. Each town has its own special version of this legendary dish.

All versions of cassoulet contain beans as well as a combination of meats. Although made from scratch in restaurants, it is often seen as a way to use up leftovers in the home. I have made a number of changes that may be noticeable to those familiar with traditional cassoulet recipes.

One reason for changing the recipe is that although I have fond memories of delicious cassoulets in southwestern France, I also remember the nights of restless sleep due to the difficulty I had digesting all the fat. I have omitted the unsmoked bacon or salt pork normally used. I have also omitted the goose or duck fat that usually accompanies the traditional confit (preserved duck or goose). The fresh duck that I use in the recipe can be skinned to remove all fat, if desired. The pork rind also found in many recipes has been omitted because it is not readily available in our markets. Also omitted are the bread crumbs normally added during the last hour of cooking to absorb the excess fat and to form a crust.

Because I have omitted so much fat from the recipe, I have dubbed it *maigre*, meaning "thin." Although the purist may be skeptical of my omissions, I hope that you will consider the ease of preparation, the healthier, lowered fat content, and the wonderful flavors of the finished recipe when passing final judgment on my version.

The preparation of the cassoulet is divided into two procedures. The beans are actually the recipe for White Beans à la Bretonne (page 184), and should be made a day or two in advance. And the cassoulet itself should be made one or two days ahead of time (an ideal dish for entertaining), because it tastes best when reheated. **SERVES 8**

1 duck (4½ to 5 pounds)
2 tablespoons butter or vegetable oil
1½ pounds boned pork shoulder, cut into 1½- to 2-inch cubes
1½ pounds boned lamb shoulder, cut into 1½- to 2-inch cubes
2 pounds Hungarian, Polish, or any good sausage, cut into 2-inch pieces
½ teaspoon salt
¼ teaspoon freshly ground pepper
⅔ cup dry white wine
2 teaspoons Meat Glaze (optional; page 309)
White Beans à la Bretonne (page 184), prepared 1 day or more in advance, at room temperature

1. Remove the legs from the duck and separate into drumsticks and thighs. Remove the breast meat by cutting next to the bone. Cut each breast in half and remove any excess fat.

2. In a large skillet, melt the butter over high heat. Working in batches, add the duck pieces, pork, lamb, and sausage and sauté until browned, about 5 minutes. Season with the salt and pepper and remove the meat from the pan. Pour off the fat.

3. Deglaze the pan by adding the white wine and stirring to loosen the caramelized bits on the bottom and sides of the pan. Reduce the liquid over high heat by half, about 1 minute. Stir in the meat glaze (if using). Stir this liquid into the beans.

4. Preheat the oven to 350°F.

5. In a large casserole, layer the meat and beans. Cover and cook until the meat is tender, about 2 hours. Adjust the heat, if necessary, so that the beans simmer gently. (The recipe can be, and is best if, made ahead of time. Let cool to room temperature, cover, and refrigerate. Reheat in a 350°F oven until the beans and meat are hot and simmering, about 1 hour.)

6. To serve, bring the casserole to the table. Spoon some of the beans and various meats on each plate and top with a piece of duck.

CHICKEN AND PORK IN A POT

[POTÉE MA FAÇON]

A POTÉE is a wonderful and warming, peasant-style dish. Although there are almost as many variations of this regional classic as there are towns in France, a *potée* almost always contains pork, cabbage, potatoes, and—usually—sausage. Then, depending on the region, it might also contain beef, lamb, rabbit, goose, duck, pheasant, or partridge—plus any number of root vegetables and sometimes dried beans.

The main meat in my version of a *potée* is chicken, which in times past would rarely have been squandered on such a humble dish because it was much too expensive. These days, just the reverse is true. The meats that used to be cooked in a *potée* are now far more costly than chicken, so my modern-day *potée* is a departure from the authentic but is in keeping with its spirit.

This dish can easily be made in advance, but shorten the cooking time in step 3 to avoid overcooking the vegetables when the dish is reheated for serving. **SERVES 10**

1 smoked pork shoulder or beef tongue
9 carrots, 1 whole and 8 cut into 2-inch lengths
5 onions, 1 whole and 4 quartered (see Note)
3 cloves
1 head of garlic
4 ribs celery, with leaves if possible
Double Bouquet Garni (page 306)
12 peppercorns
6 quarts water
1 chicken (3½ to 4 pounds), trussed (see "How to Truss a Bird," page 133)
4 white turnips, peeled and quartered
1 cabbage, cored and quartered
4 large Yukon Gold potatoes, peeled and quartered, or 16 small potatoes, peeled
1 kielbasa or other flavorful sausage, about 2 pounds
Assortment of mustards for serving

1. In a large stockpot, combine the pork shoulder (or beef tongue), 1 whole carrot, the whole onion, the cloves, head of garlic, celery, bouquet garni, peppercorns, and water and bring to a boil. Simmer uncovered for 1 hour.

2. Remove the meat and set aside. Strain the broth and discard the solids. Return the broth to the stockpot and add the chicken, pork (or tongue), the cut carrots, quartered onions, turnips, and cabbage. Bring to a boil over high heat. Reduce the heat and simmer, covered, for 15 minutes.

3. Add the potatoes and sausage and simmer until the vegetables are tender, about 30 minutes more. (The recipe can be prepared to this point in advance. Cool to room temperature, cover, and refrigerate. If making ahead, shorten the cooking time in this step by about 15 minutes. The vegetables will finish cooking when you bring this to a boil before serving.)

4. To serve: Serve the broth first, followed by platters of carved meats and vegetables accompanied by an assortment of strong, mild, and sweet mustards.

NOTE: You can replace the 4 quartered onions with 32 pearl onions to be added in step 3. Peel the pearl onions, leaving their root ends trimmed but intact so they will not fall apart.

IN ADDITION

Potée is normally served in large soup plates. The soup or broth is served first, often poured over stale or toasted French bread. The meat and vegetables follow, usually piled high on a single platter, and are eaten on the same soup plates. This is a very informal way of serving, and ideal for friends and family.

CHAPTER THREE

VEGETABLES & OTHER ACCOMPANIMENTS

THERE IS A TRADITION IN classic French cooking, that is still alive today, in which the vegetables served with a main course were an integral part of it. In fact, the name of a dish indicated what those vegetables would be. For example, a dish with Richelieu in its title always contained stuffed tomatoes and mushrooms, braised lettuces, and roast potatoes.

On the home-cooking level this is not necessarily the case. The French do not share the American belief that a main course should be served with a vegetable. The recipes in this section are designed as American-style side dishes, although several are suggested as first courses—which is how the French would treat them.

APPLESAUCE

[COMPOTE DE POMMES]

ALTHOUGH SOME might wonder what applesauce is doing in a section on vegetables, I have included it here because I use it as an accompaniment to pork, veal, ham, goose, duck, and chicken. I serve the applesauce both warm, as the French do, and cold.

Applesauce is traditionally made by quartering unpeeled apples, cooking them with water to cover, and then pushing the cooked apples through a fine-mesh sieve or food mill, leaving the skins and seeds behind. I prefer to peel and core the apples before cooking them, thus also eliminating the need for a food mill or sieve. Instead of cooking the apples in water, I cook them *à l'étuvée,* simply in their own moisture, until they are soft enough to whisk into a smooth sauce.

I still find myself making applesauce with Golden Delicious apples, but I expect this is simply from my many years of using this variety. Actually any apple you like the taste of will make a good applesauce (see what you can find at your local farmers' market). But start by making a batch with Goldens, then try the applesauce using other varieties and see what becomes your favorite.

The quantities given here are merely to give you an idea as to how much applesauce you will get from 3 pounds of apples. Obviously, you can make as much or as little as you like. Be sure you use a saucepan with a heavy bottom and tight-fitting lid.

MAKES ABOUT 3½ CUPS

3 pounds apples, peeled, cored, and cut into chunks
Sugar, to taste

1. Place the apples in a saucepan, cover tightly, and set over very low heat. Within 5 to 10 minutes steam will appear when the lid is lifted. Continue to cook, covered, stirring occasionally, until the apples are soft enough to whisk into a smooth sauce, 15 to 20 minutes.

2. Taste and add a little sugar, if necessary.

EASY WAY TO "QUARTER" AND CORE APPLES

To "quarter" and core apples for any recipe (for example, Alsatian Fruit Tart, page 216), stand the apple on end and cut off two thick slices from either side of the stem. Cut off the remaining two sections from the core. You will be left with a square-cut core and four pieces of apple.

ARTICHOKES BARIGOULE

[ARTICHAUTS BARIGOULE]

CLASSICALLY, artichokes were most often presented in French restaurants as cooked artichoke bottoms (*fonds d'artichaut*), filled with many different ingredients, such as cooked peas, mushrooms, chicken livers, and even poached eggs. They were then topped with sauce Mornay, hollandaise, or béarnaise. The filled and sauced bottoms were usually used as a garnish to accompany a main course.

Because of the time involved, I rarely serve artichoke bottoms. Instead, my favorite way of serving artichokes is to braise them.

The following recipe is an adaptation of a traditional one from the south of France called *artichauts à la Barigoule*, in which the artichokes are stuffed with ground and seasoned pork before braising.

I have omitted the stuffing because I find eating the artichokes together with the diced braising vegetables and ham much more enjoyable. Serve the artichokes in large, flat soup plates surrounded by the diced ham-vegetable mixture and braising liquid. Place a large bowl on the table for everyone to use to discard their leaves. Pluck the leaves, then dip them into the braising liquid before eating. When all the leaves are gone, eat the delectable bottom with the remaining broth, ham, and vegetable combination. **SERVES 4**

4 medium to large artichokes
½ lemon
3 tablespoons extra-virgin olive oil
2 onions, diced
2 carrots, diced
2 ribs celery, diced
¼ pound ham (boiled, baked, or smoked) in one slice (about ¼ inch thick), diced
2 cloves garlic, chopped
1 small bay leaf
½ teaspoon fresh or dried thyme leaves
⅛ teaspoon salt
⅛ teaspoon freshly ground pepper
1 cup dry white wine
2 cups beef stock, homemade or canned (see chart, page 305)

1. Wash the artichokes in cold water. Cut off the stems and top third of the leaves. (A serrated knife works best.) Rub the cut areas with the lemon to prevent discoloration. With scissors, trim the thorns from the uncut leaves.

2. Bring a large pot of water to a boil. Add the artichokes and blanch for 10 to 15 minutes to make the choke easy to remove. With a slotted spoon, lift the artichokes out and place them upside down on a plate to cool. When cool, spread the leaves apart and, using a spoon, remove the small center leaves and choke.

3. In a large Dutch oven, heat the olive oil over medium heat. Add the diced vegetables and ham and sauté until lightly browned, about 6 minutes. Stir in the garlic, herbs, salt, pepper, wine, and stock.

4. Place the artichokes bottom side down on the mixture of vegetables and ham and bring the liquid to a boil. Cover, reduce the heat to low, and simmer until a knife enters the bottom of an artichoke without resistance and the leaves pull off easily, 40 to 50 minutes. (The artichokes can be cooked ahead of time. Allow to cool uncovered, then cover and refrigerate. When ready to serve, heat to a simmer, covered, and serve.)

5. To serve: Place each artichoke in a large soup plate with some of the vegetables and braising liquid surrounding it. Serve hot.

IN ADDITION

For anyone who has never encountered an artichoke, it is helpful to know a bit about its construction. The edible portion of the artichoke is the fleshy bottom to which all the leaves are attached (each leaf, too, has a small tender and edible portion at its base). Also attached to the artichoke bottom, in its center, is a mass of hairlike fibers called the "choke," which must be removed (except in baby artichokes). If eaten, the fibers can get caught in the throat. The choke of a cooked artichoke can be easily scooped out with a spoon, although for some more elegant presentations, the choke should be removed before serving so your guests won't have to worry about it.

SERVING SUGGESTION

To round out a light meal of braised artichokes, just serve a warm baguette, a piece of cheese, and fruit.

ASPARAGUS

[ASPERGES]

THE LUSCIOUS white asparagus of France and Belgium are grown under mounds of earth to prevent them turning green (in much the same way Belgian endive is grown). I can remember in the late '60s tasting this delicately flavored vegetable for the first time and wondering why we didn't grow it in the United States. Ten years later Paris restaurants were proudly offering green asparagus on their menus in March. Heralded in the press as the first asparagus of the year, they were arriving from California by air.

Green asparagus, fresh from the garden or farm, are sweet, tender, and delicious. The season is short, so when you find locally grown asparagus in the spring, eat them as often as possible. Although imported asparagus is now available in most areas year-round, always check the label for the country of origin. Out-of-season fresh asparagus may look good on your plate, but if it has taken a long time to get there, the flavor may be disappointing. **SERVES 8**

3 pounds asparagus, washed

1. Cut or break off any dry ends from the asparagus. If the asparagus are larger than pencil thickness, peel the spears to ensure even cooking. To do this, lay them flat on a cutting board to avoid breakage, and, with a vegetable peeler, peel the entire spear from just below the tip. Tie them in eight bundles (this makes it easier to transfer a serving of asparagus from the cooking pot to the plate). If the asparagus are not to be cooked immediately, hold them in cold water.

2. Bring 5 to 6 quarts of water to a boil in a large saucepan. Add the asparagus and cook until the point of a knife penetrates the spear without resistance, 3 to 7 minutes depending on their freshness. (If you are serving the asparagus cold, refresh them in cold water to stop their cooking and to set their color.)

3. Drain the asparagus on paper towels before placing them on individual plates or a serving platter. If tied, use the string to help lift the asparagus from the water to the towels, and then to the plates where the string should be cut and removed.

IN ADDITION

Asparagus are best when freshly picked from the garden. They are sweet and tender and can be eaten raw. After a few days, however, they lose their natural sweetness, and their outer skin becomes bitter and tough. For this reason I peel all asparagus unless they are pencil thin or come freshly picked from the garden. The cooking time, as for most green vegetables, will depend on their freshness. Taste a piece of the raw asparagus; if it is sweet it will take only a few minutes to cook. If it is bitter, it may take three times as long.

SERVING SUGGESTION

At home I serve asparagus hot as a first course topped with melted butter and a little salt and pepper. On more formal occasions, I serve asparagus with Hollandaise Sauce (page 326) or *à la milanaise* (with melted butter and freshly grated Parmesan cheese). Asparagus can also be served warm or chilled with a Vinaigrette (page 336) and are good with a mayonnaise or Green Mayonnaise (page 334) when accompanying a cold poached fish.

BAKED BEETS

[BETTERAVES AU FOUR]

YOU CAN LIVE in France and never know that beets grow in the ground, or have leafy tops, or require long cooking. French markets sell beets fully cooked, ready to peel and eat. In this country, however, this convenience is not afforded the home cook.

Although most cooks boil beets, causing a good deal of the color and flavor of the vegetable to be lost, I prefer to bake them in the oven. Baking beets enhances both their color and flavor. Once cooked, they can be refrigerated for up to one week and kept for quick use—cold in salads or reheated and served as a hot side dish. **SERVES 6**

6 large beets

1. Preheat the oven to 400°F.

2. Trim beets of all stems, leaves, and roots. Wash and scrub the beets as you would a baking potato.

3. Wrap the beets in aluminum foil. (If they are not wrapped, the beet juice tends to seep and burn in the roasting pan.) Place the beets in a roasting pan and bake until a knife easily pierces the center of each beet, about 45 minutes. Remove from the oven and allow to cool.

4. When ready to use, peel away the outer skin and slice, dice, or julienne. (See Serving Suggestion for how to serve.)

IN ADDITION

In the past ten years or so several new varieties of beets have appeared in many farmers' markets and some supermarkets, including golden beets and pink-and-white-striped Chioggia beets. Their unexpected colors make them very appealing, and they are especially wonderful in a summer salad. As an added bonus, the golden beets do not "bleed" their color onto other ingredients.

SERVING SUGGESTION

The beets can be served sliced and tossed with a Vinaigrette (page 336) as a first-course salad accompanied by a warm baguette. They can also be served in Endive and Beet Salad (page 29). To serve the beets as a hot vegetable, reheat them in a covered saucepan over low heat with a small amount of butter for 5 to 10 minutes. Toss the beets to coat them with the butter and serve. I especially enjoy beets served with roasted or grilled chicken and veal.

BROCCOLI

[BROCOLI]

BROCCOLI is one of the most common American vegetables, but is rarely served in France—although Catherine de Médici brought it from Italy to France hundreds of years ago. Delicate and sweet in flavor when freshly picked, broccoli takes on a strong, disagreeable odor and flavor as it ages. Freshly picked broccoli cooks in only 3 to 4 minutes. After a few days, however, the outer skin of the stalk toughens, increasing the cooking time dramatically. For best results, I always peel broccoli stalks before cooking. It is not difficult and allows the stalk and florets to cook in the same amount of time, avoiding the problem of undercooked stalks and overcooked florets.

Although there are many ways to prepare broccoli, I enjoy it best when simply steamed or boiled and served with melted butter and a sprinkle of salt. **SERVES 4**

1 bunch broccoli
3 tablespoons butter, melted
⅛ teaspoon salt

1. Trim any dried ends from the stalks. Peel the stalks: Look at the cut end and you will see a pale green stalk with a darker green edge. Insert your knife just behind this edge and hold the peel firmly between your thumb and the blade of the knife. Pull the peel down toward the florets. If the broccoli is fresh, it will peel easily from "stem to stern." If the broccoli is not fresh, the peel will break off every inch or two, making the peeling process a little more time consuming, but all the more important.

2. Bring a large pot of water to a boil. Add the broccoli and cook until a knife penetrates the stalk easily, 3 to 7 minutes. Since cooking time is directly related to freshness, when broccoli peels easily you know the cooking time will be short. Conversely, when the peeling is difficult, the broccoli will take longer to cook.

3. Drain the broccoli on paper towels. Serve with melted butter and a sprinkle of salt.

SERVING SUGGESTION

To dress up the presentation, replace the butter with a Hollandaise Sauce (page 326) that has been flavored very lightly with lemon. Broccoli also makes an excellent purée (see page 180).

STEAMING VEGETABLES

There is a certain fallacy in the wisdom of steaming green vegetables, a cooking method that is very much in favor these days. Steaming is really only best for green vegetables that are straight out of the garden, or at least no more than two or three days from being picked. Steaming heightens a fresh vegetable's natural sweet flavors.

However, the delicate sweetness of a fresh vegetable changes soon after it is picked, and within several days is replaced by a stronger, sometimes bitter taste. (This is particularly true of broccoli and spinach.) Steaming will only accentuate this off taste, and therefore I do not recommend its use for older vegetables.

Less fresh vegetables are far better when they are boiled or blanched in large quantities of water. This method yields a more delicately flavored vegetable and is my choice for most of the green vegetables I purchase in supermarkets.

WATERLESS COOKED CARROTS

[CAROTTES À L'ETUVÉE]

OF ALL THE WONDERFUL recipes I have taught over the years, this simple preparation of carrots has received more praise from my students than any other.

The best French method for cooking the vegetable is embodied in the classic recipe *carottes Vichy*. Originally designed as part of a healthful regime for those who went to the spas in Vichy for their rejuvenating waters, the recipe calls for the carrots to be boiled in mineral water until it all evaporates. By adding a tablespoon or two of butter, the carrots become coated once the water is gone. My method of preparing carrots goes one step further, using the carrots' own moisture to cook them gently. When fully cooked, the moisture is gone, leaving the carrots with a sweeter and more intense flavor, as well as with a deeper and more vibrant color. **SERVES 6**

2 pounds carrots, sliced, diced, or julienned
2 tablespoons butter
3 sprigs parsley, chopped

1. Place the carrots and butter in a saucepan over very low heat and cover with a tight-fitting lid. The carrots will slowly steam in their own moisture. Shake the pan from time to time. To check the correct amount of heat, lift the lid after 10 minutes. You should see steam and only barely hear the carrots cooking. If there is no steam, increase the heat. If you hear sizzling or boiling, reduce the heat. As the carrots cook you will notice a combination of water and butter at the bottom of the pan.

2. Cook until the carrots are tender. Depending on their size, they will take 15 to 40 minutes. Remove the lid and increase the heat to allow any remaining moisture to evaporate quickly. There should now be only a little clear butter at the bottom of the pan.

3. Gently toss the carrots to coat with the butter. If you are not ready to serve the carrots, or if you are preparing them in advance, remove the pan from the heat. Reheat before serving over medium-high heat. Sprinkle with the chopped parsley and serve.

IN ADDITION

Over the past couple of decades the style of preparing vegetables has gravitated toward the undercooked, with many cooks going to the extreme of serving them almost raw. I enjoy both raw and cooked vegetables, but rarely have I liked those caught somewhere in between, where they have the virtues of neither. For me a perfectly cooked vegetable is one that you feel on your teeth but do not hear while eating.

VARIATIONS

Madeira-Glazed Carrots

[CAROTTES GLACÉES AU MADÈRE]

Add 2 tablespoons of Madeira when reheating the carrots in step 3. When all the liquid has evaporated and the carrots become glazed with the Madeira, they are ready to serve.

Carrots with Ginger

[CAROTTES AU GINGEMBRE]

Add 1 teaspoon (or more to taste) of chopped or julienned fresh ginger to the carrots while cooking and sprinkle with chopped cilantro instead of parsley.

Carrot Puree

[PURÉE DE CAROTTES]

Simply use a food mill or processor to purée any of the above. Add ¼ cup of milk or heavy cream to thin and smooth out the purée.

CAULIFLOWER PUREE

[PURÉE DE CHOU-FLEUR]

THERE ARE A NUMBER of ways to make French vegetable purées. One classic method mixes a thick béchamel sauce with the puréed vegetable to enrich and smooth its texture (see Creamed Spinach, page 191).

In the method I use most often, I purée the vegetable together with cooked potato or rice for body and smoothness. Most classic purées usually include large quantities of butter or heavy cream. In fact, the purées are stirred over heat to dry them out so they can be moistened with either milk or cream. I omit this step because I prefer the lighter, less rich purée that results.

Use this recipe as a guide for puréeing other vegetables. I use a ratio of potato to vegetable of 1 to 3 or, at most, 1 to 2.

SERVES 6 TO 8

1 to 1½ pounds Yukon Gold potatoes, peeled (2 to 3 large potatoes)
1 head cauliflower (about 3 pounds), cored and separated into florets
¼ to ½ cup milk (optional)
3 tablespoons butter
¾ teaspoon salt
⅛ teaspoon freshly ground pepper

1. Place the potatoes in a large pot and add water to cover by 3 inches. Bring to a boil over high heat and cook until tender, about 30 minutes. Add the cauliflower halfway through the cooking time.

2. Drain the vegetables and purée them together in a food processor. (Using a food processor to purée potatoes alone will make them pasty; puréeing them together with another vegetable works exceptionally well.) The purée should be the consistency of smooth mashed potatoes. If it isn't moist enough, add some milk.

3. Stir in the butter and season with the salt and pepper. Blend well. (The purée can be made a day or two in advance and covered with plastic wrap to prevent it from drying out. Reheat in a water bath [*bain-marie*] or microwave oven.)

IN ADDITION

I have always enjoyed cauliflower, in all the many ways it can be served. Hot, with a butter, cheese, or curry sauce; cold, with mayonnaise or vinaigrette; and raw, as a crudité. On the other hand, my family is, at best, indifferent to it. Over the years, whenever I have suggested cauliflower for dinner, I have always been outvoted; that is, until recently.

One night I made dinner and, without asking, served a purée of cauliflower with broiled chicken and string beans. The purée, which was enough for six, was devoured by four, and I now receive frequent requests for it.

When boiling vegetables for a purée, I find that very little additional liquid is necessary for the purée, and any leftover cooking liquid makes a nice, light soup.

VARIATIONS

In step 1, when you cook the cauliflower, add one or all of the following: 1 onion, diced; 2 garlic cloves, or 2 carrots, thickly sliced.

Turnip Puree

[PURÉE DE NAVETS]

Substitute 1½ pounds of turnips for the cauliflower.

Broccoli Puree

[PURÉE DE BROCOLI]

Substitute 3 pounds of broccoli for the cauliflower.

GLAZED GARLIC

[AIL GLACÉ]

THESE TENDER, glazed garlic cloves are gently boiled in beef or chicken stock. The flavor, though obviously garlic, is much milder than you might expect. They are ideal for serving with roast leg of lamb and are also good served with roast chicken or sautéed rabbit.

The glazed garlic can be prepared in advance and reheated in several additional tablespoons of stock. Make sure you boil the additional stock so that it, too, thickens to glaze the garlic. **SERVES 6**

3 medium to large heads of garlic, split into cloves and peeled
1 cup beef stock or chicken stock, homemade or canned (see chart, page 305)

1. Trim the root ends from the peeled garlic cloves and place the cloves in a small, heavy saucepan. Pour in just enough stock to cover them.

2. Bring the stock to a boil. Reduce the heat to medium and boil gently until all the moisture from the stock evaporates, about 20 minutes. Toss the garlic cloves to glaze them with the reduced stock.

PEELING GARLIC

Each clove in a head of garlic is protected by a tight-fitting skin, which can be difficult to peel. It's easy, however, if the skin is loosened. Place a garlic clove on your work surface. Put gentle, but increasing, downward pressure on the clove until you hear it snap, crack, or pop. The skin will have loosened itself from the garlic and will come away easily. Too much pressure will smash or crack the garlic (or send it flying across the room), which in many cases is fine, but if you want the cloves to retain their shape (as in Glazed Garlic) you must take care not to exert too much pressure.

Many chefs use the side of a knife blade or a cleaver to press garlic, but I find it safer to use either my fingers or a flat wooden spatula.

VARIATION

GLAZED SHALLOTS OR PEARL ONIONS

[ECHALOTES OU PETITS OIGNONS GLACÉS]

Shallots and pearl onions can be glazed in the same way as garlic. Peel them and place them in a pot with just enough stock to cover. Boil as long as needed for the stock to reduce and form a glaze. Both are good when served with steaks, roast beef, grilled or roast chicken, and veal.

GREEN BEANS

[HARICOTS VERTS]

GREEN BEANS or string beans, as they are more commonly known, are the most frequently served green vegetable in France. Although most varieties of green beans today are stringless, this was not always the case. One of the purposes of snapping off the ends of the beans was to remove the tough fibrous strands that ran down the sides of the bean. Although with today's stringless beans a number of chefs have chosen to cut off only the stem end of the bean, I continue to cut or snap off both ends for aesthetic reasons. **SERVES 6 TO 8**

2 pounds green beans, trimmed
3 tablespoons butter
¼ teaspoon salt
⅛ teaspoon freshly ground pepper

1. In a large pot, bring 5 quarts of water to a rapid boil over high heat (see Note). Add the beans and cook until tender, 5 to 7 minutes.

2. Drain the beans and refresh under cold running water to stop the cooking and set the color; drain well. (This can be done several hours in advance.)

3. To serve: Sauté (or reheat) the beans in the butter over medium to medium-high heat, tossing frequently, until they are hot and lightly coated with butter, 2 to 3 minutes. Season with the salt and pepper and serve.

NOTE: If the beans are fresh they will cook quickly and retain their bright green color. If they aren't really fresh, a teaspoon of salt added to the boiling water will help keep them green during the longer cooking time.

IN ADDITION

Serving green beans is easy when they are cooked in advance. Reheating or sautéing them in a little butter will eliminate any excess water and heighten their flavor. Sprinkle with salt and pepper just before serving.

A common belief is that the younger the vegetable, the faster it cooks, yet when picking large and small beans from the same plant, I find they are both tender with the same amount of cooking. Freshness, on the other hand, *does* make a difference. I once took 5 pounds of freshly picked beans and cooked them, a pound at a time, over a period of ten days. Each time I cooked them, it took longer to achieve the same degree of tenderness. The first day they cooked in about 3 minutes, while on the tenth day it took 7 to 8 minutes. I have bought beans in the market that have taken more than 10 minutes of cooking to become tender. When cooked this long, the beans lose their color and invariably have poor flavor.

VARIATIONS

Green Beans with Shallot Butter

[HARICOTS VERTS AUX ECHALOTES]

Gently sauté 2 finely chopped shallots (or ½ onion, finely chopped) in the butter before reheating the beans.

Green Beans Almondine

[HARICOTS VERTS AMANDINE]

Sauté ½ cup sliced or slivered almonds in the butter until lightly brown and toss with beans to reheat.

Green Beans with Garlic Butter

[HARICOTS VERTS À L'AIL]

For a delicate garlic flavor, heat 2 whole cloves of garlic in the butter before reheating the beans. Discard the garlic before serving. For a stronger garlic accent, chop 1 to 2 garlic cloves (to taste). Heat in the butter and toss with the beans before serving.

Herbed Green Beans

[HARICOTS VERTS AUX HERBES]

Sprinkle with 2 tablespoons chopped fresh parsley or 1 tablespoon chopped fresh tarragon, basil, or mint just before serving.

Green Beans with Cream

[HARICOTS VERTS À LA CRÈME]

Use ½ cup heavy cream in place of the butter to reheat the beans. Bring the cream to a boil and reduce slightly before adding the beans.

Green Beans Vinaigrette

[HARICOTS VERTS EN SALADE]

Toss chilled cooked beans in a bowl with a chopped shallot and enough Vinaigrette (page 336) to coat. These beans are excellent served with a tomato salad.

White Beans a la Bretonne

[HARICOTS À LA BRETONNE]

BRITTANY-STYLE white beans are dried white beans that are cooked and mixed with a fresh tomato sauce. They are excellent when served with roast lamb, but more important, they serve as my base for a marvelous cassoulet (Light Cassoulet, page 167).

After cooking the beans, I reduce the cooking liquid, which is usually discarded, to form a sauce. This recipe can be used to cook other dried beans and legumes (such as pinto beans, limas, chickpeas, black beans, and black-eyed peas), which can be served with or without the reduced liquid and/or the tomato sauce. **SERVES 10 TO 12**

2 pounds dried white beans, washed and drained
1 large carrot
1 whole onion, studded with 2 cloves, plus 3 onions, chopped
1 head of garlic, unpeeled, plus 4 cloves garlic, chopped
Double Bouquet Garni (page 306)
5 tablespoons butter (see Note)
2 pounds tomatoes, peeled, seeded, and chopped, or 1 can (28 ounces) canned diced tomatoes, drained
½ teaspoon salt
¼ teaspoon freshly ground pepper
3 sprigs parsley, chopped, for garnish (see Note)

1. Place the beans in a large casserole or saucepan, cover with cold water, and bring to a boil over high heat. Remove from the heat and allow to stand, covered, for 20 to 30 minutes.

2. Drain the beans, discarding the soaking water. Rinse the beans in cold water, drain, and return them to the casserole with the carrot, cloved onion, head of garlic, and one bouquet garni. Add fresh water to cover by 1 inch (2 to 2½ quarts). Bring to a boil over high heat, then reduce the heat to medium-low and simmer, partially covered, until the beans are tender yet still firm, 1 to 1½ hours.

3. Drain the beans, reserving the cooking liquid, and discard the carrot, onion, head of garlic, and bouquet garni. Reduce the liquid over high heat until it thickens and only 1 cup remains. Pour this sauce over the beans and set aside.

4. In a skillet, melt 3 tablespoons of the butter over low heat. Add the chopped onions, cover, and cook slowly until soft, about 6 minutes.

5. Add the tomatoes, chopped garlic, and remaining bouquet garni. Season with the salt and pepper, cover, and simmer gently until the tomatoes soften and a thick sauce forms, about 30 minutes. Discard the bouquet garni.

6. Add the tomato sauce to the cooked beans. (At this point the beans may be stored in the refrigerator for several days or frozen.)

7. Before serving, bring the beans slowly to a boil. Stir in the remaining 2 tablespoons butter and sprinkle with the chopped parsley. Serve hot.

NOTE: If you are making these beans to use in the Light Cassoulet (page 167), omit the final butter and parsley from step 7.

BRAISED LEEKS WITH HOLLANDAISE OR VINAIGRETTE

[POIREAUX HOLLANDAISE OU VINAIGRETTE]

LEEKS, known in France as poor man's asparagus, are generally used in America only by those who can find them. Although they are commonplace in Europe, they are not as well known here, which is a shame because this member of the onion family has a wonderful and delicate flavor.

A leek looks sort of like an enormous scallion. It has long, dark green leaves, a long white body, and white roots. A leek is usually filled with soil and needs careful washing (see "Washing Leeks," page 186). The green leaves are rarely eaten, but are used in some stocks and soups. They are also blanched, to brighten them, and then cut and used in decorating aspic-coated presentations. Many recipes call for the use of "the white part only," and in these cases the green parts can be discarded or saved for a soup.

Leeks are used as ingredients in stocks and soups, but they are also excellent on their own. **SERVES 6**

12 medium leeks (¾- to 1-inch diameter), washed
Hollandaise Sauce (page 326) or Vinaigrette (page 336)

1. Lay the leeks flat in a skillet, add ½ inch of water, bring to a simmer, and cook, covered, until tender, about 10 minutes.

2. To serve: Cut the leeks in half lengthwise and place two leeks (4 halves) on individual plates. Serve warm with hollandaise or at room temperature with vinaigrette.

LEEKS IN CREAM SAUCE

[POIREAUX À LA CRÈME]

IN THE CLASSIC version of this recipe, the white parts of the leeks are first cooked whole in boiling water for 10 to 15 minutes and then boiled in heavy cream for an additional 20 to 30 minutes, producing a very delicate but very rich vegetable dish.

In the following recipe I dice, julienne, or chop the white parts of the leeks and cook them slowly in a little butter until they are tender. I then add just enough cream to bind them.

SERVES 4

4 leeks (white parts only), washed (see below) and diced, chopped, or julienned
1 tablespoon butter
¼ cup heavy cream
Salt and freshly ground pepper

WASHING LEEKS

Leeks must be cleaned well, since dirt collects in their leaves as they grow up through the soil.

1. Cut off the roots and trim away the dried ends of the leaves. Then insert a paring knife, with its sharp edge facing up, through the white of the leek, just below where it starts to turn green. Pull the knife up through the leaves. Give the leek a quarter turn and make a second similar cut.

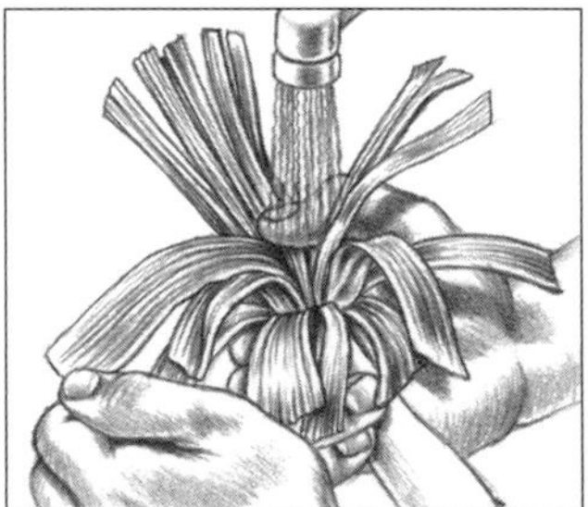

2. Spread the leaves of the leeks and wash thoroughly.

1. Place the leeks and butter in a medium-size saucepan over very low heat, cover with a tight-fitting lid, and slowly steam the leeks in their own moisture. Cook the leeks until tender, 8 to 10 minutes.

2. Remove the lid and increase the heat to allow any moisture to evaporate; the leeks will be coated with the butter.

3. Add the cream and cook, uncovered, boiling if necessary, to thicken slightly. The cream should hold the leeks together. Season to taste with salt and pepper.

SERVING SUGGESTION

I often use leeks prepared this way as a bed on which to place a grilled or sautéed pork or veal chop, or a breast of chicken. The combination is delicious. Serve the combination with buttered noodles or steamed potatoes and a chilled dry white wine.

DUXELLES

DUXELLES is one of the foundations of French cooking. It is used by itself, or mixed with chopped meats and herbs to form stuffings. To chop the mushrooms by hand is time-consuming and tedious, but a food processor will do the work in seconds.

MAKES 1½ CUPS

2 tablespoons butter
5 shallots or 1 onion, finely chopped
1 pound white mushrooms, washed, dried, and finely chopped
¼ teaspoon salt
⅛ teaspoon freshly ground pepper

1. In a large skillet, melt the butter over medium-high heat. Add the shallots or onion and cook until softened but not browned, about 2 minutes.

2. Add the mushrooms, increase the heat to high, and sauté until most of the water has evaporated and the mushrooms begin to brown, about 5 minutes. Season with the salt and pepper and remove from the heat.

SERVING SUGGESTION

Use the duxelles to stuff mushroom caps, or to flavor an omelet or a béchamel. Duxelles can also be used to make a sauce for a simple broiled chicken. When the chicken has finished cooking, remove from the broiling pan and discard the fat, but retain any glaze or browned juices in the pan. Add a couple of tablespoons of duxelles and deglaze the pan with ¼ cup of water or chicken stock. Bring to a boil and spoon the mushroom sauce over the chicken.

MUSHROOMS IN CREAM SAUCE

[CHAMPIGNONS À LA CRÈME]

ONE OF THE MOST satisfying ways to serve mushrooms, *champignons à la crème* makes an excellent first course served simply on a piece of toast, puff pastry, or—more elaborately—in a puff-pastry bouchée (see Puff-Pastry Shells Filled with Seafood in White Wine Sauce, page 76). You may also serve them as an accompaniment to sautéed veal or chicken.

SERVES 6

1 tablespoon butter
1 shallot, finely chopped
1 pound white or cremini mushrooms, washed, dried, and sliced
¼ teaspoon salt
⅛ teaspoon freshly ground pepper
¾ cup heavy cream
1 to 2 teaspoons dry sherry or Madeira, to taste (optional)
Toast, for serving

1. In a medium-size saucepan, melt the butter over medium heat. Add the shallot and sauté for about 2 minutes without browning.

2. Add the mushrooms, sprinkle with the salt and pepper, and cover tightly with a lid. Reduce the heat to medium-low and steam the mushrooms slowly in their own moisture for about 10 minutes.

3. Remove the mushrooms with a skimmer or slotted spoon and set aside. Reduce the cooking liquid over high heat until only 3 tablespoons remain, about 3 minutes.

4. Add the cream and boil, uncovered, until the sauce thickens slightly. Return the mushrooms to the sauce. (The mushrooms can be made in advance up to this point. Cover the surface with plastic wrap and refrigerate.)

5. To serve: First bring to a boil, then taste and adjust the seasoning, if necessary. Add the sherry or Madeira (if using) and spoon over warm toast.

VARIATION

WILD MUSHROOMS IN CREAM SAUCE

[CHAMPIGNONS SAUVAGES À LA CRÈME]

Use any of the many varieties of fresh wild mushrooms you find in the market in place of white mushrooms.

WASHING MUSHROOMS

Washing mushrooms is an important and often debated technique. There are those who say that mushrooms should never be washed, but merely brushed with a mushroom brush, or simply wiped with a damp towel, for if washed they will become waterlogged. Anyone trying these techniques with large quantities of mushrooms will know that they can be extremely time-consuming, and not very efficient at removing all the dirt.

Mushrooms can be quickly and easily washed to remove all traces of dirt or grit without fear of damage. It is most important, however, that the mushrooms be fresh. If the mushrooms are older, especially for those whose gills are showing, washing them will waterlog them.

To wash mushrooms, you'll need a large bowl and colander. First trim away any dried stems and place the mushrooms in a large bowl. Place the bowl under cold running water. As the bowl fills with water, use your hands to agitate the mushrooms. The mushrooms will float on the surface, while the dirt (which is heavier) falls to the bottom. Once the bowl is full, immediately lift the mushrooms out of the water and into the colander. Pour the water out, rinse out the bowl, and repeat the process. After each washing, feel the bottom of the bowl. When no trace of grit can be found at the bottom, the mushrooms are clean.

Two or three washings, taking no more than a total of 2 minutes, are all that is normally required. With this technique, you should be able to wash 1 to 3 pounds of mushrooms very quickly.

If you are sautéing the mushrooms, it is important that they be dry, so once washed, allow them to air dry, or if in a hurry, dry them with paper towels.

MUSHROOMS A LA GRECQUE

[CHAMPIGNONS À LA GRECQUE]

GREEK-STYLE marinated vegetables are served as a first course in France, but can be easily added to a summer buffet. Some chefs prepare the mushrooms with tomatoes; others do not include them. I enjoy them both ways, and use tomatoes in the summer or whenever I find them red, ripe, and full flavored.

Although mushrooms are my favorite, pearl onions are also excellent prepared in a similar fashion (see Variation).

SERVES 4 TO 6

½ cup dry white wine
¼ cup light olive oil
Juice of 1 lemon
3 shallots, finely chopped
1 clove garlic, finely chopped (optional)
2 tomatoes, peeled, seeded, and diced (optional)
Bouquet Garni (page 306)
10 peppercorns, crushed
1 teaspoon salt
Pinch of ground coriander (optional)
1½ pounds small white mushrooms, washed (if using larger mushrooms, quarter them)

1. Place all of the ingredients except the mushrooms in a large, nonreactive saucepan. Bring to a boil, reduce the heat, and simmer for 5 minutes.

2. Add the mushrooms to the simmering liquid and simmer, covered, for 5 to 6 minutes to cook the mushrooms so they release moisture and add flavor. With a slotted spoon, transfer the mushrooms to a serving bowl. Discard the bouquet garni.

3. Over high heat, reduce the liquid to approximately ¾ cup and pour over the mushrooms. Refrigerate and serve chilled.

VARIATION

PEARL ONIONS A LA GRECQUE

[PETITS OIGNONS À LA GRECQUE]

Substitute 1½ pounds of pearl onions, peeled, for the mushrooms. Add ½ cup water to the marinade in step 1. In step 2, cook the onions until tender, about 30 minutes.

CREAMED SPINACH

[PURÉE D'EPINARDS]

IN THIS TYPE of vegetable purée, a béchamel sauce is added for a rich and creamy result. **SERVES 4**

2 packages frozen spinach (10 ounces each), or 2 pounds fresh spinach (large stems removed, well washed), or 1½ pounds baby spinach
Béchamel (page 313)
¼ teaspoon salt
⅛ teaspoon freshly ground pepper
⅛ teaspoon freshly grated nutmeg

1. Prepare the frozen spinach according to the package directions. To cook fresh spinach, bring a 5-quart pot of water to a boil. Add the spinach, pushing it down into the boiling water. It will be tender in under 2 minutes of cooking (even shorter for the baby spinach). Drain into a colander and rinse under cold water to stop the cooking. Squeeze the spinach dry to remove all excess moisture.

2. In a food processor, purée the spinach. Add the béchamel, ½ cup at a time, and process just to mix after each addition.

3. Season with the salt, pepper, and nutmeg. (The purée can be prepared a day or two in advance, covered with plastic wrap to prevent it from drying out, and refrigerated. Reheat in a water bath [*bain-marie*] or microwave oven.)

BROILED TOMATOES WITH GARLIC AND HERBS

[TOMATES À LA PROVENÇALE]

WHEN TOMATOES are in season, the preparation of this recipe will fill your kitchen with the aromas of southern France. **SERVES 6**

3 medium to large tomatoes
3 tablespoons extra-virgin olive oil
2 cloves garlic, finely chopped
1 shallot, finely chopped
¼ teaspoon fresh or dried thyme leaves
5 sprigs parsley, chopped
About ⅓ cup bread crumbs
Pinch each of salt and freshly ground pepper

1. Cut the tomatoes in half crosswise and place cut side up in a roasting or broiling pan.

2. In a small saucepan, heat the olive oil over medium heat. Add the garlic and shallot and gently sauté until softened but not browned, about 2 minutes.

3. Add the thyme and remove from the heat. Stir in the parsley and enough of the bread crumbs to absorb the oil. Season with the salt and pepper.

4. Spread the bread crumb mixture over the tops of the tomatoes. (The tomatoes can be prepared to this point several hours in advance.)

5. Just before serving, preheat the broiler. Broil the tomatoes 3 to 4 inches from the heat until they are heated through and the crumbs are browned, 3 to 4 minutes. If the tomatoes are ripe they will emerge from the broiler hot (but not fully cooked), soft, moist, and flavorful.

IN ADDITION

Most recipes for these tomatoes instruct you to remove the seeds and excess juice and to fill the emptied spaces with the flavored bread crumbs. I find the tomatoes more succulent when the seeds are left intact, and have therefore eliminated this time-consuming step here.

SERVING SUGGESTION

Serve the tomatoes with roasted lamb or chicken, or with grilled lamb, chicken, steak, or fish. When available, sprinkle a little freshly chopped basil on top of the tomatoes as they come from the broiler.

RATATOUILLE

RATATOUILLE NIÇOISE is a traditional dish from the area of southern France known as Provence, specifically the city of Nice, where its few simple ingredients are grown in abundance. There are many recipes for ratatouille and although the shapes of the vegetables and the proportions used may vary, the basic ingredients do not. Onion, green pepper, eggplant, zucchini, and tomato are always used.

There are two methods of preparing ratatouille. In the first, each vegetable is cooked separately and then mixed together for serving. The liquid left over from the cooking is usually discarded.

I prefer a second method in which all the vegetables are cooked slowly in one pot, often for several hours, until they are soft. Their colors darken and blend, creating a rich, earthy hue, while their flavors and liquids blend and thicken to create a savory sauce. This method allows you to do other things as the ratatouille cooks, while the first method requires more time and attention.

There are two aspects to my technique that are important to the ratatouille's texture and richness. The first is the size of the cut-up vegetables—I cut them all into ½- to ¾-inch dice, which makes the ratatouille easier to use as a spread or a filling. Second is the way I enrich the ratatouille by reducing the excess cooking liquids to a rich, syrupy sauce for the vegetables. This simple procedure makes a world of difference. **SERVES 6**

4 tablespoons extra-virgin olive oil
2 onions, halved and diced
2 green bell peppers, stemmed, seeded, and cut into ¾-inch squares
4 cloves garlic, finely chopped
1 eggplant (about 1 pound), peeled and diced
2 zucchini (about 1 pound), peeled and diced
2 pounds tomatoes, peeled, seeded, and diced, or 1 can (28 ounces) diced tomatoes, drained
Bouquet Garni (page 306) with an extra ¼ teaspoon fresh or dried thyme leaves
¼ teaspoon salt
⅛ teaspoon freshly ground pepper
2 teaspoons tomato paste (optional)
4 sprigs parsley, chopped, for garnish

1. In a large saucepan or Dutch oven, heat the olive oil over medium heat. Add the onions and green peppers and cook until softened but not browned, about 4 minutes.

2. Add the garlic and stir several seconds. Add the eggplant and zucchini. Cover and cook gently over medium-low heat for 15 minutes. The vegetables should be partially cooked and there should be some liquid in the bottom of the pan.

3. Add the tomatoes and bouquet garni and season with the salt and pepper. Simmer gently over low heat, uncovered, stirring occasionally, until the vegetables are soft, 35 to 45 minutes.

4. By this time, the liquid in the pan should have reduced to a syrupy sauce. If your liquid is not thick enough, drain the vegetables well in a colander set over a large bowl. Discard the bouquet garni and return the liquid to the pot. Over high heat, reduce the liquid until it attains a saucelike consistency. Taste and add more salt and pepper, if necessary. If the tomatoes used were not red or flavorful enough, add the tomato paste.

5. Place the vegetables in an ovenproof dish and gently stir in the reduced liquid.

6. To serve: Reheat in a 350°F to 400°F oven for 15 to 20 minutes until bubbling. Sprinkle with the chopped parsley just before serving.

SERVING SUGGESTION

Ratatouille is an extremely versatile dish. It can be served hot as a vegetable. It can be served chilled or at room temperature as a first course, and I often serve it on crackers as an hors d'oeuvre. It can be used to fill crêpes and omelets. To serve it au gratin, sprinkle grated Swiss or Parmesan cheese on top and reheat under a broiler.

PEELING AND SEEDING TOMATOES

It is often necessary to peel and/or seed tomatoes for a recipe. Seeding tomatoes removes excess moisture and thereby also reduces the cooking time of some recipes. For example, if you don't seed the tomatoes for Tomato Sauce (page 325), it will take at least 20 minutes longer than the 5 minutes indicated in the recipe to achieve its desired consistency. In other sauces, tomatoes are added just before serving. If not seeded and well drained, the sauce will be too thin.

Tomatoes are always peeled before going into sauces in France, unless the sauce will be strained at the end. Tomatoes are not usually peeled when being cut for salads, but some varieties have thick or tough skins, and in such cases I would recommend peeling them.

PEELING: A vine-ripened tomato peels easily, but most store-bought tomatoes do not. To make peeling easy, bring a large saucepan of water to a boil. Using a paring knife held at an angle, dig around the stem end to remove the hard white core inside each tomato. With a skimmer or slotted spoon, carefully lower 3 or 4 tomatoes at a time into the boiling water. After 8 to 10 seconds, remove the tomatoes to a plate or bowl. Their skin should now be easy to peel; if it is not, return the tomatoes to the water for an additional 4 or 5 seconds. The riper the tomatoes, the less time they need in the hot water.

If you are working on a gas range, and need to peel only 1 or 2 tomatoes, use a fork to turn them over a flame. The heat from the flame will cause the skin to blister and loosen, and it will then peel easily.

SEEDING: To seed a tomato, cut it in half crosswise (through its equator and not its poles). Gently squeeze the tomato over a bowl, and shake out the seeds and excess liquid. Do not worry if a few seeds are left. Whatever you can remove by squeezing and shaking is sufficient.

ZUCCHINI STUFFED WITH MUSHROOMS AND HAM

[COURGETTES FARCIES]

ONE OF MY FAVORITE ways of preparing zucchini is to fill scooped-out halves with a combination of ham, mushrooms, and onions and top with a cheese sauce. The stuffing and sauce can be made in advance and refrigerated. The stuffed zucchini should be assembled the day of serving.

As a first course, one half zucchini is sufficient, and for a lunch or light supper I serve two together with bread, wine, and dessert. **SERVES 4 OR 8**

4 zucchini, 6 to 8 inches long, peeled if necessary (see Note)
¼ pound ham (boiled, baked, or smoked), finely chopped
¼ teaspoon fresh or dried thyme leaves
5 sprigs parsley, chopped
Duxelles (page 187)
Mornay Sauce (page 314)
2 tablespoons milk
Butter, for baking dish
2 ounces Swiss-style cheese, such as Gruyère or Emmentaler, grated (about ⅔ cup)

1. Preheat the oven to 475°F with the rack in the upper third of the oven. Bring 4 quarts of water to a boil in a large pot over high heat.

2. Cut the zucchini in half lengthwise and scoop out the seeds with a teaspoon.

3. Place the zucchini halves in the boiling water and blanch until tender, 3 to 5 minutes, depending on freshness. Drain on paper towels.

4. Stir the ham, thyme, and parsley into the duxelles. If the Mornay sauce was made ahead of time, reheat it. Thin the sauce with the milk and bring to a boil. Whisk well. Stir 5 to 6 tablespoons of the hot sauce into the stuffing.

5. Butter a baking dish or ovenproof platter that will hold all the zucchini. Fill each zucchini half with stuffing and place in the baking dish. Spoon the sauce over the stuffed zucchini and sprinkle with the grated cheese. (The dish can be prepared to this point up to 1 day in advance and refrigerated.)

6. Bake until the sauce is bubbling and the cheese begins to brown, 6 to 8 minutes.

NOTE: Zucchini skin is sweet when it is very fresh, but can turn bitter when it's older. While trimming the stem, I cut off and taste a piece of the skin. If it's bitter, I peel the zucchini. If it's sweet, I just wash it. Peeled zucchini is fragile when cooked, and care should be taken in handling it.

IN ADDITION

There are many possible fillings for a stuffed zucchini. Cooked chicken, lamb, or ground beef can replace the ham in this recipe. Cooked rice or bread crumbs can be added when unexpected guests appear. Or use a fresh Tomato Sauce (page 325) with or in place of the cheese sauce.

SAUTEED POTATOES

[POMMES DE TERRE SAUTÉES]

CLASSICALLY, sautéed potatoes are parboiled before being cooked in butter and browned. The initial cooking softens the starch, allowing the potatoes to brown easily when sautéed. Most European potatoes are of the firm, waxy variety, and remain firm after boiling, making this procedure easy to handle. I simplify this technique and save cleaning an extra pot, by sautéing potatoes as follows. **SERVES 6**

6 large Yukon Gold potatoes
4 tablespoons (½ stick) butter, or more as needed
¼ teaspoon salt
Pinch of freshly ground pepper
3 sprigs parsley, chopped, for garnish

1. Peel the potatoes and cut them into ½-inch dice. Soak in cold water until ready to use.

2. In a 12-inch nonstick skillet, melt the butter. Drain the potatoes and place in the skillet over medium-low heat. Cover the pan and steam the potatoes for 2 to 5 minutes. They should be tender, but not brown.

3. Uncover, turn the heat to medium-high or high, and sauté, shaking the pan frequently, until the potatoes brown, about 10 minutes. If not shaken, the potatoes may stick and not brown evenly. If the pan seems dry, add more butter, 1 tablespoon at a time. (The potatoes can be prepared up to 1 hour in advance and reheated by sautéing over medium-high heat just before serving.) Season with the salt and pepper and sprinkle with the chopped parsley to serve.

STEAMED POTATOES

[POMMES DE TERRE À LA VAPEUR]

PERHAPS THE EASIEST WAY to prepare potatoes is to steam them. In classical French cooking, steamed potatoes are served with all poached fish, as well as being added to many *ragoûts* (stews). I also serve steamed potatoes with grilled, sautéed, and roasted meats, although their traditional partners are sautéed or fried potatoes. **SERVES 6**

18 small Yukon Gold or red-skinned potatoes
3 tablespoons butter, melted (optional; see Notes)
Salt to taste
Chopped parsley

1. Peel the potatoes, if desired (see Notes); otherwise just wash them. Place them in a steamer basket set over boiling water and cover with a lid.

2. Steam until tender, 20 to 30 minutes. Insert a small knife into a potato; if the potato does not cling to the knife, it is done. (If the potatoes are cooked in advance, reheat for several minutes in the steamer before serving.)

3. Transfer the potatoes to a warm bowl. Coat with the melted butter (if using) and sprinkle lightly with the salt and chopped parsley.

NOTES: If steamed potatoes are going to be served as an accompaniment to a dish with a sauce, I generally omit the butter.

In formal settings, potatoes are traditionally served peeled; leaving them unpeeled is more informal and adds some texture.

FRENCH-FRIED POTATOES

[LES POMMES FRITES]

THE FRENCH are famous for their fried potatoes. Most Americans probably know only plain *pommes frites,* which are like skinny American French fries. But the French have a whole range of fried potatoes, each with a different shape, size,

YELLOW POTATOES

One reason for the superior results the French achieve with fried potatoes is the yellow potato. Yellow potatoes are used extensively in Europe, where they are prized for their flavor, creamy texture, and superb cooking qualities. In this country, the most common yellow potato available is the Yukon Gold, but keep your eye out for other varieties, such as Yellow Finn, Saginaw Gold, Donna, Delta Gold, Banana, and Golden Delite.

and name: *chips, julienne, pailles* (straws), *allumettes* (matchsticks), *Pont-Neuf* (thick-cut), *gaufrettes* (waffled), and *soufflées* (puffed).

The general method for deep-frying potatoes below is followed by specific instructions for preparing and cooking the individual varieties of *pommes frites.* **SERVES 4 TO 6**

8 large Yukon Gold potatoes, peeled
2 to 3 quarts light vegetable or peanut oil, for deep-frying
Salt

1. Trim one side of the potato so it rests flat on your cutting board. Keep trimming the sides and turning the potato until four sides are square. Trim the ends. You will now have a classically trimmed potato, ready for slicing. (Don't let those potato scraps go to waste; see Note.)

2. Prepare the potatoes according to the style of French-fried potato you want (see Variations), and soak the potatoes in a bowl of cold water until ready to use.

3. Place the oil in a deep-fryer with a frying basket and heat to the temperature specified for the style of potato you are making (see Variations). Temperatures will range from 320°F to 400°F, depending on the thickness of the prepared potato.

4. Drain the potatoes and dry between several layers of paper towels. Place about two handfuls of potato pieces in the frying basket (any more and the temperature of the oil will drop, increasing the frying time and causing the potatoes to absorb too much oil). Slowly lower the potatoes into the hot oil. If the potatoes are wet, the oil may boil violently. Remove the basket at once. In such cases it may be necessary to lower the basket in steps to avoid excess spattering, which can be dangerous. Shake the basket frequently to prevent the potatoes from sticking.

5. The potatoes are done when they are golden brown and tender. Drain them in the frying basket, then on paper towels. Sprinkle with salt and serve while still hot. Though best served hot from the fryer, they can be kept warm in a 300°F oven for a short time.

NOTE: When trimming potatoes for any of the fried potato recipes (step 1), do what a professional cook would do: Save the potato scraps to use in soups or to make mashed potatoes. Throw the scraps into a bowl of cold water as you work to prevent them from discoloring.

IN ADDITION

When I am asked why potatoes fried in America don't taste like the potatoes fried in France, I reply that both our potatoes and the oil we use to fry them differ. The best flavor is achieved when a combination of animal fats (beef, veal, and pork) is used. Since animal fats are unhealthy, however, we avoid frying with them, sacrificing that true French flavor. The texture of fried potatoes in America also differs from the French because most of ours are made from brown-skinned russets (baking potatoes), while the French use a yellow potato closer in texture to our Yukon Gold potatoes (see "Yellow Potatoes," facing page).

VARIATIONS

Thick-Cut French Fries

[POMMES PONT-NEUF]

These are 3½-inch-long French fries cut ½-inch square that need to be fried at two temperatures. First fry them at 350°F until the potatoes are cooked but not browned, about 7 minutes. A potato pressed between thumb and forefinger should crush. (If you are unaccustomed to handling very hot food, do not attempt this test. Instead, use the back of a spoon to crush the potato on a plate or counter.) This first frying can be done several hours ahead of time. Just before serving, fry the potatoes again at 390°F to 400°F until golden brown, 1 to 2 minutes.

French Fries

[POMMES FRITES]

This term generally refers to potatoes cut into strips ¼ inch square and about 2½ inches long. They can either be fried like the *pommes Pont-Neuf*, requiring only about 5 minutes for the initial frying and about 1 minute to brown at the higher temperature, or they can be fried all at once at 350°F until they color, 7 to 8 minutes.

Puffed Sliced Potatoes

[POMMES SOUFFLÉES]

These little air-filled crunchy pillows take care and time to prepare, but are a guaranteed hit. The potatoes should simply be peeled, not squared. Slice them lengthwise into ⅛- to 3⁄16-inch-thick ovals, taking care to cut them evenly. Cooking in small batches, drop the slices by the handful into 325°F oil. When the

WAFFLED FRENCH FRIES: *Pommes Gaufrettes*

To make *gaufrettes,* you will need a vegetable slicer with a ripple blade. Peel but don't square the potatoes and slice them ⅛ inch thick. Make the first cut with the ripple slicer, then rotate the potato one-quarter turn to make the next cut. Continue to rotate the potatoes one-quarter turn back and forth as they pass across the rippled blade to give them the traditional open basket-weave design that resembles a waffle. Cook as for the Potato Chips on page 200, about 3 minutes.

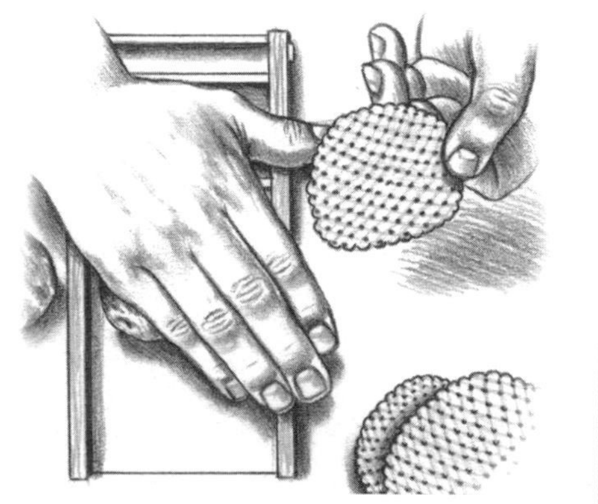

bubbling of the oil ceases, use a frying skimmer to remove the slices and drain on paper towels. At this point, the potatoes should have little or no color. Increase the temperature of the oil to 400°F, add the potatoes, and they should immediately puff and brown. If they have not browned sufficiently, they will collapse on cooling. Should this happen, refry them and some will puff again. Not all slices will puff. These potatoes need to be practiced on your family and friends before attempting to impress guests. Serve the potatoes salted, in a napkin-lined serving dish.

Potato Chips

[POMMES CHIPS]

The potatoes should simply be peeled, not squared, and thinly sliced (a food processor works well), then fried in very hot oil (390°F to 400°F). The chips should be golden brown in about 2 minutes.

Julienned Potatoes

[POMMES JULIENNE]

The potatoes are first thinly sliced and then cut into thin julienne and fried as for potato chips (this page).

Potato Straws and Matchsticks

[POMMES PAILLES ET ALLUMETTES]

Both are cut about ⅛ inch thick; *allumettes* (matchsticks) are 2 inches long and *pailles* (straws) are as long as the potato will allow. Fry at 375°F until golden brown, about 3 minutes.

Gratin Dauphinois

A GRATIN IS A DISH having a crusted or browned surface. Originating in the region of the Alps known as the Dauphiné, this simple and easy potato dish is truly one of France's great gratins and is ideal to serve with roast beef, lamb, and poultry.

Many different versions of this gratin recipe exist. Some are made with cream and cheese, while others are made with milk, eggs, and cheese. I think the best are made just with a combination of milk and cream, which I heat before baking to cut the oven time in half. (If you are not in a rush, you can eliminate this step, but cook the potatoes for 1 hour.) **SERVES 6**

Butter, for baking dish
4 pounds large Yukon Gold potatoes (about 8), peeled and cut into ⅛-inch-thick slices
1 clove garlic, chopped
1 teaspoon salt
⅛ teaspoon freshly ground pepper
1 cup milk
1 cup heavy cream

1. Preheat the oven to 450°F with the oven rack in the middle position. Butter a large (9 x 14 inches) baking dish.

2. Layer the sliced potatoes in the baking dish and sprinkle with the garlic, salt, and pepper.

3. In a small saucepan, combine the milk and cream and bring to a boil over medium heat. Pour over the layered potatoes.

4. Bake the potatoes until their tops are brown and they are tender (a knife will easily penetrate them), 35 to 40 minutes. The potatoes should simmer or gently boil while in the oven. If they begin to boil rapidly, or the top browns before they are tender, reduce the heat by 25 to 50 degrees.

5. Remove the dish from the oven and serve. The potatoes will stay hot for about 30 minutes. (The gratin can be made ahead of time. Let cool to room temperature, cover, and refrigerate. Reheat by bringing back to room temperature and then placing in a 350°F oven for 15 minutes.)

IN ADDITION

Recipes differ in how the potatoes for a *gratin dauphinois* are prepared. Some chefs insist on slicing and soaking the potatoes in cold water to rid them of their surface starch before baking. Others, including myself, believe the starch is necessary for the creamy consistency of the potatoes. However, if you prepare the potatoes ahead of time, they do need to be soaked to prevent them from discoloring. Therefore, for this recipe, if you slice the potatoes in advance, soak them in the milk and cream in which they will be cooked so as not to lose the starch.

VARIATION

Sprinkle 2 ounces grated Swiss-style cheese (about ⅔ cup), such as Gruyère or Emmentaler, over the gratin in step 3.

POTATOES A LA BOULANGERE

[POMMES DE TERRE À LA BOULANGÈRE]

IT WAS THE PRACTICE on Sundays in many towns throughout France to leave a piece of meat with the town *boulangère* (baker) to be roasted. The roast would be dropped off at the baker's shop on the way to church and picked up, fully cooked, on the way home.

The baker would place the meat on racks in his bread ovens and position baking dishes filled with sliced potatoes and onions beneath the roasts to catch their juices while cooking. Sometimes the bakers would roast the meat directly on top of the sliced potatoes and onion. The potatoes were simply moistened with water, but would pick up flavor from the dripping fat and meat juices. Thus, the origin of the name *à la boulangère,* or "in the style of the baker."

I have specified that the onions be sautéed, a step that slightly increases your work but substantially increases the flavor of the finished dish. **SERVES 6**

1 tablespoon butter
2 onions, chopped
4 pounds large Yukon Gold potatoes (about 8), peeled and cut into ⅛-inch-thick slices
1 teaspoon salt
⅛ teaspoon freshly ground pepper
2 cups chicken or beef stock, homemade or canned (see chart, page 305)

1. Preheat the oven to 450°F.

2. In a skillet, melt the butter over medium-high heat. Add the onions and sauté until lightly browned, about 4 minutes.

3. Layer the potatoes and onions in an ovenproof casserole or baking dish and season with the salt and pepper.

4. In a saucepan, bring the stock to a boil and

POTATOES SAVOYARDE: *Pommes de Terre Savoyarde*

You can turn *pommes de terre à la boulangère* into a hearty main dish from the Savoy, high in the French Alps, by combining with 3 ounces of diced ham or cooked bacon and ⅔ cup of grated Swiss-style cheese (about 2 ounces), such as Gruyère or Emmentaler. When served with a green salad and fruit for dessert, these potatoes become a wholesome meal.

pour it over the potatoes and onions. Bake the casserole in the oven until the potatoes are tender, about 45 minutes. Adjust the oven temperature if necessary so that the stock boils gently. (These potatoes are best served hot from the oven, but may be cooked in advance and reheated. When reheating, add 2 tablespoons stock or water.)

POTATO PUFFS

[POMMES DE TERRE DAUPHINE]

MADE FROM mashed potatoes and cream-puff pastry, *pommes de terre dauphine* are potato puffs that are fried just before serving. They are good served with roasted meats like beef, lamb, chicken, and turkey. The batter can be prepared up to a day in advance to make their preparation easier. It is important to dry the mashed potatoes to extract any excess moisture. If the potatoes are too wet, the puffs will be heavy instead of light. For the same reason, make sure any ingredients mixed with the batter (see Variations) are also dry. **SERVES 4 TO 6**

1½ pounds Yukon Gold potatoes, peeled, boiled, and mashed (see Note)
Savory Cream-Puff Pastry (page 221)
½ teaspoon salt
¼ teaspoon freshly ground pepper
2 quarts light vegetable or peanut oil, for deep-frying

1. Dry the mashed potatoes a little by stirring them in a saucepan over medium heat until they begin to lightly coat the pan.

2. Mix the potato and cream-puff pastry together and season with the salt and pepper.

3. In a deep-fryer, bring the oil to 375°F. Drop the mixture by teaspoonfuls into the hot oil and cook until puffed and a rich brown color, 2 to 3 minutes.

4. Drain on paper towels and sprinkle with salt to taste. Serve very hot.

NOTE: Do not use a food processor to mash the potatoes or they will be pasty.

VARIATIONS

In addition to the specific variations below, you can also mix 2 tablespoons chopped fresh herbs, ¼ pound chopped cooked ham or chicken, or ¼ pound grated cheese or combinations of any of the above into the pastry mixture.

Potato Puffs with Spinach

[POMMES DE TERRE ELISABETH]

Add ¼ pound spinach that has been cooked, squeezed dry, and chopped to the potato and pastry mixture.

Truffled Potato Puffs

[POMMES DE TERRE IDÉALES]

Add 1 large julienned truffle to the potato and pastry mixture.

Roasted Potatoes

[POMMES DE TERRE RÔTIES]

TRADITIONAL *pommes de terre rôties* are small potatoes—or large potatoes cut to resemble small ones—that are roasted and served with roast beef, roast lamb, and roast chicken.

Always remember to shake the pan frequently to make sure none of the potatoes stick. Once cooked, remove the potatoes from the hot pan. If you are not ready to serve them, they can be reheated in a hot oven for 5 minutes. **SERVES 6**

6 tablespoons (¾ stick) butter
18 small Yukon Gold potatoes, peeled, or 6 large potatoes, peeled and quartered
¼ teaspoon salt
Pinch of freshly ground pepper

1. Preheat the oven to 475°F.

2. In a roasting pan large enough to hold the potatoes in one layer, melt the butter in the oven or on top of the stove. Add the potatoes, shaking the pan to coat them with butter.

3. Place the pan in the oven. Shake the pan frequently, about every 10 minutes, making sure none of the potatoes stick to the pan. Turn the potatoes if necessary, to brown evenly. Cook until well browned, crisp on the outside, and tender when pierced with a knife, about 45 minutes. Remove the potatoes from the hot butter, sprinkle with the salt and pepper, and serve.

IN ADDITION

Another method of preparing the potatoes is to place them in a large roasting pan surrounding a roast, and, in 45 minutes to 1 hour, the potatoes will be crisp and brown on the outside and soft and tender inside.

GARLIC MASHED POTATOES

[PURÉE DE POMMES DE TERRE À L'AIL]

MASHED POTATOES are always popular, and this version, with its added delicate flavor of garlic, never fails to delight.

A classic French purée of potatoes is first dried by being stirred over heat before it is moistened with milk or cream and enriched with butter. Although delicious, I prefer to save all those calories for dessert. The following recipe uses only the flavorful cooking water to produce a light and healthful purée that can be consumed without guilt. When the flavor of garlic does not complement the rest of your meal, simply omit it.

If preparing the potatoes in advance, cover the surface with plastic wrap or a little milk to prevent them from drying out. Keep warm or reheat in a water bath (*bain-marie*) to prevent the potatoes from scorching on the bottom of the pan. **SERVES 6 TO 8**

8 large Yukon Gold potatoes
8 cloves garlic, peeled
¾ teaspoon salt
Milk (optional)
⅛ teaspoon freshly ground pepper

1. Peel the potatoes and cut them into large chunks. Place them in cold water until you are ready to cook them.

2. To cook, place the potatoes and garlic in a 4-quart pot and barely cover with water (the tips of several potatoes will not be covered). Add ½ teaspoon of the salt and bring to a boil over high heat.

3. Boil, uncovered, over medium-high heat until tender, 20 to 30 minutes. The potato is tender when a point of a knife goes in and out without the potato clinging to it. Drain the potatoes and garlic, reserving the cooking liquid (about ⅔ cup).

4. Purée the potatoes and garlic using a potato masher, food mill, or similar device. Do not use a food processor as it will cause the potatoes to become pasty. Moisten the purée with the reserved cooking liquid until the desired consistency is reached. If more liquid is necessary, use milk. Season with the remaining salt and the pepper.

BOILED WHITE RICE

[RIZ AU BLANC]

THIS IS THE EASIEST METHOD I know of preparing fluffy white rice. It is ideal to serve with any sauce, but is especially suited to white sauces. It is also the best way to cook rice that is destined for a stuffing or a salad. Classically, the rice is first cooked in a large quantity of water, then drained, rinsed, and either towel dried or steam dried in an oven. The rice can be cooked in advance and reheated for serving. I simplify the drying and reheating process by steaming the rice quickly just before serving. Some people prefer their rice firmer than others, and I have indicated a cooking time of 15 to 18 minutes. Start tasting the rice after 15 minutes, and stop the cooking when the rice reaches the texture you prefer. The only equipment needed for steaming is a metal strainer. **SERVES 4**

1½ quarts water
½ teaspoon salt
1 cup long-grain white rice

1. In a medium-size saucepan, bring the water to a boil over high heat. Add the salt and the rice and stir, making sure none sticks to the bottom of the pan. Boil for 15 to 18 minutes. The water needs to boil constantly to keep the rice moving so it does not stick to the pan. Taste the rice to determine when you want to stop the cooking.

2. Drain the rice into a metal strainer and rinse well under warm or cold water to remove the excess starch. Place the strainer over the pan used for cooking the rice and allow to drain.

3. To reheat and serve: Fill the pan with at least 1 inch of water. Place the strainer in the pan and cover with a lid. (The strainer should not touch the water.) Steam the rice for about 5 minutes, or until hot. Blot the bottom of the strainer with several layers of paper towel or a folded kitchen towel to absorb any excess moisture, and then empty the strainer of rice into a hot bowl and serve.

RICE PILAF

[RIZ PILAF]

RICE PILAF is a basic recipe with great versatility. The standard ratio of liquid to rice is 2 to 1. If you prefer your rice softer and moister, add another ½ cup of liquid. If you prefer the rice to be firmer, use ¼ cup less.

Once you know the basic technique, you can create your own variations to complement whatever you are serving. Here are a few suggestions: You can use chicken, beef, fish, or vegetable stock; and you can flavor the stocks with herbs, or spices such as curry or saffron. You can cook a few sliced mushrooms or some diced ham with the rice, or you can chop up dried fruit and nuts and add them to the rice before serving. Don't use all of these suggestions in one recipe, but experiment with combinations. **SERVES 4**

2 tablespoons butter
½ onion, chopped
1 cup long-grain white rice
2 cups water or stock
¼ teaspoon salt
⅛ teaspoon freshly ground pepper

1. In a medium-size saucepan, melt the butter over medium heat. Add the onion and cook several minutes until softened but not browned. Add the rice and stir with a wooden spoon until the rice takes on a milky opaque appearance, 1 to 2 minutes.

2. Add the water or stock, salt, and pepper and bring to a boil. Stir, making sure the rice does not stick to the pan. Reduce the heat, cover tightly, and cook for 18 minutes over very low heat.

3. Remove the pan from the heat. (The rice will remain hot for 20 minutes and can be kept warm in a water bath [*bain-marie*] or 200°F oven.)

4. To serve: Fluff the rice with a fork, adjust the seasoning, if necessary, and transfer to a warm serving bowl.

IN ADDITION

You can also bake the pilaf. In step 1, sauté the onion and rice in the butter in a flameproof casserole or ovenproof saucepan. Add the stock, salt, and pepper, bring to a boil, cover tightly, and bake in a 300°F oven for 18 minutes.

QUICK STOCKS FOR RICE PILAF

When making a rice pilaf, you can make a quick, light stock to use in place of the water. For example, you may have some poultry parts (not the livers) or shrimp shells left over from another recipe that together with some onion and mushroom trimmings and a few sprigs of parsley can be simmered in 2½ cups of water to produce a light, flavorful stock in less than 20 minutes.

Wild Rice with Mushrooms

[RIZ SAUVAGE FORESTIÈRE]

WILD RICE, a purely North American product still harvested to a large degree by Native Americans, is becoming a present-day classic in France. Some of their finest restaurants import it to offer on their menus. I find that its earthy color and flavor, combined with its slightly crunchy texture, make it an ideal companion for duck, squab, and game birds in general.

SERVES 8

8 ounces wild rice, rinsed in cold water
4 tablespoons (½ stick) butter
1 small onion or 3 shallots, chopped
¾ pound cultivated or wild mushrooms, washed, dried, and chopped
4 chicken livers, chopped (optional; see Note)
¼ teaspoon salt
⅛ teaspoon freshly ground pepper
10 sprigs parsley, chopped

1. Place the wild rice in a large saucepan with 5 quarts of water. Bring to a boil and cook until the rice grains open and are tender, 45 minutes to 1 hour. Drain and rinse the rice under cold water. Set aside.

2. In a 12-inch skillet, melt the butter over medium-low heat. Add the onion and cook until softened but not browned, about 3 minutes. Add the mushrooms, turn the heat to high, and cook until lightly browned, about 3 minutes. Add the livers and cook quickly, about 30 seconds. Season with the salt and pepper and add the mixture to the rice. Stir in the parsley; taste and adjust the seasoning, if necessary.

3. Reheat the rice mixture, covered, in a water bath (*bain-marie*) or in a 200°F oven until hot, about 15 minutes, stirring occasionally. Serve.

LADLES

Most people probably don't realize that ladles come in sizes and can be used to measure ingredients. A 1-cup ladle is the most common size, although I also use ½-cup and ¼-cup ladles. The size is often marked (in ounces) on the ladle's handle.

A ladle is particularly useful for transferring a measured amount of hot liquid from one pot to another. Instead of pouring the hot liquid into a measuring cup and then into your pan or work bowl, simply ladle out what you need.

I often use a ladle for making rice pilaf, which is made with two parts water or stock to one part rice. Just measure the rice in the ladle, then scoop up twice as much liquid to pour over the rice.

USING A MICROWAVE OVEN FOR REHEATING

Although many recipes can be reheated in a microwave oven, I was surprised and disappointed to find that when reheating wild rice this way, it had lost its good flavor. For this reason, I do not recommend using the microwave oven to reheat any wild rice recipes. It is, however, especially good for reheating vegetable purées, sauces, *ragoûts,* and dishes with a dense consistency that take longer to reheat, such as the Light Cassoulet (page 167).

NOTE: The liver can be left out, but if you like liver and you are serving squabs, ducks, or game birds, use their livers in the recipe. If you are serving this dish with game birds, in addition to using the liver from the bird in place of the chicken livers, also add ¼ teaspoon thyme to the mushrooms while they are cooking. You can also sprinkle the rice with a tablespoon or two of Madeira when reheating it.

CHAPTER FOUR

PASTRIES & DESSERTS

IN MY VIEW, a meal is never complete without a dessert, be it cake, fruit, ice cream, or pastry. When serving a meal, try to pace the courses so your guests will be satisfied after finishing the entrée, yet will still be looking forward to dessert. Children seem to do this naturally, and in our home, no matter what the main course has been, my girls—even though they are now grown women—always ask, "What's for dessert?"

In the following chapter, I have included most of my favorites, omitting only those that take an excessive amount of time to make. Most of these pastries and desserts can be made either completely or partially in advance, while others need only a quick, final assembly before serving. Since the final course often determines the success of a meal, knowing that you already have a marvelous dessert ready allows you to relax and prepare the rest of the meal with confidence.

PASTRIES

BEFORE THE EARLY '70S, French restaurants offered chocolate mousse, crème caramel, poached fruit, and the like for dessert, but rarely offered pastry. The average restaurant chef in France prepared only those desserts known as entremets. Pastry chefs did their work in pastry shops and large hotels. Today no top restaurant can reach a high standing or maintain it without a superb pastry chef.

The recipes and techniques I have developed can make home cooks comfortable in an area once the sole domain of the pastry chef.

Successful pastry-making requires accuracy in measuring ingredients. Hence, the use of gram measurements in this chapter (see also "The Metric System in Cooking and Pastry Making," page 360).

TART PASTRY

[PÂTE BRISÉE]

FRENCH TART PASTRY is designed to be self-supporting when baked, and is firmer and crunchier than American pie crust—qualities that come in part from a more thorough incorporation of fat and flour in a blending/kneading process called *fraisage* (see illustration, page 214).

Although *pâte brisée* is traditionally made by hand, the food processor method included below makes an excellent tart pastry and takes much of the risk out of the procedure for the novice (inexperienced bakers tend to overwork the pastry, causing it to be tough and to shrink when baked).

Both *pâte brisée,* which is unsweetened, and *pâte sucrée* (a sweetened version, which follows) call for a whole egg (although many recipes for tart pastry call for no egg or the yolk only). The egg white acts as a sealant, preventing liquids baked in the tart from being absorbed or from seeping through the crust. The yolk enriches the pastry and adds color.

MAKES ENOUGH FOR A 10- TO 11-INCH TART

FOOD PROCESSOR METHOD

1⅓ cups (190g) all-purpose flour
8 tablespoons (1 stick; 115g) cold, unsalted butter, cut into 8 pieces
1 egg
⅛ teaspoon salt
1½ tablespoons cold water

HAND METHOD

1⅓ cups (190g) all-purpose flour
8 tablespoons (1 stick; 115g) cold, unsalted butter, cut into ½-inch cubes
1 egg
⅛ teaspoon salt
2 to 3 tablespoons cold water

1. Food processor method: Place all of the ingredients in the bowl of a food processor fitted with a metal blade and process until the mixture blends together to form a mass, about 20 seconds. If it doesn't form a mass after 25 seconds, add another teaspoon of water.

Hand method: Place the flour on a work surface, or in a large bowl, and form a well in the center. Add the butter, egg, salt, and 1 tablespoon of the water to the well and mix with a pastry blender. The pastry should have a coarse, granular texture and be moist enough to begin to stick together. If it is too dry, add up to 2 tablespoons more water, 1 teaspoon at a time.

2. Turn the pastry out onto a lightly floured work surface, dust the pastry lightly with flour, and begin the blending or kneading process (see Note) known as *fraisage:* With the heel of your hand, push the pastry down and away from you a little at a time and repeat this process three or four times or until the pastry is smooth and does not stick to the work surface.

3. Lightly dust the pastry with flour and shape it into a flat round, much like a thick hamburger.

The pastry can be used immediately unless it is too warm and soft, in which case wrap it in plastic wrap and refrigerate for 10 to 20 minutes.

NOTE: The processor does such a good job of blending that most cooks do not see the purpose of kneading at this point. However, if not kneaded the pastry will be too fragile and will break either while you are lining the pan or later after baking.

VARIATION

SWEET TART PASTRY

[PÂTE SUCRÉE]

The techniques for making and handling *pâte sucrée* are identical to those for *pâte brisée.* The only changes are in the ingredients: ¼ cup (50g) sugar is added and the salt is omitted. If you have never made *pâte sucrée,* start by using only 1 tablespoon (15g) of sugar. The more sugar you add (you can use up to 5 tablespoons or 75g), the more fragile the pastry will be.

FRAISAGE

To thoroughly incorporate the fat and flour in tart pastry dough, use the heel of your hand to push the pastry down and away from you a little at a time. Repeat this process three or four times or until the pastry is smooth and does not stick to the work surface.

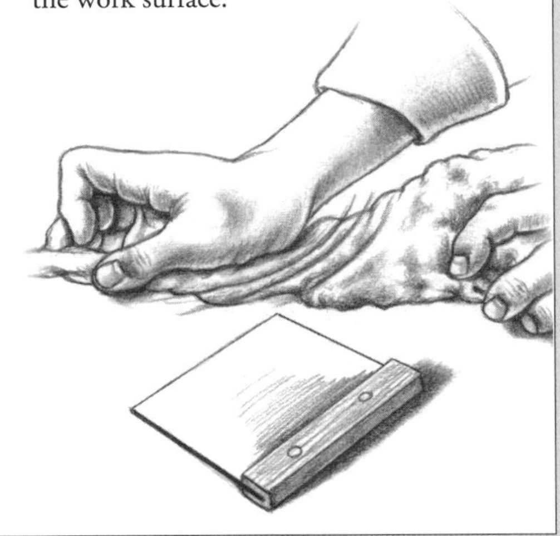

BLUEBERRY TART

[TARTE AUX MYRTILLES]

IN FRANCE, where blueberries in a fresh fruit tart are usually uncooked, I have always missed the wonderful, juicy cooked-berry taste of an American blueberry pie. For the best of both worlds, my *tarte aux myrtilles* consists of cooked blueberries in a traditional French tart pastry, and unlike American blueberry pie, is not too sweet. The natural flavors and sweetness of the fruit are complemented by a currant jelly glaze (*glaçage à la gellée de groseille*).

SERVES 6 TO 8

Butter, for tart pan
Sweet Tart Pastry (facing page)
2 tablespoons (20g) cornstarch
2 pints fresh blueberries
2 to 3 tablespoons (30g to 45g) sugar (optional; see Note)
Currant Jelly Glaze (page 354), hot

1. Preheat the oven to 475°F with the oven rack in the lowest position. Lightly butter a 9½- to 10-inch tart pan with a removable bottom. Line the pan with the tart pastry (see "How to Line a Tart Pan," page 65). Prick the bottom of the pastry several times with the point of a sharp knife to prevent it from puffing during baking. Refrigerate or freeze the shell until you are ready to fill and bake it.

2. Sprinkle the cornstarch over the bottom of the tart shell and fill with the blueberries. At this point the blueberries will mound slightly above the rim of the tart. Sprinkle with the sugar (if using).

3. Bake the tart for 10 minutes. Reduce the temperature to 425°F and continue baking until the berries are gently boiling and the rim of the tart is dark brown, an additional 30 to 35 minutes.

4. Unmold the tart as soon as possible and allow to cool on a wire rack (see "Unmolding a Tart or Quiche," page 218).

5. To serve: When the tart has cooled, dab the hot currant jelly glaze over the surface of the tart with a pastry brush. Slide the tart off the rack and onto a serving platter. (When you cut into the tart, the berry juice should run very slowly. If the juice does not run at all, use a little less cornstarch when next making the tart. Similarly, should the juice be too liquid, use more cornstarch.)

NOTE: If your berries are sour, you may want to sprinkle them with 2 to 3 tablespoons of sugar before baking, although I usually opt for the tartness.

VARIATIONS

Peach and Raspberry Tart

[TARTE AUX PÊCHES ET AUX FRAMBOISES]

In place of the blueberries, use about 2½ pounds of peaches, peeled and cut into large, 1-inch thick slices, and ½ pint raspberries. Starting at the outer edge of the tart, overlap the peach slices in concentric circles and place the raspberries in the center. Sprinkle the fruit with 1 to 2 tablespoons of sugar, depending on the sweetness of the fruit. After it's baked, glaze the peaches with hot Apricot Jelly Glaze (page 354) and the raspberries with hot Currant Jelly Glaze (page 354).

Italian Prune Plum Tart

[TARTE AUX QUETSCHES]

Replace the blueberries with 2½ pounds of washed, pitted, and halved Italian prune plums. Use only 1½ tablespoons of cornstarch. Starting at the outer edge of the tart, overlap the plums, flesh side up, in a clockwise or counter-clockwise direction, covering the entire surface of the tart. Sprinkle the plums with 1 to 2 tablespoons of sugar, depending on the sweetness of the fruit, and bake for a total of 40 minutes. Glaze with hot Currant Jelly Glaze (page 354).

ALSATIAN FRUIT TART

[TARTE ALSACIENNE AUX FRUITS]

ALSACE is an area of France that produces a great variety of fruit. Fruit tarts from this area include a custard made with flour, eggs, and heavy cream—they are sort of a fruit quiche. The custard holds the fruit in place when cut, which makes serving this tart very easy. I have generally found these tarts to be a bit too heavy and rich for my taste, and rather rustic looking. In the recipe that follows, I have lightened the texture of the custard by using powdered almonds in place of some of the flour, egg yolks instead of whole eggs, and milk rather than heavy cream. I also glaze this tart, something usually not done, because I think it both improves the flavor of the tart and enhances its appearance.

You can use any of the fruits grown in Alsace—apples, apricots, cherries, pears, peaches, and plums—and the only thing that will change in the recipe will be the glaze: currant jelly glaze for dark fruits (such as plums and cherries) and apricot glaze for light fruits. I sometimes make this tart with raspberries, and when doing so, I omit the glaze, finding the flavor better. My favorite Alsatian tart is made with fresh sour cherries. If you are fortunate enough to find sour cherries in the market, or if you or a neighbor has a tree in the backyard, I encourage you to make one. Frozen unsweetened sour cherries are almost as good, but the canned are not. **SERVES 6 TO 8**

Butter, for tart pan (see Notes)
Sweet Tart Pastry (page 214)
⅓ cup (50g) whole blanched almonds
¼ cup (50g) sugar
1 tablespoon (10g) all-purpose flour
2 egg yolks
½ cup milk
½ teaspoon pure vanilla extract
1 tablespoon fruit eau-de-vie or brandy (optional; see Notes)
2 pounds fruit (apples, apricots, cherries, pears, peaches, or prune plums)
Apricot or Currant Jelly Glaze (page 354), hot

1. Preheat the oven to 500°F with the oven rack in the lowest position. Lightly butter a 9½- to 10-inch tart pan with a removable bottom. Line the pan with the tart pastry (see "How to Line a Tart Pan," page 65). Prick the bottom of the pastry several times with the point of a sharp knife to prevent it from puffing during baking. Refrigerate or freeze the shell until you are ready to fill and bake it.

2. Using a food processor, grind the almonds and sugar into a fine powder. Add the flour and egg yolks, creating a paste. Add the milk slowly and process until smooth. Flavor this custard mixture with the vanilla and eau-de-vie (if using).

Arranging Apples in an Alsatian Fruit Tart

When cutting apples (or pears or peaches) for a tart, it's important to keep the slices together. Since the slices have a tendency to stick to the knife blade and not stay put, I cut with just the point of the knife, held up at a 45-degree angle, drawing the tip through quickly. This way the fruit doesn't have enough surface to cling to and the slices remain on the cutting board.

1. "Quarter" and core the apples as shown.

2. Cut the two round pieces into thin slices, keeping them together.

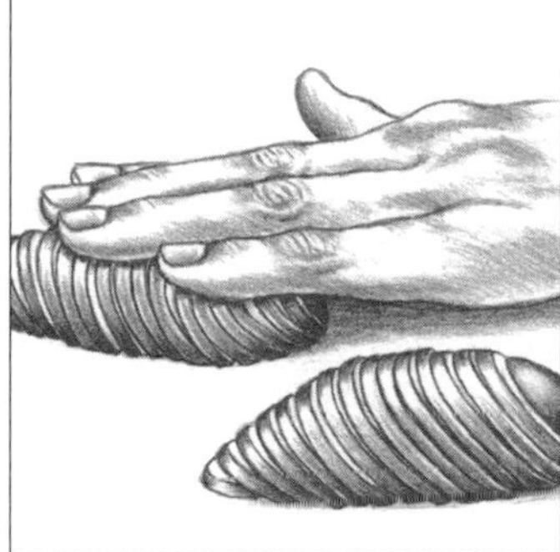

3. Spread out and flatten the apple slices with your hand.

4. Transfer the flattened slices to the tart shell.

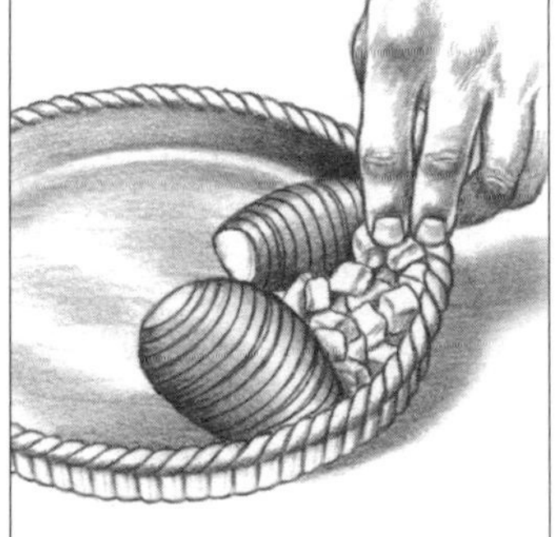

5. Dice the remaining apple pieces and place in between the flattened apple slices.

6. The finished tart.

3. Prepare your chosen fruit: Peel, core, and slice the apples or pears. Pit cherries, and halve and pit apricots, peaches, and prune plums; slice the peaches. Fill the tart shell with the fruit. (For how to arrange apples, pears, or peaches, see "Arranging Apples in an Alsatian Fruit Tart," above.) Cherries are put in whole. Prune plums and apricots are put in cut side down. Pour the custard over the fruit.

4. Bake the tart for 10 minutes. Reduce the heat to 425°F and bake until the crust is golden brown, an additional 20 minutes.

5. Unmold the tart as soon as possible and allow to cool on a wire rack (see "Unmolding a Tart or Quiche," below).

6. To serve: Coat the cooled tart with the hot currant jelly or apricot glaze. Slide the tart from the rack to a serving platter.

NOTES: Use less than ¼ teaspoon butter to give the pan a light varnish. Too much butter causes the pastry to slide down the side of the pan.

If you are making an apricot or peach tart, use Cognac. For an apple tart, use Calvados. For a cherry tart, use kirsch. For a pear tart, use Poire Williams. For a plum tart, use quetsch.

UNMOLDING A TART OR QUICHE

A tart should be unmolded while it is hot so that the pastry dries as it cools. A tart pan with a removable bottom makes unmolding possible. Because of the false bottom, it is important to lift and move the tart pan by holding the outer rim only.

The procedure shown here may seem difficult, and many people prefer not to try it. However, if you choose not to do it, the tart will have a soggy bottom. It may take you two or three tarts to master the technique, but the results are well worth it. Once the tart has cooled, it can slide easily from its rack to a flat tart plate or platter for presentation and serving.

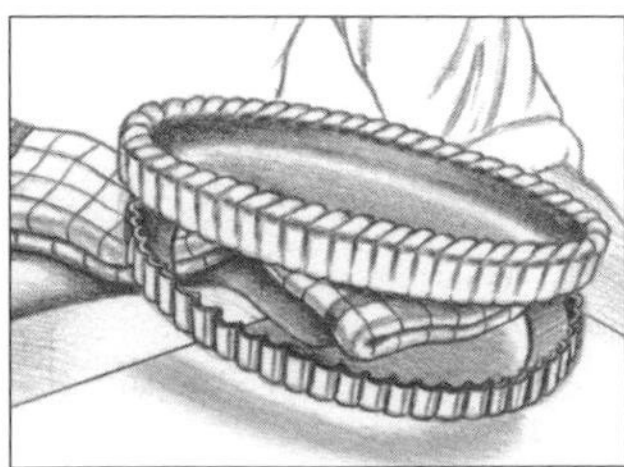

1. When the tart has finished baking, place it on your countertop. Fold a kitchen towel to cover your hand and forearm. Slide the tart pan off the countertop and onto your hand.

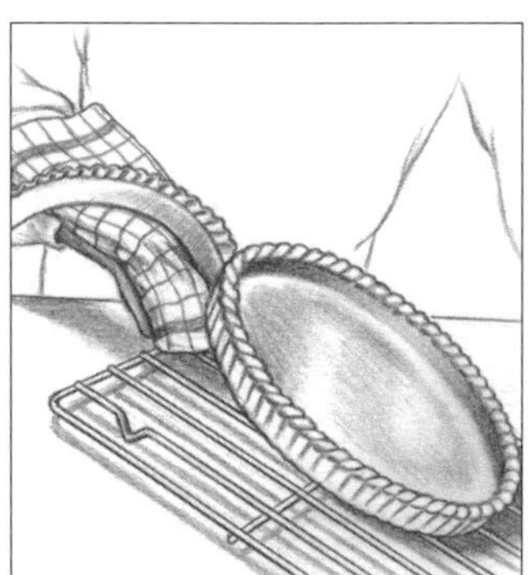

2. The rim will drop away and hang on your wrist. Transfer the tart on its metal bottom to a wire rack. The removal of the metal bottom is a little more difficult but also essential.

3. Slide a long, narrow metal spatula between the metal bottom and the tart. It should slide freely

across the bottom. (If the spatula sticks in the middle, the pastry has not been sufficiently cooked, and you should return the tart, rack and all, to the oven for a few minutes of additional baking.) Holding on to the edge of the metal bottom with one hand, raise it, tilting it 10 to 15 degrees. Again, slide the spatula underneath the pastry and pull the metal bottom away, while supporting the tart with the spatula, as you lower the tart to the rack.

TARTE TATIN

TARTE TATIN, an upside-down caramelized apple tart, was made famous by the Tatin sisters, who served this tart in their hotel restaurant in the early 1900s. It has been a very popular dessert ever since and is my favorite apple dessert.

Every chef has his own way of making this tart. Some bake it totally in the oven, while others cook the apples on top of the stove and finish baking it with its pastry in the oven. I use the second method.

The pastry used in this recipe is normal tart pastry, but if you have puff pastry in your freezer, by all means use it, as do most restaurants in France. A half recipe of *pâte brisée* is exactly the amount of dough needed, and the remainder can be frozen for another use. If, however, you are not sure of your pastry-rolling skills, use the whole recipe and roll out until ⅛ inch thick before using.

I use less butter and sugar than most tarte tatin recipes call for. **SERVES 8**

10 Golden Delicious apples (about 4½ pounds; see Note)
7 tablespoons (100g) butter
½ cup plus 3 tablespoons (150g) sugar
1 tablespoon freshly squeezed lemon juice or water
½ recipe Tart Pastry (page 213) or ½ pound Rough Puff Pastry (page 230)
Whipped cream or crème fraîche (optional)

1. Preheat the oven to 425°F with the oven rack in the upper third.

2. Peel, halve, and core the apples. With the cut side down, trim off a small slice from one side of each apple half so it can stand on its side.

3. In a 10-inch ovenproof skillet, melt the butter over medium heat. Add the sugar and lemon juice (if the apples are sour, use water instead) and mix well. (The sugar will not be completely dissolved at this point.)

4. Starting at the outside of the pan, stand the apple halves on their sides, one next to the other, filling the skillet tightly. Once the outer circle is complete, place two halves together in the center and then continue placing the apples around until all are tightly packed. There may be one or two large holes that should be filled by cutting a piece of apple to fit. At this point, the apples should stand a little above the rim of the skillet (after a few minutes of cooking, the apples will begin to soften and you may be able to wedge additional pieces into the pan).

5. Continue cooking over medium to medium-high heat for 25 to 30 minutes. The juice from the apples will first dissolve the sugar, then evaporate, and the sugar will slowly cook to the caramel stage. When the sugar bubbling around the apples is pale brown in color, place the skillet in the oven for 5 minutes. The apples will settle in the skillet.

6. Remove the skillet from the oven and increase the heat to 475°F.

7. Roll out the pastry as you would for a tart, keeping it round. When it is large enough to fully cover the top of the skillet, about 12 inches in diameter, roll it up onto your rolling pin and unroll it over the top of the apples. The pastry will drape down the sides of the skillet. Run a paring knife around the edge, trimming off the excess pastry.

Preparing Apples for a Tarte Tatin

Peel, halve, and core the apples. With the cut side down, trim off a small slice from each apple half so they will stand on their sides.

There is a special pan sold in France, and imported by a few companies in the United States, called a tarte tatin mold. Made of copper with relatively high, gently sloping sides and no handle, it is very expensive. I use a heavy aluminum or cast-iron skillet with a handle that can withstand high temperatures.

While cooking the apples on the stove, the sugary juice tends to bubble over the side of the pan, so if you have a choice of pans, choose the one with the highest sides.

8. Place the skillet in the oven and bake until the pastry is lightly browned, 15 to 20 minutes.

9. Remove the tart from the oven and run your knife around the inside edge of the skillet to make sure that the apples and pastry are not stuck to it. Holding a round *heat-resistant platter* (never crystal) inverted over the pastry with one hand, and the handle of the skillet (wrapped in a pot holder) with the other, turn the skillet upside down and place the platter on the counter. Slowly lift off the skillet, unmolding the tart. The apples will have some spaces between them. Run a long metal spatula around the outside of the apples several times, drawing them toward the center. A border of pastry will be revealed as the apples are compressed. Use the spatula to smooth the top of the tart.

10. A tarte tatin is best when served warm and can be reheated if necessary. Serve with whipped cream or crème fraîche, if desired.

NOTE: Depending on the size of the skillet and the apples, you may need as many as two more or fewer apples than called for in this recipe.

VARIATION

Pear Tarte Tatin

[TARTE TATIN AUX POIRES]

Use an equal weight of Bosc pears, peeled and halved, in place of the apples.

SWEET CREAM-PUFF PASTRY

[PÂTE À CHOUX SUCRÉE]

CREAM-PUFF pastry is the most versatile of French pastry doughs. It can be baked in a multitude of forms, from profiteroles (miniature cream puffs) or éclairs to elaborate dessert creations, such as Paris-Brest (page 228).

I have used the terms sweet (*sucrée*) and salted (*salée*) to differentiate between the dessert version and the savory version (see Variation) of this dough. Although the French would certainly add sugar to a cream-puff dough used to make a dessert and salt to a dough used for a savory dish, they would call both doughs simply *pâte à choux.* **MAKES 20 TO 25 PROFITEROLES OR A PARIS-BREST**

½ cup water
4 tablespoons (½ stick; 55g) unsalted butter
2 tablespoons (25g) sugar
¼ teaspoon pure vanilla extract
½ cup (70g) all-purpose flour
2 large eggs

1. In a medium-size saucepan, bring the water, butter, sugar, and vanilla to a boil over medium-high heat, stirring occasionally. Remove from the heat.

2. Sift the flour into the liquid and stir with a wooden spoon. The pastry should resemble mashed potatoes at this point. Return to the heat and continue stirring for about 20 seconds. The pastry will dry slightly, forming a smooth mass when shaken in the pan. Remove it from the heat.

3. Add the eggs, one at a time, stirring well after each addition. The pastry should cling to the sides of the pan and to the wooden spatula once all the eggs have been added. Lift your spatula and check the pastry. It should hang down 2 to 3 inches from the spatula. If the pastry clings to the spatula but does not hang, it is still a little stiff and requires a bit more egg. If the pastry runs down from the spatula, you have added too much egg, and although you could add more flour to stiffen the pastry at this point, the texture of your finished pastry would not be as good as it will be if you start again.

4. At this point the pastry is ready to be formed. Once the pastry is formed it can be refrigerated or frozen on the baking sheet until ready to bake. However, as most home cooks do not have enough freezer space for this, you might opt for baking and then freezing for future use.

VARIATION

SAVORY CREAM-PUFF PASTRY

[PÂTE À CHOUX SALÉE]

Substitute ¼ teaspoon salt and ⅛ teaspoon freshly ground pepper for the sugar and vanilla.

USING A PASTRY BAG

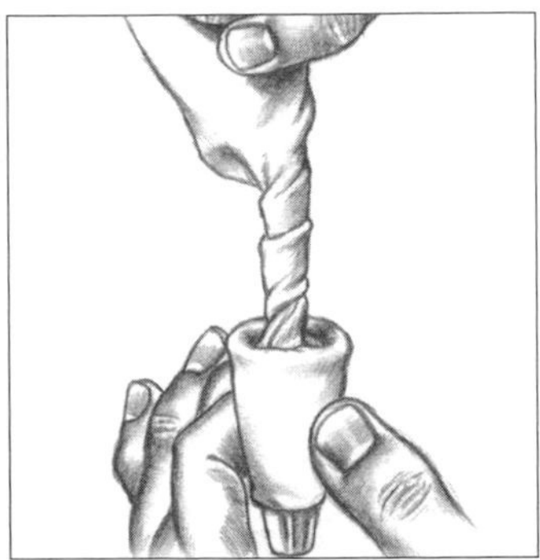

1. Place the tube inside the bag and push or shake it down so its tip pokes out of the small opening at the bottom of the bag. (If the opening is too small, cut off a piece of the bag.) To keep your batter or icing from leaking out while you fill the bag, simply twist the bag right above the tube and push the twisted portion inside the tube.

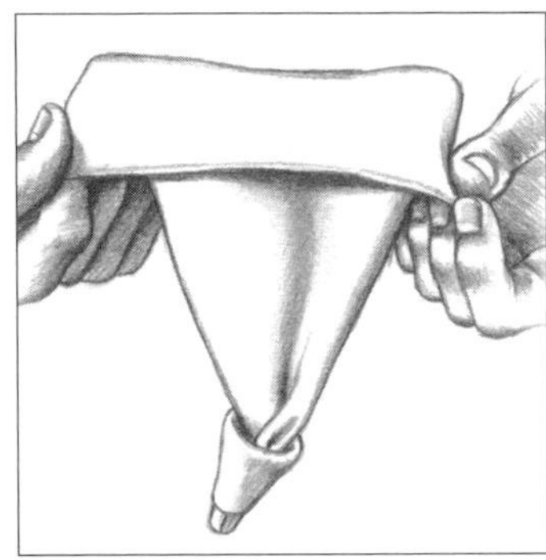

2. Fold the top of the bag down to form a 3- to 4-inch cuff.

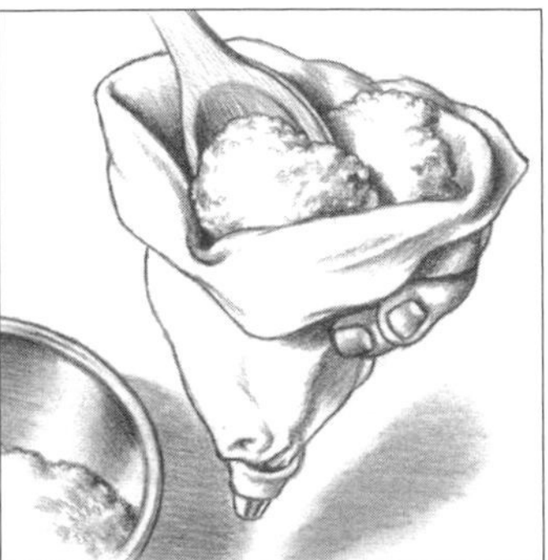

3. Slip one hand underneath the cuff while you fill the bag.

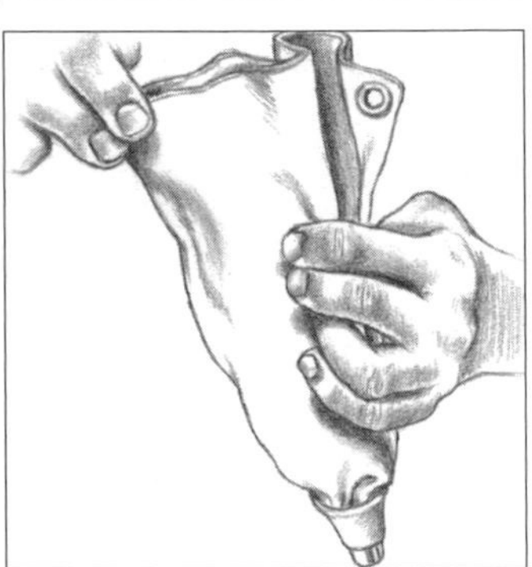

4. After the bag is filled, unfold the cuff and make an accordion pleat.

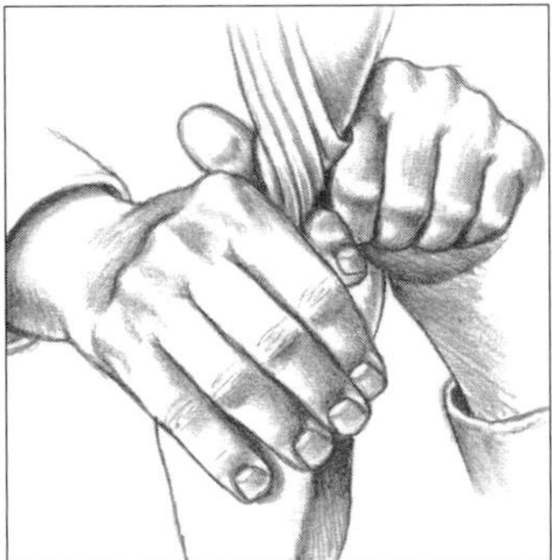

5. Twist the pleated area, forcing the filling down in the bag. Tightly grasp the twisted portion of the bag directly above the filling with your thumb and forefinger.

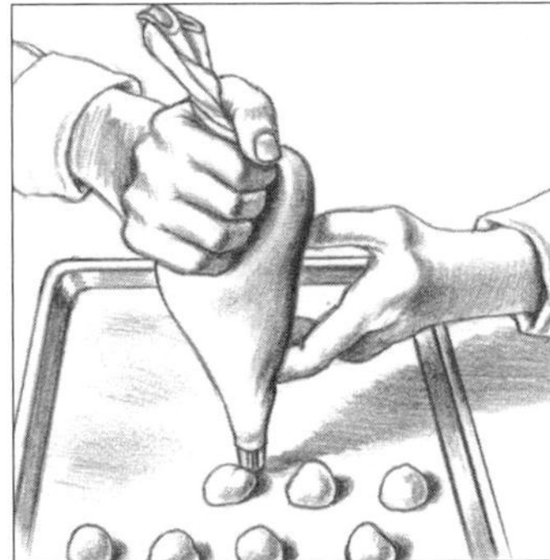

6. Use your other fingers of that hand to squeeze the mixture out. Use your second hand to guide the tip of the tube. When you no longer can comfortably squeeze the bag, stop and twist the bag again, grasping it lower. Continue squeezing with the same hand.

RUM-FLAVORED BANANA FRITTERS

[BEIGNETS SOUFFLÉS AUX BANANES]

ORDINARILY, a *beignet de banane* would be a piece of banana dipped in batter and fried. For a lighter version, I make *beignets soufflés* (luscious fritters made from cream-puff pastry and diced banana and served with a hot apricot sauce). Rum adds a Caribbean touch and complements the banana flavor. **SERVES 6**

1 cup apricot jam
3 tablespoons dark rum
2 tablespoons water
1 banana, diced
1 teaspoon (5g) granulated sugar
½ recipe Sweet Cream-Puff Pastry (page 221)
2 to 2½ quarts vegetable oil, for deep-frying
Confectioners' sugar, for dusting

1. In a small saucepan, bring the apricot jam, 2 tablespoons of the rum, and the water to a boil over medium-high heat. Strain and keep warm.

2. Place the banana in a bowl, sprinkle with the granulated sugar and the remaining rum, and set aside while you make the cream-puff pastry.

3. In a deep-fryer, heat the oil to 365°F.

4. Gently stir the banana-rum mixture into the cream-puff pastry. Drop the batter by tablespoonfuls into the hot oil. The fritters will puff and turn themselves over several times. They are done when they have turned a deep brown color and stopped turning over, about 5 minutes.

5. To serve: Drain the fritters on paper towels. Place them on a plate or in individual serving bowls. Sprinkle with confectioners' sugar and serve with the hot apricot sauce.

CHOCOLATE-DIPPED PROFITEROLES

[PROFITEROLES AU CHOCOLAT]

PROFITEROLES are small dessert cream puffs. They are classically filled with vanilla pastry cream and stacked in a pyramid-shaped mound. A chocolate sauce is poured over the pyramid, making an attractive display.

The presentation I use is simpler and easier to serve. Instead of making a pyramid and then covering it with sauce, I dip each profiterole into a thick chocolate sauce and arrange them on a round platter so that each can be picked up easily.

The profiteroles can be filled 4 to 6 hours in advance and allowed to stand at room temperature. (If you have any left over at the end of the meal, be sure to refrigerate them.) **SERVES 8**

Butter and all-purpose flour, for baking sheet (optional)
Sweet Cream-Puff Pastry (page 221)
1 egg, lightly beaten with a pinch of salt
Pastry Cream, at room temperature (page 347; see Note)
Chocolate Sauce (page 344), made with ¼ cup water, cooled to room temperature

1. Preheat the oven to 475°F with the oven rack in the middle position. Use a nonstick baking sheet or prepare a regular baking sheet by coating it with butter and flour or lining it with a silicone liner or parchment paper.

ICE CREAM–FILLED PROFITEROLES: *Profiteroles à la Glace*

Restaurants often serve profiteroles filled with ice cream and topped with a hot chocolate sauce. I am not a fan of ice-cold cream-puff pastry, but it is certainly an easy presentation. Let the ice cream get semisoft (or use still-soft homemade ice cream straight from the ice-cream machine) and use a pastry bag to fill the cream puffs. Place the filled puffs in the freezer until ready to serve.

EGG SIZES

USDA Grade A Large eggs weigh 60 to 65 grams, or about 2 ounces each. Although egg size is supposed to be the same throughout the country, I have bought boxes of "Large" eggs containing eggs weighing as little as 50 grams and as much as 75 grams. I recall this happening to me while teaching in Charlotte, North Carolina. I was making cream-puff pastry on two consecutive days, and noticed that on the second day my raw pastry was considerably softer than on the first. I asked my assistant to show me the cartons from the eggs, thinking that she might have accidentally purchased Extra Large, but on examining the cartons, I found that the eggs used on the first day had come from a farm in North Carolina, while on the second day we had used eggs from South Carolina. This is not to say that all South Carolina eggs are larger than those produced in North Carolina, but it is possible for you to buy larger or smaller eggs than you intended.

2. Fill a pastry bag fitted with a ½-inch (#6) plain tube with the cream-puff pastry. Form small cream puffs the size of a quarter, about 1 inch in diameter. (You can also form them with a spoon, although they will be rougher looking.) Lightly brush the cream puffs with the beaten egg.

3. Place the baking sheet in the oven for 5 minutes. Lower the heat to 400°F and bake until the cream puffs are evenly colored and firm to the touch, about 25 minutes. No moisture should be heard escaping from the pastry when the oven door is opened.

4. Remove the cream puffs from the oven and place on a wire rack. While they are still warm, make a small hole in their bottoms or sides with either the point of the pastry tube or a knife.

5. Place the pastry cream into a pastry bag fitted with a 3⁄16-inch (#1) plain tube and fill the cream puffs.

6. To serve: Dip the filled cream puffs into the cooled chocolate sauce to coat the tops and place on a doilied platter.

NOTE: For an easier version, substitute whipped cream for the pastry cream.

VARIATION

CHOCOLATE-DIPPED PROFITEROLES WITH GRAND MARNIER

[PROFITEROLES AU CHOCOLAT GRAND MARNIER]

Add 2 tablespoons (or more to taste) Grand Marnier to the chocolate sauce and/or pastry cream.

CREAM PUFFS FILLED WITH CHOCOLATE SOUFFLE

[CHOUX SOUFFLÉS AU CHOCOLAT]

YOU CAN USE a cream puff as a container in which to bake any soufflé. In this recipe, I use my basic chocolate mousse recipe and treat it like a soufflé (which is also how I make my Chocolate Soufflé with Grand Marnier on page 266). Once the cream puffs are filled with the mousse mixture, they can be frozen and baked several days later. Since the puffs are small, they do not need to be thawed first. The filled *choux soufflés* can be eaten hot or cold—unbaked with a mousse filling or baked with a hot soufflé filling. **SERVES 8**

Butter and all-purpose flour, for baking sheet (optional)
Sweet Cream-Puff Pastry (page 221)
1 egg, lightly beaten with a pinch of salt
½ cup (50g) sliced almonds
Chocolate Mousse (page 275)
Confectioners' sugar
Crème Anglaise (page 346)

1. Preheat the oven to 475°F with the oven rack in the middle position. Use a nonstick baking sheet or prepare a regular baking sheet by coating it with butter and flour or lining it with a silicone liner or parchment paper.

2. Fill a pastry bag fitted with a ½-inch (#6) plain tube with the cream-puff pastry. Form cream puffs 1½ inches in diameter on the baking sheet. (You can use a spoon, but the cream puffs will be rougher looking.) Brush lightly with the beaten egg and sprinkle with the sliced almonds.

3. Place the baking sheet in the oven for 5 minutes. Lower the temperature to 400°F and bake until the cream puffs have colored evenly and are firm to the touch, 25 minutes. No moisture should be heard escaping from the pastry when the oven door is opened.

4. Cool the cream puffs on a wire rack. When cool, use a serrated knife to cut off the tops one-third of the way down. Set the tops aside.

FRENCH WOODEN SPATULA

A French wooden spatula is basically a flat wooden spoon. It has a rounded but flat blade and a flat handle. (American wooden spatulas are square-bladed.) It is ideal for mixing and stirring batters, as well as for general kitchen use. Anytime I call for a wooden spoon in my recipes, I use my French wooden spatula instead.

5. Increase the oven temperature to 475°F.

6. Use a spoon or a pastry bag fitted with a ½-inch (#6) plain tip to fill the puffs with the chocolate mousse. Replace the tops of the cream puffs. (The cream puffs can be made ahead to this point and frozen. Bake without defrosting.)

7. Bake the cream puffs until the soufflé begins to rise, lifting the cream-puff tops by about ¼ inch, 3 to 4 minutes. Sprinkle with confectioners' sugar and serve each cream puff on a plate surrounded by crème anglaise, or pass the sauce separately.

IN ADDITION

Any problems that people have making cream-puff pastry are due to inaccurate measurements, so a scale is very helpful. Also, if there is not enough egg, the pastry will not puff; if too much is added, it may be too runny to bake or may puff with a concave rather than a flat bottom. It is important to measure carefully and to have the correct-size eggs.

CREAM PUFFS: Variations on the Theme

The various desserts that use cream-puff pastry are many, and as with much of French cooking, each variation has its own prescribed size, shape, and name.

PROFITEROLES: The smallest member of the cream-puff family is the profiterole. They are small and round, usually about 1 to 1½ inches in diameter, and filled with a vanilla pastry cream, ice cream, or whipped cream. They are most often served with a chocolate sauce.

CHOUX GRILLES: These are the same size as profiteroles, or larger, and are coated with chopped almonds before baking. They are filled with coffee pastry cream and dusted with confectioners' sugar before serving.

CROQUEMBOUCHE: This spectacular dessert is made from profiteroles that have been stuck together with hot caramel to form a hollow pyramid (constructed around a special cone-shaped mold). The pyramid is self-supporting and will not collapse if a puff is plucked from the center.

SALAMBOS: Salambôs are oval cream puffs, traditionally filled with a kirsch-flavored pastry cream. The filled cream puffs are dipped into hot caramel and then into chopped pistachios.

ECLAIRS: An éclair is a 4½- to 5-inch-long cream puff filled with either vanilla-, coffee-, or chocolate-flavored pastry cream and coated with a chocolate or coffee sugar icing. I coat them with the same sauce I use on profiteroles.

CAROLINES: Carolines are shaped like small éclairs and are about 2 inches long. They are traditionally filled with either vanilla- or coffee-flavored pastry cream and then coated with chocolate or coffee sugar icing.

PARIS-BREST

THIS BEAUTIFUL and delicious cream-puff pastry dessert is one of my favorites. It is a marvelous example of a masterpiece that is created from ordinary ingredients (though it is not a dessert for beginners).

The Paris-Brest is made by baking cream-puff pastry in the form of a crown or wheel. The top of the crown is removed and the pastry is filled and decorated with a praline-flavored *crème St.-Honoré* (also called *crème Chiboust*).

To make the cream filling rise above the edges of the ring, without having to mound the ring with an excessive quantity of filling, here's a little trick I learned as a student in Paris: Bake a few extra cream puffs at the same time as the ring. Cut the puffs into quarters and place them in the ring after filling halfway with the cream filling. Then pipe the filling over the supporting pieces to create a lovely dessert. **SERVES 6 TO 8**

Butter and all-purpose flour, for baking sheet (optional)
Sweet Cream-Puff Pastry (page 221)
1 egg, beaten with a pinch of salt
¼ cup (25g) sliced almonds
4 egg whites
⅛ teaspoon cream of tartar
Praline Pastry Cream (page 348)
Confectioners' sugar, for dusting

1. Preheat the oven to 475°F with the rack in the middle position. Coat a nonstick or regular baking sheet with butter and flour, or line it with parchment paper.

2. Fill a pastry bag fitted with an 11/16-inch (#9) plain tube with the cream-puff pastry. Use a pot lid 6 inches in diameter to draw the outline of a circle on the baking sheet with a pencil or toothpick. Squeeze 5 or 6 small cream puffs onto the baking sheet. Squeeze a ring of pastry about 1 inch wide just inside the circle you drew on the baking sheet (figure 1, facing page). Brush the ring lightly with the beaten egg and cover with the sliced almonds.

3. Place the pastry in the oven for 5 minutes. Reduce the heat to 400°F and bake until medium brown all over, another 25 to 30 minutes. Allow the pastry to cool on a wire rack. Using a serrated knife, cut off the top one-third of the pastry and reserve. Cut the cream puffs into quarters.

4. In a bowl, beat the egg whites with the cream of tartar until stiff peaks form. (If you've made the pastry cream ahead of time, reheat gently at this point.) Pour the hot pastry cream into the egg whites and fold rapidly until smooth to produce a firm yet light, soufflé-like mixture. The filling should be firm enough to support a spatula in an upright position.

5. To assemble: Spoon half of the pastry cream mixture into the bottom of the pastry ring and top with the cream-puff pieces so their rounded ends stand up to give added height. Fill a pastry bag fitted with a ¼-inch (#2) or 5⁄16-inch (#3) star tube with the remaining pastry cream and decorate by squeezing ribbons of cream back and forth over the top, forming loops that hang over the sides of the pastry (figure 2, below).

6. To serve: Replace the top of the pastry ring gently and sprinkle with confectioners' sugar (figure 3, below). Using two long metal spatulas, gently lift the dessert onto a serving platter lined with a doily. When serving, hold the top ring in place as you cut through it with a serrated knife.

IN ADDITION

If you are eager to try this dessert, but are unsure of your ability, I suggest that you make the pastry in the form of cream puffs or éclairs. With their tops cut off and filled with the praline-flavored *crème St.-Honoré,* they will taste the same as the Paris-Brest but will be easier to make and can even be made without pastry bags and tubes.

MAKING A PARIS-BREST

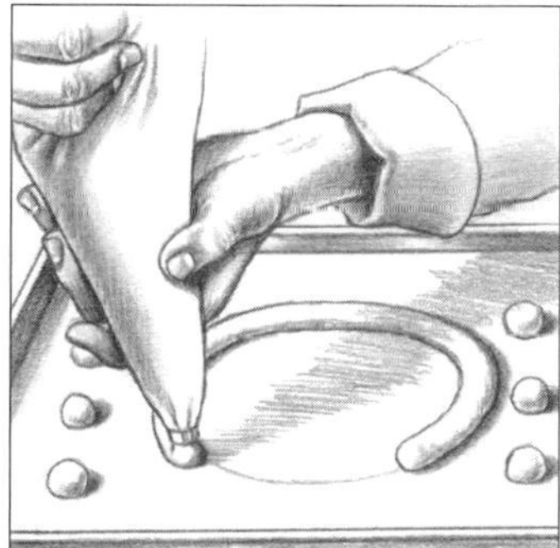

1. Squeeze five or six small cream puffs onto the baking sheet. Then squeeze a ring of pastry onto the baking sheet and bake.

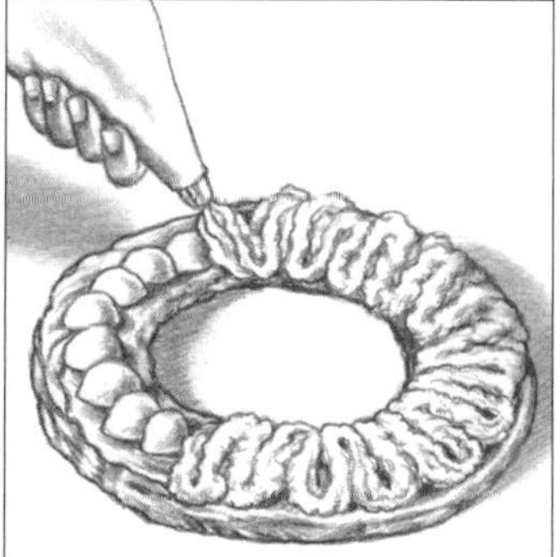

2. Pipe the remaining cream over the cream-puff pieces in the partially assembled Paris-Brest to form ribbons that overlap the edge of the pastry.

3. Dust the assembled pastry with confectioners' sugar.

ROUGH PUFF PASTRY

[PÂTE DEMI-FEUILLETÉE]

PUFF PASTRY is often thought of as the most difficult of French pastry doughs. And, in fact, it is a long, drawn-out procedure that involves rolling and rerolling a flour and water dough with a block of butter to produce the more than one thousand individual layers of dough and butter that, when baked, rise to produce flaky layers of pastry.

In between all the rolling, the dough must rest to relax the elasticity built up while rolling. It is these resting times that make classic puff pastry so time consuming.

A second method, which makes what is called rapid, rough, or half-puff pastry, shortens the resting time considerably. The butter, instead of being kept completely separated between layers of dough, is interspaced in chunks throughout the dough. This creates much less elasticity. The dough, which looks very rough at first, can be rolled without resting and used shortly thereafter. The end results are so good that I rarely teach the classic version anymore.

If you have an ounce/gram scale, you can make this pastry in any quantity desired. Use equal weights of flour and butter, and the amount of water is half the weight of the flour. Use only a small amount of salt so the pastry can be used for savory as well as dessert recipes.

Because of the quantity of butter involved, working on a cold surface is important for success. If you don't have a large plastic pastry board (about 16 x 20 inches) to chill, fill one or two large roasting pans with ice and place them on your countertop to chill it.

Using plastic wrap, as I do to initially form the pastry, alleviates the need to handle it with warm hands, and makes the beginning stages of making the pastry less sticky.

MAKES 2½ POUNDS

3 cups (450g) all-purpose flour (see Note)
1 teaspoon (5g) salt
1 cup cold water
1 pound (4 sticks; 450g) cold unsalted butter, cut into ½-inch cubes

1. Place the flour in a large bowl and make a well in the center. Place the salt, water, and butter in the well. Quickly and gently blend all of the ingredients together using your fingertips.

2. As soon as all of the ingredients begin to stick together, transfer the contents of the bowl to a sheet of plastic wrap and, with your hands, form the mass into a rectangle about 7 x 10 inches. Wrap tightly in the plastic and run your rolling pin over the surface of the wrapped dough to make it tighter and more compact. Refrigerate for 15 minutes or freeze for 5 minutes. At this point, the dough will be very rough looking.

PATE DEMI-FEUILLETEE: Helpful Hints

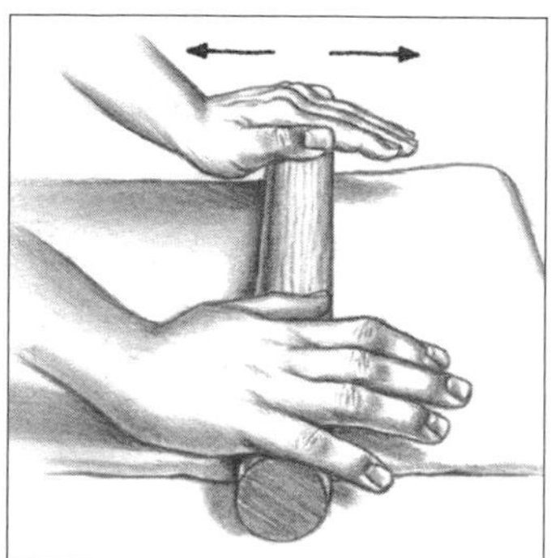

1. Roll out the dough into a 8 x 20-inch rectangle.

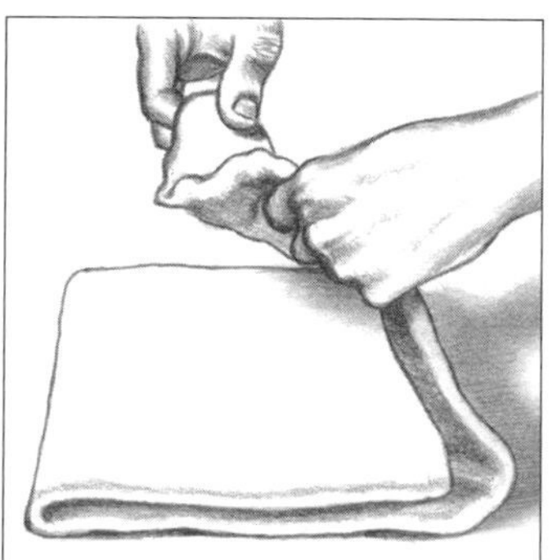

2. Fold the dough into thirds as you would a letter.

3. Mark the finished dough into five pieces.

3. Working on a cold, lightly floured surface, give the dough four "turns" as follows: Remove the plastic wrap and roll out the dough into a 8 x 20-inch rectangle with one short side facing you (figure 1, above). Fold in thirds as you would a letter (figure 2, above) and give it one-quarter turn to the right or left. You have now given the dough one "turn." Repeat this rolling and turning process three more times. Keep the work surface, dough, and rolling pin lightly floured, but brush off any excess flour from the dough before folding.

4. Rewrap the dough and refrigerate for 15 minutes (or longer). It can be used after these four "turns," or it can be given two additional "turns" before use. The pastry will rise just as much with four "turns" as with six, but the layers after six "turns" will be thinner, making the finished pastry more tender.

5. The pastry will keep for 3 to 4 days in the refrigerator, or for several months in the freezer. It should be kept tightly wrapped in plastic wrap. If you think you will use less than the 2½ pounds of dough, mark the finished dough into five equal portions (figure 3, above). Each piece will be ½ pound of pastry. Cut off the amount you need for the recipe you are working on, and wrap and store the remainder.

NOTE: To make even finer pastry, replace ⅔ cup of all-purpose flour (100g) with ½ cup plus ⅓ cup cake flour (100g).

IN ADDITION

French pastry shops have refrigerated surfaces (a marble work surface placed on top of a large horizontal refrigerator) designed specifically for working with puff pastry. The marble top is actually a part of the refrigerator, serving as one of its four walls, and the refrigeration unit in turn keeps the marble very well chilled.

STRAWBERRY-TOPPED PUFF-PASTRY TARTLETS

[FEUILLETÉ AUX FRAISES]

SOME OF THE FINEST fruit tarts are those made with puff pastry, fresh strawberries or raspberries, and a currant jelly glaze. But they are always made ahead of time and served at room temperature. Unfortunately, this does not take advantage of puff pastry's best feature: the flaky, buttery taste it has when it's still warm. By changing the presentation of a traditional puff-pastry tart slightly, this magnificent dessert results. Small individual squares of puff pastry are baked ahead of time, then reheated just before serving and topped with fresh berries and warm currant jelly.

The optional addition of toasted sliced almonds adds a delicate crunch and harmonizing flavor. **SERVES 8**

Butter, for baking sheet
1½ pounds Rough Puff Pastry (page 230) or 1 pound store-bought puff pastry
1 egg, beaten
1 jar (8 ounces) red currant jelly
1 to 2 tablespoons kirsch, to taste
3 pints strawberries, quartered if large
¼ cup (25g) sliced almonds, toasted (optional; see Note)

1. Preheat the oven to 400°F with the oven rack in the middle position. Lightly butter a baking sheet.

2. Roll the pastry out into a square about 12 x 12 inches and cut it into nine 4-inch squares.

3. Trim ½-inch strips off two opposite sides of each square (these are the "long" strips). Then trim ½-inch strips off the two remaining sides (the "short" strips). You should have 3-inch squares. Brush the surface lightly with the beaten egg and place the two "short" strips on opposite edges of the square, pressing gently to attach the strips to the square. Brush lightly with the egg wash. Attach the two "long" strips to the other edges, again pressing gently. Brush again with the egg wash. Trim off any excess pastry at the corners of the square. If desired, decorate the surface of the border by making diagonal slashes with a knife just through the top surface of the pastry.

4. Place the pastry squares on the baking sheet and prick the centers several times with the point of a knife. Bake until the pastry has risen and is evenly colored, 20 to 25 minutes.

5. Allow to cool on a wire rack. With a sharp paring knife, following the inside edges of the rim, cut out the pastry in the center, going down about ½ inch. Gently lift this piece out with the tip of the knife and set aside to use as a lid. With your fingers, pull out the remaining excess pastry in the center, leaving a well to be filled. (This can be done several hours in advance. Before assembling the dessert, reheat the pastry in a 350°F oven, about 3 minutes.)

6. In a small saucepan, heat the currant jelly over medium heat until it melts and comes to a boil. Add the kirsch.

7. Place the warm pastry on individual serving plates and fill to overflowing with strawberries. Spoon or brush on the hot currant jelly glaze and sprinkle with the toasted sliced almonds (if using).

NOTE: Don't use slivered almonds in place of sliced ones; the thicker-cut almonds are too firm for the combination of textures in this delicate dessert.

VARIATION

Raspberry-Topped Puff-Pastry Tartlets

[FEUILLETÉ AUX FRAMBOISES]

Use 2 pints of raspberries in place of the strawberries.

Making Feuilletes: A Second Method

Another way to make a tartlet: Roll out and cut the dough into 4-inch squares as described in the recipe. Brush lightly with the egg wash. With the tip of a paring knife, cut ½ inch in from the edge along all 4 sides, but stopping ¼ inch from two opposing corners (top, right). Pick up the corners that have been cut all the way through and cross them over one another (left). Press the edges down at each of the four corners to seal (bottom, right).

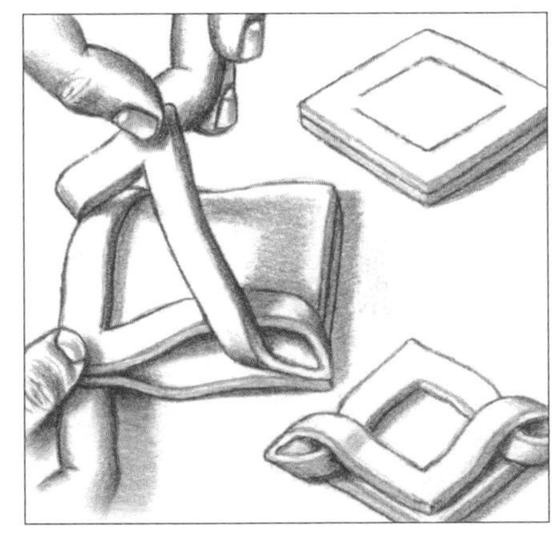

NAPOLEONS

[MILLE-FEUILLES]

THE MOST DELICIOUS mille-feuille I ever ate was served to me by Jean and Pierre Troisgros when I had lunch with them many years ago in their three-star restaurant in Roanne. The pastry had just emerged from the oven and was served with a room-temperature pastry cream.

To serve a Napoleon warm requires the hands of a veteran chef. Pastry cream at room temperature is very soft and makes the cutting and serving of this layered pastry difficult. For this reason, most Napoleons are refrigerated before they are cut. When refrigerated, the pastry becomes less flaky and loses some of its allure. In order to get as close as possible to the wonderful warm mille-feuilles of my memory, I do not refrigerate them, and assemble them only 3 to 4 hours before serving. Make your pastry cream and prepare the puff pastry up to the point of baking it the day before and the process will be easy. **SERVES 6**

Butter, for baking sheet
1½ pounds Rough Puff Pastry (page 230) or 1 pound store-bought puff pastry
Double recipe Liqueur-Flavored Pastry Cream (page 348), chilled
Confectioners' sugar, for dusting

1. Preheat the oven to 400°F with the oven rack placed in the middle position. Lightly butter a 14 x 17-inch baking sheet.

2. Roll the pastry out to fit the baking sheet. The pastry should be less than ⅛ inch thick.

3. Sprinkle the baking sheet with water. Roll the pastry onto a rolling pin and unroll it onto the baking sheet. Trim off any excess pastry.

4. Prick the pastry all over with the tines of a fork. Refrigerate it for 15 minutes or more.

5. Place the pastry in the oven and bake until the pastry is golden brown and dry, 20 to 25 minutes. Allow it to cool on a rack.

6. Use a serrated knife to trim the pastry and to cut it lengthwise into three equal strips.

7. Whisk the chilled pastry cream to make it smooth and easy to spread. Spread two of the puff-pastry strips with pastry cream and place one on top of the other, pastry cream–side up. Place the last strip of pastry, bottom side up, on top. Sprinkle confectioners' sugar on top.

8. Use two long metal spatulas to lift the pastry to a doily-covered serving platter. When you are ready to serve, hold the top layer as you cut through it with a serrated knife to form six individual Napoleons. (This can be done no more than 3 to 4 hours ahead. Do not refrigerate the pastries before serving. However, do refrigerate any leftovers, which will keep for 1 to 2 days.)

GENOISE

GÉNOISE is the most popular all-purpose cake in France. Once you master the techniques for making this cake, the possibilities are endless. Basically a sponge cake made with butter, it is used to make round cakes, square cakes, and jelly rolls. Because of its firm texture, it can be cut into thin layers that—when layered with a variety of buttercreams, whipped creams, liqueur- or coffee-flavored syrups, sugar icings, toasted nuts, praline, and ganache—transform it into elaborate and delicious creations (see "Les Gâteaux," page 236). For two good examples, try Chocolate Génoise with Grand Marnier Ganache (page 240) and Gâteau Moka (page 241), which is a vanilla génoise with a coffee buttercream.

In the technique for making a classic génoise, there are two areas that can cause problems for cooks, inexperienced and experienced alike. The first is in the initial beating of eggs over heat—the warmth helps the eggs to increase their volume but can also be awkward and time consuming. And the second problem area arises when melted butter must be folded into this lightened egg mixture without deflating it.

To make the whole procedure easier, and to reduce the risk of failure, I do two things. Instead of beating the eggs over heat, I simply warm the eggs (in the shell) in a bowl of hot tap water while I assemble the other ingredients. Then I pour the water out of the bowl, dry the bowl, and crack the eggs into it while they are still warm. I then beat them with the sugar to produce a thick, firm batter in a relatively short time (5 to 8 minutes).

When it comes time to incorporate the butter, I use soft, partially melted butter in place of the traditional fully melted butter. And instead of adding it directly to the batter, I blend a small amount of batter into the butter first to make its consistency similar to the batter, and thereby easier to fold back in.

If you are familiar with French cake recipes, you will notice that I have reduced the amount of sugar in the classic sugar syrup by at least 75 percent, since I find most classical French cakes too sweet. **MAKES 1 LAYER**

Butter and all-purpose flour, for cake pan

FOR A 9-INCH ROUND CAKE

4 large eggs
3 tablespoons (45g) unsalted butter, cut into 4 pieces
½ cup (110g) sugar
1 teaspoon pure vanilla extract or 1 teaspoon orange or lemon juice and the grated zest of 1 small orange or lemon
⅔ cup (100g) all-purpose flour

FOR AN 8-INCH ROUND CAKE

3 large eggs
2½ tablespoons (35g) unsalted butter, cut into 3 pieces
⅓ cup plus 1 tablespoon (85g) sugar
¾ teaspoon pure vanilla extract or ¾ teaspoon orange or lemon juice and the grated zest of 1 small orange or lemon
½ cup (70g) all-purpose flour

1. Preheat the oven to 350°F with the oven rack in the middle position. Butter and flour an 8- or 9-inch round cake pan.

2. Place the unbroken eggs in a large bowl filled with hot tap water.

3. In a small saucepan, warm the butter over low heat. When the pieces are about half melted, remove the pan from the heat and stir until completely melted; the butter should be the consistency of light cream. Set the saucepan aside. When you are ready to use the butter, it will have cooled further, and should be the consistency of heavy cream or light mayonnaise.

4. Remove the eggs from the bowl, pour out the water, and dry the bowl. Crack the eggs into the bowl and beat with the sugar and vanilla until they triple in volume, 5 to 8 minutes. The batter should be very thick. It will fall slowly from the beaters and stand on the surface.

5. Sift the flour one-third at a time onto the surface of the batter. Using a rubber/silicone spatula, fold the flour in gently. Fold no more than 10 to 12 times after each addition. After

LES GATEAUX: Layer Cakes

Though the combinations of flavors, fillings, and icings in French cakes are infinite, there are a great number of cakes whose fillings and decorations are well defined. In fact, the name is often written on top of the cake, or the icing decoration will be so particular to that cake that when you see it in the pastry shop you know exactly what the inside will be like.

MASCOTTE PRALINEE: Génoise layers filled with praline buttercream, coated with toasted almonds, and dusted with confectioners' sugar.

LUTETIA: Génoise layers filled with walnut buttercream and coated with apricot glaze. Walnut halves are embedded in the top and sides of the cake, and the cake is iced with chocolate fondant. It is decorated with a vanilla-flavored chestnut purée.

FINANCIER: Génoise layers made from almonds and flour and baked with a layer of candied fruits in the batter. Topped with confectioners' sugar.

REGENT: Three génoise layers filled with buttercream or a thick chestnut purée, are coated with apricot jam, decorated with candied fruits, then frosted with rum fondant. The outlines of the fruits shows through the fondant.

CLUNY: Génoise layers filled with pistachio and Benedictine buttercream, coated with apricot jam, and topped with Benedictine fondant and roasted hazelnuts. Decorated with chocolate.

SIFTING FLOUR

The only time I ever sift flour is when I want to prevent lumping when adding it to a liquid, or to keep it light while folding it into a cake batter, such as génoise. In these instances, or anytime you need to sift flour, there is no need for a special flour sifter. Just use an everyday kitchen strainer, tapping the outer rim against the palm of your hand. Any lumps or foreign matter will be left in the strainer.

the last addition you may still see a small amount of flour; this will disappear when the butter is added.

6. Fold approximately 1 cup of the batter into the creamy butter until well blended. Pour this mixture back into the remaining batter and fold gently no more than 10 to 12 times. The batter will begin to fall and you may see streaks of butter. A completely smooth batter is not necessary.

7. Pour the batter into the prepared pan, filling it three-quarters full. Tap the filled pan firmly on a counter several times to make sure no large air bubbles have been trapped in the batter.

8. Place the pan in the oven and bake for 25 to 35 minutes, until the cake begins to come away from the sides of the pan and is golden brown and springy to the touch.

9. Unmold the cake onto a rack and allow it to cool, covered with the cake pan. (If not used immediately, the cake should be wrapped in plastic. It can be refrigerated for several days or frozen for up to 2 months.)

IN ADDITION

I call for all-purpose flour in the génoise recipe (and in fact for all the cakes in the book), because this is the type of flour that most people have at home and I want to encourage you to try these desserts without having to buy special ingredients. However, for those who are bakers—or who have tried the génoise already and would like to make it even better—I would recommend making it with cake flour. Cake flour is made from a softer wheat (one with less gluten in it), and the resulting cake will have a finer, more delicate texture.

Use the same amount of cake flour as the all-purpose flour called for. Be absolutely sure you do this by *weight,* with a scale, and *not* by cup measures, because the volumes of the two flours will not be the same.

VARIATION

CHOCOLATE GENOISE

[GÉNOISE AU CHOCOLAT]

For an all-purpose chocolate cake that can be used in the same way as the plain génoise, simply replace one-third of the flour in the preceding recipes with cocoa powder. Mix the flour and cocoa together before sifting into the batter. The measurements are as follows: for an 8-inch cake, ⅓ cup (50g) all-purpose flour and ¼ cup (20g) unsweetened cocoa powder; for a 9-inch cake, ½ cup (70g) all-purpose flour and ⅓ cup (30g) unsweetened cocoa powder.

Decorating a Cake with Ganache and Royal Icing

Before attempting to use Ganache (page 349) and Royal Icing (page 352) together, simply coat a cake with ganache first to make sure you can frost the cake successfully.

To use royal icing and ganache together to make a design, it is important to have both at a similar consistency before starting. As soon as the cake has been coated with the ganache icing, place the royal icing in a decorating cone (see "Making and Using a Decorating Cone," page 353) and use it to make the following designs:

HERRINGBONE: Squeeze horizontal lines the size of spaghetti on the top of the cake, leaving a ½- to ¾-inch space between bands. The royal icing should sink into the ganache at this point. Immediately draw the point of a small knife, like a paring knife, down the center and perpendicular to the lines. As the knife tip passes through

HERRINGBONE DECORATION

1. Coat the assembled cake with an even layer of ganache.

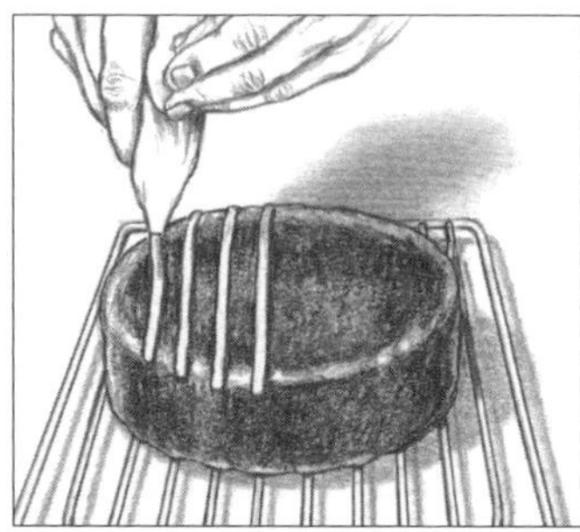

2. Apply horizontal lines of royal icing ½ to ¾ inch apart.

3. Draw the point of a knife through the center of the lines. Repeat this at an equal distance from both sides of the first line.

4. Turn the cake 180 degrees and make four equally distanced cuts through the icing.

the two icings, it should draw the band of white down into a V-shaped design. Working quickly, repeat this at equal distances from both sides of the first line.

Turn the cake 180 degrees and draw a knife through the frosting to make four equally distanced cuts.

If the consistencies of the two icings are just right, and you work quickly, you will have a beautiful herringbone design. If the icings are not of the same consistency, the following can happen:

- If the white bands run down the side of the cake, the chocolate icing was too thin.
- If the white bands crack instead of flowing smoothly, the royal icing was too stiff.
- If the cut marks made by the knife are visible, you probably did not work fast enough and the chocolate stiffened. It should be soft enough to flow back to cover up the knife marks.

SPIDERWEB DESIGN:

Make a spiral design with the royal icing on top of the soft ganache. Start at the center and spiral the icing out to the outer edge of the cake, leaving a ½- to ¾-inch space between the lines of the spiral. Immediately draw the point of your paring knife from one side of the cake to the other through the center of the spiral. Turn the cake 90 degrees and repeat the cut from edge to edge. Divide each quarter by making similar cuts for a spiderweb design.

The same problems as mentioned at left can occur. But in time, you will be making perfect designs.

SPIDERWEB DECORATION

1. Starting at the center, spiral a line of icing out to the edge of the cake.

2. Draw the point of a knife through the icing from one side of the cake to the other through the center. Turn the cake 90 degrees and cut the design into quarters. Then divide the quarters in half or into fourths.

CHOCOLATE GENOISE WITH GRAND MARNIER GANACHE

[GÂTEAU CHOCOLAT AU GRAND MARNIER]

THE LAYERS in this delicious chocolate cake are moistened with orange juice and Grand Marnier in place of the traditional sugar syrup. You can serve it just as is, or decorate it with Royal Icing (page 352) or candied orange peel. **SERVES 8 TO 10**

½ cup orange juice
2 tablespoons Grand Marnier
Chocolate Génoise (8 or 9 inches; page 237), batter flavored with the grated zest of 1 orange
Ganache (page 349), flavored with Grand Marnier

1. Combine the orange juice and Grand Marnier.

2. Using a serrated knife, cut the chocolate génoise into two layers (see page 242). Turn the top layer cut side up on the rack. Using a pastry brush, moisten both layers with the flavored orange juice. (Several tablespoons of juice will remain when making an 8-inch cake.)

3. Place the cake, on the wire rack, over a baking sheet. Spread an even layer of ganache over the bottom layer.

4. Replace the top layer. Pour the remaining ganache over the top of the cake so it runs down the sides. Tap the rack on the pastry sheet to help the ganache fall evenly. If there are spots that were missed, coat them with the excess ganache from the pastry sheet, using your spatula.

5. Refrigerate or freeze the cake on the rack. When the icing is firm, transfer the cake to a doilied serving plate. (The cake will keep refrigerated for several days, or can be frozen for several weeks. Bring to room temperature before serving.)

IN ADDITION

Before placing your cake on a serving plate, refrigerate or freeze it, still on the wire rack, to set the frosting. When it has set, carefully move the cake with a long metal spatula from the rack to a serving plate. Use one hand to support the bottom of the cake while moving it.

VARIATIONS

SACHERTORTE

This cake, which I usually find too dry, is moist and delicious in this variation. Using raspberry jam provides yet another dimension. After moistening the layers with the orange juice, coat with strained raspberry jam or some Apricot Glaze (page 354). Spread some of the ganache on the bottom layer. Replace the top layer. Coat the top and sides with more apricot or raspberry glaze and refrigerate to set. Finally, coat with the remaining ganache.

Chocolate Genoise with Mocha Ganache

[GÂTEAU CHOCOLAT AU CAFÉ]

Omit the orange zest from the chocolate génoise. Make a light coffee syrup (see Gâteau Moka, step 1, below) flavored with 1 tablespoon Cognac, rum, or Kahlúa to use in place of the Grand Marnier–flavored orange juice. Flavor the ganache with Coffee Essence (page 358) or Quick Coffee Essence (page 359)—2 tablespoons for an 8-inch cake, 3 tablespoons for a 9-inch. Moisten the cake layers with the coffee syrup and frost with the ganache. Or, instead of the ganache, you might want to try a Coffee Buttercream (page 351).

Gateau Moka

THIS IS A LIGHT vanilla cake with an irresistible coffee buttercream. As with most cakes made with génoise and buttercream, it can be made several days or even weeks ahead (and it freezes well).

SERVES 8 TO 10

½ cup boiling water
2 tablespoons (30g) sugar
2 tablespoons (10g) instant coffee granules
Génoise (8 or 9 inches; page 235), made with vanilla extract
Coffee Buttercream (page 351)
⅔ cup (100g) chopped toasted almonds (see Note)

1. Make a light coffee syrup: In a small bowl, combine the boiling water, sugar, and instant coffee. Stir to dissolve.

2. Using a serrated knife, cut the cake into two layers (see page 242). Turn the top layer cut side up on the cake rack. Using a pastry brush, moisten both layers with the syrup. (Several tablespoons will remain when making an 8-inch cake.)

3. Spread a thin, even layer of coffee buttercream over the bottom layer. Replace the top layer.

4. Ice the top and sides of the cake with a thin layer of the remaining buttercream. If you have a pastry bag and starred decoration tube, you can use them to make a decorative border on top of the cake.

5. Scoop up the toasted almonds in your hand and press them gently onto the sides of the cake. Refrigerate or freeze the cake on the rack. When the icing is firm, transfer the cake to a doilied serving plate. (The cake will keep refrigerated for several days, or can be frozen for several weeks. Let the cake return to room temperature before serving.)

NOTE: To toast the whole almonds (before chopping), preheat the oven to 400°F. Spread the nuts on an ungreased baking sheet and roast until the nuts are beige and shiny, 5 to 7 minutes. Do not let them burn.

VARIATIONS

GATEAU MOKA WITH CHOCOLATE GANACHE

[GÂTEAU MOKA À LA GANACHE]

This cake combines two of my favorite flavors. Follow the preceding recipe through step 4 without making a decorative border. Chill in the refrigerator until firm and then pour a coating of Ganache (page 349) over the buttercream. If desired, decorate the top of the cake with any leftover coffee buttercream. Omit the almonds, or sprinkle them on the buttercream layer in step 4. Try this same treatment with a chocolate génoise.

ORANGE GENOISE WITH GRAND MARNIER BUTTERCREAM

[GÂTEAU AU GRAND MARNIER]

Flavor the cake batter with the grated zest of 1 orange and moisten the layers with Grand Marnier–flavored orange juice (see Chocolate Génoise with Grand Marnier Ganache, page 240, step 1). Make a Buttercream (page 350) flavored with the grated zest of 1 orange and ¼ cup Grand Marnier, adding it, 1 tablespoon at a time, in step 3 of the buttercream recipe.

HOW TO CUT A GENOISE INTO LAYERS

A génoise is a firm cake that is baked in one layer and then cut into thinner layers to be built into traditional French-style cakes. A long, wide serrated spatula (see figure 1, below) or knife works well for cutting the cake.

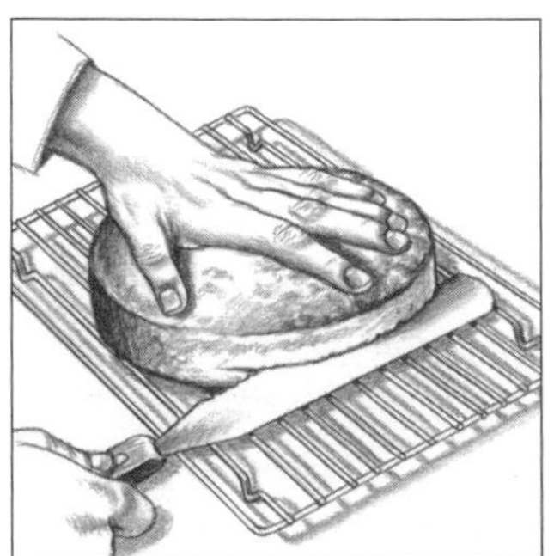

1. Score the cake around the outside edge with a serrated spatula or knife.

2. Holding the cake gently, cut through along the scored line.

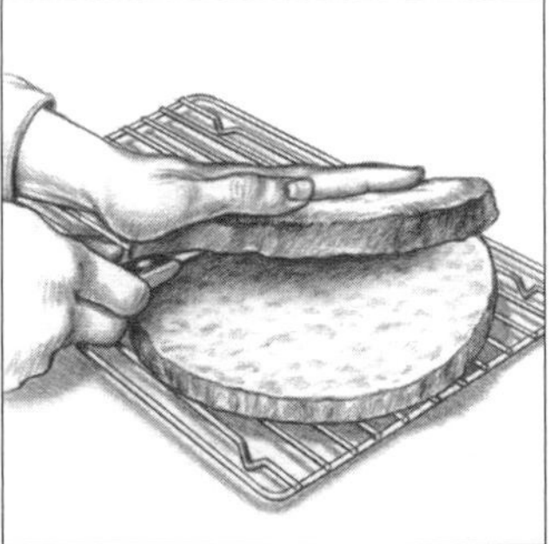

3. Using the flat of the spatula, turn the top layer over, cut side up, onto the cake rack.

Apricot Jam Roll

[BISCUIT ROULÉ À L'ABRICOT]

THE CLASSIC jelly roll is made with a *biscuit,* or French sponge cake batter, similar to a génoise but made without butter and with egg yolks and egg whites beaten separately. The resulting batter is quite stiff. I have found that for jelly rolls the batter does not have to be as thick as tradition has dictated. So, I simplify the recipe by using a butterless génoise, modifying the génoise recipe slightly by adding 2 tablespoons of liquid, which both lightens and moistens the resulting sponge cake. **SERVES 6**

4 eggs
Butter and all-purpose flour, for jelly-roll pan
½ cup (110g) granulated sugar
2 tablespoons orange juice
Grated zest of 1 small orange
⅔ cup (100g) all-purpose flour
1 jar (8 ounces) apricot jam (see Note)
¼ cup (25g) sliced almonds, toasted
Confectioners' sugar, for dusting (optional)

1. Place the unbroken eggs in a large bowl filled with hot tap water.

2. Preheat the oven to 350°F with the oven rack in the middle position. Lightly butter the bottom of a 17 x 11 x 1-inch jelly-roll pan and line with waxed paper. Butter and lightly flour the waxed paper and the sides of the pan.

3. Remove the eggs from the bowl, pour out the water, and dry the bowl. Crack the eggs into the bowl and beat with the granulated sugar, orange juice, and orange zest until tripled in volume, 5 to 8 minutes. The batter should be very thick. It will fall slowly from the beaters and stand on the surface.

4. Sift the flour, one-third at a time, onto the surface of the batter. Using a rubber/silicone spatula, gently fold the flour in until smooth.

5. Pour the batter into the prepared pan, spreading to fill the pan evenly. Tap the filled pan firmly on a counter several times to make sure no large air bubbles are trapped in the batter.

6. Place the pan in the oven and bake until the cake begins to come away from the sides of the pan and is golden brown and springy to the touch, 10 to 12 minutes.

7. Run a knife around the sides of the pan, making sure that the cake is not sticking. Unmold the cake onto a clean kitchen towel lined with waxed paper. The waxed paper that had lined the pan will be attached to the surface of the cake. Remove this paper, then replace it loosely on the surface of the cake. Roll the cake up in the towel between the layers of waxed paper and allow to cool. You may roll the cake in whichever direction you prefer to produce either a long, thin cake or a short, thick one. (The cake can be made to this point 1 day in advance and refrigerated as is.)

8. A few hours before serving, warm the jam in a saucepan on the stove (or in a bowl in the microwave) until it is thin enough to spread easily.

9. Unroll the cake and remove the top layer of waxed paper. Spread a thin layer of jam evenly over the surface of the cake. Reroll the cake, peeling away the waxed paper as you go. Trim the ends, and transfer to a serving platter. Coat the outside of the cake with a thin layer of jam. Sprinkle the almonds over the sides and top of the cake and dust with confectioners' sugar, if desired.

NOTE: Buy lightly sweetened preserves, or make your own Apricot Jam (page 356) for jelly rolls so that the end results will be full of the fruit flavor and not overly sweet. This is an easy dessert to make and is popular with children and adults alike.

VARIATIONS

The apricot jam can be replaced by 2 cups of flavored whipped cream or buttercream.

The recipe can also be used to make a 10-inch round cake.

ALMOND CAKE WITH A RASPBERRY PUREE

[PAIN DE GÊNES SUR COULIS DE FRAMBOISE]

PAIN DE GÊNES is an almond cake that is traditionally served with tea in France. When I first tasted it I found the cake dry, but enjoyed its rich almond flavor. Classically made with three eggs, I found myself short an egg one day, but made the cake anyway. The result was a moist and delicious cake that became an instant hit.

Although good by itself, this simple cake turns into an elegant dessert when served surrounded with raspberry coulis (purée).

SERVES 6 TO 8

1 tablespoon kirsch, framboise, or Cointreau (optional)
Raspberry Coulis (page 345)
1 tablespoon melted butter and all-purpose flour, for cake pan
⅔ cup (100g) whole blanched almonds or ¾ cup (100g) slivered almonds
½ cup plus 1 tablespoon (125g) granulated sugar
¼ cup (40g) all-purpose flour
8 tablespoons (1 stick; 115g) unsalted butter
2 eggs
1 teaspoon pure vanilla extract
2 tablespoons dark rum
Confectioners' sugar, for dusting

1. Add the kirsch, framboise, or Cointreau to the raspberry coulis. (The coulis can be made a day in advance and refrigerated until used.)

2. Preheat the oven to 350°F with the oven rack in the middle position. Cut a round of waxed paper to fit the bottom of an 8- or 9-inch cake pan. Brush the bottom of the pan with the melted butter and place the paper in it. Butter and lightly flour the waxed paper and the sides of the pan.

3. Combine the almonds with half the granulated sugar in a food processor and grind to a fine powder. Add the flour to this mixture and set aside.

4. In a food processor, cream the 8 tablespoons of butter and the remaining granulated sugar. When smooth, add the eggs, one at a time, mixing well after each addition. Blend in the vanilla and rum. Add the almond-flour mixture and process quickly just until smooth.

5. Pour the batter into the cake pan. (It will fill only about one fourth of the pan.) Bake for 30 to 35 minutes, or until the cake is golden brown in color and comes slightly away from the edge of the pan. Unmold onto a wire rack, remove and discard the waxed paper, and allow to cool.

6. To serve: Dust with confectioners' sugar to coat the surface of the cake. Cut into 8 wedges. Pour about 3 tablespoons of raspberry coulis onto each serving plate. Tilt the plates so the sauce coats them evenly, then place a slice of cake in the center of each plate.

ALMOND CAKE WITH SORBET AND FRUIT:
Pain de Gênes au Sorbet et aux Fruits

In summertime, with sorbet in the freezer and fresh fruit readily available, I make an extra-special presentation of this dessert. For example, I simply add a scoop of Pineapple Sorbet (page 288) on one side of the cake and several tablespoons of blueberries on the other. The raspberry coulis complements all, and you'll have a dessert that any fine French restaurant would be proud to serve. This cake goes nicely with other fruit purées. Try strawberry, blueberry, or peach.

CHOCOLATE MOUSSE CAKE

[GÂTEAU MOUSSE AU CHOCOLAT]

THIS LIGHT and luscious mousse cake combines both baked and unbaked chocolate mousse. All flavor variations that work for the mousse recipe can be used for this cake. It can be made a day or two in advance and can be frozen for later use, if desired. **SERVES 8**

Butter, for cake pan
Double recipe of Chocolate Mousse (page 275)
Unsweetened cocoa powder and whipped cream for decoration (optional; see Note)

1. Preheat the oven to 350°F with the oven rack in the middle position. Butter a 9-inch cake pan.

2. Pour three-fourths of the chocolate mousse mixture into the pan. (Refrigerate the remainder until ready to use.) Bake for 30 to 35 minutes. The cake will rise at first; when it falls back, it is done.

3. Unmold onto a wire rack to cool. When cooled, the cake will have a concave center. Transfer the cake, with the aid of a long metal spatula, to a serving platter and fill the center with the remaining mousse mixture. Refrigerate until the mousse sets, about 1 hour.

NOTE: If desired, decorate the cake before serving by dusting the mousse center with cocoa powder and piping whipped cream around the outer edge.

RUM-SOAKED SAVARIN

[SAVARIN AU RHUM]

THE YEAST DOUGH that is used to make this delicious rum-soaked cake is the same that is used for *baba au rhum.* Babas are baked in small metal cups or baba molds, while a savarin is baked in a ring-shaped savarin mold. Once risen, baked, and unmolded, babas or savarins are soaked with rum and a hot sugar syrup. Finally, they are glazed with hot apricot jam and decorated with sliced almonds and candied fruits.

Those who have tasted a savarin will find my recipe far less sweet. The light sugar syrup is one-quarter as sugary as the usual French syrup. **SERVES 16**

2 tablespoons butter, melted, for mold
2 packages active dry yeast or 1 ounce fresh yeast
¼ cup (50g) sugar
6 tablespoons warm (90°F to 115°F) water
2 cups plus 2 tablespoons (300g) all-purpose flour
4 eggs
7 tablespoons (100g) unsalted butter, melted
1 teaspoon pure vanilla extract
4 cups Light Sugar Syrup (page 359)
¾ cup dark rum
Apricot Glaze (page 354)
¼ cup sliced almonds and/or candied fruit and violets, for decoration

1. Completely coat the inside of a 9½-inch savarin mold with the 2 tablespoons melted butter.

2. Dissolve the yeast and 1 tablespoon of the sugar in the warm water. Let sit for 2 to 5 minutes, or until foamy and showing signs of life. If the yeast does not foam, discard and start again with new yeast.

3. In a food processor, combine the remaining 3 tablespoons sugar, the flour, eggs, 7 tablespoons melted butter, vanilla, and yeast mixture and process until a smooth, sticky batter forms, about 1 minute.

4. Preheat the oven to 400°F with the oven rack in the lowest position.

5. Drop the batter, 1 tablespoon at a time, into the mold, taking care not to drip batter on the sides of the mold. The mold should be filled halfway. Place a towel on the counter and bang the filled mold several times firmly on the towel to level the batter and to bring any air bubbles to the surface. Cover the mold with a large inverted bowl or pot and let rise until the batter reaches to within ⅛ inch of the top, about 30 minutes.

6. Place the mold in the oven and immediately lower the temperature to 350°F. Bake until the cake has risen and is dark brown on top and golden brown on the bottom and sides, 40 to 45 minutes. Unmold the savarin onto a wire rack and let cool, 20 to 30 minutes.

7. Place the light sugar syrup in a small saucepan over high heat and bring to a boil.

SAVARIN MOLD

Savarins are baked in special tinned-steel ring molds (below, at right) with a center rim that rises higher than the outer rim, helping the cake to rise straight. Although you can use a regular ring mold (below, left), the savarin may sink in the center.

8. Place the savarin, on its wire rack, over a large bowl or deep pan. (A roasting pan or sauté pan works well.) Spoon or slowly pour the boiling sugar syrup over the savarin and repeat until most of the syrup has been absorbed, 8 to 10 applications. As the syrup cools, reheat it.

9. When there is only about ½ cup of syrup remaining, stop and slowly spoon the rum over the savarin. Follow the rum with the remaining syrup. (Save any syrup that drips into the bowl or pan under the rack.)

10. In a small saucepan, bring the apricot glaze to a boil over medium heat. Using a pastry brush, coat the entire savarin with a layer of the glaze. Decorate as desired.

11. Using two long metal spatulas, transfer the savarin to a large rimmed serving platter. Pour any remaining syrup around the savarin.

IN ADDITION

The savarin is a sticky yeast dough that is made in seconds using a food processor, although the dough then must rise for about 30 minutes. To make the preparation of this dessert even easier, I often bake the cake itself the night before I plan to serve it.

VARIATION

Kirsch Cake with Fruit and Whipped Cream

[SAVARIN CHANTILLY AUX FRUITS]

This elegant dessert will serve 18 to 20 because of the additional ingredients. Prepare the savarin as in the preceding recipe, replacing the rum with an equal amount of kirsch. Fill the center of the savarin with 1 cup whipped cream. Place 1 pint of strawberries, raspberries, or blueberries around the outside and in the center of the ring, on top of the cream.

Almond Meringue Layer Cake with Coffee and Chocolate Buttercream

[GÂTEAU AUX FONDS À SUCCÈS]

THERE ARE a number of cakes in France made with layers of baked meringue, or meringue and ground nuts, that are filled and frosted with buttercream. If the meringue is made with almonds, the layers are called *fonds à succès.* Layers made with almond-hazelnut meringue are *fonds de progrès.* (Another variation can be made with pecans.) The layers are light, sometimes chewy, and have a wonderful roasted-nut flavor.

One of the nicest features of this cake—apart from its luscious taste and wonderful combination of creamy and chewy textures—is that it can be made well ahead of time and in stages. The layers can be kept wrapped airtight in plastic for a week or more. The completed cake keeps for several days in the refrigerator and also freezes well. **SERVES 12 TO 14**

Butter and all-purpose flour, for baking sheets (optional)
1¼ cups (150g) slivered almonds, untoasted, plus ½ cup (60g) slivered almonds, chopped and toasted
3 tablespoons plus ½ cup (150g) sugar
2 tablespoons (20g) cornstarch or all-purpose flour
6 egg whites
Coffee Buttercream (page 351), for an 8-inch cake (see Note)
Chocolate Buttercream (page 351), for an 8-inch cake (see Note)

1. Preheat the oven to 350°F with the oven rack in the middle position. Use two or more baking sheets and prepare them by lightly coating with butter and flour or lining with parchment paper.

2. Cut a piece of cardboard into a 10 x 3½-inch rectangle to serve as the pattern for the layers. Mark the outline of the pattern six times on the baking sheets with a pencil or toothpick. Leave ½ to ¾ inch of space between each.

3. In a food processor, grind the 1¼ cups untoasted slivered almonds, the 3 tablespoons sugar, and the cornstarch to a powder.

4. In a large bowl, beat the egg whites until soft peaks form, about 1 minute. Add the ½ cup sugar and beat until very stiff, about 2 minutes. Fold in the almond powder until smooth.

5. Using a pastry bag fitted with a ⅜-inch (#4) plain tube, squeeze the nut-meringue mixture out to completely fill in the outlined rectangles.

PASTRY BAGS: An Important Tool for Bakers

Pastry bags and tubes make the forming and filling of pastries quick and easy. The simplest dough to work with is cream-puff pastry (see page 221), and once you have mastered the technique you can move on and use pastry bags and tubes to make ladyfingers and meringue-nut layers and to make simple decorations with buttercream and whipped cream. They are often confused with decorating bags and tubes, which are much smaller and are used for more intricate decorations.

Traditional pastry bags are 14 to 16 inches long and are made of light canvas or nylon. More and more, pastry chefs and home cooks are using disposable plastic bags. The simplest pastry tubes have plain or starred tips and come in various sizes. For the recipes in this book, I have used #1, #4, #6, and #9 plain tubes, and #2 and #3 starred tubes.

6. Bake one sheet at a time until evenly browned, 20 to 25 minutes. (Although you can bake two sheets at one time if you change their positions after 8 to 10 minutes, you will get better results if you bake only one at a time.)

7. Slide a long metal spatula under the layers to remove them while hot and place them on a flat surface. The layers, which will initially be soft, stiffen quickly. While the layers are soft, place the cardboard pattern on top of each layer, and trim the edges square with a serrated knife. Let the layers cool.

8. Assemble the cake by coating the top of five layers with a thin (about ⅛ inch) layer of coffee buttercream. Place one layer on a flat surface, place the other coated layers on top. Top with the uncoated layer. Holding the cake in one hand or resting it on a wire rack, coat it all over with the chocolate buttercream.

9. Scoop the chopped toasted almonds in the palm of your hand and gently press them onto the sides of the cake. Hold the cake over a bowl to catch the excess nuts as they fall. Refrigerate the cake until 15 minutes before serving.

10. Serve ½-inch-thick slices on individual dessert plates.

NOTE: You may have buttercream left over. Freeze the rest for another use; it will keep for months.

IN ADDITION

Nut meringue and buttercream are delicious together, but are very rich. I used to bake this as a round cake and serve very small wedges, just enough to enjoy without too many added calories. But many students complained that the servings looked too small on their plates. My solution to this was to make the layers rectangular instead of round, constructing a loaf-shaped cake whose slices appear satisfyingly large.

VARIATIONS

Almond Meringue and Ice-Cream Layer Cake

[SUCCÈS À LA GLACE]

Use softened homemade or store-bought ice cream in place of the buttercream to make an ice-cream cake.

Pecan Meringue Layer Cake with Coffee and Chocolate Buttercream

[SUCCÈS AUX PACANES]

You can make the meringue layers using an equal amount of pecans in place of the almonds, but process for only 15 to 20 seconds in step 3 or they will become pasty instead of powdery.

CHOCOLATE ROLL WITH WHIPPED CREAM

[GÂTEAU ROULÉ AU CHOCOLAT]

A CHOCOLATE ROLL is usually made with a chocolate sponge, but I make a light, flourless chocolate roll with my basic chocolate mousse. When baked, chocolate reacts a little like flour, resulting in a cakelike consistency.

I roll the cake to produce a long, relatively thin chocolate roll, and I generally serve 2 to 3 slices per person. If you like thick chocolate rolls, simply roll the cake in the opposite direction. **SERVES 8**

Butter, for jelly-roll pan
1½ recipes Chocolate Mousse (page 275)
2 cups heavy cream
3 tablespoons orange liqueur, such as Cointreau or Grand Marnier (see Note)
Confectioners' sugar
Unsweetened cocoa powder, for dusting

1. Preheat the oven to 400°F with the oven rack in the middle position. Butter a 17 x 11 x 1-inch jelly-roll pan well and line it with waxed paper.

2. Pour the mousse into the prepared jelly-roll pan, spreading it evenly with a spatula. Bake until the cake has begun to come away from the sides of the pan, 10 minutes.

3. Run a knife around the sides of the pan, making sure that the cake is not sticking. Unmold the cake onto a clean kitchen towel lined with waxed paper. The waxed paper that had lined the pan will be attached to the top surface of the cake. Remove this paper, then replace it loosely on the surface of the cake. Roll the cake up in the towel between the layers of waxed paper and cool. You may roll the cake in whichever direction you prefer to produce either a long, thin cake or a short, thick one.

4. In a bowl set into a larger bowl of ice and water, whip the cream and orange liqueur until stiff. Add confectioners' sugar to taste.

5. Unroll the chocolate roll and remove the top layer of waxed paper (don't worry if it cracks a little). Coat the roll with half of the whipped cream. Reroll the cake, peeling away the waxed paper as you go. Trim the ends, and lift it onto a serving platter. Coat with the remaining whipped cream and dust the top with cocoa powder. Or use a pastry bag and a starred tip to coat the roll in long strips or bands of whipped cream. Refrigerate until ready to serve.

NOTE: You can flavor the whipped cream with vanilla, unsweetened cocoa powder, instant coffee, or coffee liqueur in place of the orange liqueur.

ALMOND TUILES

[TUILES AUX AMANDES]

TUILES are without question France's best cookie. The reputations of many French pastry chefs have been made or broken by the quality of their *tuiles*. These extremely thin, crisp almond cookies, which are formed to resemble the roof tiles (*tuiles*) found in Mediterranean countries, are often served with dessert in the finest restaurants. The memory of an otherwise superb meal can be flawed by poor-quality *tuiles*, and imperfections in a meal can be forgiven if it ends with outstanding ones.

From the small number of ingredients in these cookies, it might seem unlikely that there could be so much variation in taste, texture, and quality. But there is. One teaspoon of butter or one tablespoon of sugar one way or the other and you've appreciably altered the *tuiles'* consistency.

After years of tasting and testing, I've finally arrived at what I consider to be the perfect proportions for this cookie. If you follow this recipe exactly—I hope using a scale to measure the ingredients—you will have a *tuile* that you could proudly offer to a three-star pastry chef.

One thing to keep in mind, though, is baking time. You must find the baking time that works best for your baking sheet, oven, and thickness of cookies. Use my baking times first, but if they don't work, try a slightly different time (it may be a matter of only 15 to 30 seconds) and when you find the time that works, make a note of it and use that.

You may not bake perfect *tuiles* at first—although chances are pretty good that you will—but even the mistakes make good eating. **MAKES 20 TO 24**

Butter, for baking sheets
3 tablespoons (45g) unsalted butter
½ cup minus 2 teaspoons (100g) sugar
2 egg whites
¼ teaspoon pure vanilla extract
3 tablespoons plus 1 teaspoon (30g) all-purpose flour
1 cup (100g) sliced blanched almonds

1. Preheat the oven to 400°F with the oven rack in the middle position. Heavily butter two baking sheets.

2. In a small saucepan, melt the 3 tablespoons butter and remove from the heat.

3. In a small bowl, combine the sugar, egg whites, and vanilla and, without beating, mix together with a whisk. Stir in the flour with the whisk until smooth. Add the melted butter and stir with the whisk until smooth. Using a rubber/silicone spatula, fold in the sliced almonds.

4. Drop teaspoonfuls of the batter onto a baking sheet. With the back of the spoon, spread each thinly to about 3 inches in diameter (you

SHAPING TUILES

You can make these cookies by cooling them on a rack and serving them flat, but part of their glory is their shape. Special *tuile* molds do exist, made up of four or five U-shaped sections, but I have found that French bread pans, especially the baguette size, do the job equally well. You can also form the *tuiles* on top of a rolling pin, or over the side of a wine bottle, but it is not as easy as turning them into the bread pans. If you like these cookies, it is worthwhile buying the bread pans solely for the purpose of forming them.

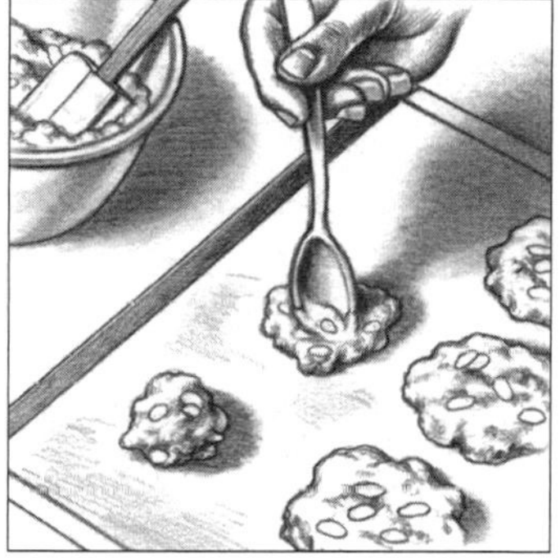

1. Spread the cookie batter thinly to about 3 inches in diameter, leaving 2 inches between each cookie.

2. Quickly remove the cookies with a long metal spatula.

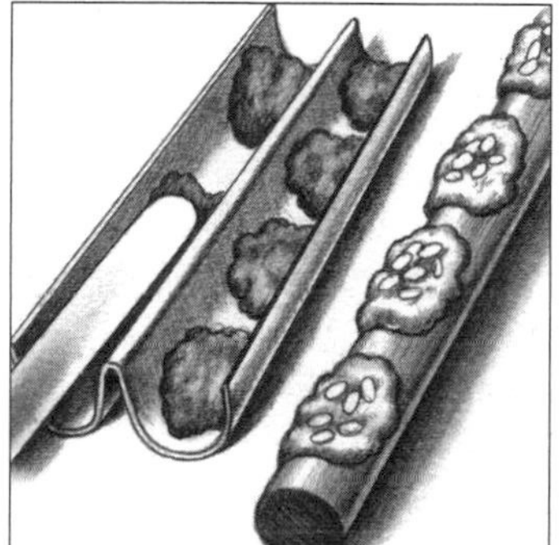

3. Invert the cookies into the baguette mold or lay over a rolling pin.

will see the baking sheet through the thin layer of batter), leaving 2 inches between each cookie.

5. Bake until the edges are browned, 4 to 7 minutes.

6. Using a long metal spatula and working quickly, remove the cookies from the sheet and invert them into a French bread (baguette) pan. (If you don't have a French bread pan, you can lay them over a rolling pin.) If the cookies harden before you have a chance to remove them from the baking sheet, place the sheet back in the oven for 20 to 30 seconds to soften them.

7. When cooled, remove the tuiles from the baguette pan or rolling pin. As soon as one batch is finished, bake the next.

8. Serve the tuiles on a doilied platter in overlapping rows. If you are not serving the cookies for several hours, keep them dry in an airtight tin or jar, because humidity can render this thin, crunchy cookie limp, sticky, and chewy.

MADELEINES

MADELEINES are little tea cakes that are good served with fruit or ice cream for dessert. They are classically made from a pound cake batter that is baked in small, shell-like molds appropriately named madeleine molds.

However, I deviate from classic madeleines by using the technique I use for making génoise rather than that for pound cake. As with génoise, folding the melted butter into the batter can be difficult, even for professionals, for the butter is heavy and rapidly collapses the batter. Softening the butter to the consistency of creamy mayonnaise, as I have instructed, makes this procedure easier and the results lighter and more delicate than the denser pound-cake variety. **MAKES 2 DOZEN**

3 eggs
8 tablespoons (1 stick; 115g) unsalted butter, cut into 8 pieces
½ cup plus 1 tablespoon (120g) sugar
Grated zest of 1 small lemon or orange or ¾ teaspoon pure vanilla extract
½ teaspoon baking powder
¾ cup plus 1 tablespoon (120g) all-purpose flour

1. Preheat the oven to 375°F with the oven rack in the middle position.

2. Place the unbroken eggs in a large bowl filled with hot tap water.

3. In a small saucepan, begin to melt the butter over low heat. When the pieces are about half melted, remove the pan from the heat and stir until completely melted; the butter should be the consistency of light cream. Set the saucepan aside. When you are ready to use the butter, it will have cooled further and should be the consistency of heavy cream or light mayonnaise.

4. Brush two madeleine molds well with about 1½ tablespoons of the melted butter.

5. Remove the eggs from the bowl, pour out the water, and dry the bowl. Crack the eggs into the bowl and beat with the sugar and zest (or vanilla) until they triple in volume, 5 to 8 minutes. The batter should be very thick. It will fall slowly from the beaters and stand on the surface.

6. Mix the baking powder with the flour and sift it, one-third at a time, onto the batter, folding gently after each addition. Stop folding while a little of the flour is still visible.

7. Gently fold one-third of the batter into the creamy butter. Pour this butter mixture back into the remaining batter and fold gently no more than 8 to 10 times. The batter will begin to fall and you may see streaks of butter. A completely smooth batter is not necessary.

8. Spoon a heaping tablespoonful of the batter into each of the buttered molds, filling each three-quarters full. (If you have beaten and folded well, you may have a tablespoon of excess batter.)

9. Bake the madeleines until golden brown, 13 to 14 minutes. Unmold immediately and cool them on a wire rack. If the cakes do not fall out when inverting the mold, give one end a firm tap on the countertop. Although madeleines are best eaten within hours of being baked, they can be stored in a cookie tin for 3 or 4 days, or frozen for up to a month.

BIARRITZ

AFTER THE ALMOND TUILES (page 252), these are my favorite French cookies. Most versions are made using only almonds, but I use half almonds and half hazelnuts for a more unusual cookie. I also bake my cookies on a baking sheet that is only buttered, instead of buttered and floured, producing a slightly thinner cookie than the original. If your cookies are too fragile and break often while you are coating them with the chocolate, bake your next batch on a floured cookie sheet. The cookies can be frozen for several months. **MAKES 5 TO 6 DOZEN**

⅓ cup (50g) blanched hazelnuts
⅓ cup (50g) whole blanched almonds
Butter, for baking sheets
½ cup minus 2 teaspoons (100g) sugar
7 tablespoons (100g) unsalted butter
¼ teaspoon pure vanilla extract
2 egg whites
¼ cup (40g) all-purpose flour
8 ounces (230g) semisweet chocolate

1. Preheat the oven to 400°F with the oven rack in the middle position.

2. Place the hazelnuts and almonds in a rimmed baking sheet and roast until the nuts are lightly browned, 5 to 6 minutes. Allow the nuts to cool, about 15 minutes.

3. Increase the oven temperature to 450°F. Lightly butter two baking sheets.

4. In a food processor, grind the hazelnuts and almonds with the sugar until a powder forms, about 45 seconds. Add the butter and blend until smooth, about 30 seconds. Add the vanilla and egg whites and blend until the batter is smooth, about 15 seconds. Turn the processor off and add the flour. Process quickly, on and off, to mix in the flour, about 5 seconds.

5. Using a pastry bag fitted with a ¼-inch (#1) plain pastry tube, pipe out mounds about the size of a quarter, or drop scant teaspoonfuls onto the baking sheets, leaving 1 inch between the cookies.

6. Bake for 6 to 8 minutes, or until the edges are lightly browned. Remove the cookies with a long metal spatula to a rack to cool.

7. Melt the chocolate (see "Melting Chocolate," page 294). When smooth and cool to the touch, use a knife or small metal spatula to coat the flat side of each cookie with a thin layer of the chocolate. Place the cookies on a plate or pastry rack. Chill until the chocolate hardens. Serve cool or at room temperature.

BAKING OR COOKIE SHEETS

There are many different types of baking or cookie sheets available. There are coated and uncoated sheets, light metal and dark metal sheets, thick and thin metal sheets; and each will affect your baking differently to some degree.

Nonstick coatings are excellent in that they usually eliminate the steps you must normally take to prevent sticking. These coatings are easily damaged, however, and care must be taken not to cut on their surfaces. For recipes where cutting is necessary, an uncoated sheet is needed.

Light metal (mostly aluminum) sheets bake cooler than the dark ones, and in most cases are the ones I have used. If you are using a dark sheet, it will probably be necessary to reduce your oven temperature from between 50 to 75 degrees to prevent burning.

Most thin sheets buckle when they go into a hot oven, and although this normally doesn't cause any major damage, it is always disconcerting when it happens. When buying a baking sheet, try to find one that is sturdy and not too flexible.

Just remember, if the bottom of your pastry is burning, reduce your oven temperature or move the baking sheet higher in the oven.

CHOCOLATE-ALMOND MACAROONS

[MACARONS AU CHOCOLAT]

I HAVE ALWAYS found macaroons too sweet. Most recipes contain at least twice as much sugar as almonds, and I have reduced the sugar to a point where many would no longer call them macaroons (although I feel that much of the cookies' original character still remains). The cocoa adds to the subtle, semisweet nature of this cookie. **MAKES 5 DOZEN**

1⅓ cups (200g) whole blanched almonds or 1⅔ cups (200g) slivered almonds
½ cup plus 3 tablespoons (150g) sugar
⅓ cup (30g) unsweetened cocoa powder
2 to 3 egg whites

1. Preheat the oven to 350°F with the oven rack in the middle position. Use a nonstick baking sheet or line a regular baking sheet with parchment paper or a nonstick silicone liner.

2. In a food processor, grind the almonds and sugar to a powder. Mix in the cocoa.

3. Add 2 egg whites and mix by pulsing the processor several times to avoid overmixing. Add enough of the third egg white, if necessary, to form a sticky paste.

4. Fill a pastry bag fitted with a ½-inch (#6) plain tube and form cookies the size of a quarter on the prepared baking sheet, or drop by teaspoonfuls.

5. Bake the cookies until they have puffed slightly, 12 to 14 minutes. Let cool on the baking sheet. Remove from the sheet and store in an airtight container.

IN ADDITION

Similar nut cookies can be made using pecans, macadamia nuts, or hazelnuts. Also try making them with either toasted or unblanched almonds, both of which will change the flavor and character of the cookie.

VARIATION

MACAROONS

[MACARONS]

Omit the cocoa powder for a purer almond flavor.

PALM LEAF COOKIES

[PALMIERS]

ALTHOUGH THESE DELICIOUS, lightly caramelized pastries are called cookies, they really belong in a class by themselves. Sometimes called "elephant ears" in English, *palmiers* (which means "palm trees") are a perfect way to use up any scraps of puff pastry you may have—although once you've tasted a *palmier,* you're likely to make fresh puff pastry so you can bake a larger batch. **MAKES 25 TO 30**

About ⅓ cup (75g) sugar
¾ pound Rough Puff Pastry (page 230) or ½ pound store-bought puff pastry (see Note)
Butter, for baking sheets

1. Sprinkle the work surface with a light layer of sugar. Place the block of puff pastry on it and sprinkle it with a light layer of sugar.

2. Roll the pastry out into a rectangle about 10 inches long and ⅛ inch thick. Continue sprinkling sugar on the dough to make sure the dough is well coated on both sides. Trim the ends square.

3. With a pastry brush or your fingers, lightly sprinkle the surface of the dough with water (this will ensure that the folds stick together when baked). Fold two ends to meet at the center so that the 10-inch side now measures 5 inches. With a rolling pin, roll the pastry slightly to flatten the folded edges.

4. Sprinkle the surface again lightly with water and fold in half so that the 5-inch side now measures 2½ inches. Roll lightly again to flatten the folded edge. Cover with plastic wrap and refrigerate for at least 30 minutes.

5. Preheat the oven to 475°F with the oven rack in the middle position. Butter two baking sheets.

6. Cut the chilled dough, across the folds, into ¼-inch-wide strips. Lay the slices cut sides down on baking sheets, leaving 1½ to 2 inches between them.

7. Bake for 5 minutes. Turn the cookies over and bake until glazed and golden brown, another 2 to 3 minutes. Cool on a rack and keep them dry in an airtight container until served. Serve on a doily-covered plate.

NOTE: I find, and you may too, that using store-bought puff pastry produces cookies saltier than those made with my recipe.

LADYFINGERS

[BISCUITS À LA CUILLÈRE]

LADYFINGERS are made from a light sponge cake batter that's firm enough to hold its shape when formed with a pastry bag and large plain pastry tube. They are best eaten within several hours of baking, and are ideal for serving with fresh fruit or sorbet. Ladyfingers are used to line molds for desserts like the Chocolate Marquise (page 293), and are often moistened with liqueurs to become a part of a dessert, as they do in the Marquise Alice (page 271).

A problem often encountered is a runny batter that does not hold its shape when formed on the pastry sheet. This is often caused by the use of vanilla extract in the recipe. For this reason I call for a very small amount. Other ways of avoiding the use of liquid vanilla are to use vanilla sugar (sugar in which a vanilla bean has been stored to give the sugar flavor) or to flavor the batter with grated orange or lemon zest. In France, powdered vanilla is used, eliminating the problem. **MAKES 20**

3 eggs, separated
⅓ cup (75g) granulated sugar
¼ teaspoon pure vanilla extract or grated zest of 1 orange or lemon
⅛ teaspoon cream of tartar
½ cup plus 2 teaspoons (75g) all-purpose flour
Confectioners' sugar, for dusting

1. Preheat the oven to 375°F with the oven rack in the middle position. Line two baking sheets with waxed paper, parchment paper, or nonstick silicone liners.

2. In a small bowl, beat the egg yolks and granulated sugar until very thick. Beat in the vanilla.

3. In a medium-size bowl, beat the egg whites with the cream of tartar until stiff peaks form.

4. Sift the flour into the yolk mixture. Add half the beaten egg whites and fold until partially mixed. Add the remaining egg whites and fold until smooth.

5. Fill a pastry bag fitted with an 11⁄16-inch (#9) plain pastry tube with the batter. Form the ladyfingers 4 inches long by squeezing the batter from the bag while holding the tube about ½ inch above the surface of the baking sheet. As the batter falls to the sheet, draw your hand in a steady line until the prescribed length has been reached. Stop squeezing, and with a quick down-and-up motion of the pastry tube, cut the batter off.

6. Sprinkle the ladyfingers twice with confectioners' sugar and bake until lightly colored, 10 to 15 minutes.

7. Let the ladyfingers cool on the paper, and then gently pry them off. If not using immediately, store in an airtight container.

DESSERTS

Coming as they do at the end of a meal, desserts have the ability to turn an otherwise ordinary dinner into a memorable one; yet if mischosen, they can ruin the memory of a splendid one. Follow an elegant meal with an elegant dessert, such as Chocolate Marquise (page 293), but a rich meal with a light dessert, such as Pear Sorbet (page 288).

Although I have in many cases reduced the amount of sugar, butter, and cream used in updating the classic desserts, I also make a point of serving my guests small portions.

Many of the desserts in this chapter can be made partially or totally in advance. By following the advance preparation suggestions, you can make entertaining easy.

DESSERT OMELET WITH COINTREAU

[OMELETTE AU COINTREAU]

WITHOUT QUESTION, my most successful omelet is an *omelette au Cointreau.* By adding alcohol and sugar to the eggs, they become lighter and have a creamy custard consistency when cooked to perfection. The sugar in my version of this traditional dessert is one-third of that used in the original.

Depending on the size pan you use, and the number of people you serve, you can easily increase or decrease this recipe. For each egg, use 1 teaspoon sugar and 1 tablespoon Cointreau. **SERVES 2**

3 eggs
1 tablespoon granulated sugar
2 to 3 tablespoons Cointreau, to taste
½ tablespoon butter
Confectioners' sugar, for dusting

1. In a bowl, beat the eggs, granulated sugar, and Cointreau together until smooth.

2. In a 7- or 8-inch nonstick omelet pan, melt the butter over medium-high heat.

3. Add the egg mixture to the pan and rapidly and constantly stir with a wooden spoon. If you can, gently shake the pan at the same time. When the eggs are nearly set, yet a little liquid still remains, stop stirring and shake the pan for a couple of seconds, making sure that the bottom of the pan is completely covered by the egg. At this point, the eggs should be set, yet still moist. Stop shaking the pan and allow the bottom of the omelet to firm slightly, 4 to 5 seconds. (After making several omelets, you will be able to stir and shake the pan simultaneously.)

4. Fold the omelet into thirds by lifting the handle and tilting the pan at a 30-degree angle (see "How to Fold an Omelet," page 37). With the back of the spoon, fold the portion of the omelet nearest you toward the center of the pan. Gently push the omelet forward in the pan so the unfolded portion rises up the side of the pan. Using the spoon, fold this portion back into the pan, overlapping the first fold. Turn the omelet out onto a serving plate so that it ends up folded side down. Dust with confectioners' sugar and serve immediately.

VARIATIONS

DESSERT OMELET WITH RUM

[OMELETTE AU RHUM]

Substitute rum for Cointreau.

Strawberry-Filled Dessert Omelet with Cointreau

[OMELETTE AUX FRAISES ET AU COINTREAU]

Place 3 tablespoons diced strawberries across the center of the omelet before folding in step 4. Decorate with 2 strawberry halves.

Strawberry Breakfast Omelet

[OMELETTE AUX FRAISES]

By omitting the Cointreau from the above variation, the omelet becomes a breakfast treat for any member of the family.

Apple Omelet with Calvados

[OMELETTE VALLÉE D'AUGE]

Substitute 2 tablespoons Calvados for the Cointreau. Place a few tablespoons of sautéed apples down the center of the omelet before folding in step 4. Decorate with additional slices of sautéed apple.

Orange Souffleed Omelet

[OMELETTE SOUFFLÉE À L'ORANGE]

THIS IS A QUICK, elegant—and often overlooked—dessert that will impress and satisfy your guests whenever you have not had time to prepare one in advance.

By beating the egg yolks and whites separately, and then folding them together, an *omelette soufflée,* which is usually cooked in an omelet pan, puffs and browns like a soufflé.

The orange souffléed omelet I serve for dessert is baked in the oven and looks very much like a Baked Alaska. The fluffy egg mixture is first mounded on an *unbuttered* ovenproof platter, and then, using a pastry bag, it is decorated with swirls of the omelet soufflé batter. Browned quickly in a hot oven, the omelet soufflé is served warm, moist, and frothy, a light, delicate ending suitable for a full or rich meal. **SERVES 6 TO 8**

6 eggs, separated
½ cup plus 3 tablespoons (150g) granulated sugar
Grated zest of 2 oranges
Confectioners' sugar, for dusting

1. Preheat the oven to 475°F with the oven rack in the middle position.

2. In a bowl, beat the egg yolks with half of the granulated sugar until thickened. Stir in the orange zest.

3. Beat the egg whites until soft peaks form. Add the remaining sugar and beat until the egg whites are very stiff. Fold the egg whites into the yolk-sugar mixture.

4. With a spatula, mound the mixture on an ovenproof platter. Decorate the surface of the omelet using a pastry bag filled with one-sixth of the omelet mixture and fitted with a 5⁄16-inch (#3) star tube.

5. Bake until the souffléed omelet colors but does not rise, 4 to 5 minutes.

6. Dust with the confectioners' sugar and serve immediately.

IN ADDITION

There are also first-course or savory souffléed omelets. For example, a souffléed cheese omelet can be prepared by mixing grated cheese with beaten egg yolks and folding stiffly beaten egg whites into this mixture. Pour into a buttered omelet pan and cook for a few minutes over medium heat, then finish in a hot oven with a little cheese sprinkled on top. Slide the souffléed omelet from the pan to a warm serving plate or platter and serve.

APRICOT SOUFFLE

[SOUFFLÉ À L'ABRICOT]

THIS IS AN EXAMPLE of a fruit soufflé made without the traditional pastry-cream base. Fruits with a lot of pulp and not much liquid, such as apricots, produce a thick base when puréed. The base can then be simply sweetened and mixed with beaten egg whites to produce a very light and luscious dessert. Fruit soufflés prepared this way are lighter and will rise faster than traditional pastry-cream soufflés and require less baking time. Generally they will rise in 8 minutes or less.

For this recipe I use the principle of puréed fruit as a soufflé base, but substitute dried California apricots (I find their flavor more intense than the Turkish variety) for fresh ones because they are available year-round. The apricots are puréed in a blender with hot water to replace the fruit's natural moisture and to soften them.

Other fruits you can try are mangoes, pears, and papayas. With fresh fruit it is not necessary to add water. If the fruit needs sweetening, the sugar should be beaten with the stiff egg whites to dissolve it, or use Heavy Sugar Syrup (page 359) instead. **SERVES 4**

Butter and granulated sugar, for the soufflé mold
About ¾ cup (100g) dried California apricots
¼ cup plus 1 tablespoon (75g) granulated sugar
¾ cup hot water
2 tablespoons orange liqueur, such as Triple Sec, Cointreau, or Grand Marnier
5 egg whites
⅛ teaspoon cream of tartar
Confectioners' sugar, for dusting

1. Preheat the oven to 475°F with the oven rack in the lowest position. Butter and sugar a 4-cup soufflé mold.

2. Place the apricots in a blender (see Note). Dissolve the granulated sugar in the hot water and add to the blender. Add the orange liqueur. Blend until smooth. Transfer to a large bowl.

3. In second large bowl, beat the egg whites with the cream of tartar until stiff peaks form. With a whisk, fold one-third of the stiffly beaten egg whites into the apricot mixture to lighten it. With a rubber spatula, fold the remaining whites into the mixture until it is smooth. Pour the soufflé batter into the prepared mold and level the surface with a spatula. Run your thumb around the top of the mold to clean off any excess batter.

4. Bake the soufflé for 5 minutes. Lower the temperature to 425°F and bake until the soufflé has risen 3 to 4 inches above the top of the mold and is springy to the touch, another 3 to 4 minutes.

Preparing Souffles for the Oven Ahead of Time

To find out just how far in advance you can make your soufflés, I suggest that you try the following: Make any of the soufflés in the book up to the point of baking, and instead of pouring the batter into a 4-cup mold, pour it into individual (¾- to 1-cup) molds. Place one of the molds in your freezer, one in your refrigerator, one on your kitchen counter, and one in your oven. Baking time is only about 5 minutes. You should have no problems with the first one baked. Bake the one that is sitting on your counter 2 hours later, the one in the refrigerator the next day for lunch, and the one from the freezer the following week. If all bake as well as the first, your advance preparation can be done at any time.

Note: The freezer method works only for individual-size molds. The surface of the larger ones tends to dry out and crack in the freezer, preventing them from rising when baked.

5. Dust the soufflé with confectioners' sugar and serve immediately.

NOTE: If you have only a food processor, soften the apricots in the hot water first before puréeing them (with the water).

GRAND MARNIER SOUFFLE

[SOUFFLÉ AU GRAND MARNIER]

ONE OF THE MOST POPULAR dessert soufflés is the *soufflé au Grand Marnier,* yet it is but one of many soufflés that can be made with liqueurs. Use any of your favorite liqueurs in place of the Grand Marnier and produce a soufflé with the name of the liqueur. (Don't be tempted to add any more liqueur than called for in the recipe, for if too much is added, it will fall out of suspension and end up on the bottom of the soufflé dish in a liquid or pasty mass.) **SERVES 4**

Butter and granulated sugar, for the soufflé mold
1 cup milk
3 egg yolks
¼ cup minus 2 teaspoons (50g) granulated sugar
3 tablespoons (25g) all-purpose flour
4 egg whites
⅛ teaspoon cream of tartar
¼ teaspoon pure vanilla extract
Grated zest of 1 orange
¼ cup Grand Marnier
Confectioners' sugar, for dusting

1. Preheat the oven to 475°F with the oven rack in the lower third. Butter and sugar a 4-cup soufflé mold.

2. In a small saucepan, bring the milk to a boil over medium heat.

3. While the milk is heating, whisk the egg yolks and granulated sugar together in a small bowl. Add the flour and mix well, until smooth and free of lumps.

4. Thin the egg yolk mixture with about ¼ cup of the warm milk. When the remaining milk begins to boil, add it to the egg yolk mixture and stir well. Return the mixture to the saucepan and whisk rapidly over medium-high heat, making sure to whisk the bottom and the sides of the pan until the mixture thickens and boils, about 1 minute.

5. Cook the pastry cream an additional 2 minutes over medium heat, whisking while it boils gently, until it becomes shiny and is easier to stir. Remove the pan from the heat and cover to keep warm.

6. In a large bowl, beat the egg whites with the cream of tartar until stiff peaks form.

7. Pour the pastry cream into a large bowl and stir in the vanilla, grated orange zest, and Grand Marnier.

8. Fold one-third of the stiffly beaten egg whites into the pastry cream with a whisk to lighten it. Fold the remaining whites into the mixture with a rubber spatula until it is smooth. Pour the soufflé batter into the prepared mold and level the surface with the spatula. Run your thumb around the top of the mold to clean off any excess batter. (The soufflé can be made ahead to this point; see "Preparing Soufflés for the Oven Ahead of Time," page 264.)

9. Bake the soufflé for 5 minutes. Lower the temperature to 425°F and bake until the soufflé has risen 3 to 4 inches above the top of the mold and it is golden brown in color and springy to the touch, another 4 to 5 minutes.

10. Dust the soufflé with confectioners' sugar and serve immediately.

IN ADDITION

As with most soufflés, the center of this Grand Marnier soufflé will be soft and creamy when cooked to perfection. Although a sauce is never necessary with a creamy-centered soufflé, I realize that many people feel that a soufflé is not complete without one. For those of you who are so inclined, Grand Marnier–flavored Crème Anglaise (page 346) or fresh Raspberry Coulis (page 345) should suit the purpose admirably.

VARIATIONS

MOCHA SOUFFLE

[SOUFFLÉ MOKA]

Omit the vanilla, orange zest, and Grand Marnier. Add Coffee Essence (page 358) or instant coffee to taste to the warming milk in step 3. Taste the pastry cream in step 4, and if the coffee has made it too bitter, add up to 2 tablespoons sugar to the beaten egg whites in step 6 and beat again until stiff. Serve the soufflé with chocolate sauce made from 4 ounces (115g) semisweet or bittersweet chocolate, ⅓ cup water, and 2 tablespoons Cognac (optional).

STRAWBERRY SOUFFLE

[SOUFFLÉ AUX FRAISES]

Replace the orange zest and Grand Marnier with 2 tablespoons kirsch and add to the pastry cream in step 7. Fold 1 cup diced strawberries into the pastry cream with the second half of the beaten egg whites in step 8.

CHOCOLATE SOUFFLE WITH GRAND MARNIER

[SOUFFLÉ AU CHOCOLAT ET AU GRAND MARNIER]

THIS IS AN EXTREMELY light chocolate soufflé made from my basic chocolate mousse recipe with the addition of orange zest and Grand Marnier. A plain chocolate soufflé can be made by omitting them.

The soufflé mixture can also be baked in a water bath (*bain-marie*) for a little bit longer, to give you a *pudding au chocolat,* a wonderful, dense fallen soufflé dessert (see Variation).

SERVES 4

Butter and granulated sugar, for the soufflé mold
4 ounces (115g) semisweet or bittersweet chocolate
4 tablespoons (½ stick; 60g) unsalted butter
4 eggs, separated
Grated zest of 1 orange
2 tablespoons Grand Marnier
⅛ teaspoon cream of tartar
Confectioners' sugar, for dusting

1. Preheat the oven to 475°F with the oven rack in the lowest position. Butter and sugar a 4-cup soufflé mold.

2. In a small saucepan, combine the chocolate and butter and melt over low heat. Remove from the heat, whisk in the egg yolks, and pour into a large bowl. Stir in the grated orange zest and Grand Marnier.

3. In a large bowl, beat the egg whites with the cream of tartar until stiff peaks form.

4. With a whisk, fold one-third of the beaten egg whites into the chocolate mixture. Fold in the remaining egg whites with a rubber spatula. Pour into the prepared soufflé mold and level the surface with a spatula. Run your thumb around the top of the mold to clean off any excess batter. (The soufflé can be prepared ahead to this point; see "Preparing Soufflés for the Oven Ahead of Time," page 264.)

5. Bake the soufflé for 5 minutes. Lower the temperature to 425°F and bake until the soufflé has risen 3 to 4 inches above the top of the mold and is springy to the touch, another 4 to 5 minutes.

6. Dust the soufflé with confectioners' sugar and serve immediately.

IN ADDITION

I usually make this soufflé in advance and refrigerate it. When it is time for dessert, I ask my guests if they would like a chocolate mousse or soufflé. If the majority want a soufflé, I bake it. If they want mousse, it is served cold.

VARIATION

Fallen Chocolate Souffle

[PUDDING AU CHOCOLAT]

A French *pudding* is basically a fallen soufflé. Follow the soufflé recipe through step 4, buttering a 4-cup soufflé dish or charlotte mold. Pour the soufflé mixture into the prepared mold. Place the mold in a deep roasting pan and fill with enough boiling water to come halfway up the sides of the mold. Place in the oven, reduce the temperature to 400°F, and bake for 15 to 20 minutes. Remove from the oven and allow to cool. (The inflated puffed portion will drop back into the mold.) To serve, unmold onto a platter. The pudding can be served warm or cold and can be accompanied by Crème Anglaise (page 346).

Any of the soufflés in this book can be baked and unmolded using this method, if desired.

CREME CARAMEL

[CRÈME RENVERSÉE AU CARAMEL]

CRÈME RENVERSÉE *au caramel,* commonly called *crème caramel* and known as *flan* in Spanish, is one of the world's most popular desserts. It is a vanilla custard cooked in a caramel-lined mold, so that when it is unmolded it is covered with a liquid caramel sauce.

I make a classic custard with 2 eggs per cup of milk. In the following recipe, I have removed two egg whites, creating a fragile yet rich-tasting custard. Although you can bake the custard in almost any size mold, I have chosen a cake pan so that the finished dessert will be no higher than 1½ inches. If you want the custard to be higher, use a deeper mold and give it added strength by including the 2 egg whites otherwise removed. The custard can be made with milk, heavy cream, or a mixture of the two, and many people serve it with whipped cream, although I find that unnecessary.

Always unmold the crème caramel just before serving, because if it's unmolded too early, it will look dull and dry instead of shiny and bright. **SERVES 8 TO 10**

THE COLOR OF CARAMEL

The color of the cooked caramel for crème caramel is very important. If it is too pale, it will have little or no flavor. If it is too dark, it will taste bitter or burnt. I cook the sugar until it is a deep amber color and is just about to smoke, and often tell students to wait until they begin seeing smoke before pouring the hot sugar into their mold. After making the dessert several times, you can determine for yourself the color required for the flavor desired.

CARAMEL

¼ cup water
½ cup (110g) sugar
2 to 3 drops lemon juice (optional, see Note)
Butter, for mold (optional)

CUSTARD

3 cups milk
⅔ cup (140g) sugar
4 whole eggs
2 egg yolks
2 teaspoons pure vanilla extract

1. Make the caramel: Place the water in a small saucepan and add the sugar. Cook, without stirring, over medium-high heat until the sugar turns amber in color, about 5 minutes.

2. Immediately pour the caramel into an 8-inch round cake pan and, using pot holders, turn it until the bottom and sides of the pan are coated. (If you are unable to fully coat the sides of your mold, wait for the caramel to cool and then lightly butter the sides not coated.) Set aside. (As the caramel cools, it will harden. When the pan cools, the caramel may crack. This is normal and will not affect the dessert.)

3. Preheat the oven to 350°F with the oven rack in the lowest position.

4. Make the custard: In a small saucepan, bring the milk and sugar to a boil over medium heat.

5. In a bowl, whisk the 4 whole eggs and 2 egg yolks until smooth. Stirring constantly, pour the hot milk mixture slowly into the eggs. Stir in the vanilla.

6. Place the caramel-coated cake pan in a small roasting pan, which will serve as a water bath (*bain-marie*). For a perfectly smooth custard, strain the mixture into the cake pan. Fill the roasting pan with enough boiling water to come halfway up the sides of the cake pan.

7. Bake until a cake tester or toothpick placed in the center of the custard comes out clean, not milky, 25 to 30 minutes. Allow the custard to cool. Refrigerate for 2 hours or more.

8. To serve: Unmold the custard onto a large round plate or platter just before serving. To do so, run the point of a knife around the edge of the custard to make sure that it is not stuck to the pan. Place a serving platter upside down on top of the cake pan, and while holding the two firmly together, invert quickly. Remove the cake pan and allow the caramel sauce to flow on top of the custard. Use a cake server to cut and serve the custard.

NOTE: The lemon juice slows the hardening of the sugar and gives you more time to coat the pan in step 2. If you have experience working with caramel, you can leave it out.

THE EVER-CHANGING CUSTARD

Custard is one of the foundations of French dessert making. In varying proportions, it is a combination of milk or cream, eggs, and sugar. At its thinnest and most refined, it is used as a sauce, called Crème Anglaise (page 346). It can be served with cake, poached fruit, or as part of a meringue dessert such as Floating Island with Raspberry Sauce (page 274). When you freeze a crème anglaise, it becomes ice cream (see page 290). When you add whipped cream and gelatin to it, it becomes a rich dessert called Bavarian cream (see Marquise Alice, page 271, or Riz à l'Impératrice, page 273).

Then there are the baked custards, ranging from the simple and always satisfying Crème Caramel (facing page) to the silky and smooth *pots de crème* (see page 270). For most custards, but particularly for the very rich recipes such as *pots de crème,* I have reduced egg yolks, cream, and sugar where possible without destroying the satisfying nature of these desserts.

VANILLA AND COFFEE POTS DE CREME

[POTS DE CRÈME: VANILLE ET CAFÉ]

THE CLASSIC RECIPE for *pots de crème* calls for 1 quart of heavy cream, 12 egg yolks, and about 1½ cups sugar. This is basically the same formula that is used for crème brûlée, a rich vanilla custard served with a crust of melted brown sugar. Although I enjoy these rich custards and will share one at a restaurant, I cannot, in good conscience, make and serve anything so high in cholesterol and calories.

The following recipe is made lighter by the reduction of yolks, the addition of egg whites, and the use of milk instead of cream. I have also reduced the sugar considerably, yet it still tastes rich and delicious. **SERVES 6**

3 cups milk
½ cup plus 3 tablespoons (150g) sugar
2 eggs
5 egg yolks
2 teaspoons pure vanilla extract
1½ teaspoons instant coffee granules

1. Preheat the oven to 350°F with the oven rack in the lowest position.

2. In a small saucepan, bring the milk and sugar to a boil over medium heat.

3. In a bowl, whisk the whole eggs and yolks together lightly. Stirring constantly, pour the

POTS DE CREME: What's in a Name?

Pots de crème gets its name from the small pots this rich custard is traditionally baked and served in. These little ceramic cups with lids have a ⅓-cup capacity and were often served three per person, one each of chocolate, vanilla, and coffee. Even with my lightened custard, I find three too much to eat, and serve only two: vanilla and coffee (I omit the chocolate because it is grainy and tends to produce a dull rather than shiny surface).

hot milk-and-sugar mixture slowly into the eggs. Stir in the vanilla.

4. Divide the custard into 2 equal portions. Add the coffee to one portion and stir until dissolved.

5. For a perfectly smooth custard, strain the mixtures into 6 small *pot de crème* "pots" or ½-cup ramekins. Be sure that all of the foam is spooned from the top of each.

6. Place the *pots* into a roasting pan. Add boiling water to the roasting pan to come halfway up the sides of the *pots.* Bake until a cake tester or toothpick inserted in the custard comes out dry or clean, 20 to 30 minutes. Do not let the custard boil. If the custard begins to puff, an indication that it is beginning to boil, remove it from the oven immediately.

7. Allow the *pots* to cool and then refrigerate for 2 hours or more. (The custard can be made a day ahead. Keep refrigerated.)

8. Serve one vanilla and one coffee *pot* to each person.

MARQUISE ALICE

A BAVARIAN CREAM (*bavarois*) is a molded dessert made from a crème anglaise base to which gelatin and whipped cream are added. A *marquise Alice* is a praline-flavored Bavarian cream with kirsch-moistened ladyfingers buried in the center. The unmolded cream is traditionally covered with whipped cream and decorated with currant jelly.

Although the white-covered Bavarian cream with its deep red decoration is most attractive, I have saved calories by simply serving the unmolded, undecorated dessert surrounded by a band of currant jelly. You can also use small metal molds to make individual servings. **SERVES 6 TO 8**

Kirsch
4 to 6 Ladyfingers (page 259) or store-bought ladyfingers
Crème Anglaise (page 346), hot
1 envelope unflavored gelatin softened in ¼ cup cold water
½ teaspoon pure vanilla extract
2 rounded tablespoons (50g) Praline Paste (page 356)
¾ cup heavy cream
½ cup red currant jelly
2 teaspoons water

1. Sprinkle enough kirsch over the ladyfingers to moisten them.

2. Place the hot crème anglaise in a medium-size metal bowl and add the softened gelatin, vanilla, and praline paste.

3. Set the bowl in a larger bowl of ice and water (see "Over Ice," below) and stir until cool to the touch, being sure to scrape the sides and bottom of the bowl. Remove the custard from the ice.

4. In another bowl, set in the ice and water, beat the cream until stiff. Fold the whipped cream into the cooled custard. (This is now a Bavarian cream.) Place the bowl containing the Bavarian cream over the ice and continue folding until the mixture is thick and smooth.

5. Pour half of this mixture into an 8-inch round cake pan. Make a layer of ladyfingers, placing them no closer than ¼ inch from the edge. Cover the ladyfingers with the remaining Bavarian cream. Refrigerate for at least 2 hours before unmolding.

6. In a small saucepan, melt the currant jelly and water over low heat. Bring to a boil, remove from the heat, and add 2 teaspoons kirsch. Allow to cool at room temperature, yet remain liquid.

7. To unmold: Run the point of a knife around the custard and dip the mold into hot water for 5 to 10 seconds. Place a chilled cake platter upside down over the cake pan. Holding the pan and platter together, invert. Remove the cake pan. If the dessert does not unmold easily after one or two immersions in hot water, give both the plate and the mold a firm downward shake. (This can be done several hours before serving. Keep refrigerated.)

8. Just before serving, spoon the currant jelly onto the platter around the dessert.

"OVER ICE": Controlling the Cooling Process

Stirring mixtures "over ice" is an extremely useful technique. It is used when working with gelatin in order to speed up the jelling process and at the same time give you control over it so it doesn't jell too much (which might happen if you leave the gelatin mixture in the refrigerator). You can also use it any time you want to cool down a hot mixture quickly.

To cool things over ice, place the saucepan or a metal or glass bowl containing the mixture in question in a larger bowl filled with ice and a little water. The water is needed in order to completely surround the saucepan or bowl with cold. If you are cooling a hot mixture or thickening a gelatin mixture, you must stir it, which both speeds up the cooling process and, in the case of gelatin, prevents uneven jelling.

Use the same method when whipping cream, because the cold temperature prevents the cream from turning to butter before the cream is stiff.

RIZ A L'IMPERATRICE

THE CLASSIC *riz à l'Impératrice* is a vanilla-flavored rice pudding mixed with Bavarian cream (crème anglaise, gelatin, and whipped cream) and preserved fruits and molded in a ring mold. It is served unmolded with kirsch-flavored currant jelly around it.

I have reduced by half the amount of egg yolks and heavy cream originally used. I have also eliminated the preserved fruits, which I find too sweet, and use a raspberry sauce sweetened with currant jelly in place of the jelly on its own. My choice of a cake pan instead of a ring mold is mainly for presentation. I find a wedge of the dessert looks better than a section of a ring. **SERVES 8**

½ cup (100g) long-grain white rice
3 cups milk
½ cup minus 2 teaspoons (100g) sugar
1 vanilla bean or 1 tablespoon pure vanilla extract
2 egg yolks
1 envelope unflavored gelatin softened in ¼ cup cold water
½ cup heavy cream
½ recipe Raspberry Coulis (page 345), sweetened with red currant jelly to taste

1. In a small saucepan, cook the rice in 2 or more cups of boiling water for 15 minutes and drain.

2. In a 2-quart saucepan, bring the milk, sugar, and vanilla bean (if using vanilla extract, add it in step 3) to a boil. Add the rice, cover, and cook over low heat for 30 minutes. Not all of the milk will be absorbed; about 1 cup should remain. Remove the vanilla bean, if used.

3. Remove the rice from the heat and whisk in the egg yolks, softened gelatin, and vanilla extract, if using. Pour into a medium-size metal bowl and place in a larger bowl of ice and water (see "Over Ice," facing page). Stir until cool to the touch, being sure to scrape the sides and bottom of the bowl. Set aside.

4. In another bowl, set into the ice and water, whip the cream until stiff. Fold the whipped cream into the rice mixture. Return the rice to the ice and water and continue folding until the mixture begins to set or thicken. Pour into an 8-inch round cake pan or other metal mold. Refrigerate for at least 2 hours before unmolding.

5. To unmold: Run the point of a knife around the rice mixture and dip the mold into hot water for 5 to 10 seconds. Place a chilled cake platter upside down over the cake pan. Holding the pan and platter together, invert. Remove the cake pan. If the rice does not unmold easily after one or two immersions in hot water, give both the plate and the mold a firm downward shake. (This can be done several hours before serving. Keep refrigerated.)

6. To serve: Pour a little of the raspberry coulis around the unmolded rice and serve the remaining sauce in a pitcher or bowl. You can also serve the dessert sliced and surrounded with the sauce on individual plates.

FLOATING ISLAND WITH RASPBERRY SAUCE

[ILE FLOTTANTE CARDINALE]

ILE FLOTTANTE and *oeufs à la neige* are both desserts made from poached meringue and served with crème anglaise. In the case of *oeufs à la neige,* large egg-shaped spoonfuls of meringue are poached in simmering milk or water, while the *île flottante* meringue is molded and poached in the oven. When unmolded, the meringue becomes an island floating on the crème anglaise.

Ile flottante often has crushed praline mixed into or layered with the meringue. I find the praline too sweet in this dessert, so I add chopped toasted almonds instead. I also use raspberry sauce to coat the surface of the floating island and have added the name *cardinale,* which is classically used to describe a dish robed in red.

The dessert can be made up to one day in advance and assembled before serving.

SERVES 6

Butter, for the soufflé mold
3 egg whites
¼ cup plus 2 tablespoons (90g) sugar
¼ teaspoon pure vanilla extract
⅓ cup (40g) chopped toasted almonds
Crème Anglaise (page 346)
Raspberry Coulis (page 345)

1. Preheat the oven to 350°F with the rack in the lowest position. Lightly butter a 4-cup soufflé mold.

2. In a bowl, beat the egg whites until soft peaks form, about 30 seconds. Add the sugar and vanilla extract and beat until very stiff, about 1 minute. Fold in the chopped toasted almonds.

3. Pour the meringue mixture into the prepared mold and bake in a water bath (*bain-marie*) for 20 minutes, or until springy to the touch and lightly colored on top.

4. Allow the meringue to cool in the mold. Refrigerate for at least 1 hour before unmolding and serving.

5. Present the unmolded meringue on a deep platter surrounded by crème anglaise and covered with raspberry coulis. Serve each guest a slice accompanied by a little of each sauce.

IN ADDITION

Many years ago I was asked by my friends Tim and Nina Zagat to bring a light dessert to a dinner party at which Paul Bocuse was to be the honored guest. When it was announced that the Floating Island that was about to be served was mine, I was told by my dinner partner, who was a close friend of the great chef, that I shouldn't be upset if Monsieur Bocuse merely tasted it, for he rarely ate desserts. I was pleased when he ate not only the portion served, but asked for more.

THE CHOCOLATE MOUSSE: Marvelous and Multifaceted

Since chocolate behaves much like flour when baked, it is possible to use this basic chocolate mousse recipe to make several desserts that normally contain flour. For example, baked in a cake pan it makes Chocolate Mousse Cake (page 246). If you bake it in a jelly-roll pan, you have a chocolate roll (see page 251). Baked in a soufflé mold, it is Chocolate Soufflé (page 266). For a delicious Fallen Chocolate Soufflé (page 267), the mousse is baked in a soufflé mold in a water bath (*bain-marie*). You can also make a wonderfully simple variation of the chocolate mousse by freezing it and serving it in slices (see Chocolate Marquise, page 293).

CHOCOLATE MOUSSE

[MOUSSE AU CHOCOLAT]

THIS SIMPLE CLASSIC is one of the most versatile recipes that I have ever taught. Not only is it a fabulous chocolate mousse, but it can also be baked to make a soufflé, a cake, a chocolate roll, or a French-style chocolate pudding (see "The Chocolate Mousse," above).

A mousse is light and airy and can be made with beaten egg whites or whipped cream, but I make mine with egg whites alone. I find that the chocolate, butter, and egg yolks in the recipe supply all the richness needed.

A refreshing variation can be made by adding the finely grated zest of 1 orange. If you want to flavor the mousse with coffee, rum, Grand Marnier, or another liqueur, add only 1 to 2 tablespoons (to taste) just before incorporating the egg whites. If you add more you may lose the light consistency that makes this recipe so good. **SERVES 6**

4 ounces (115g) semisweet or bittersweet chocolate
4 tablespoons (½ stick; 60g) unsalted butter
4 eggs, separated
⅛ teaspoon cream of tartar

1. In a heavy-bottomed saucepan, melt the chocolate and butter over low heat. Stir occasionally until smooth.

2. Remove the chocolate mixture from the heat and whisk in the egg yolks until blended. Immediately pour the mixture into a large bowl. (The melted chocolate and butter will be hot enough to poach the egg yolks, which will lightly thicken the mixture.)

3. In a large bowl, beat the egg whites with the cream of tartar until stiff peaks form.

4. With a whisk, fold one-third of the stiffly beaten egg whites into the chocolate mixture to lighten it. Using a rubber spatula, fold the remaining whites into the chocolate mixture until smooth.

5. Pour the mousse into a crystal serving bowl or individual glasses and refrigerate until set, 2 hours or longer. Serve chilled.

LIME MOUSSE

[MOUSSE AU CITRON VERT]

CLASSIC FRUIT MOUSSES are made with fruit purées sweetened with sugar syrup and then folded with whipped cream, molded, and refrigerated. This version uses half whipped cream and half stiffly beaten egg whites. For lime mousse, fruit juice is used instead of a purée and gelatin is used to thicken it.

The tartness of limes varies, and I prefer this mousse on the tart side. If, when you combine the sugar syrup and the lime juice in step 4, you find it too tart, sweeten it to taste by adding confectioners' sugar.

This wonderfully refreshing dessert can be made a day in advance. Refrigerate until served. **SERVES 8 TO 10**

8 to 10 limes
1 cup (220g) granulated sugar
½ cup water
1½ envelopes unflavored gelatin softened in ½ cup cold water
1 cup heavy cream
4 egg whites
Confectioners' sugar

1. Remove the zest from one of the limes to make 10 to 12 lime zest knots for garnish (see "How to Make Zest Knots," facing page). Cover the knots with plastic wrap.

2. Squeeze the limes to obtain 1 cup of juice.

3. In a small saucepan, bring ½ cup of the granulated sugar and the water to a boil, making sure the sugar is dissolved. Remove from the heat and stir in the softened gelatin to dissolve it.

4. Add the gelatin-sugar mixture to the lime juice and place in a metal bowl set into a larger bowl filled halfway with ice and a little water (see "Over Ice," page 272). Stir the juice until it is cool (see "Cool to the Touch," page 350), about 1 minute. Remove from the ice and set aside.

5. In a medium-size bowl set into the ice and water, beat the cream until stiff, about 1 minute. Set aside.

6. In a large bowl, beat the egg whites until soft peaks form, about 30 seconds. Add the

How to Make Zest Knots

Any type of citrus peel—lime, lemon, orange, grapefruit—can be used to make an attractive knot for a garnish. Using a vegetable peeler, peel strips of zest from the citrus fruit with a sawing motion from top to bottom, trying to make the strips as long as possible. With a sharp paring knife, trim off the ragged edges of the strips and cut the zest into long 1⁄16-inch-wide "strings." Gently tie a knot in the center of each string.

remaining ½ cup granulated sugar and beat until stiff peaks form, about 1 minute.

7. Refresh the ice-and-water mixture by pouring off excess water and adding more ice to return it to its original proportions. Place the juice mixture over the ice and water and stir with a metal spoon, being sure to scrape the sides and bottom of the bowl, until it is very cold and the consistency of heavy cream, 4 to 5 minutes.

8. Fold in half of the beaten egg whites, then three-quarters of the whipped cream. Follow this with the remaining egg whites. The mixture should be smooth and have the consistency of sour cream. Pour into a serving bowl and refrigerate until set, about 30 minutes. (This can be done up to 1 day before serving.)

9. To decorate the mousse: Whisk a little confectioners' sugar into the remaining whipped cream to sweeten to taste. Fill a pastry bag fitted with a 3⁄16-inch (#1) starred tube with the whipped cream and pipe rosettes over the top of the mousse. Place one lime zest knot in the center of each rosette.

VARIATION

Lemon Mousse

[MOUSSE AU CITRON]

Replace lime zest and juice with lemon zest and juice.

DESSERT CREPES

[CRÊPES SUCRÉES]

DESSERT CRÊPES are made with sweetened batter. In addition to the sugar and vanilla in the recipe, other flavorings can be added to the batter to match the crêpes to the filling. A touch of freshly grated nutmeg or ground cinnamon for an apple filling, or a little grated lemon zest when filling with a lemon-flavored pastry cream, are just two examples.

This recipe was a favorite of my daughters growing up. It became a Saturday morning ritual and something all their friends knew about. When they were old enough to make them with me, crêpe cooking lessons in the morning were part of sleepover dates. They enjoyed, and still do, spreading a thin layer of Apricot Jam (page 356) or Raspberry Jam (page 355) on the crêpes and then folding or rolling them to eat.

Traditionally, crêpes are made in small steel pans that must be seasoned and lubricated with butter or oil after every few crêpes. I find using nonstick pans much easier and less messy, and therefore recommend their use. **MAKES 16 TO 24 SIX-INCH CRÊPES**

MAKING CREPES

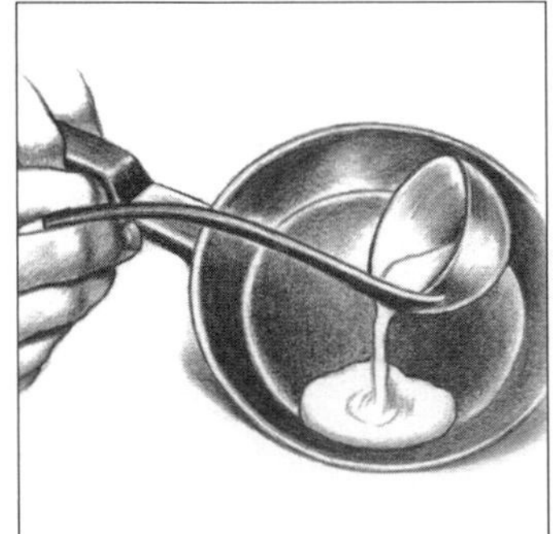

1. Tilt the crêpe pan slightly and ladle approximately 2 tablespoons of batter into the pan where the sides and bottom meet.

2. Turn the pan in a circular motion to spread the batter evenly.

3. When the edges of the crêpe begin to brown, flip it.

1 cup plus 1 tablespoon (150g) all-purpose flour
3 eggs
2 tablespoons (25g) sugar
½ teaspoon pure vanilla extract
1½ cups milk
3 tablespoons (45g) melted butter or vegetable oil

1. Put the flour in a bowl (see Note) and add the eggs, sugar, vanilla, and ½ cup of the milk. Whisk slowly until a smooth batter is formed. Add the remaining 1 cup milk and whisk well. If time permits, allow the batter to rest 30 minutes. (As the batter rests, the granules of flour absorb the milk and swell, creating a smoother batter and a slightly stronger crêpe than if used right away.)

2. Whisk in the butter just before using the batter.

3. Heat a nonstick pan with a 6-inch surface over medium-high heat. The pan is ready when a drop of water dances on the hot surface. Hold the pan in one hand, tilting it slightly. Using a small ladle or coffee measure, pour about 2 tablespoons of batter into the pan where the sides and bottom meet. Now turn the pan in a circular motion to spread the batter evenly. The amount of batter used should just coat the bottom of the pan. Any excess should be poured back.

4. Cook the crêpe until the edge begins to brown, 30 to 45 seconds. Turn the crêpe with a spatula or flip it (see Savory Crêpes, step 4, page 60). Cook the second side for only 10 seconds and slide the crêpe onto a plate. (The surface of the crêpe should be medium brown in color, which is darker than a savory crêpe because of the sugar in the batter. If after making two crêpes you find the color either too dark or too light, adjust your heat accordingly. At the same point, if you find the crêpe is too thick, thin the batter with a little more milk.) If at any point a crêpe sticks to the pan, use a light brush of oil before making the next one. Repeat until all the crêpes are made, stacking them one on top of the other, and allow them to cool.

NOTE: The batter can be made in a blender without worry of lumps forming. Place all ingredients in the container of the blender and cover. Then turn the blender on and off again. Scrape down the flour that has stuck to the sides of the blender and blend until smooth.

Neutral Crepe Batter

If you prefer, you can make crêpes to be used in either savory dishes or desserts by making a crêpe batter flavored with only ¼ teaspoon salt (leaving out the sugar and vanilla).

CREPES SUZETTE

CRÊPES SUZETTE is one of those desserts whose flavor lingers in your memory long after you have finished eating. The combination of orange, butter, sugar, and Cognac provides a delicious sauce for the thin, delicately flavored French pancakes.

Those who are familiar with making crêpes will notice that for this dessert I have removed 2 egg whites from the traditional dessert crêpe batter, which creates softer and richer-tasting crêpes. They are wonderful to eat, but more fragile (having lost the strength provided by the egg whites). If you have problems with the crêpes tearing, use 3 whole eggs the next time.

Choose an attractive ovenproof platter for serving, and make sure that it has a rim high enough to contain the sauce created by the melting butter. Although this dessert is customarily flambéed, I choose not to do so in order to make advance preparation and serving easy. When making crêpes for a large party, I use two crêpe pans to speed the process.

SERVES 6 TO 8

DESSERT CREPE VARIATIONS

Most classic dessert crêpes are filled—unlike Crêpes Suzette, which are simply folded and served with a flavored butter sauce. The basic fillings for dessert crêpes are Pastry Cream (page 347), whipped cream, and Ice Cream (page 290). Diced fruit and chopped nuts are often mixed with the various cream fillings, and raspberry, vanilla, and chocolate sauces are served over the crêpes.

A crêpe filled with a soufflé batter and baked becomes a *crêpe soufflée.* You can fill the crêpes with Grand Marnier Soufflé (page 265) or Chocolate Soufflé with Grand Marnier (page 266). To make the *crêpes soufflées,* spoon about 3 tablespoons soufflé batter down the middle of the crêpe. Fold the two sides of the crêpe over the filling and place the filled crêpes, seam side down, on a well-buttered ovenproof platter. Bake at 475°F for 4 to 5 minutes, until they double in size. Serve the *crêpes soufflées* with Crème Anglaise (page 346), flavored to enhance the soufflé filling.

Dessert Crêpes (page 278)
1 tablespoon plus ¼ cup Grand Marnier
8 tablespoons (1 stick; 115g) unsalted butter, softened to room temperature
¼ cup (50g) sugar
Grated zest and juice of 1 orange, at room temperature

1. Prepare the crêpes using 1 egg and 2 egg yolks in place of 3 eggs. In step 2 of the crêpe recipe, whisk in the 1 tablespoon of the Grand Marnier along with the melted butter.

2. Make the Suzette butter (see Note): In a food processor, cream the butter. Add the sugar and process until the mixture is smooth and white. Add the orange zest and gradually add the juice. (If the orange juice is cold it will stiffen the butter, making this procedure more difficult.)

3. Add the ¼ cup Grand Marnier a little at a time. Do not worry if the butter does not hold all the liquid.

4. Assemble the dessert: Turn the stack of crêpes over so that the lighter side is on top. Spread each crêpe with 1 teaspoon of the Suzette butter and fold in half and then in half again, forming a quarter-circle wedge. Arrange attractively on an ovenproof platter and spread any remaining butter and liquid over them. (At this point, the crêpes can be covered and refrigerated or frozen. Bake unthawed.)

5. To serve: Preheat the oven to 425°F. Place the platter of crêpes in the oven for 10 to 15 minutes, or until the butter is bubbling. Serve 2 to 3 crêpes per person.

NOTE: It is best to make the Suzette butter while the crêpe batter is resting, for although the butter can be made ahead and refrigerated, it must be brought back to room temperature before using.

IN ADDITION

Crêpes Suzette was originally designed to be a restaurant spectacle, with the maître d' flaming them for you at the table. I prefer to sip Cognac or Grand Marnier with coffee following dessert instead. However, if you wish to flame the crêpes, simply warm an additional ¼ cup of Grand Marnier and pour it over the crêpes hot from the oven. Carefully ignite the flaming sauce and use a long kitchen spoon to baste the crêpes with the sauce until the flames die. If all the alcohol has not evaporated, the delicate balance of flavors can be upset. (See also "How to Flambé," page 282.)

BANANAS FLAMBEED WITH RUM

[BANANES FLAMBÉES AU RHUM]

FOR PEOPLE who like bananas, *bananes flambées* is a certain winner. Although your guests may enjoy the drama of this dessert, the flaming of the bananas is not just for show, and in fact is most easily done in the kitchen, away from the guests. In addition to cooking off the alcohol, flaming browns the bananas and caramelizes the sugar.

A simple variation can be made by serving half a banana cut lengthwise with a scoop of vanilla ice cream. Also try plain or toasted grated coconut with or in place of the almonds. **SERVES 4**

HOW TO FLAMBE

When a recipe calls for flaming, a distilled liquor (like rum, Cognac, or gin) or a liqueur (like Grand Marnier or Cointreau) is used. The alcohol is added to a hot pan, causing fumes to rise. The fumes are then ignited and the alcohol is allowed to burn off.

In restaurant kitchens, a chef will usually ignite the alcohol by tilting the pan so that the gas flames of the burner ignite the fumes. For the home kitchen, it is safer to take the pan off the flames and ignite the fumes with a match. Of course, if you have an electric stove, you will have to use a match anyway.

When the alcohol is ignited while the pan is still over the heat, the flames will be quite high. Off the heat the flames will be lower, but it is still wise to stand back and keep your face averted when you light the alcohol. A long match (like a fireplace match) works well.

Never use more than about ¼ cup of alcohol for flaming. If you use more, it will take too long for the flames to die down.

Anyone who has had difficulty flaming a dessert at the table will find flaming in the kitchen much easier. Before you take your pan off the heat, be sure to have the alcohol you're adding at hand, and the match ready to strike so the alcohol won't all evaporate before you're ready to ignite it.

⅓ cup (70g) sugar
4 tablespoons (½ stick; 60g) butter
Juice of 1 lime or lemon
½ cup dark rum
4 small bananas (see Note), peeled
¼ cup (25g) sliced almonds, toasted

1. In a large skillet, stir the sugar over medium-high heat until it melts and lightly caramelizes. Remove the pan from the heat.

2. Stir in the butter, lime juice, and ¼ cup of the rum. Return the pan to low heat.

3. Place the bananas in the pan and baste with the sauce. Cover and cook over low heat until tender, 5 to 10 minutes.

4. To flame: Pour the remaining ¼ cup rum into the pan; remove from the heat. Keeping your face and anything flammable well away from the pan, carefully ignite the rum by touching a match to the pan's edge. Baste the bananas until the flames die. Transfer to a serving platter or plates, sprinkle with toasted almonds, and serve immediately.

NOTE: Use bananas that still have a little green at the stem.

IN ADDITION

There are many rums with varying flavors. Most of the rum used in France comes from the island of Martinique, and its flavor differs from that of most other rum-producing islands. As hard as I tried to develop an appreciation for it while living in France, I never did. My preference is for one of the dark, full-flavored blended rums from Puerto Rico or Jamaica, and my favorite rum is a Demerara rum from Guyana, but it is hard to find and I regularly use Myers's dark rum. If you use an ultra-high-proof rum, be careful of the added fire power when flaming.

STRAWBERRIES WITH SABAYON

[FRAISES AU SABAYON]

THE FRENCH *sauce sabayon* is fashioned after the Italian zabaglione. In Italy it is made with Marsala, a sweet Italian wine, while in France it is made with a dry white wine and often flavored with an eau-de-vie or liqueur. Sabayon can be served warm, cold, or frozen, and is excellent with both fresh and poached fruit. **SERVES 6**

2 pints strawberries
3 egg yolks
¼ cup plus 2 tablespoons (90g) sugar
⅓ cup dry white wine
1 to 2 tablespoons kirsch or Grand Marnier, to taste
½ cup (50g) sliced almonds, toasted

1. Place the berries in individual glass or crystal compote dishes or goblets.

2. Bring a saucepan filled with water to a gentle simmer. Place the egg yolks, sugar, and wine in a metal or heatproof glass mixing bowl and set the bowl over the simmering water. (Or use a 2-quart double boiler.)

3. Using an electric hand mixer or whisk, beat the egg-and-sugar mixture until it is thick and foamy, about 5 minutes. At this point the sauce will be warm to the touch. Beat in the kirsch.

4. Serve the sabayon either warm or cold. If it is to be served cold, place the bowl into a larger bowl of ice and water and continue beating until it is chilled. (A sabayon to be served cold can be made 24 hours in advance and frozen. Pour the cold sauce into a cold bowl or container and freeze. When frozen, the sauce will be thick and can be spooned over the berries.)

5. To serve: Pour the sabayon over the berries, sprinkle with the almonds, and serve.

TOASTING NUTS

Toasting nuts heightens their flavor. You can toast them in the oven, under the broiler, or in a toaster oven. Spread them out on a pan and toast at 400°F to 425°F for 3 to 4 minutes, shaking the pan once or twice. The nuts will start to give off a wonderful, rich aroma, and they will become darker in color and sometimes take on a shine as the oil comes to the surface. Take care not to go too far or they will smell burnt and have an unpleasant flavor. Pour the nuts out of the baking pan as soon as they're done to keep them from continuing to cook.

PEARS POACHED IN PORT WINE

[POIRES AU PORTO]

SEVERAL YEARS AGO, when it seemed as though everyone was poaching pears in red wine, I was reminded of Fernand Point's recipe for prunes poached in red wine and port (see Variation) and was inspired to try pears instead. By poaching in port, which has a certain sweetness, you can eliminate a large quantity of the sugar normally used in poaching fruit. You can use any kind of port, but if you have only a top-quality bottle, you might want to invest in a less-expensive port for use in cooking.

Serve the pears with Madeleines (page 254) or Almond Tuiles (page 252). Any excess poaching liquid remaining after the pears have been served can be refrigerated or frozen for future use in poaching pears. **SERVES 6**

6 pears, preferably Comice or Bosc, peeled
3 cups dry red wine
1½ cups port
½ cup minus 2 teaspoons (100g) sugar
Peeled zest and juice of 1 orange
Peeled zest and juice of 1 small lemon

1. Place the pears upright in a deep pan just large enough to hold them. Add all of the other ingredients and bring to a boil over medium-high heat. Reduce the heat and simmer gently, uncovered, until the pears are tender, 15 to 20 minutes for unripened pears and 5 to 10 minutes for ripened, ready-to-eat pears. Allow the pears to cool in the poaching liquid.

2. Place the pears in a serving bowl and strain the liquid over them. Refrigerate for 2 hours or more. (This can be done a day or two in advance.)

3. Serve 1 pear per person in a bowl or on a plate with some of the poaching liquid.

VARIATION

PRUNES POACHED IN PORT WINE

[PRUNEAUX AU PORTO]

Substitute 2 pounds of pitted prunes for the pears. In step 1, cook the prunes until tender, about 10 minutes. Serve 3 or 4 prunes in wine glasses with some of the poaching liquid. If desired, drizzle each serving with 1 tablespoon heavy cream.

ORANGES IN CHAMPAGNE

[ORANGES AU CHAMPAGNE]

WHILE A FRENCH COOK would never dream of making this simple, elegant, classic dessert with anything but French Champagne, I find that Champagne-style sparkling wines produced in this and other countries are very suitable for it.

I like to add to the elegance of this dessert by serving it in a cut crystal bowl or in individual goblets. And to gild the lily, I usually accompany the oranges with Ladyfingers (page 259) or Almond Tuiles (page 252).

The best oranges to use are seedless so the sections will be solid and not left with holes made by the seeds. The navel, the familiar

HOW TO SECTION AN ORANGE

Sectioning an orange—or grapefruit, lemon, or lime—means releasing the segments of fruit from their membranes. The resulting segments will be more attractive: shiny, bright in color, and tender (so your guests won't have to chew through the fruit's tough membrane). Though the sectioning process takes a bit of time, it can absolutely make the dish, as in Oranges in Champagne (page 285), Duck à l'Orange (page 131), or Endive and Pink Grapefruit Salad (page 28).

PEELING METHOD ONE: Start by cutting off one end of the orange so you can see the exposed flesh. With a sharp knife, follow the fruit's contours and slice off strips of peel, taking care to remove the membrane but without removing too much flesh.

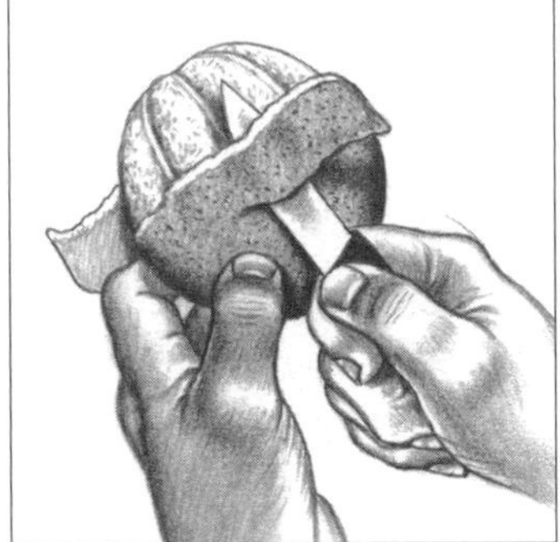

PEELING METHOD TWO: Hold the paring knife as you would to peel an apple, but instead of just drawing your knife along the flesh, carefully move it up and down with a sawing motion at the same time to cut through the thick skin more easily. Keep the knife under the membrane but as close to it as possible so as not to cut away too much flesh. Continue cutting around the orange until all the skin and membrane are removed.

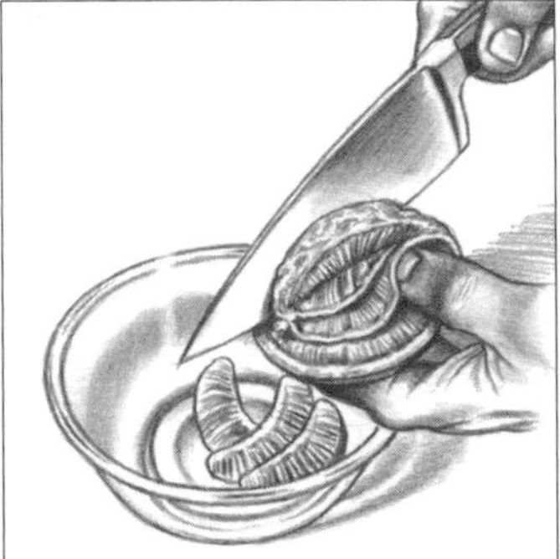

SECTIONING: Section the oranges by carefully cutting toward the center as close to each sectional membrane as possible. This will yield shiny, smooth individual orange segments. Once all the segments have been removed, squeeze the membranes that are left to extract any juices.

seedless orange, is known in France as the Thompson, after the man who developed it. Use oranges in the winter months, at the height of their season, when they are deep orange in color and full of flavor. In addition to the navel, a number of other citrus fruits work well for this dessert, even though they have some seeds. Some of these are Valencia oranges, Mineola and other tangelos, and blood oranges. **SERVES 8 TO 10**

8 oranges, preferably a seedless variety, such as navel
1 bottle demi-sec Champagne or similar sparkling wine

1. Peel and section all of the oranges, making sure they are completely free of all membranes (see "How to Section an Orange," facing page, but reserve the juice for another use—or drink it on the spot, as I do). Place the oranges in a colander (they will hold their shape better than if allowed to sit in their own juice) and refrigerate until ready to serve.

2. Place the sectioned oranges in a serving bowl or individual dessert bowls and bring to the table with a chilled bottle of Champagne.

3. Pour the Champagne over the oranges and serve.

SORBET

A FRESH FRUIT sorbet captures the essence of fruit in a frozen state. It provides an ideal ending for a meal, especially during the summer months when the variety and quality of fresh fruit is at its best.

Easy to make, sorbets are simply sweetened fruit purées frozen in an ice-cream machine. They will keep in your freezer for several weeks.

In most cases I use a very heavy sugar syrup to ensure a smooth sorbet (see Note), but I add it to taste, according to the fruit being used. This recipe, which is constructed loosely in order to give you freedom, will make as much or as little sorbet as you want or as the size of the fruit dictates. The fruit quantities given in the flavor variations that follow will produce about 1 quart of sorbet. **SERVES 8 TO 10**

Fruit (see Variations)
Heavy Sugar Syrup (page 359)
Lemon juice (optional)

1. Purée the fruit using a food processor or blender.

2. Strain only when necessary to remove large seeds or fibrous content, for example for raspberries, pineapple, or citrus juices.

3. Sweeten to taste with the heavy sugar syrup. If you add too much sugar, adjust the sweetness with lemon juice. Keep in mind that the purée will taste a little less sweet when frozen.

4. Freeze following the directions for your ice-cream machine. If you do not have a machine, you can use a food processor (see "Making Ice Cream the New Old-Fashioned Way," page 292).

5. Store sorbets in covered plastic containers in the freezer for up to a month. If the sorbet becomes too hard or icy, let it melt and refreeze in your ice-cream machine.

NOTE: The amount of sugar added to the purée plays a large role in the consistency of the finished sorbet. If too little sugar is added, the sorbet will be hard and icy; if too much is added, it will not freeze. In classic French cooking, the sugar required to achieve the proper consistency is added without regard for the natural sweetness of the fruit, often resulting in an overly sweet purée. When this happens, lemon juice is added to adjust the sweetness.

VARIATIONS

Raspberry Sorbet

[SORBET AUX FRAMBOISES]

I make raspberry sorbet more often than any other kind. It is excellent when served with other sorbets, with vanilla or coffee ice cream, and with fresh fruit. For about 1 quart, use 2 pints fresh raspberries or 2 packages (10 ounces each) unsweetened frozen.

Blueberry Sorbet

[SORBET AUX MYRTILLES]

I like the taste of both fresh and cooked blueberries (the flavor of blueberry pie). For cooked blueberry sorbet, after puréeing and sweetening the fruit, bring it to a boil, then chill before freezing. I often add a tablespoon or two of crème de cassis (black currant liqueur), which creates an unusual flavor. For about 1 quart, use 2 pints of fresh blueberries or 2 packages (10 to 12 ounces each) unsweetened frozen.

Strawberry Sorbet

[SORBET AUX FRAISES]

Use dark red, full-flavored berries. For about 1 quart, use 2 pints of fresh strawberries or 2 packages (10 ounces each) unsweetened frozen.

Pineapple Sorbet

[SORBET À L'ANANAS]

Pineapple makes an excellent sorbet when the fruit is ripe and full of flavor. Choose a pineapple that has a sweet, ripe smell to it. This sorbet is excellent served with fresh raspberries, strawberries, blueberries, or mango, or with sorbets made from these fruits. To surprise your guests, hollow out a pineapple and fill it with sorbet. For about 1 quart, use a medium pineapple, peeled, cored, and cubed.

Pear Sorbet

[SORBET AUX POIRES]

Use ripe, juicy Comice pears when in season. Purée with a little lemon juice and sugar syrup to retard discoloration. For about 1 quart, use 4 pears.

Lemon or Lime Sorbet

[SORBET AU CITRON OU AU CITRON VERT]

Both juices create extremely refreshing sorbets. Strain the pulp and dilute the juice with an equal amount of water before sweetening. You can increase the flavor of all citrus sorbets by adding the grated zest of the fruit; you can leave the zest in or strain just before freezing. Lemon and raspberry sorbet served together are a wonderful combination. For about 1 quart, use 4 cups of diluted and sweetened juice.

GRAPEFRUIT SORBET

[SORBET AU PAMPLEMOUSSE]

This sorbet is extremely easy to make with freshly squeezed grapefruit juice, which is available at most supermarkets. Try it flavored with a little white vermouth or Campari. If you squeeze your own grapefruits for this, you can add the grated zest for a more pronounced flavor; leave the zest in or strain just before freezing. Although I do not serve sorbets between courses as a palate refresher, grapefruit sorbet would work well for this purpose. For about 1 quart, use 4 cups of sweetened juice.

MELON SORBET

[SORBET AU MELON]

Melon sorbet is good only when melons are truly at their perfection, otherwise it is not worth making. For about 1 quart, use 1 cantaloupe (or similar quantity of another melon).

MANGO SORBET

[SORBET À LA MANGUE]

When ripe and full of flavor, mangoes make a marvelous sorbet. This purée requires very little sugar, and its flavor is improved with a touch of lime juice. For about 1 quart, use 4 ripe mangoes.

TROPICAL FRUIT SORBET WITH RUM

[SORBET TROPICAL]

For about 1 quart, use 3 bananas, 3 cups orange juice, and 6 tablespoons dark rum. Add sugar syrup (page 359), if needed, or adjust sweetness with either lemon or lime juice.

SERVING SORBETS

I find sorbets so easy to make, especially as quantities don't really matter and sugar is added to taste, that I make sorbets whenever fruit looks particularly good or is in season. I often have a whole range of flavors in my freezer to choose from and will serve several together.

If you have a variety of flavors, use a small scoop (1½ inches in diameter) and fill a wine glass with the different flavors. If you're planning this in advance, take the colors of the sorbets into consideration to help make an attractive arrangement.

To serve a single flavor of sorbet, use a large ice-cream scoop and, if desired, surround the sorbet with fresh fruit.

Even better for sorbets is an oval scoop that will produce "eggs" of sorbet 1¾ to 2 inches long. You can also shape these restaurant-style servings of sorbet by using two large dessert spoons to scoop and mold. Arrange the scoops on a cold dessert plate, with or without added fresh fruit. When using this scoop, I generally serve 3 scoops per person.

CHOCOLATE-ORANGE SORBET

[SORBET AU CHOCOLAT ET À L'ORANGE]

THIS RECIPE is for all those who want their chocolate without cream. I often flavor the sorbet with a little Coffee Essence (page 358) or Grand Marnier before freezing. I also make another wonderful variation by adding a cup of raspberry purée.

MAKES ABOUT 1 QUART

6 ounces (170g) unsweetened or semisweet chocolate
½ cup water
2 cups fresh orange juice, strained
Heavy Sugar Syrup (page 359)

1. In a small saucepan, melt the chocolate in the water over medium heat. Bring to a boil and whisk into a smooth sauce. Remove from the heat and cool.

2. Blend the chocolate sauce with the orange juice and sweeten to taste with heavy sugar syrup.

3. Freeze, following the directions for your ice-cream machine. If you do not have a machine, you can use a food processor (see "Making Ice Cream the New Old-Fashioned Way," page 292).

ICE CREAM

[LES GLACES]

FRENCH ICE CREAM is simply frozen crème anglaise. This produces a rich ice cream, which many chefs make richer by using cream in place of the milk.

When making ice cream, I use one part heavy cream to three parts milk, and reduce both the number of egg yolks and the amount of sugar normally found in a crème anglaise.

Here is my basic ice-cream recipe, followed by the various flavors I make. Because the canisters of ice-cream makers can make anything from 1 cup to 2 quarts, the flavoring instructions are given per cup of ice-cream base. This way you can make as little or as much as you like of each flavor.

MAKES 5 CUPS BASE/ ABOUT 1½ QUARTS ICE CREAM

3 cups milk
1 cup heavy cream
½ cup minus 2 teaspoons (100g) sugar
6 egg yolks

1. In a large saucepan, bring the milk, cream, and sugar to a boil over medium-high heat, about 3 minutes.

2. Place the egg yolks in a bowl. Slowly beat in about 1 cup of the hot milk. Return the mixture to the saucepan and whisk rapidly over medium-high heat for several seconds. Do not boil. Remove the pan from the heat. The mixture should thicken sufficiently to coat a spoon. If the mixture is too thin, return the pan to the heat and whisk several more seconds. This procedure should take no more than 15 seconds.

3. Strain into a large bowl and allow to cool. Refrigerate until cold.

4. Freeze following the directions for your ice-cream machine, or use a food processor (see "Making Ice Cream the New Old-Fashioned Way," page 292).

VARIATIONS

Vanilla Ice Cream

[GLACE À LA VANILLE]

I often serve vanilla ice cream with a variety of fruit sorbets, and it is a perfect match for ripe cantaloupe. A few well-known French desserts use vanilla ice cream as a base: *Coupe Jacques* or *Royale* is simply diced fresh fruit with vanilla ice cream. *Poires* or *Pêches Belle Hélène* is poached pears (*poires*) or peaches (*pêches*) with vanilla ice cream that is topped with chocolate sauce. Peaches, pears, or strawberries with vanilla ice cream and a raspberry sauce are called *Cardinal* or *Melba.*

To make vanilla ice cream, add 1½ teaspoons vanilla extract to each cup of base. (Or, flavor the base with a vanilla bean when you cook it. Add a vanilla bean to the milk when you bring it to a boil in step 1. Then remove the vanilla bean, split the pod, and scrape the seeds into the milk.)

Chocolate Ice Cream

[GLACE AU CHOCOLAT]

Use 1½ ounces of your favorite semisweet chocolate for every cup of base. Although you can simply melt the chocolate in the base, the ice cream will be smoother if you make a chocolate sauce first. Use 1½ tablespoons water for every 1½ ounces of chocolate to make the sauce. Bring the chocolate and water to a boil. Stir until smooth and add to the ice-cream base.

Chocolate Ice Cream with Toasted Almonds

[GLACE AU CHOCOLAT ET AUX AMANDES GRILLÉES]

The lightly toasted and thinly sliced almonds give a wonderful flavor and delicate crunch to the Chocolate Ice Cream (above). For each cup of base used, add ¼ cup (25g) lightly toasted sliced almonds to the ice cream while it is still soft but nearly frozen.

Mocha Ice Cream with Toasted Pecans

[GLACE MOKA AUX PACANES GRILLÉES]

This is one of my favorites. I flavor Chocolate Ice Cream (above) with 1 teaspoon Coffee Essence (page 358) or instant coffee granules per cup of base. When the mixture is nearly frozen, I add ¼ cup (25g) chopped, toasted, *unsalted* pecans per cup of base used. The combination is truly delicious.

Coffee Ice Cream

[GLACE AU CAFÉ]

Use about 1 tablespoon Coffee Syrup (page 358) or 1 tablespoon sugar and 1 tablespoon instant coffee granules for each cup of base. By using decaffeinated espresso coffee beans for the coffee syrup, I can make a strongly flavored ice cream that won't keep children and grandparents awake at night. Coffee ice cream is outstanding with Raspberry Sorbet (page 288) and with Chocolate Sauce (page 344).

Praline Ice Cream

[GLACE PRALINÉE]

Add 1 tablespoon Praline Paste (page 356) to each cup of base. Use praline ice cream for a marvelous *Poires Belle Hélène* (poached pears with ice cream and chocolate sauce).

Rum-Raisin Ice Cream

[GLACE AU RHUM ET AUX RAISINS SECS]

No commercial rum raisin ice cream can ever match the homemade variety. Soak the raisins for 2 or more hours in your favorite rum. Add ¼ cup rum-soaked raisins to each cup of base used. It is tempting to add more of the liquid, but the alcohol acts as an antifreeze and makes the ice cream more difficult to freeze. If you add just the raisins, the ice cream will be delicious but soft.

Armagnac-Prune Ice Cream

[GLACE AUX PRUNEAUX À L'ARMAGNAC]

Use Armagnac-Soaked Prunes (page 298) for this delicious ice cream. For each cup of base, use 2 to 3 finely chopped or puréed prunes. As with the Rum-Raisin (at left), do not add extra liquid.

Making Ice Cream the New Old-Fashioned Way

For those without an ice-cream machine, try this easy method for ice cream made with a food processor. It stands up surprisingly well to the machine-made.

Place the ice-cream base in a bowl or other container and place in the freezer until frozen. (If you taste it, you will notice that large ice crystals have formed, making it crunchy.) Place the frozen base in a processor and process until smooth, 1 to 2 minutes. Pour the smooth mixture back into the cold container from which it came and place in the freezer for another 2 to 3 hours, until frozen. The ice cream may still have a few tiny ice crystals, but not enough to keep you from enjoying it and proudly serving it to guests.

I generally reserve ice cream making for special flavors, since for the more ordinary flavors—such as vanilla, chocolate, and coffee—I find many commercial brands quite acceptable.

Chocolate Marquise

[MARQUISE AU CHOCOLAT]

MY VERSION of this classic dessert is simply a chocolate mousse that is frozen in a ladyfinger-lined mold. When unmolded, it is sliced and served with a crème anglaise. The classic version—which I first tasted many years ago at Lasserre, then the top restaurant in Paris—is made with a chocolate buttercream and is refrigerated, not frozen. My marquise is a lot lighter and easier to digest after a big meal.

This make-ahead dessert may look complicated but it is actually quite easy to make. Bake your ladyfingers one day (or use store-bought) and complete the dessert the next. It can be made several days in advance.

I designed this dessert for a 5-cup French loaf pan, which is longer and narrower than ours, but you can use any 5-cup loaf pan. **SERVES 6 TO 8**

1½ recipes Ladyfingers (page 259) or about 30 store-bought ladyfingers
Chocolate Mousse (page 275)
Whipped cream and/or candied violets, for decoration
Crème Anglaise (page 346), chilled

1. Line the bottom of a 5-cup loaf pan with waxed paper. Trim the ladyfingers at one end and on each side to fit tightly together and flush against the bottom of the pan. With cut ends down, line the sides of the loaf pan with the ladyfingers.

2. Pour the chocolate mousse into the lined loaf pan. Refrigerate for 2 hours to set, and then freeze. (If frozen immediately, the mousse will contract.)

3. Before serving, trim the ladyfingers off at the level of the chocolate and unmold the marquise onto a rectangular platter, peel off the waxed paper, and decorate the top with whipped cream and/or candied violets. Freeze until ready to use.

4. To serve: Cut ½-inch slices, place in the center of a dessert plate, and surround with the chilled crème anglaise.

VARIATION

Chocolate Marquise with Berries

[MARQUISE AU CHOCOLAT CARDINALE]

Fill the ladyfinger-lined mold halfway with the mousse mixture, then add a layer of raspberries or whole small strawberries and cover them with the remaining mousse. In addition to the crème anglaise, serve with a Raspberry Coulis (page 345).

MELTING CHOCOLATE

If chocolate is melted alone, at a temperature that is too high, two things can happen. The first and most damaging effect is that the chocolate can scorch, dry out, and stiffen. The second, which is noticeable only when using the chocolate for coating, is that the cocoa butter comes out of suspension or separates, causing the chocolate to be streaky and grayish and to lose its gloss.

Theoretically, chocolate should be melted at a temperature below 120°F to keep it from drying out, and below 90°F to prevent the separation of the cocoa butter from occurring. In practice, I have melted chocolate at much higher temperatures without damaging effects. Following either of the two methods given here for melting will prevent the chocolate from scorching, and if you stir it well while it is cooling for coating, any cocoa butter that may have separated will be mixed back into suspension. If you make lots of chocolate candy, a stricter control of melting and the maintenance of temperature may be advisable, but for the recipes in this book it is not necessary.

What *is* necessary, however, is making sure that no moisture mixes with the chocolate when you melt it. Chocolate *can* be melted with liquids—water, milk, or cream—to makes sauces and icing. But the liquids have to be in the right proportion to the chocolate: at least 1 tablespoon liquid per ounce of chocolate. A smaller amount of liquid—a mere drop or two—that falls into a pan or bowl of melted chocolate will cause it to stiffen and make it useless for coating. The following methods keep this from happening.

IN THE MICROWAVE: Melt cut-up chocolate in a microwave-safe bowl in 30-second bursts, stirring after each burst. It's important to stir because with the microwave method, the chocolate keeps its shape. The only way to know if it's melted is to stir it.

IN A WATER BATH OR DOUBLE BOILER: Heat water to a depth of 1 inch in an 8- to 10-inch skillet until it comes to a simmer. Turn off the heat and place a saucepan, with the chocolate in it, in the hot water. Stir occasionally until melted, about 5 minutes. If you are using a double boiler, the chocolate should also be melted off the heat, over hot, not simmering, water.

IN A WARM OVEN: When I'm not in a rush, I use the gentle heat of an oven lightbulb to melt chocolate. The advantage to this method is that it does not involve any tending and the chocolate cannot be scorched. Place the chocolate in a saucepan and place the pan in your oven with the light on. In about 20 minutes the chocolate should be melted and ready to use. If your oven light does not generate enough heat, turn the oven to "warm," or whatever the lowest setting is. You can leave the chocolate in the oven for several hours with no ill effect to the chocolate.

Choosing a Cooking Chocolate

The process of making chocolate is in some ways similar to the process of making coffee. Both cocoa and coffee beans are roasted and then blended to produce a desired flavor, and with each, manufacturers develop a variety of flavors. The quality of the chocolate varies, depending on its percentage of cocoa butter and the amount of time spent refining it.

When choosing a cooking chocolate, I look for one that tastes good, is smooth on my tongue as it melts, leaves a good aftertaste, and is neither too sweet nor too bitter. (A further consideration when the chocolate is to be used for candy making is to find one that is both dark and shiny.)

In general, Americans prefer eating milk chocolate to the dark, semisweet, or bittersweet varieties. Cooks, on the other hand, prefer dark chocolate. The terms "semisweet" and "bittersweet" are often synonymous, and the actual sweetness varies among manufacturers. If a company produces both, its bittersweet will be less sweet than its semisweet chocolate. On the other hand, you may find a bittersweet chocolate made by one company that is sweeter than a semisweet made by another. The only true test is in the tasting.

Many chocolate manufacturers now designate the percentage of cacao. I prefer chocolate in the 65% to 75% range. You can also buy quality chocolate in bulk at candy stores and specialty food shops. This can often save you money, and offers you a variety of flavors to choose from.

Ganache Truffles

[TRUFFES AU CHOCOLAT À LA CRÈME]

CHOCOLATE FORMED to resemble truffles, as they emerge from the earth covered with "dirt," have been a Christmas specialty in French candy shops for decades. Their worldwide popularity has spawned truffle shops and candy companies specializing only in truffles—although many of the confections carrying this name hardly resemble their namesake. It now seems that anything round and chocolate is called a truffle.

The original chocolate truffles were made of a sturdy, fudgelike mixture, concocted of chocolate, butter, and egg yolks, that can be formed by hand and stand at room temperature without melting. But the contemporary chocolate truffle is made with a combination of chocolate and fresh cream (called ganache) and must be handled carefully and refrigerated, for it melts at room temperature.

Because they melt easily when handled, the soft, creamy chocolates, when formed into balls, are dipped in chocolate to lightly coat and protect them. They are then rolled in cocoa powder, which tastes much better than the soil it represents. Biting into a finished chocolate truffle provides a wonderful combination of sensations. Bitter cocoa covers a thin layer of crunchy bittersweet chocolate, which surrounds a creamy, meltingly soft chocolate center. Only those with incredible willpower can refuse a second one.

Trying to make the truffles in one day can be difficult and frustrating, but doing a little work over a two- to three-day period makes truffle-making easy and enjoyable.

In addition to the Grand Marnier flavoring used in the following recipe, truffles can be flavored with Coffee Essence (page 358), rum, Cognac, or mint extract. If you enjoy the flavor of praline, try mixing ¼ to ½ cup (50g to 100g) of Praline Paste (page 356) with the ganache for a delicious combination.

MAKES 80 TO 90 PIECES (2 POUNDS)

TRUFFLE MIXTURE

12 ounces (340g) semisweet or bittersweet chocolate

1 cup heavy cream

3 tablespoons Grand Marnier or other liqueur

CHOCOLATE COVERING

1 pound (450g) semisweet or bittersweet chocolate

2 ounces (60g) unsweetened cocoa powder

1. Make the truffle mixture: In a saucepan, heat the chocolate and heavy cream over low heat, stirring occasionally until the chocolate is melted.

2. Remove from the heat and pour into a bowl. Stir in the Grand Marnier. Place the mixture in the refrigerator until it is firm, a minimum of 2 hours.

3. Cover a baking sheet with a piece of waxed paper. Using two spoons, scoop out and drop mounds of ½ to 1 teaspoonful, depending on the size you wish to make, onto the paper. Refrigerate overnight.

4. When cold, loosen the mounds from the paper and use your fingers to make them as round as you can, if not already so. Refrigerate until ready to coat.

5. Make the chocolate covering: In an ovenproof saucepan, melt the chocolate in a very low oven (see "Melting Chocolate," page 294).

6. When the chocolate has melted, stir it well from time to time as it cools to body temperature. (This is determined when you notice no difference in temperature when you touch the chocolate with the knuckle of your smallest finger.)

7. Sift the cocoa powder evenly onto a chilled jelly-roll pan or plate.

8. Remove the truffles from the refrigerator and drop two at a time into the coating chocolate. Using two forks, turn the truffles, coating them well with chocolate. Lift a truffle with one fork, tapping that fork with the other to knock off excess chocolate, then drop the coated truffle onto the pan containing the cocoa powder. Using a spoon, quickly roll and coat with the powder, then push it to the side.

9. When the coating has cooled and the truffles are firm enough to handle, transfer them to a bowl and refrigerate or freeze until ready to serve. (They will keep well in the refrigerator for about 2 weeks and can be stored in the freezer for several months.)

10. To serve: Mound the truffles in a serving dish. They are delicious when served at room temperature or cold from the refrigerator.

IN ADDITION

When using melted chocolate as a coating for candy or chocolate-dipped fruits, it's important to stir it as it cools. Generally, when you melt chocolate the cocoa butter floats to the surface, as butter would in a sauce. When it cools and sets, it leaves a dull white film on the surface. By stirring the chocolate well as it cools, you keep the cocoa butter mixed in, and the chocolate remains smooth and even-colored.

CHOCOLATE-DIPPED FRUIT

[FRUITS GLACÉS AU CHOCOLAT]

SOME OF THE MOST delicious candies are very simple to make. For example, chocolate-coated dried and fresh fruits, as well as assorted nuts, add an elegant touch to the end of a meal when served with coffee or Cognac. All you need to do is melt chocolate, stir it well as it cools (see In Addition, above), dip the fruit to coat, and let it cool on waxed paper. You can use either semisweet or milk chocolate for these candies.

When dipping, the chocolate should feel cool to the touch. The chocolate will be thick and close to setting. Chill a plate or baking sheet and cover it with waxed paper. The chilled surface helps the chocolate set once dipped. The chocolate-covered fruits should be kept covered in a cool room or in the refrigerator, but should be served at room temperature.

To make chocolate-dipped fruits, melt the chocolate in a low oven (see "Melting Chocolate," page 294) and use any of the following suggestions.

APRICOTS: Choose deep orange, dried California apricots. Stretch them gently, if necessary, to flatten them. Dip them only halfway into the chocolate and allow the excess to drip off before placing the coated apricots on the waxed paper.

PRUNES: Take large, soft, pitted prunes and cut them into two to four pieces. Drop the pieces into the chocolate and use two forks to turn and coat each piece. Lift a piece out of the chocolate with one fork and tap with the other fork to knock off any excess chocolate. Drop the coated prune onto the waxed paper.

CANDIED GINGER OR CANDIED CITRUS PEEL: Coat the same way you coat the prune pieces (above).

NUTS AND RAISINS: Toasted unsalted nuts and raisins are delicious when coated with chocolate. I enjoy eating clusters made with a combination of both. Stir enough nuts and raisins into your melted chocolate so they become lightly coated. Drop them by teaspoonfuls onto the waxed paper.

STRAWBERRIES: Leave the stems on the strawberries, wash, and make sure they are completely dried before dipping. If water gets into your chocolate, it will stiffen and become unusable for this purpose. Use paper towels to pat dry and then air-dry the strawberries for several hours before dipping. For best results, dip the berries the day you serve them.

ARMAGNAC-SOAKED PRUNES

[PRUNEAUX À L'ARMAGNAC]

PRUNES soaked in Armagnac (or Cognac) are a delicacy to be shared with guests after dinner, with coffee. The longer the prunes sit in the alcohol, the better they get. If you find you enjoy these "stewed" prunes as much as I do, store them in an attractive jar that can be brought to the table. **MAKES 1 POUND**

1 pound pitted prunes
Armagnac or Cognac

1. Place the prunes in an attractive jar and cover them with Armagnac or Cognac.

2. Set aside the jar to allow the prunes to absorb the Armagnac, adding more as necessary to keep them covered. When the level of Armagnac remains constant, the prunes are ready to serve. This takes about 1 week.

3. Serve 2 or 3 prunes per person in a wine glass with a little of the Armagnac from the jar.

VARIATION

Madeira-Soaked Prunes

[PRUNEAUX AU MADÈRE]

For a slightly milder version with a different but equally interesting taste, marinate the prunes in Madeira.

CHAPTER FIVE

BASICS

CLASSIC SAUCES provide much of the glory of French food. Although many beginning cooks are often intimidated by even the idea of sauce making, once they realize the relative ease with which a few basic sauces can be prepared—and the wonderful elegance they add to the simplest dishes—they'll soon find themselves making them often.

In this section are the stocks and sauces that are basic to French cooking, including the sweet sauces used in a number of different dessert recipes. Pastry Cream, Crème Anglaise, and icings are also here because they are important components of many French desserts. The following recipes form a cornerstone of most of French cooking.

STOCKS

MOST BOOKS on the subject of French cooking stress the importance of making your own stocks to use in soups and sauces. Stocks themselves are not difficult to make, and I encourage you to make them to learn their delicate flavors. Then try reducing them to a richer, more intense glaze (*glace*) to better understand their full potential. Knowing the characteristics of homemade stocks and glazes will enable you to use store-bought products successfully when homemade ones are not available (see "Using Canned Stocks," page 305).

Over the years I have found that only about 25 percent of serious home cooks regularly make their own stock. They tell me that they have difficulty finding the bones and the time necessary for making it. The time problem can be alleviated by shortening the cooking process, as I have done here, but because of the way meat and fish are currently being processed, unless you live in one of the major cities on either coast, chicken bones may be the only bones you can easily find. Don't let this discourage you, for chicken stock and glaze can take the place of beef stock and glaze in many recipes with excellent results.

Meat glaze (*glace de viande*)—like chicken glaze (*glace de volaille*), fish glaze (*glace de poisson*), and game glaze (*glace de gibier*)—is an essential part of fine sauce making. It is the essence of stock and the result of a long reduction. Its full flavor and body add character and color to sauces. By reducing stock until it has practically no water, glaze can be stored in your refrigerator or freezer until you are ready to use it. A hot glaze has the consistency of a thick syrup; when cold, it will be firm and gelatinous.

Unlike stocks, glazes are not readily available in the supermarket, and for this reason I have made their use in my recipes optional. Most of the recipes call for only 1 to 2 teaspoons of meat glaze. Without it, the sauce will be very good; with its addition, it will be even better.

Economical Beef Stock

[FONDS BRUN ECONOMIQUE]

A CLASSIC brown beef stock is made with meat and bones and is simmered for eight hours. Without the meat it becomes less expensive and hence more economical. The bones and vegetables are usually cooked whole or in large pieces, which helps to keep the stock clear, but they require a long cooking time to extract their flavor. In this recipe I cut the bones and vegetables into smaller pieces, thus reducing the cooking time by more than half.

Once the stock has come to its initial boil, it is important to adjust the heat to prevent rapid boiling during the lengthy cooking time. If the stock boils vigorously, it will become cloudy, and it may even appear as though milk has been added. The cloudy stock can be used, but when a clear one is needed, it will have to be clarified (see "Clarifying," below).

To make this recipe, you will need a 16- to 20-quart stockpot. If one is not available, the ingredients can easily be halved to fit the size pot you have. It is important to leave the stock uncovered while it is cooling. Trapped warm air can make a stock sour, rendering it unusable. **MAKES 5 TO 6 QUARTS**

Clarifying

When a stock needs to be absolutely clear, as when making aspic or Chicken Consommé (page 17), it should be clarified. To clarify a stock, add 1 egg white per quart of stock and stir constantly while the stock reheats. When it begins to boil, stop stirring, reduce the heat, and simmer gently for 5 to 10 minutes. As the egg white cooks, it will float to the top of the stock, carrying with it the particles that would otherwise cloud the stock; you can then remove it easily with a spoon or a skimmer.

8 to 10 pounds beef or veal bones, cut into 2-inch pieces (see Note)
4 tablespoons vegetable oil or butter
4 carrots, thickly sliced on the diagonal
4 onions, halved and sliced ¼ inch thick
8 quarts cold water
4 ribs celery, with leaves if possible
2 leeks, washed and diced (optional)
1 turnip, cut into 4 pieces, each piece stuck with 1 clove
4 cloves garlic
Double Bouquet Garni (page 306)
15 peppercorns

1. Preheat the oven to 500°F.

2. Place the bones in a large roasting pan and brown in the oven, 45 minutes to 1 hour.

3. Meanwhile, in a stockpot, heat the oil over high heat. Add the carrots and onions and cook, occasionally scraping the browned bits from the bottom of the pan, until well browned, 20 to 25 minutes.

4. Add the browned bones to the stockpot and cover with the water. Add all the remaining ingredients and bring to a boil (this will take 30 to 45 minutes).

5. Reduce the heat and simmer, uncovered, for 3½ hours. Skim the surface several times during the simmering to remove any foam that appears.

6. Strain and allow the stock to cool uncovered before refrigerating. Remove any fat from the surface when cold, or before using. Freeze the portion not used, or reduce to form Meat Glaze (page 309). Four quarts of stock will reduce to yield about 1½ cups of meat glaze.

NOTE: Beef bones have become increasingly hard to find in supermarkets, since meat is now cut and packaged at a central warehouse and shipped to local stores without bones. When bones are not available, use 2 pounds beef shank, oxtail, or short ribs, and 6 pounds of chicken backs or necks.

VARIATIONS

Quick Beef Stock

[FONDS BRUN RAPIDE]

This version of beef stock cuts the preparation time by about 1 hour. Place all the ingredients, without browning, into a pot, cover with water, and bring to a boil. While the stock comes to a boil, blacken an onion as follows: Cut the onion in half and place both halves, cut side down, in a hot, dry (without butter or oil) skillet. The onion will blacken within 3 to 4 minutes. Adding the blackened onion to the stockpot will give the stock the brown color it would otherwise be missing.

Although the flavor of this quick stock is slightly different, it works perfectly well as a brown beef stock. One word of caution: The time saved by not browning the bones and vegetables may be equaled by the effort needed to clean your skillet after blackening the onion.

Game Stock

[FONDS DE GIBIER]

Follow the steps in the beef stock recipe to make a game stock, using 6 pounds of game meat and 7 pounds of bones. Brown the meat when you brown the bones (use two roasting pans if necessary). Add 10 juniper berries and 2 sage leaves. Use 16 quarts of water.

Using Canned Stocks

A properly made stock has a delicate flavor that does not overwhelm the dishes it is in. Most people using a store-bought broth follow the directions on the label and unfortunately end up using too strong a stock.

If, for example, you use a can of Campbell's beef broth diluted with 1 can of water, as the manufacturer instructs, you will taste this product in all your finished recipes. If, however, you use additional water (see chart below), you will have a liquid to use that will be equivalent in strength (although not in taste) to a homemade beef stock. Other brands of commercial beef stock, and some chicken stock, may be less concentrated and require less extra water. The chart below lists just some of the broths that were tested for this book, and shows how to dilute them for both a "normal-strength" stock, which you can use any time stock is called for, as well as a "double-strength" stock, which is used to make consommé (see pages 17–18). For the beef stock, there is also an extra-fortified dilution used to make Quick Brown Sauce (page 320).

When using a brand of stock not in the chart, keep in mind that in most cases you're better off with an overdiluted canned stock than one that is too strong.

BRAND	RATIO OF BROTH TO WATER (REGULAR STRENGTH)	RATIO OF BROTH TO WATER (DOUBLE STRENGTH)
BEEF STOCK		
Progresso Beef Broth	1 to 3	1 to 1½
Swanson Fat-Free Beef Broth	1 to 3	1 to 1½
College Inn Low-Sodium Beef Broth	1 to 3	1 to 1½
Campbell's Beef Broth	1 to 6	1 to 3
CHICKEN STOCK		
Swanson Chicken Broth	1 to 3	1 to 1½
Campbell's Chicken Broth	1 to 4	1 to 2
College Inn Chicken Broth	1 to 2	1 to 1
College Inn Light & Fat-Free Chicken Broth	1 to 1	1 to ½

Bouquet Garni

A bouquet garni consists of 4 to 5 sprigs of parsley, 1 bay leaf, and 2 to 3 sprigs of fresh thyme (or ¼ teaspoon dried leaves), which I tie up in a celery rib cut in half. The reason for tying the ingredients together is to enable you to discard them easily once the cooking is finished. If you plan to strain the stock or sauce in which the bouquet garni has been cooking, it is not necessary for you to tie up the ingredients, although it makes skimming easier.

1. Place the fresh or dried thyme in the hollow of the celery rib half and cover with the bay leaf and parsley sprigs.

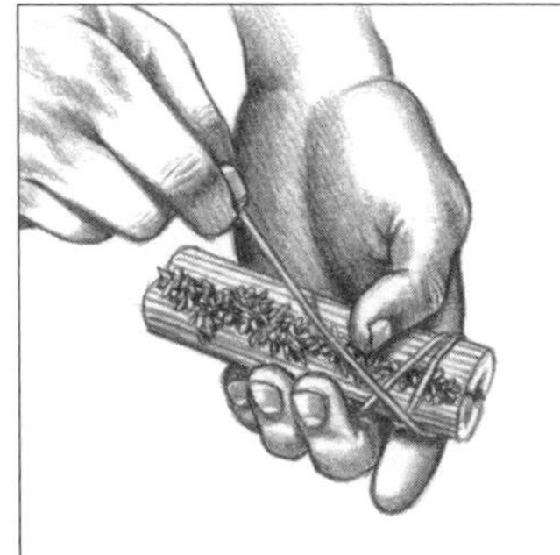

2. Cover with the remaining celery rib half and tie together.

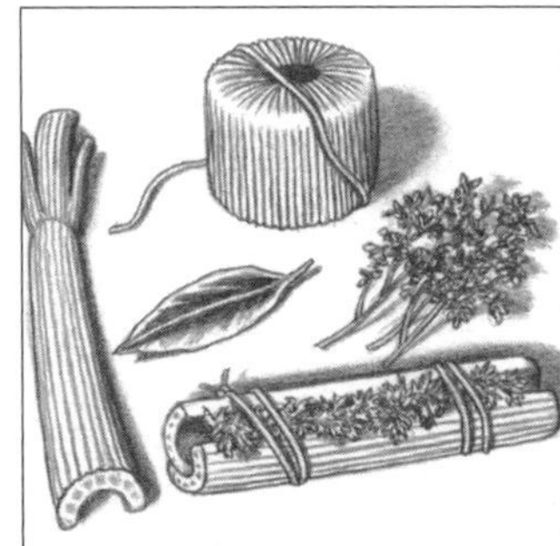

3. Double Bouquet Garni: If a recipe calls for a double bouquet garni, just double the herbs and tie with the same celery rib.

Fish Stock

[FUMET DE POISSON]

FISH STOCK (*fumet de poisson*), can be made from the bones and heads of any fresh fish you buy. It is used when cooking fish and for making soups and sauces. The fish stock can also be reduced to a syrupy Fish Glaze (page 310), which can be stored and used for sauces and soups when stock is not available.

Fresh whole fish may be difficult to find and bones nonexistent. In such cases, search for a fish wholesaler in the area. Although most fish is being processed on the two coasts and flown minus heads and bones throughout the country, many wholesalers buy large whole fish, because they remain fresher in that condition. They fillet them locally before selling in smaller portions. You may be able to buy bones from these wholesale markets for your stock.

MAKES ABOUT 3 CUPS

2 pounds fish bones and heads (avoid oily, strong-flavored fish such as mackerel and bluefish)
2 tablespoons butter
1 onion, sliced
¼ pound white mushrooms, light parts only (see Note), sliced (optional)
10 sprigs parsley
¾ cup dry white wine
3 cups water

1. Cut away and discard all traces of the liver and the gills from the bones and fish heads. If you have time, soak them in ice water for at least 20 minutes to extract any remaining blood.

2. In a large saucepan, melt the butter over medium heat. Add the onion, mushrooms (if using), and parsley and gently sauté over medium heat until the onion is softened but not browned, about 3 minutes.

3. Add the fish heads and bones, cover, and cook for 15 minutes.

4. Add the wine, increase the heat to high, and reduce the liquid, uncovered, by half, about 3 minutes.

5. Add the water, bring to a boil, reduce the heat, and simmer, uncovered, for 15 minutes.

6. Strain the stock and allow it to cool uncovered before refrigerating.

NOTE: If using mushrooms, do not use the dark brown undersides of the cap (the gills); use only the light-colored portions of the cap and stems.

IN ADDITION

Shrimp shells and lobster shells can also be used to make a quick flavorful stock for seafood dishes. For that reason, I often throw shrimp shells or lobster shells into a bag in the freezer to have on hand.

CHICKEN STOCK

[FONDS DE VOLAILLE]

CHICKEN STOCK is easier to make than beef stock because chicken parts are more readily available today than are beef bones. Although I occasionally use a whole chicken or parts to make the stock (and then use the cooked meat for chicken salad), I normally use backs and necks, which are more economical. Hearts and gizzards can also be used, but not the liver, which has too strong a flavor.

The cautions on pot size, boiling, and cooling stock are the same here as they are for Economical Beef Stock (page 303).

MAKES ABOUT 3½ QUARTS

1 chicken (4 pounds) or 4 pounds chicken parts, rinsed
4 quarts cold water
1 leek (white part only), washed
2 onions, each studded with a clove
3 carrots
3 ribs celery, with leaves if possible, halved
Bouquet Garni (page 306)
6 peppercorns

1. Place the chicken in a stockpot. Cover with the water and bring to a boil over high heat, 15 to 20 minutes. Skim the foam from the surface and reduce the heat.

2. Add the remaining ingredients and simmer, uncovered, for 2 hours, occasionally skimming any more foam.

3. Strain the stock and allow it to cool uncovered before refrigerating. Remove the fat from the surface when it is cold or before using. Freeze the portion not used, or reduce to form Chicken Glaze (page 310), which can be stored in the refrigerator or freezer. Two quarts of stock will reduce to yield approximately ¾ cup chicken glaze.

VEGETABLE STOCK

[FONDS BLANC DE LÉGUMES]

VEGETABLE STOCK can be made more quickly than those made with meat and bones, because extracting flavor from bones takes a long time. To get the most flavor out of vegetables in a shorter cooking time, they should be coarsely chopped into small pieces. Do not boil or cook too long, for the smaller pieces can break up and make the stock cloudy.

The object in making a light vegetable stock (*fonds blanc*) is to have subtle, not overpowering, vegetable flavors. For this reason I remove the dark gills from the mushrooms (though they are fine in a brown vegetable stock; see Variation). And although I encourage you to try other vegetables here, I also recommend that you avoid the strong tastes of turnips and members of the cabbage family. **MAKES ABOUT 3½ QUARTS**

10 ounces white mushrooms, washed
3 leeks, washed and coarsely chopped
3 onions, coarsely chopped
4 carrots, thickly sliced
3 celery ribs, with leaves if possible, coarsely chopped
6 cloves garlic, coarsely chopped
Bouquet Garni (page 306)
6 black peppercorns
4 quarts cold water

1. Pull off the mushroom stems and set aside. Slice off the mushroom gills and discard. Coarsely chop the caps and stems.

2. Place the mushroom pieces, leeks, onions, carrots, celery, garlic, bouquet garni, and peppercorns in a stockpot. Cover with the water and bring to a boil over high heat, 15 to 20 minutes. Skim any foam from the surface and reduce the heat.

3. Simmer, uncovered, for 1 hour, occasionally skimming any additional foam.

4. Strain the stock and allow it to cool uncovered before refrigerating. Freeze the portion not used.

VARIATION

Brown Vegetable Stock

[FONDS BRUN DE LÉGUMES]

In the stockpot, sauté the carrots and onions in 2 tablespoons of light olive oil over medium-high heat until they are well browned, but not burned, 10 to 12 minutes. Add the remaining vegetables and sauté for 2 to 3 minutes over medium heat without browning. Add the remaining ingredients and cover with the water. Proceed as above. Skim any oil from the surface after straining.

MEAT GLAZE

[GLACE DE VIANDE]

I ENCOURAGE YOU to make stock in order to use it to make meat glaze. A meat glaze is homemade beef stock (see page 303) that has been reduced so that nearly all the water in it is removed. When hot, the glaze has a thick, syrupy consistency; when cold, it is firm yet springy. It can be cut into chunks that can be added to soups and sauces to increase their flavor, or used like a bouillon cube to be reconstituted as a stock. Meat glaze is a convenient way to store large quantities of stock.

Continue using the store-bought stocks you use for your soups and sauces, but have meat glaze on hand to add to them to improve their flavor.

If you make chicken stock frequently and beef stock rarely, reduce your chicken stock to make Chicken Glaze (see Variations), and use it whenever meat glaze is called for. Although you will be adding a different flavor, you will be contributing a richness and intensity to your sauce that otherwise would be missing.

MAKES 1 TO 1½ CUPS

4 quarts Economical Beef Stock (page 303)

1. After removing all the fat from the surface of the stock, boil it uncovered over medium-high heat until only 3 cups remain, about 1½ hours. Skim the stock as it reduces to remove all foam and impurities.

2. Strain the stock into a small heavy-bottomed saucepan and continue reducing over medium heat until the liquid thickens to coat a spoon, about 30 minutes. The liquid will at this point be dark and shiny and will bubble slowly.

3. Pour the hot glaze into a heatproof custard cup or bowl and refrigerate. When cold it will be firm and can be easily unmolded. Invert the cup or bowl, and with your thumb, push or pull the glaze from the edge of the cup toward the center. This will loosen the glaze and allow it to fall into your hand.

4. Wrap the glaze well in plastic wrap and refrigerate or freeze it. To use, simply cut off teaspoon-size chunks, and rewrap the unused portion. A glaze will keep this way for many months.

IN ADDITION

After making a glaze, allow a small piece to melt in your mouth and notice the wonderful intense flavor that is released. You will find the glaze salty, even though no salt was added when making the stock. The salt you taste is the natural salt extracted from the bones and vegetables used in making the stock.

VARIATIONS

Chicken Glaze

[GLACE DE VOLAILLE]

Make Chicken Stock (page 307) and reduce to about 1 cup of glaze.

Fish Glaze

[GLACE DE POISSON]

Triple the recipe for Fish Stock (page 306) and reduce to about ¾ cup.

Game Glaze

[GLACE DE GIBIER]

Make Game Stock (page 304) and reduce to about 1 cup.

SAUCES

FRENCH COOKING'S FAME is in great part due to its many superb sauces. A plain piece of poached fish takes on elegance when served with a *sauce beurre blanc*; an ordinary steak becomes anything but ordinary with a béarnaise sauce, and a simple chicken is transformed into a delicate masterpiece when served with a *sauce suprême à l'estragon.*

The repertoire of classic sauces available to a trained chef is so vast that a mere listing of their names baffles a beginner. Learning a few basic sauces, however, will give you the ability and freedom to produce many others.

A sauce is a flavorful liquid that has been thickened. An unthickened liquid is called a *jus* (or juice). A sauce can be created separately from the main dish—as is hollandaise sauce—or it can be an integral part of the dish.

A sauce can be thickened by simple reduction (rapid boiling to evaporate excess liquid), or it can be thickened by the addition of a starch, egg yolks, or cream. There are even some sauces, rarely made today, that use animal blood as the thickening agent.

By far the majority of classic sauces are thickened by a starch. Most of these sauces are rarely found in restaurants today because of the nouvelle cuisine movement of the early '70s, when a small group of prominent chefs decided to eliminate starch as a thickening agent on the premise of producing simpler sauces. They opted instead for sauces thickened or enhanced with butter or cream, often relying on meat glazes.

Although doubtful that restaurant-goers miss the old-fashioned, classic starch-based sauces, there are good reasons why the home cook should not forget them. Those flour- or roux-based sauces can be successfully made with store-bought stocks, making them easier to create at home.

Although you can use store-bought stocks successfully, it is my hope that while learning the sauces in this book you will progress to homemade ones.

A brief description of the classic basic sauces follows.

BASIC SAUCES: French Kitchen Essentials

Sauces fall into two general categories, hot and cold; within the hot sauce category, there are white sauces and brown sauces. Sauces are further divided by the way they are thickened. For a better understanding of the following definitions, it is helpful to know what a roux is. A roux is flour cooked in butter, and is the base for most classic sauces. A white roux is flour cooked in butter until the flour is pale yellow and frothy. A brown roux is cooked until the flour turns a reddish brown.

HOT WHITE SAUCES

VELOUTÉ: White stock (veal, chicken, or fish) thickened with a white roux. Recipe on page 315.

ALLEMANDE/PARISIENNE: A velouté enriched by egg yolks. See Sole Fillets with Poached Mushrooms and Shrimp Sauce (page 95).

SUPRÊME: A velouté enriched by heavy cream. See Creamy Poule au Pot (page 115).

BÉCHAMEL: A sauce made with a white roux and milk. Recipe on facing page.

CRÈME: A sauce made with a reduction of a dish's cooking liquids and heavy cream. See Steak au Poivre (page 141) or Chicken with Riesling (page 119).

HOLLANDAISE: The classic butter sauce made from an emulsion of egg yolks and butter (page 326). Other sauces in the same family include Béarnaise Sauce (page 327), *sauce choron* (Béarnaise with Tomatoes, page 329), and *sauce paloise* (Béarnaise with Mint, page 329).

BEURRE BLANC: This is the contemporary butter sauce made without egg yolks. Recipe on page 329.

HOT BROWN SAUCES

DEMI-GLACE: The basic brown sauce made with a brown roux, a brown stock, a browned mirepoix (diced vegetables), and tomatoes.

JUS LIÉ: A brown beef stock lightly thickened with arrowroot, potato starch, or cornstarch. Recipe on page 318.

TOMATE: A tomato sauce. Recipe on page 325.

COLD SAUCES

MAYONNAISE: An emulsion of egg yolks and oil (page 331). Other sauces in the mayonnaise family include Aioli (page 332) and Green Mayonnaise (page 334).

VINAIGRETTE: A sauce with a base of vinegar and oil. Recipe on page 336.

BECHAMEL

[SAUCE BÉCHAMEL]

BÉCHAMEL SAUCE is the classic white "cream" sauce, made from milk and a white roux. Although it has been replaced in most restaurants today by a sauce made completely of heavy cream, it still has a number of important uses. A béchamel is used whenever you want a creamy sauce without using cream. It may be mixed with puréed vegetables for richness without many added calories. Add cheese and transform it into a Mornay Sauce (page 314) for a gratin or to coat vegetables or crêpes. When made correctly, it is smooth and creamy; poorly made, it will be thick and pasty.

Simple variations of the sauce can be made by adding tomato paste, mustard, or curry powder to taste.

MAKES 2 CUPS TO SERVE 8

2½ tablespoons butter
3 tablespoons all-purpose flour
2 cups milk
¼ teaspoon salt
⅛ teaspoon freshly ground pepper

1. In a medium-size saucepan, melt the butter over medium-high heat. Add the flour and cook, stirring frequently, until the roux is pale yellow and frothy, 30 to 45 seconds. Add the milk and stir well with a whisk until the sauce thickens and comes to a boil, 2 to 3 minutes.

2. Reduce the heat to maintain a gentle simmer and season with the salt and pepper. Whisk vigorously for about 10 seconds. Simmer gently, whisking the sauce well from time to time, until the sauce is a little thicker than heavy cream, 2 to 3 minutes. Skim off any butter that rises to the surface. (The sauce can be made ahead and refrigerated for several days or frozen for later use. Cover the surface with plastic wrap. Before using, bring to a boil and check the consistency and seasoning. If the sauce is too thick, add a little milk or water to thin it.)

Mornay Sauce

[SAUCE MORNAY]

A MORNAY is a cheese-flavored béchamel that can be used with poached eggs, crêpes, vegetables, and meat. In France, the cheese used for the sauce is usually Gruyère, or a combination of Gruyère and Parmesan. Any Swiss-style cheese can be used; if you use other than a Swiss-style cheese, such as Camembert, the sauce takes on the name of the cheese. Classically, a Mornay is made with an addition of 3 to 4 tablespoons of butter just before serving. I find this added richness unnecessary and have eliminated it with today's eating habits in mind. When browning the sauce as in a gratin, I always sprinkle additional cheese on top. **MAKES 2 CUPS TO SERVE 8**

2½ tablespoons butter
3 tablespoons all-purpose flour
2 cups milk
⅛ teaspoon salt
⅛ teaspoon freshly ground pepper
Pinch of freshly grated nutmeg
2 ounces Swiss-style cheese, such as Gruyère or Emmentaler, grated (about ⅔ cup) or 1 ounce each Gruyère and Parmesan cheese, grated

1. In a medium-size saucepan, melt the butter over medium-high heat. Add the flour and cook, stirring frequently, until the roux is pale yellow and frothy, 30 to 45 seconds. Add the milk and stir well with a whisk until the sauce thickens and comes to a boil, 2 to 3 minutes. (This is a béchamel sauce.)

2. Reduce the heat to maintain a gentle simmer and season with the salt, pepper, and nutmeg. Whisk vigorously for about 10 seconds. Simmer gently, whisking the sauce well from time to time, until the sauce is the consistency of heavy cream, 2 to 3 minutes. Skim off any butter that may rise to the surface.

3. Stir in the cheese and bring to a boil while whisking. At this point the sauce should be slightly thicker than heavy cream and is ready to use. (The sauce can be made in advance and refrigerated for several days or frozen for later use. Cover the surface with plastic wrap. To reheat, bring to a boil and check the consistency and seasoning before using. If the sauce is too thick, thin it with a little milk or water.)

VELOUTE

[SAUCE VELOUTÉ]

A VELOUTÉ is a velvety smooth sauce that is made with a white roux and a white stock (veal, chicken, fish, or vegetable). It is one of the finest sauces to come from the classic French kitchen. In this sauce, perhaps more than any other, the quality of the stock is very important. Although veloutés can be made with canned stock, those made with fresh stock are far preferable, and for this reason I have used veloutés in this book only when a stock is made as a part of the recipe; for example, Creamy Veal Stew with Morels (page 154).

Classically, veloutés are slowly simmered for an hour or more, with additional stock added as needed to achieve a beautifully smooth consistency. During this time the sauce is skimmed frequently to remove the butter and impurities that rise to the surface. While the sauce cooks, the flavor develops and intensifies.

Normally I shorten the process and simply reduce some of the stock rapidly to make a glaze, then add it to the sauce. With careful skimming, and vigorous whisking, a beautifully smooth and flavorful sauce can be made quite rapidly. Just keep in mind that the more you whisk, the smoother and shinier your sauce becomes. **MAKES 2 CUPS TO SERVE 8**

3 cups Chicken Stock (page 307), Fish Stock (page 306), or Vegetable Stock (page 308)
2½ tablespoons butter
3 tablespoons all-purpose flour
¼ teaspoon salt
⅛ teaspoon freshly ground pepper

VARIABLE VELOUTES

When making a velouté, look around your kitchen for any liquids to use in preparing the stock for your sauce. As an example, besides the fish stock used in a recipe such as Sole Fillets with Poached Mushrooms and Shrimp Sauce (page 95), you may have liquid created while steaming oysters and mussels. You may also have flavorful liquid from poaching fresh mushrooms, or from soaking dried ones. There may be some tomato liquid collected while seeding tomatoes. Taste these liquids to determine which will complement your final dish. If they are strong or salty, just add a little. If they are mild, reduce to strengthen, and taste again before adding them to your sauce. Spices like saffron and curry, and herbs like tarragon and chives can be added for color and flavor shortly before serving. Use all these potential flavorings as an artist uses the many colors of his palette.

1. In a small saucepan, reduce 1 cup of the stock over high heat until reduced to 1 tablespoon of glaze. Remove from the heat and reserve.

2. In a medium-size saucepan, melt the butter over medium-high heat. Add the flour and cook, stirring frequently, until the roux is pale yellow and frothy, 30 to 45 seconds. Add the remaining 2 cups of stock and stir well with a whisk until the sauce thickens and comes to a boil, 2 to 3 minutes.

3. Reduce the heat to maintain a gentle simmer and season with the salt and pepper. Add the reserved glaze and whisk vigorously for about 10 seconds. Simmer gently, whisking the sauce from time to time, until the sauce has the consistency of heavy cream, 2 to 3 minutes. Skim off any butter that rises to the surface. (The sauce can be made in advance and refrigerated for several days or frozen for later use. Cover the surface with plastic wrap. To reheat, bring to a boil and check its consistency and seasoning before using. If the sauce is too thick, add a little additional stock or water to thin it.)

TOMATO-FLAVORED VELOUTE

[SAUCE AURORE]

TOMATO-FLAVORED velouté can be made with either chicken or fish stock, depending on what you intend to serve it with. A classic *sauce aurore* recipe calls for tomato purée, whereas this recipe uses a more concentrated tomato paste. This reduces the cooking time necessary to achieve the desired consistency of the sauce. I use Tomato-Flavored Velouté mainly with poached fish and Basic Fish Mousseline (page 48), but it is also an excellent accompaniment to crab, lobster, or poached chicken.

MAKES 2 CUPS TO SERVE 8

3 tablespoons butter (plus more for finishing the sauce; see below)
¼ cup all-purpose flour
3 cups Fish Stock (page 306) or Chicken Stock (page 307)
¼ teaspoon salt
⅛ teaspoon freshly ground pepper
1 tablespoon tomato paste
3 tablespoons butter or ⅓ cup heavy cream (optional; see Note)

1. In a small saucepan, melt the 3 tablespoons butter over medium-high heat. Add the flour and cook, stirring frequently, until the roux is pale yellow and frothy, 30 to 45 seconds. Add the stock and stir well with a whisk until it thickens and comes to a boil, 2 to 3 minutes.

2. Reduce the heat and simmer gently, whisking the sauce well from time to time, until the sauce has the consistency of heavy cream, 10 to 15 minutes. Skim off any butter that rises to the surface.

3. Season with the salt and pepper. Add the tomato paste and whisk until smooth. Simmer for 5 minutes longer. The sauce will have thickened slightly and should be smooth and creamy. (The sauce can be made ahead to this point. Cover the surface with plastic wrap, let cool, and refrigerate for several days or freeze for later use.)

4. Just before serving, bring the sauce to a boil and whisk in the 3 to 4 tablespoons butter or ⅓ cup cream. If you use butter, do not boil the sauce once it has been added.

NOTE: The butter or cream enriches the sauce and softens the flavor a bit. Taste the sauce before adding. You may choose not to add the calories.

Skimming Sauces

Skimming is used to remove foam, fat, and impurities from the surface of liquids. It is one of the most important and often overlooked steps in preparing fine sauces, soups, and jams. In most cases, it should be done during the cooking process. The importance of skimming can easily be understood by tasting the foam or fat removed. You can also notice the difference it makes while cooking jam. If not skimmed, the foam will cause a jam to be cloudy and dull instead of clear and shiny. If you make skimming a regular habit, you will find it improves the general quality of your cooking.

Saffron Sauce with Fresh Tomatoes

[SAUCE AU SAFRAN À LA TOMATE FRAÎCHE]

If you like the flavor of saffron, you will probably find this transformation of a classic *sauce velouté* to be one of your favorites to serve with poached fish or Basic Fish Mousseline (page 48). I use two large pinches of saffron for this sauce, but you may want to start with only one and see if you like the flavor. I have made this sauce a little thicker than a normal velouté, but it will thin to a perfect consistency, a little lighter than heavy cream, after the tomatoes have been added.

MAKES 2 TO 2½ CUPS TO SERVE 8 TO 10

5 tablespoons butter
¼ cup all-purpose flour
3 cups Fish Stock (page 306)
2 large pinches of saffron threads (see Note)
¼ teaspoon salt
Pinch of freshly ground pepper
2 tomatoes, peeled, seeded, chopped, and drained
2 to 3 tablespoons chopped fresh chives, basil, tarragon, or parsley, to taste

1. In a small saucepan, melt 3 tablespoons of the butter over medium-high heat. Add the flour and cook, stirring frequently, until the roux is pale yellow and frothy, 30 to 45 seconds. Add the stock and stir well with a whisk until it thickens and comes to a boil, 2 to 3 minutes.

2. Reduce the heat to maintain a gentle simmer and season with the saffron, salt, and pepper. Whisk vigorously for about 10 seconds. Simmer gently, whisking the sauce well from time to time, until the sauce is slightly thicker than heavy cream, 30 to 45 minutes. Skim off any butter that rises to the surface. (The sauce can be made to this point up to a day ahead. Cover the surface with plastic wrap, let cool, and refrigerate for several days or freeze for later use.)

3. Just before serving, bring the sauce to a boil. Off the heat, whisk in the remaining 2 tablespoons butter. Gently stir in the tomatoes and all but 1 teaspoon of the herbs. Heat for several seconds, but do not boil.

4. Sprinkle the sauce with the remaining herbs just before serving.

NOTE: The saffron slowly dissolves into the sauce, and when the threads are translucent it is completely dissolved. If you wish to add more saffron near the end of the cooking time, crush the threads to speed the dissolving.

THICKENED BEEF STOCK

[JUS LIÉ]

WHENEVER I NEED a basic brown sauce (called a demi-glace), but do not have the time to make one, I use a thickened beef stock called a *jus lié.* Since my beef stock is very mild, I reduce the stock by half and add some meat glaze to heighten its flavor. To thicken the stock, I use arrowroot, potato starch, or cornstarch (in that order of preference), dissolved in a little cold water.

The tomato traditionally found in a classic demi-glace is omitted from this thickened stock, giving the sauce a greater clarity, which

DEMI-GLACE

Demi-glace, the basic brown sauce that was once the mainstay in the classic French kitchen, has all but vanished from today's top French restaurants. The classic demi-glace, or *espagnole* as it was known, took at least two days to make.

The principles used in making demi-glace are still used in such dishes as Duck à l'Orange (page 131). But in most instances where a brown sauce is called for, I use Thickened Beef Stock (facing page), which makes a thinner and clearer brown sauce that I find more refined (and certainly less time-consuming) than the classic sauces made with demi-glace.

is characteristic of contemporary brown sauces. Note that while I've made meat glaze optional in all other recipes, in this recipe it is critical.

If you don't have time to make home-made stock, you might want to try the Quick Brown Sauce (page 320) made with canned stock. **MAKES 2 CUPS TO SERVE 12**

1 quart Economical Beef Stock (page 303)
3 tablespoons Meat Glaze (page 309)
2 tablespoons arrowroot, potato starch, or cornstarch, dissolved in 2 tablespoons cold water
¼ teaspoon salt
⅛ teaspoon freshly ground pepper

1. In a medium-size saucepan, bring the stock and meat glaze to a boil over medium-high to high heat. Boil gently, uncovered, until the stock reduces by half, 15 to 20 minutes, skimming off any fat and impurities as they rise to the surface.

2. Whisk the dissolved arrowroot into the gently boiling stock. Whisk vigorously until the sauce thickens and lightly coats a spoon, 15 to 20 seconds, and remove from the heat. Season with the salt and pepper. (This thickened stock can be made in advance. Cover the surface with plastic wrap, let cool, and refrigerate for several days or freeze for later use.)

VARIATIONS

MADEIRA SAUCE

[SAUCE MADÈRE]

For a very simple sauce, bring 1 cup of Thickened Beef Stock to a boil and add ¼ cup Madeira. Serve with veal, chicken, or turkey.

PORT SAUCE

[SAUCE PORTO]

For a quick port sauce, bring 1 cup of Thickened Beef Stock to a boil and add ¼ cup port. Serve with pork, beef, or duck.

QUICK BROWN SAUCE

[JUS LIÉ RAPIDE]

FOR AN ALMOST instant brown sauce, when you don't have time to make beef stock, use this sauce made with canned broth. In this recipe, the meat glaze is optional; in the preceding one, it is not.

MAKES ABOUT 2 CUPS TO SERVE 12

2 cups canned beef broth, diluted to extra-fortified strength (see Note)
3 tablespoons Meat Glaze (optional; page 309)
2½ tablespoons arrowroot, potato starch, or cornstarch dissolved in 2½ tablespoons cold water
¼ teaspoon salt
⅛ teaspoon freshly ground pepper

1. In a medium-size saucepan, bring the stock and meat glaze (if using) to a boil over medium-high to high heat. Reduce the heat to medium.

2. Whisk the dissolved arrowroot into the gently boiling stock. Whisk vigorously until the sauce thickens and lightly coats a spoon, 15 to 20 seconds, and remove from the heat. Season with the salt and pepper. (This thickened stock can be made in advance. Cover the surface with plastic wrap, let cool, and refrigerate for several days or freeze for later use.)

NOTE: For this sauce, use the following ratios to dilute beef broth to the extra-fortified strength needed here: Progresso, Swanson Fat-Free, and College Inn Low-Sodium are all 1 part broth to 1 part water. Campbell's Beef Broth is 1 part broth to 2½ parts water.

BORDELAISE SAUCE

[SAUCE BORDELAISE]

THIS RICH RED wine sauce is a perfect match for beef. It is traditionally served with slices of beef marrow that have been poached in water and a little vinegar. In a classic kitchen, if the sauce were intended to go with a roast, the marrow would be added to the sauce along with fresh parsley just before serving. However, since marrow can be difficult to find, I have omitted it as well as the parsley, but have kept a small amount of butter to round out this full-bodied sauce.

MAKES ABOUT 1¼ CUPS TO SERVE 6

2 shallots, finely chopped
1 sprig fresh thyme or a pinch of dried leaves
¼ bay leaf
1 tablespoon Meat Glaze (optional; page 309)
⅛ teaspoon freshly ground pepper
¾ cup red Bordeaux wine or any dry red wine
1½ cups Thickened Beef Stock (page 318)
2 teaspoons Cognac
1 tablespoon butter

1. In a small saucepan, combine the shallots, thyme, bay leaf, meat glaze (if using), pepper, and wine. Over high heat, reduce the liquid by two-thirds, about 5 minutes.

2. Add the thickened beef stock and simmer until the liquid lightly coats a spoon, 5 to 7 minutes. Whisk gently occasionally and skim if necessary. Strain the sauce through a fine-mesh sieve. (The sauce can be made in advance up to this point. Cover the surface with plastic wrap, let cool, and refrigerate for up to a week or freeze for later use.)

3. Just before serving, bring the sauce to a boil over medium-high heat and add the Cognac. Remove the sauce from the heat and whisk in the butter.

Reducing Liquids

Sauce recipes will often instruct you to "reduce by half" or "reduce until only 1 cup remains." The reasons for reducing are to intensify flavors and to thicken or reduce the quantity of a liquid. Most reductions are done in an uncovered pan rapidly over high heat. To increase the speed of reduction, transfer the liquid to a larger pan. The greater the surface area, the faster the evaporation. Conversely, when reducing a sauce or soup slowly, which helps to develop deep flavors, you should use as small a pan as possible. The smaller the surface area, and the greater the depth, the more slowly a liquid will evaporate.

SAUCE ROBERT

THIS MUSTARD-FLAVORED brown sauce is ideal to serve with sautéed or roasted pork, and can be used with sautéed rabbit and chicken as well. The amount of mustard you use will depend on your personal taste, but I always use less when serving the sauce with chicken. A pinch or two of sugar is often added to cut the bite of the vinegar. Although I have never found this necessary, you might.

MAKES 1 CUP TO SERVE 6

1 small onion, finely chopped
¾ cup dry white wine
¼ cup white (distilled) or white wine vinegar
1 cup Thickened Beef Stock (page 318)
1 teaspoon Meat Glaze (optional; page 309)
1 to 2 tablespoons Dijon mustard, to taste
¼ teaspoon sugar (optional)
4 to 5 sprigs parsley, chopped (see Note)

1. In a small saucepan, combine the onion, wine, and vinegar. Bring to a boil over high heat and cook until the liquid is reduced by two-thirds, about 5 minutes.

2. Add the thickened beef stock and meat glaze (if using). Reduce the heat to low and simmer, uncovered, until the sauce thickens enough to lightly coat a spoon, 2 to 3 minutes. If necessary, skim during the simmering.

3. Strain the sauce, and stir in the mustard. Taste and adjust the seasoning, adding the sugar, if necessary. (The sauce can be kept warm in a water bath [*bain-marie*].) Stir in the parsley just before serving.

NOTE: When preparing the sauce to be used with Pork Medallions with Sauce Robert (page 166), omit the parsley (for a more elegant look).

GAME SAUCE WITH PEPPER

[SAUCE POIVRADE]

THIS CLASSIC GAME SAUCE and its two variations, *chevreuil* and *grand veneur,* are traditionally served with venison, elk, antelope, hare, and wild boar. The aromatic *sauce poivrade* goes well with all these meats, while the *chevreuil* and *grand veneur,* a little milder and sweeter than the *poivrade,* are especially good with venison.

All three sauces include the game marinade, which for the purposes of this book I've used to marinate a leg of lamb (see Venison-Style Leg of Lamb, page 160). Although game is becoming more and more available (much of it being raised on ranches and shipped precut and packaged to the markets), you can experiment with game marinades and game sauces by serving them with the leg of lamb before venturing on to venison.

MAKES ABOUT 3 CUPS TO SERVE 16

Game Marinade (page 324)
2 tablespoons butter or vegetable oil
½ pound ground game or lamb (optional; see Note)
¼ cup Madeira
3 cups Thickened Beef Stock (page 318)
1 tablespoon tomato paste
30 peppercorns, crushed, or 1½ teaspoons freshly ground pepper
6 tablespoons (¾ stick) butter, softened

ADDING BUTTER TO A SAUCE

Butter is often added to sauces just before serving. The purpose is to make strong sauces milder, light sauces richer, or sharp sauces smoother. The sauce should never boil after the butter has been added, although it may be boiling at the moment you add it. Boiling will cause the butter to come out of suspension and float to the surface. I have often been asked, "Why skim butter from the surface of a sauce during cooking if you plan to beat butter in at the end?" Butter used in cooking tastes like oil and detracts from the sauce's flavor, whereas butter added at the end contributes a fresh buttery flavor. Butter that has been at room temperature beats into a sauce more easily than does butter taken directly from the refrigerator. For this reason, take the butter from the refrigerator when beginning your recipes.

1. If you have not already done so, strain the marinade and set the marinade and vegetables aside.

2. In a heavy-bottomed 4- to 4½-quart saucepan, melt the 2 tablespoons butter over medium-high to high heat. Add the reserved vegetables and the ground meat (if using). Cook, stirring only occasionally, until the meat and vegetables begin to brown, about 10 minutes.

3. Add 2 cups of the marinade and the Madeira. Cook over high heat, stirring occasionally, and reduce until no liquid remains, 15 to 20 minutes. Pour off any excess fat.

4. Add the thickened beef stock, another ½ cup of marinade, and the tomato paste. Stir well and bring to a boil. Reduce the heat and simmer gently for 15 minutes, skimming off butter and impurities as they rise to the surface. Add the crushed peppercorns and continue simmering until the sauce thickens to lightly coat a spoon, 10 to 15 minutes longer.

5. Strain the sauce through a fine-mesh sieve, taste, and adjust the seasoning, if necessary. (The sauce can be made ahead to this point and refrigerated for several days or frozen for later use.)

6. Just before serving, bring the sauce to a boil. Remove from the heat and beat in the 6 tablespoons softened butter, 1 tablespoon at a time. Do not allow the sauce to boil again once the butter has been added. Keep hot in a water bath (*bain-marie*). (The sauce can be made ahead and refrigerated for several days or frozen. Reheat in a water bath.)

NOTE: If you are making these sauces to go with the Venison-Style Leg of Lamb (page 160), the ground meat can be made from the excess meat trimmed from the H-bone (see "French-Style Leg of Lamb," page 161).

VARIATIONS

CREAMY PEPPER GAME SAUCE

[SAUCE CHEVREUIL]

Prepare the recipe through step 5. Just before serving, bring the sauce to a boil. Add

¾ cup heavy cream and simmer 10 to 15 minutes. Skim the sauce and adjust the seasoning, if necessary. (The sauce can be made ahead and refrigerated for several days or frozen. To reheat, bring to a boil.)

Creamy Currant-Pepper Game Sauce

[SAUCE GRAND VENEUR]

Prepare the recipe through step 5. Just before serving, bring the sauce to a boil. Add 4½ teaspoons currant jelly and ¾ cup heavy cream and simmer 10 to 15 minutes. Skim the sauce and adjust the seasoning, if necessary. (The sauce can be made ahead and refrigerated for several days or frozen for later use. To reheat, simply bring to a boil.)

A Trio of Game Sauces

You can make just one of the game sauces or, because they are really just slight variations on one another, you can make all three. I suggest that the first time you make the recipe you do this to decide which is your favorite. Prepare the Game Sauce with Pepper recipe through step 5 and divide this sauce base in thirds. Follow the directions for making each of the sauces, using these adjustments:

- **POIVRADE:** Add 2 tablespoons softened butter.
- **CHEVREUIL:** Add ¼ cup heavy cream.
- **GRAND VENEUR:** Add 1½ teaspoons currant jelly and ¼ cup heavy cream.

Game Marinade

[MARINADE POUR GIBIER]

THIS MARINADE is classically made with white wine, but I prefer making it with red wine, because I find it less acidic and the resulting sauces have a richer color and smoother flavor. Either version can be used to flavor the meat of such game as venison, elk, antelope, hare, and wild boar. I use a marinade whenever I have meat cut from animals that have not been aged.

Since most people do not prepare game at home, I have adapted the marinade for use with a leg of lamb (see Venison-Style Leg of Lamb, page 160). While the lamb is roasting, I use the marinade to prepare one of three sauces, also traditionally served with game.

Depending on the amount of meat to be marinated, you can easily increase the quantities shown below. **MAKES ABOUT 4 CUPS/ ENOUGH FOR ABOUT 5 POUNDS OF MEAT**

1 small onion, halved and sliced
1 carrot, sliced
2 shallots, sliced
1 rib celery, sliced
2 cloves garlic, smashed
3 sprigs parsley
3 to 4 sprigs fresh thyme or ¼ teaspoon dried leaves
1 small sprig fresh rosemary or ¼ teaspoon dried
1 bay leaf, crumbled
8 juniper berries, crushed
5 peppercorns, crushed, or ¼ teaspoon freshly ground pepper
1 whole clove or whole allspice berry
1 bottle (750 ml) dry red wine
½ cup white (distilled) vinegar
½ cup vegetable oil

1. Mix all the ingredients together in a large bowl or deep roasting pan and place the meat you are using in it. The meat should be at least half covered by the marinade. Cover with plastic wrap and marinate in the refrigerator for 2 to 4 days. Turn the meat in the marinade twice a day.

2. When you are ready to cook the meat, drain the marinade (see Note), and dry the meat before browning.

NOTE: If you are making any of the game sauces (see facing page), reserve the marinade and the vegetables.

IN ADDITION

If you are fortunate enough to have game, marinate it for several days and then either braise it, using a little of the marinade together with some game stock as the braising liquid, or make *ragoût* (stew) using the same combination of liquids.

TOMATO SAUCE

[SAUCE TOMATE]

THIS SIMPLE, chunky tomato sauce can be used with pasta, veal, chicken, or fish. When your tomatoes are not as ripe or as red as you may wish them to be, add 2 teaspoons of tomato paste or ½ cup tomato purée to improve both the color and flavor of the sauce (or use canned tomatoes). A variation can be made by using a blender or processor to purée the cooked sauce to make it smooth. **MAKES 2 CUPS TO SERVE 6**

3 tablespoons extra-virgin olive oil
1 onion, chopped
3 cloves garlic, chopped
3 pounds tomatoes, peeled, seeded, chopped, and drained, or 3 cans (14.5 ounces each) diced tomatoes, drained
¼ teaspoon salt
⅛ teaspoon freshly ground pepper
10 to 12 fresh basil leaves, chopped, or 1 teaspoon dried basil

1. In a large skillet, heat the oil over medium heat. Add the onion and sauté until softened but not browned, about 2 minutes.

2. Add the garlic and the tomatoes, increase the heat to high, and cook the sauce until most of the moisture has evaporated, leaving a medium-thick sauce, 4 to 5 minutes. Season with the salt and pepper. (The recipe can be prepared ahead to this point 1 to 2 days in advance. Cover and refrigerate. Bring back to a boil before proceeding.)

3. Remove the sauce from the heat and stir in the basil. Use at once.

HOLLANDAISE SAUCE

[SAUCE HOLLANDAISE]

THE CLASSIC hollandaise sauce, an emulsion of egg yolks and butter flavored with lemon, is a perfect match for fish. The sauce is also used with poached eggs and with vegetables. For eggs I omit the lemon juice completely, and I use only a touch of lemon when serving with vegetables. I like to vary the sauce by adding chopped fresh chives when available.

The sauce is most often made in a double boiler. This technique is tedious and the resulting sauce is quite heavy. When made with the following technique, hollandaise is much lighter and quick to prepare. It will help if you have a small, heavy saucepan that conducts heat well, preferably one with a core of either aluminum or copper. Also important is a good 8-inch wire whisk with several layers of wire loops.

Once made, the sauce can be kept warm in a water bath (*bain-marie*) for 15 to 20 minutes while you put the finishing touches on the meal. The water in the water bath should never be hotter than warm to the touch. If the water gets too hot, the sauce will curdle.

MAKES 1¼ CUPS TO SERVE 8 TO 10

2 egg yolks
2 tablespoons water
12 tablespoons (1½ sticks) butter, melted
¼ teaspoon salt
A few drops of lemon juice, or more to taste
1 to 2 tablespoons chopped fresh chives, to taste (optional)

1. In a small, heavy saucepan, whisk the egg yolks and water together over medium heat until thick and fluffy, 2 to 3 minutes. As soon as the sauce thickens enough so you can see the bottom of the pan while whisking, remove it from the heat. (Too much heat at this point can cause the yolks to set and look like scrambled eggs.

If this happens, start again.) Continue whisking the mixture off the heat for several seconds. The sauce should be thick enough to cling to your whisk.

2. Allow the pan to cool for a minute before slowly adding the melted butter, which should be no hotter than the egg yolks. Whisk constantly while adding the butter, a little at a time, as you would for a mayonnaise. Add the salt and lightly flavor with lemon juice. Stir in the chopped chives (if using) and keep warm in a water bath (*bain-marie*) for 15 to 20 minutes.

IN ADDITION

Most classic recipes for hollandaise call for the butter to be clarified. To clarify butter, it must be heated sufficiently to separate the milk solids from the fat, yielding clear butter. When this is done, the sweet, fresh taste of butter is destroyed. For this reason, I am careful to just melt the butter, and often remove my pan from the heat before the butter is completely melted.

REPAIRING A CURDLED HOLLANDAISE

Should your sauce curdle, try one of the following:

✦ Place a fresh egg yolk in a clean bowl and slowly whisk in the curdled sauce a little at a time, making sure the sauce is smooth before adding more curdled sauce.

✦ Put 1 to 2 teaspoons of cold water in a clean bowl and slowly whisk in the curdled sauce a little at a time, making sure the sauce is smooth before adding more curdled sauce.

In both cases, the sauce should return to its emulsified state provided the egg yolk has not set. If that is the case, strain the sauce and serve the flavored butter.

BEARNAISE SAUCE

[SAUCE BÉARNAISE]

A BÉARNAISE SAUCE is essentially a hollandaise sauce made with a reduction of tarragon, chervil, shallots, pepper, wine, and vinegar instead of lemon juice. Its delicious blend of flavors makes it one of France's most popular sauces. Although usually served with grilled steak, it is also ideal with other grilled meats, fish, and poultry.

Classically, the shallots are first sautéed to soften, and only vinegar is used in the reduction. I do not sauté the shallots, creating a slightly stronger flavor, which I find most people enjoy. Adding white wine to the vinegar reduction rounds out the flavor.

Leftover béarnaise is excellent on sandwiches made with leftover roasts, and I often serve the sauce at room temperature with cold, sliced fillet of beef.

MAKES 1½ CUPS TO SERVE 8 TO 12

2 shallots, finely chopped
2 teaspoons chopped fresh tarragon or crushed dried tarragon
1 teaspoon chopped fresh chervil or crushed dried chervil
⅛ teaspoon freshly ground pepper
2 tablespoons tarragon vinegar or white (distilled) vinegar
2 tablespoons dry white wine
2 tablespoons water
2 egg yolks
12 tablespoons (1½ sticks) butter, melted
¼ teaspoon salt

1. Place the shallots, tarragon, chervil, pepper, vinegar, and wine in a small saucepan. Over high heat, reduce until only 1 teaspoon of liquid remains, about 2 minutes. Remove from the heat. (This can be done several hours in advance.)

2. Add the water and egg yolks and whisk constantly, over medium heat, until thick and fluffy, 2 to 3 minutes. As soon as the sauce thickens enough so you can see the bottom of the pan while whisking, remove it from the heat. (Too much heat at this point can cause the yolks to set and look like scrambled eggs. If this happens, start again.) Continue whisking the mixture off the heat for several seconds. The sauce should be thick enough to cling to your whisk.

3. Allow the pan to cool for a minute before slowly adding the melted butter, which should be no hotter than the egg yolks. Whisk constantly while adding the butter, a little at a time, as you

USING A WATER BATH

It is often necessary to keep things warm at temperatures well below the boiling point, and a water bath (*bain-marie*) is ideal for this purpose. The temperature of the pan is kept below boiling by placing it in another pan containing water (this second pan is the water bath). Even if the water in the water bath boils, the contents of the pan will not. (A double boiler works similarly to a water bath.)

When making a water bath, use a pan considerably larger than the one you want to heat or keep warm. For example, I would choose an 8-inch square cake pan as the water bath for a 1-quart saucepan, or a 10-inch skillet for a 3-quart saucepan. By using large pans, you can easily monitor the temperature of the water in the water bath.

would for a mayonnaise. Add the salt. The sauce should taste of tarragon and have a slight bite from the vinegar and a hint of salt. If necessary, add 1 to 3 drops of vinegar, additional tarragon, and a sprinkle of salt. Keep warm in a water bath (*bain-marie*) for 15 to 20 minutes.

VARIATIONS

BEARNAISE WITH MINT

[SAUCE PALOISE]

Substitute an equal amount of mint for the tarragon.

BEARNAISE WITH TOMATOES

[SAUCE CHORON]

This delightful variation of béarnaise is wonderful with roast or grilled lamb as well as with grilled fish. Use it in the summer when you are sure to get a full-flavored, ripe tomato. Peel, seed, and finely chop 1 tomato before placing it in a fine strainer to drain well. If the pulp is not well drained, it will thin the béarnaise too much. The sauce should remain thick enough to lightly coat the meat or fish. Mix in ¼ cup chopped fresh tomato pulp or 2 heaping teaspoons tomato paste just before serving.

BEARNAISE SAUCE WITH MEAT GLAZE

[SAUCE FOYOT/VALOIS]

A béarnaise with the addition of meat glaze is known by either the name *Foyot* or *Valois* and is served primarily with beef. Just before serving, add 1 tablespoon Meat Glaze (page 309) and salt to taste to the béarnaise. I have made similar sauces using chicken glaze or fish glaze to serve with grilled chicken and grilled fish, but I have never seen names for these sauces. This sauce can also be made with the reduced deglazed liquid from a roasting pan.

BEURRE BLANC

[SAUCE BEURRE BLANC]

BEURRE BLANC NANTAIS, now known simply as beurre blanc, is a velvety white butter sauce, traditionally made from a reduction of vinegar and shallots to which butter is added. It was created in the area of the Loire Valley between the towns of Angers and Nantes to serve with the pike, shad, and salmon that populate the Loire River.

The recipe that follows, which is based on the original and uses only vinegar, will surprise those familiar with a contemporary beurre blanc that uses wine or a combination of wine and vinegar. It is wonderful with all forms of fish. Although flavored vinegars can be used, I generally use plain white (distilled) vinegar. Freshly chopped herbs, or even puréed herbs, can be added at the end to vary the flavor and appearance of the sauce.

MAKES 1 CUP TO SERVE 6 TO 8

2 shallots, finely chopped
½ cup white (distilled) vinegar
16 tablespoons (2 sticks) salted butter (see Note), softened to room temperature

1. In a small, heavy saucepan, cook the shallots slowly in the vinegar over medium-low heat until only 1 tablespoon of liquid remains, about 10 minutes.

2. Remove the pan from the heat. Whisk in the butter 2 tablespoons at a time, waiting for each addition to melt before adding the next. The sauce will be warm and thick enough to lightly coat a spoon. Keep the sauce warm in a water bath (*bain-marie*) until ready to use.

NOTE: You will note that I use salted butter for beurre blanc in place of the unsalted I normally use. When made with unsalted butter, the sauce tends to be a little thinner.

IN ADDITION

In the early '70s, Paul Bocuse and other chefs abandoned hollandaise sauce, the butter sauce of the classic French kitchen, and started using beurre blanc exclusively. Variations developed, with wine being used in place of the traditional vinegar. Even red wine was used to create a *beurre rouge* (red butter sauce). Beurre blanc soon became the mainstay of nouvelle cuisine, and is still popular today with fish, veal, chicken, and vegetables.

VARIATIONS

Basil Beurre Blanc

[BEURRE BLANC AU BASILIC]

Stir in 1 to 2 tablespoons chopped fresh basil at the end of step 1.

Chive Beurre Blanc

[BEURRE BLANC À LA CIBOULETTE]

Stir in 2 to 3 tablespoons chopped chives at the end of step 1.

Tarragon Beurre Blanc

[BEURRE BLANC À L'ESTRAGON]

Stir in 2 to 3 tablespoons chopped fresh tarragon at the end of step 1.

Watercress Beurre Blanc

[BEURRE BLANC AU CRESSON]

Make a dry purée of watercress (see step 1 of Fresh Green Pasta, page 81), using only 1 bunch of watercress. Whisk in enough of the puréed watercress to lightly color the sauce.

MAYONNAISE

STORE-BOUGHT mayonnaise serves me well for everyday uses, but whenever a special sauce merits it, or a large quantity is called for, I whisk up a homemade one especially for the occasion.

Mayonnaise is an emulsified sauce. Egg yolk is used to hold oil in suspension, and vinegar or lemon juice is used to thin and to add flavor and acidity to the sauce. Besides adding salt and pepper to season the mayonnaise, you can add any number of other seasonings to change or enhance its flavor. The most common addition is Dijon mustard. Others include curry powder, tomato paste, horseradish, saffron, a purée of fresh herbs and greens for Green Mayonnaise (page 334), and garlic for Aioli (page 332).

My technique for making mayonnaise differs from most cookbook writers' in one significant way. Most start by combining the egg yolk and vinegar before adding the oil, whereas I add the oil before the vinegar. My reason is simple. I find the egg yolk holds the oil in suspension more easily when it is thick, and I can add the oil faster with less danger of separation than when the yolk is first thinned with vinegar. It is difficult to separate a mayonnaise once a good emulsion is formed. I add the vinegar or lemon juice when the sauce becomes too thick to stir. While adding the vinegar, I taste the mayonnaise, making sure not to add too much. If the mayonnaise tastes good yet is still too thick, simply thin it with a little water.

Although the classic mayonnaise is made only with egg yolks, it is just as easy to make it with a whole egg, producing a lighter, slightly less rich version. As in traditional mayonnaise, the eggs in this sauce are uncooked (see "Egg Safety," page 333).

One egg yolk will hold up to 1 cup of oil in suspension, and I frequently make mayonnaise with only ¾ cup of oil per egg yolk. The more oil you use, the thicker the mayonnaise becomes. **MAKES 2½ CUPS**

1 egg
1 egg yolk
½ teaspoon salt
¼ teaspoon freshly ground pepper
2 cups light olive or other vegetable oil
2 to 3 teaspoons vinegar or lemon juice

FLAVOR VARIATIONS

Oil is the major component of a mayonnaise, and will lend its taste to the sauce. I prefer to make a mayonnaise for general use with a light-flavored oil, but there are times I will add some stronger flavors. Nut oils such as hazelnut and walnut are very strong, but can add an interesting accent when used in small amounts.

Traditionally either lemon juice or plain white (distilled) vinegar is used for making mayonnaise, but with all the various flavored vinegars now available, you may wish to try one if you feel its flavor will add to your presentation.

Repairing a Separated Mayonnaise

If a mayonnaise separates, it is usually due to one or more of the following:

✦ Oil is added too rapidly at first.

✦ The egg or the oil is too cold.

✦ Too much oil was added for the amount of egg used.

The easiest way to restore it is to beat the curdled sauce, slowly at first, into a bowl containing either a fresh egg yolk or 1 teaspoon of Dijon mustard. If your problem is due to temperature, you can first try beating the curdled sauce vigorously while adding 1 tablespoon of boiling water.

1. Place the whole egg, egg yolk, salt, and pepper in a food processor or blender. Process until well blended.

2. With the machine running, slowly pour in the oil, gradually increasing the amount added as the sauce thickens. As soon as the sauce is very thick, thin with 2 teaspoons of the vinegar, followed by the remaining oil.

3. Stop the machine and taste the mayonnaise. Add more vinegar, if necessary, and adjust the seasoning to taste. Cover the surface of the mayonnaise with plastic wrap. It can be stored in the refrigerator for up to 2 weeks.

NOTE: You can also make mayonnaise by hand with a whisk or electric beater.

Aioli

AIOLI, the "butter" of Provence, is found in every restaurant in the south of France. The region, which traditionally is not known for its dairy products, uses this strong garlic mayonnaise instead of butter in many instances. Spread on bread and lightly toasted, it makes wonderful garlic bread. It can be used as a dip for raw vegetables, or be spread on a piece of fish and broiled, and it is a must to serve with Mediterranean Fish Soup (page 21) or American Bouillabaisse (page 99).

The sauce is easily made in a blender, by first puréeing the garlic and then adding the yolk, salt, and oil, and thinning it in the end with lemon juice. Note that I use extra-virgin olive oil for its heightened flavor, which reminds me of Provence. **MAKES 1 CUP**

1 egg yolk
Salt
5 cloves garlic, crushed through a press or finely chopped (see Note)
¾ cup extra-virgin olive oil
Juice of 1 lemon

1. In a small bowl, whisk the egg yolk with a pinch of salt. Add the garlic.

EGG SAFETY

There are numerous sauces and dishes in classic French cooking that are made with raw or barely cooked eggs. Because eggs can carry a strain of bacteria called *Salmonella* (though the rate of contamination is only 1 in 20,000 eggs), it's best to take some precautions. Buy very fresh eggs and keep them well refrigerated. Or look for pasteurized eggs if you're concerned. And never serve raw eggs to very young children, the elderly, pregnant women, or anyone whose immune system is impaired.

2. Whisking, slowly begin adding the oil, drop by drop at first. As the mixture thickens, more oil can be incorporated more rapidly.

3. Thin the sauce with some lemon juice when it becomes very thick and follow with the remaining oil. Whisk in salt and additional lemon juice to taste. The aïoli should be the consistency of mayonnaise.

NOTE: If you find the sauce too strong on garlic, simply use less the next time and thin your first batch with a little plain mayonnaise.

VARIATIONS

ROUILLE

This spicy garlic mayonnaise is traditionally served with bouillabaisse. Rouille gets its rusty color (*rouille* means rust) and its fiery hotness from a crushed, small fresh red chili pepper. When not available, I use a crushed small dried red chili pepper or add cayenne powder to taste (¼ teaspoon or more). The traditional recipe also calls for soup-soaked bread or potato, but I leave it out.

BASIL AIOLI

[AÏOLI AU BASILIC]

Add 10 to 15 chopped fresh basil leaves (to taste) to make a delicious basil and garlic mayonnaise. Try it as a dip for shrimp or vegetables.

GREEN MAYONNAISE

[SAUCE VERTE]

SAUCE VERTE is a green mayonnaise served with cold poached fish and seafood. The sauce is made with a variety of greens and herbs that are first briefly blanched and refreshed to heighten their color, then squeezed dry and chopped along with the mayonnaise ingredients in a blender or food processor. It is not always possible to find all the herbs listed (see Note).

If you already have some homemade mayonnaise on hand, simply chop the herbs after squeezing them dry and mix them with the prepared mayonnaise. **MAKES 2 CUPS**

12 leaves spinach, stemmed, or 30 to 40 baby spinach leaves
25 chives or 2 scallions
15 sprigs watercress, stemmed
4 sprigs fresh tarragon or 1 teaspoon dried tarragon
6 sprigs fresh parsley
12 sprigs fresh chervil
6 fresh basil leaves
1 egg
1 egg yolk
½ teaspoon salt
⅛ teaspoon freshly ground pepper
1½ cups light olive oil
2 to 4 teaspoons tarragon vinegar or lemon juice

1. Drop all the greens (including all the fresh herbs) into a small pot of boiling water for 30 to 45 seconds. Drain and refresh under cold running water. Press or squeeze the greens to extract their moisture. Place in paper towels and squeeze dry.

2. Place the greens together with the egg, egg yolk, salt, and pepper in a food processor. Process until well blended.

3. With the processor running, slowly pour in the oil, gradually increasing the amount added as the sauce thickens. As soon as the sauce is very thick, thin with the vinegar or lemon juice to taste.

4. Stop the machine and taste the mayonnaise. Add more vinegar or lemon juice, if necessary, and adjust the seasoning to taste. Serve with poached fish. Cover the surface of the mayonnaise with plastic wrap and refrigerate if storing.

NOTE: Try to use at least four different herbs. The proportions can vary, and the amounts given in the ingredients are to be used as a guide. The greater the variety of greens and herbs, the better the sauce will be. I have not given dried equivalents for the fresh chervil and basil in the recipe, for I do not like them in this sauce.

REMOULADE SAUCE

[SAUCE RÉMOULADE]

THIS CLASSIC French sauce, similar to a tartar sauce, is also a member of the mayonnaise family. It is excellent with both fried and cold poached fish and seafood. Try mixing it with mussels, crabmeat, shrimp, or tuna for seafood salads with a new twist. Cornichons are small sour French gherkin pickles, which can be found in the imported food section of most supermarkets.

MAKES 1¼ CUPS TO SERVE 8 TO 10

6 medium cornichons, finely chopped
1 tablespoon capers, finely chopped
2 teaspoons Dijon mustard
1 sprig fresh tarragon, chopped (see Note)
3 sprigs fresh parsley, chopped
1 cup mayonnaise, homemade (see page 331) or store-bought

Mix all ingredients together in a small bowl. Refrigerate, with the surface covered in plastic wrap, until ready to serve.

NOTE: If fresh tarragon is not available it can be omitted entirely, but if you are making your own mayonnaise, use tarragon vinegar to add more flavor.

COLD HORSERADISH SAUCE

[SAUCE RAIFORT]

THIS CREAMY horseradish sauce is ideal to serve with cold roast beef. I also like to use it with sliced cold beef that's been boiled, braised, or corned.

The classic version of this sauce is made with bread crumbs, which are moistened in milk and then squeezed dry; then mustard, fresh horseradish, vinegar, sugar, and heavy cream are added.

The interpretation that follows does away with the bread crumbs, vinegar, and sugar. I whip the cream to replace the body the bread crumbs add to the sauce.

MAKES 1 CUP TO SERVE 8

1 cup heavy cream, whipped
1 teaspoon Dijon mustard
2 to 3 tablespoons prepared horseradish, to taste

Mix all the ingredients together and serve chilled.

VINAIGRETTE

[SAUCE VINAIGRETTE]

IN ITS SIMPLEST FORM, a vinaigrette, or French salad dressing, is one part vinegar or lemon juice to three or four parts olive or vegetable oil. It is seasoned with a little salt and pepper. Mixed extremely well just before using, the vinaigrette is smooth and delicate tasting; if not well blended, it can be harsh and oily. If the oil and vinegar used have excellent flavor, nothing else is needed to dress a mixed green salad.

Dijon mustard is used as a basic vinaigrette ingredient by many chefs. Besides adding flavor, it also acts as an emulsifier, holding the oil and vinegar in suspension longer. Other ingredients added to a vinaigrette are chopped fresh herbs, chopped shallots, chopped hard-cooked egg, and garlic.

I generally keep a bottle of vinaigrette in the refrigerator ready to use, shaking it well just before pouring it over a salad.

Using the proportions shown here, it's easy to scale this recipe up or down. I use a blender whenever making large quantities of the dressing. **MAKES 1¾ CUPS**

3 tablespoons tarragon vinegar
3 tablespoons lemon juice
1 to 2 teaspoons Dijon mustard, to taste
1 clove garlic, halved (see Notes)
¼ teaspoon salt
⅛ teaspoon freshly ground pepper
1¼ cups light olive or other vegetable oil

1. In a small bowl or jar, mix the vinegar, lemon juice, mustard, garlic, salt, and pepper together.

2. Add the oil and mix all ingredients until well blended and smooth. Blend well again just before using.

NOTES: Because garlic can overpower a salad, add a halved garlic clove instead of chopped garlic to the dressing. In this way you can remove it when the dressing has acquired sufficient garlic flavor.

When entertaining, I make the dressing keeping in mind what I am serving before and after the salad. For example, if garlic is not present in the other dishes, I do not use it in the vinaigrette.

BREADS

THE FIRST THING you are served in a French restaurant is bread and butter. And it continues to be an important feature of the meal all the way through to the cheese course.

Only a very few restaurants make their own bread or rolls, for there is usually a bakery within a few blocks that makes good bread, but the top restaurants all have their special bakeries. And with such good bakeries around, it is the rare home cook who makes bread.

In some areas of the United States, finding a well-made, freshly baked loaf of French bread may be a rarity and is sufficient reason to make your own. Bread making is easy with the aid of a food processor. And except for the time required for rising, it is also quick.

BREAD BASICS

FLOUR: This is the most important ingredient in bread. I prefer unbleached flour to bleached. If the flavor or texture of your bread is not up to your expectations, try making your next loaf with 50 percent bread flour. Bread flour contains more gluten (the protein in flour) than all-purpose, so a dough made from it is more elastic, and the bread chewier. I find that bread made with 100 percent bread flour is too difficult to work with, so I mix it half-and-half with all-purpose flour.

When forming loaves made with bread flour, you may find them springy and hard to form. When this happens, stop working, cover the dough with plastic wrap, and let it rest for 2 to 5 minutes to allow the tension in the dough to relax.

YEAST: The other vital component in bread making, yeast needs to be dissolved in a warm liquid, usually water, and most recipes provide a temperature range. If you do not have a thermometer, just put your finger into the warm water. If the water feels warm or even very warm, it is in a good range; it should not feel hot.

I have used both fresh and active dry yeast with equally good results, so try both to see if you have a preference. Fresh yeast can be stored in the freezer for 2 to 3 months. I do not recommend "quick rising" yeast; the difference in rising time is not appreciable and the flavor is not as good as in breads made with traditional yeasts.

WATER: If your local water contains chemicals, you may find the flavor of your bread improved by using bottled (or filtered) water.

CAUSES AND EFFECTS: Yeast dough has a tendency to be temperamental and inconsistent in its behavior. Being aware of the factors that may affect the dough will help you handle its moods.

Occasionally, you may find that your dough is stiffer or softer than usual, and that the amount of rising time it needs increases or decreases substantially. (A stiff dough takes longer to rise than a softer one.) Both the type of flour and the amount of humidity in the air play a role in determining the amount of water your dough may need, so don't hesitate to add up to ¼ cup more if you feel the dough is too stiff. And if the dough is too soft and sticky, add more flour.

Other things that may influence rising time are altitude and room temperature. High altitudes can reduce both the rising and baking times, so keep an eye on your dough. Similarly, a dough left to rise in a warm place will rise more quickly than one left in a cold or drafty room.

A final, perhaps more obvious, factor that will affect your bread is oven temperature. French bread is baked at relatively high temperatures to give color, flavor, and crunch to the crust. If you find the temperature too high, lower it 25 to 50 degrees. If you are using black pans or baking sheets, this is a good rule of thumb anyway.

French Bread

[PAIN FRANÇAIS]

ALTHOUGH I DO NOT consider myself a bread baker, never having formally studied the subject nor worked in a bakery, I do pride myself on the recipe and techniques I've put together for teaching French bread making to American home cooks. By following the suggestions in the recipe, your first loaf of bread will be a certain success.

The first step in bread making is combining the flour, water, and yeast to form a dough. Mixing these basic ingredients by hand can be a difficult and messy task, but with a food processor it becomes a snap.

Many bread recipes produce a sticky dough that needs to be formed on a floured surface and kneaded with floured hands to keep from sticking. Working with dough in this way can be difficult and messy for the novice. In my recipe the dough is rarely sticky, eliminating the need for additional flour and making the forming process much easier and neater.

Once the dough is mixed, it must rest to give the yeast time to grow. While the yeast grows, it emits carbon dioxide, which causes tiny air pockets to appear in the dough. This rising or leavening of the dough takes several hours and should not be rushed, because it is during this rising period that the bread also develops some of its flavor. Once the dough has risen to two or three times its original volume, it needs to be deflated, or punched down, and kneaded to release the gas. If the dough is left inflated too long, the bread will have a strong taste similar to baking soda from overexposure to carbon dioxide.

Many bakers allow their dough to rise three or four times, the flavor changing slightly with each rise. I have found that most people are unable to tell the difference in taste between two and three rises, so I suggest that you form your bread after the first rise to considerably shorten the time needed for making it. When you have the time, give it the additional rises, and determine for yourself if they are beneficial.

Traditionally, once formed and risen, and just before going into the oven, a loaf of bread's surface is slashed with a sharp knife or razor blade to enhance its beauty and fullness when baked, and to prevent the crust from bursting as the moist interior expands more rapidly than the drier exterior. Slashing a fully risen, fragile loaf can cause it to deflate, producing both a low loaf and a low spirit. I recommend that you slash about halfway through the rise, when the loaf is more resilient, until you become more confident in your slashing. Should you forget to slash, there is no need to panic. Even if your loaf is not picture perfect, it will still taste great.

Many French bakeries use bread ovens that inject steam to moisten the surface of the bread as it bakes, creating a thicker and crunchier crust. Home bakers have tried to simulate the professional steam oven in a variety of ways. Some have put pans of boiling water in their ovens to create steam; some open their oven door to spray their baking loaves with a plant mister; others put ice cubes on the bottom of their hot ovens, while others merely brush their loaves with water to produce the thicker crust. However, if the surface of your dough has been kept moist by being well covered throughout the rising process (in my method, I use plastic wrap instead of the usual kitchen towel, which lets air dry out the dough's surface), no additional moisture is needed to produce a crisp and crunchy crust.

To bake baguettes, the typical 16- to 18-inch-long loaves of French bread, you can use baking sheets or, if you have them, baguette pans, special long loaf pans designed for French bread.

MAKES 2 TO 3 BAGUETTES

1 package active dry yeast or ½ ounce fresh yeast
1 teaspoon sugar
¼ cup warm (90°F to 115°F) water
3¼ cups (455g) unbleached all-purpose flour, or half bread flour and half all-purpose (see "Bread Basics," page 338)
1 teaspoon salt
¾ cup plus 2 tablespoons cold water
Oil for baguette pans or all-purpose flour for baking sheet

1. In a small bowl, dissolve the yeast and sugar in the warm water. Let sit until foamy and showing signs of life, 2 to 5 minutes. If the yeast is not active, discard and start again with new yeast.

2. Place the flour and salt in a food processor and add the dissolved yeast. With the processor running, add the cold water in a steady stream and process until the mixture forms a smooth dough, 40 to 60 seconds.

3. Turn the dough out onto a work surface. It should be soft, smooth, and easy to knead. To test it, squeeze the dough in one hand, lift it into the air, and let it fall back onto the work surface. If the dough leaves your hands clean, it is perfect. If it sticks to your hands, sprinkle it with a little flour and knead until smooth and no longer sticky. If the dough is too firm or dry, dip your fingers into water and plunge them into the dough. Knead the dough and repeat the process until the dough has softened.

4. Tuck the edges of the dough underneath itself, and press to form into a flat round or disc. Place the dough in a large bowl or saucepan (4- to 5-quart) and cover tightly with plastic wrap or a lid (the plastic should not touch the dough). Allow the dough to rest in a cool room until doubled in size, 1½ to 2 hours. The dough is ready when a clear impression remains when a finger is inserted into its center.

5. While the dough rises, oil your baguette pans. If using a baking sheet, sprinkle enough flour on it to prevent the dough from touching it.

COATING BAKING SHEETS

If you are baking your loaves on a baking sheet, do not oil it as you would a bread pan, or they will spread out rather than up. Instead, coat the sheet with enough of a layer of flour to keep the bread from touching the sheet. The flour will not change the bread's flavor, but if you feel so inspired, try coating your baking sheet with cornmeal, sesame seeds, caraway, or poppy seeds to add another dimension to your bread.

6. Punch down the dough and turn it onto the work surface. Knead about 30 seconds, to force out air bubbles that formed during the rising. (If desired, the dough can now be given one to two additional risings in the bowl.)

7. Cut the dough into two or three equal portions, each weighing ½ to ¾ pound, depending on the size of your pans, and cover the pieces you are not working on with plastic wrap to keep them from drying out.

8. Flatten one of the portions of dough with your fingers into a rectangular shape, pressing out the air bubbles as they move to the edge of the dough. Depending on the width of your rectangle, fold the dough in half or in thirds lengthwise to form a long, narrow piece of dough about 2 inches wide. Press down on the edges as you fold the dough to seal them and to break any air bubbles that may still appear. Elongate the dough by rolling it back and forth with the flat palms and extended fingers of your hands, and at the same time moving your hands from the center down to the ends. The dough should resemble a piece of rope, measuring approximately 1 inch in diameter, and be the same length as your baguette pan or baking sheet.

9. If using baguette pans, place the loaves into the prepared pans and cover completely with plastic wrap. If using a baking sheet, cover the loaves with a deep roasting pan. Neither the plastic wrap nor the roasting pan should touch the rising dough. If they do, the dough will stick. In such cases, you should remove the plastic wrap (carefully to prevent the loaves from falling) and then carefully re-cover the dough. Let the loaves rise about 30 minutes, or until risen by half.

10. Uncover the loaves and make three or four diagonal slashes in each loaf with a sharp knife—a serrated knife works well. Each slash should be 3 to 4 inches long and about ½ inch deep, and, if possible, the blade should be held at a 45-degree angle to the loaf. Re-cover the loaves and allow them to continue rising until doubled or tripled in size, about 45 minutes.

11. Preheat the oven to 450°F with the oven rack placed in the lowest position.

12. Remove the plastic or roasting pan and bake the loaves until evenly browned, 20 to 25 minutes. If they begin to brown more on top than on the bottom, turn them over in the pans or baking sheet for the last 5 minutes.

13. Transfer the loaves to a rack to cool. Do not be concerned if you hear the crust cracking. When the bread is completely cool, freeze any that is not to be eaten within 24 hours. (Frozen bread will keep for several weeks, well wrapped in plastic or aluminum foil. To serve, reheat until the crust crackles when squeezed: 10 minutes at 350°F if frozen, 5 minutes at 400°F if thawed.)

VARIATIONS

Pita Bread

[PAIN LIBANAIS]

Pita is definitely not French, but is common in France because of the large numbers of North African and Middle Eastern immigrants. It doesn't need a final rising before baking and bakes in just a few minutes.

Follow the recipe through step 4. Preheat the oven to 500°F and place an uncoated baking sheet or baking stone on the lowest rack of the oven. Omit step 5 and after following step 6, form the dough into a long sausagelike shape and cut off 2- to 4-ounce pieces. Keep the pieces covered with plastic wrap when not being worked with. Flatten each piece with your fingers until it is as thin as possible. Place (or toss) these flat, pancakelike pieces of dough onto the hot sheet or stone. The pita will puff and bake in about 4 minutes. If they are beginning to get too brown, turn them after 3 minutes. Cool on a rack.

Round Loaf

[BOULE]

Follow the recipe through step 7 and form one round loaf as illustrated (at right). Preheat the oven to 425°F with the rack placed in the lowest position. Place the loaf on a baking sheet (sprinkled with flour), cover with a bowl or pot, and let rise until doubled or tripled in size, about 1 hour. Just before placing in the oven, make a slash about 1 inch deep through the center. Bake until evenly browned, 25 to 30 minutes. Cool on a rack.

Whole-Wheat Bread

[PAIN COMPLET]

Substitute half whole-wheat flour and half bread flour for the unbleached all-purpose flour. The rest of the recipe is the same; or shape it into a *boule* (see illustration, at right).

Forming a Boule

A *boule,* or ball-shaped loaf of bread, with its tight, smooth outer surface is not hard to form, but takes a little practice to make perfect.

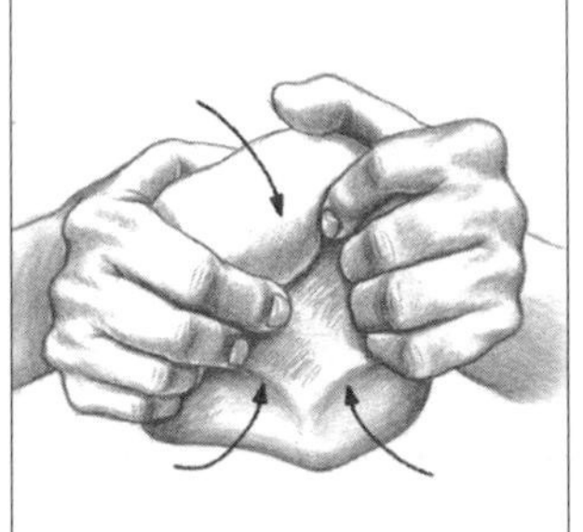

1. Tuck the edges of the kneaded dough underneath itself.

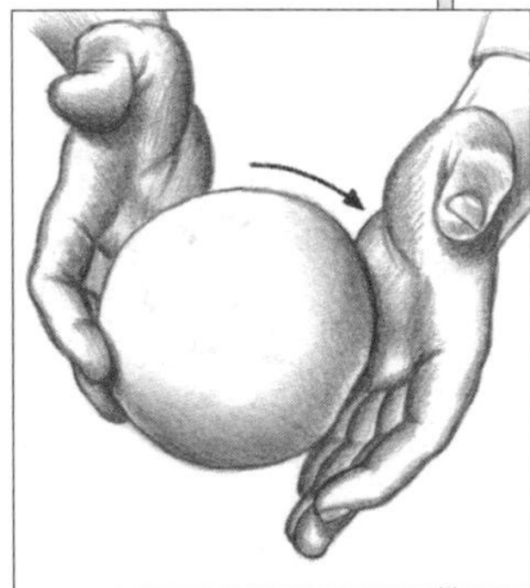

2. Shape the dough into a smooth round ball.

DESSERT SAUCES

HERE ARE THE BASIC SAUCES, fillings, icings, and flavorings that you will need to make the desserts in this book. I have also included my recipe for quick and easy homemade jam, which is only lightly sweetened and intense with fruit, and my sugar syrups (used for moistening cakes and making sorbets). You will notice that for all of my dessert sauces, I use less sugar than most classic recipes call for.

Although some of the recipes that follow are not strictly "sauces," they are the basic dessert-building tools of a classic pastry chef. Once you have made them successfully and begin to see the many uses they have, I recommend that you commit them to memory (this is what a chef in training must do). Learning the structure and the proportions of a pastry cream or a crème anglaise, for example, will give you the freedom to quickly make dessert soufflés, filled cream puffs, ice cream, and dessert sauces whenever you want to.

CHOCOLATE SAUCE

[SAUCE AU CHOCOLAT]

IF YOU START with a good-tasting chocolate, it is a simple matter to make a good sauce. A chocolate sauce can be made with water, milk, or cream. In the following recipe, I use the most convenient and least caloric of these liquids to produce a dark, shiny sauce.

You can create a thin or thick sauce by merely changing the amount of liquid used. The amount shown in the recipe below produces a sauce that is thin when hot and thicker when cold, the proper consistency whenever a chocolate sauce is called for. It is also an ideal consistency for flavoring ice creams, custards, and the like. Using *half* the amount of liquid produces a thick, hot sauce that becomes fudgy when cold. In this form, it is perfect for pouring over ice cream, and at room temperature mixes well with buttercreams and makes a wonderful coating for cream puffs and éclairs.

You can add a teaspoon or two of Cognac, rum, Grand Marnier, or liqueur to change the flavor of your sauce, or make it richer by using milk or cream, instead of water. **MAKES ¾ CUP**

4 ounces (115g) semisweet or bittersweet chocolate
½ cup water (see Note)

1. In a small saucepan, melt the chocolate with the water over medium heat, about 2 minutes. When the water and chocolate come to a boil, stir gently with a whisk until smooth.

2. If the sauce is too thin, cook it longer. If it is too thick, add more liquid and stir to blend well.

3. Remove the sauce from the heat and serve hot or cold. Refrigerate any leftovers.

NOTE: Use only ¼ cup water for a thick sauce.

IN ADDITION

Over the years, I have been told by chefs, cooking teachers, and cookbook writers that you can't mix water and chocolate and boil it to make a sauce. It is true that when melting chocolate, a drop of water will cause the chocolate to seize up, but if enough liquid is used you won't have a problem. I often use a microwave oven to make this sauce. I put the water and chocolate into a glass or ceramic bowl, and when the water boils, there will be enough heat to melt the chocolate, allowing you to stir it to make a smooth sauce. If too thin, use the microwave to boil the sauce to thicken.

Raspberry Coulis

[COULIS DE FRAMBOISE]

A RASPBERRY COULIS, or purée, is an extremely versatile sauce. Its flavor and color can dramatically alter a dessert and, in effect, create a new one. More than a century ago Auguste Escoffier did so when he created his now famous *pêche Melba* by adding a sweetened raspberry purée to a poached peach perched on top of vanilla ice cream. The addition transformed the simple peach and ice cream into an extraordinary dessert.

Raspberry coulis is great served over other fruits like strawberries or blueberries, or over ice creams such as chocolate or coffee. And the coulis can be frozen into a great sorbet.

MAKES 1½ CUPS

2 boxes (4 ounces each) fresh raspberries or 1 package (10 ounces) frozen unsweetened raspberries, thawed but undrained

Confectioners' sugar, Sugar Syrup (page 359), or red currant jelly, to taste

1 tablespoon kirsch or framboise (optional)

In a food processor or blender, purée the raspberries. Taste and add confectioners' sugar, sugar syrup, or currant jelly if too tart. Add the kirsch (if using) and strain through a fine-mesh sieve to remove the seeds. (This sauce can be made a day in advance and refrigerated until used.)

Straining the Coulis

As you strain the raspberry purée, tap the side of the strainer to encourage the purée to go through, but leave the seeds behind. When you use a spoon to push the purée through a strainer, you risk pushing the seeds through as well.

CREME ANGLAISE

CRÈME ANGLAISE is a vanilla custard sauce with many uses. It is usually used as a sauce and served both warm and cold to accompany cakes, French *puddings,* crêpes, fruit, and soufflés. It is the base from which both French Ice Cream (page 290) and Bavarian cream desserts (such as Marquise Alice, page 271) are made, and it can be easily flavored with chocolate, coffee, or any variety of liqueur.

The classic technique for making a crème anglaise requires beating the egg yolks and sugar to the "ribbon" stage, adding warm milk, and stirring over simmering water until the sauce thickens enough to coat a spoon. This procedure takes between 10 and 20 minutes.

For my crème anglaise, I skip the beating of the egg yolks and sugar and eliminate the use of the double boiler. Once the milk and sugar come to a boil, it takes no more than 10 seconds to make the sauce. The classic technique leaves the surface of the sauce smooth and shiny, while this one leaves it with many small bubbles. The bubbles are easily removed with a spoon (but if you're using the crème anglaise in ice cream or a Bavarian cream, don't worry about the bubbles).

MAKES 1½ CUPS TO SERVE 4 TO 6

1 cup milk
3 tablespoons (40g) sugar
3 egg yolks
¾ teaspoon pure vanilla extract

1. In a small, good heat-conducting saucepan, bring the milk and sugar to a boil over medium-high heat.

2. Place the egg yolks in a bowl. While whisking, add the hot milk slowly. Return the mixture to the saucepan and whisk rapidly over the heat for several seconds. Do not boil. Remove the

"THICK ENOUGH TO COAT A SPOON"

Many recipes instruct the reader to cook a sauce until it is "thick enough to coat a spoon." To use this test, dip a spoon into your sauce; remove it, and draw your finger down the center of the back of the spoon. If a clear, clean path has been left by your finger, the sauce has thickened sufficiently. The thickness, however, can vary. A sauce must be thick enough to coat whatever it is accompanying. Sauces like beurre blanc and crème anglaise are thin and are meant to coat lightly, while a Mornay sauce, for example, provides a heavier coating.

pan from the heat. The sauce should have thickened enough to lightly coat a spoon. If the sauce is too thin, return the pan to the heat and whisk several seconds more. This procedure should take less than 10 seconds.

3. Strain the sauce into a bowl and flavor with the vanilla. The sauce can be served hot or cold. If it is to be served cold, cover the surface with plastic wrap and refrigerate. The sauce will be slightly thicker when cold.

IN ADDITION

When using the rapid technique in the Crème Anglaise recipe, it is helpful to have a good whisk and a good heat-conducting saucepan (see "Pots and Pans," page 11). If the sauce boils, it will curdle, so make it first in small quantities to learn the technique before trying larger amounts.

PASTRY CREAM

[CRÈME PÂTISSIÈRE]

A CLASSIC pastry cream— the creamy filling used in éclairs and Napoleons, as the base for most dessert soufflés, and as the filling for many fruit tarts—is made by boiling milk, flour, sugar, and egg yolks together until a smooth, thick, and creamy sauce is formed.

One of the most common mistakes in making a pastry cream is to undercook it. People generally stop cooking when the pastry cream first comes to a boil. If you follow the method below and cook and whisk the pastry cream an additional minute or two, you will notice a dramatic change in its consistency. The pastry cream will become shiny, smoother, and thinner, instead of thick and pasty, with the disagreeable raw-flour taste of an undercooked pastry cream.

Since many people do not cook this pastry cream sufficiently, I am including another, widely used version, using cornstarch (page 349). I normally use the classic version because I prefer the taste. However, you may find the recipe with cornstarch easier to make because it requires less cooking time. If it is undercooked, it will not have the grainy taste that the flour-based recipe would have.

Pastry cream will keep, well covered with plastic wrap, for several days in the refrigerator, and it can be frozen. **MAKES 1¼ CUPS**

1 cup milk
3 egg yolks
3 tablespoons (40g) sugar
3 tablespoons (25g) all-purpose flour
1 teaspoon pure vanilla extract

1. In a small saucepan, bring the milk to a boil over medium heat.

2. Meanwhile, whisk the egg yolks and sugar together in a small bowl. Add the flour to the egg yolks and mix well, until smooth and free of lumps.

3. Thin the egg-yolk mixture with approximately ¼ cup of the warm milk. When the remaining milk begins to boil, add it to the egg-yolk mixture and stir well. Return the mixture to the saucepan and whisk rapidly over high heat, whisking the bottom and the sides of the pan until the pastry cream thickens and boils, about 1 minute. Turning the pan as you whisk helps to easily reach all areas of the pan.

4. Reduce the heat to medium and cook an additional 2 minutes, whisking as the pastry cream gently boils. It will become shiny and easier to stir.

5. Pour the pastry cream into a bowl and stir in the vanilla. Place plastic wrap directly on the surface of the pastry cream (this prevents a skin from forming on the surface) and allow it to cool. Refrigerate or freeze if not using right away.

IN ADDITION

A pastry cream can be lightened with beaten egg whites, creating *crème Chiboust* or *crème St.-Honoré,* and it can be mixed with softened butter to produce a rich buttercream filling. Or to turn a pastry cream into a sauce to toss with fruit (for a crêpe filling, for example), just thin it by stirring in a bit more milk.

VARIATIONS

PRALINE PASTRY CREAM

[CRÈME PÂTISSIÈRE AU PRALIN]

Add 3 tablespoons of Praline Paste (page 356) in step 4.

LIQUEUR-FLAVORED PASTRY CREAM

[CRÈME PÂTISSIÈRE AUX LIQUEURS]

Stir in 2 tablespoons of Grand Marnier, rum, or kirsch in step 4.

PASTRY CREAM WITH CORNSTARCH

[CRÈME PÂTISSIÈRE À LA MAÏZENA]

IF YOU ARE having trouble making a classic pastry cream, try this version, which many people find easier. **MAKES 1¼ CUPS**

1 cup milk
3 egg yolks
3 tablespoons (40g) sugar
2 tablespoons (15g) cornstarch
1 teaspoon pure vanilla extract

1. In a small saucepan, bring the milk to a boil over medium heat. Meanwhile, whisk the egg yolks and sugar together in a small bowl. Add the cornstarch to the egg-yolk mixture and mix well, until smooth and free of lumps.

2. When the milk boils, add it to the egg-yolk mixture and stir well. Return the mixture to the saucepan and whisk rapidly over high heat, whisking the bottom and the sides of the pan until the pastry cream thickens and boils, about 1 minute. Turning the pan as you whisk helps to easily reach all areas of the pan.

3. Reduce the heat to medium and cook an additional 1 minute, whisking as the pastry cream gently boils. It will become shiny and easier to stir.

4. Pour the pastry cream into a bowl and stir in the vanilla. Place plastic wrap directly on the surface of the pastry cream, and allow it to cool. Refrigerate or freeze if not using right away.

GANACHE

GANACHE is a creamy, smooth chocolate icing that is basic to French pastry making. For the most part, it has taken the place of the more classic chocolate fondant or sugar icing. It can be poured over cakes, yielding a dark, rich finish, or it can be whipped, when cool, to produce a lighter, fluffier icing that can be used like a chocolate buttercream. I also use a ganache for the centers of my Ganache Truffles (page 295).

Ganache can be flavored with strong coffee, rum, Cognac, Cointreau, Grand Marnier,

Kahlúa, or another liqueur or brandy of your choice. Adding liqueurs will thin the ganache, and you will need to wait until it is cold, instead of cool, to the touch before pouring it.

TO COVER AN 8-INCH CAKE

6 ounces semisweet chocolate
½ cup heavy cream
2 tablespoons liqueur, rum, or Cognac (optional)

TO COVER A 9-INCH CAKE

9 ounces semisweet chocolate
¾ cup heavy cream
3 tablespoons liqueur, rum, or Cognac (optional)

1. Place the chocolate and cream in a small saucepan over low heat. When the chocolate begins to melt, about 2 minutes, stir gently until it is nearly melted. Do not allow to boil. Remove from the heat and stir until the chocolate is completely melted and smooth.

2. Slowly add the liqueur (if using) and stir gently until smooth. Be sure to be gentle when you stir the ganache; overzealous stirring will cause air bubbles to form, which can end up causing small holes in the icing once the cake is coated.

3. When the chocolate is cool to the touch, it should thicken and be ready to use. To see if the ganache is ready to pour, spoon some out of the saucepan and pour it back. If it remains on the surface for a few seconds, it is ready. It should be thin enough to pour, but not so thin that it runs right off your cake. If not ready, cool the ganache for a bit longer. Ganache will keep at room temperature for a day; refrigerate for longer periods. (If it is too stiff by the time you use it, reheat gently over low heat, stirring occasionally.)

"COOL TO THE TOUCH"

The knuckle of your little finger is very sensitive to temperature. Use the knuckle to test the temperature of liquids. When a gelatin mixture feels cool, for example, it will be close to setting.

BUTTERCREAM

[CRÈME AU BEURRE]

BUTTERCREAM, one of France's most famous culinary creations, is used for frosting cakes and as a filling for chocolates. A well-made buttercream is velvety smooth and melts in your mouth. It also spreads easily and makes beautiful designs when piped through the decorating tube of a pastry bag.

Although there are several methods for making buttercream, the one that follows produces the best results.

TO COVER AN 8-INCH CAKE

½ cup minus 2 teaspoons (100g) sugar
2 tablespoons water
3 egg yolks
12 tablespoons (1½ sticks; 170g) butter, softened

TO COVER A 9-INCH CAKE

½ cup plus 2 tablespoons (135g) sugar
2½ tablespoons water
4 egg yolks
16 tablespoons (2 sticks; 225g) butter, softened

1. In a small, heavy-bottomed saucepan, bring the sugar and water to a boil over medium-high heat, about 2 minutes. Stir several times to dissolve the sugar. When fully dissolved, the mixture will be clear and boiling rapidly.

2. In a small bowl, with an electric mixer, start beating the egg yolks slowly while adding the hot sugar syrup. Continue beating at high speed until the mixture is cool, 5 to 6 minutes. The mixture will be thick and pale yellow.

3. Beat in the softened butter until smooth. Flavor the buttercream to taste (see Variations). Buttercreams are best used at room temperature, but are often served chilled. (They can be made in advance and kept in the refrigerator for several days or frozen for months.)

IN ADDITION

Made from butter, egg yolks, and sugar, buttercream is undoubtedly one of the richest preparations you can eat. When compared with the imitation buttercream often found on commercial cakes, the "real thing" is so superior that you will forgo all the others. Use it sparingly, and save it for special occasions.

VARIATIONS

VANILLA BUTTERCREAM

[CRÈME AU BEURRE À LA VANILLE]

Beat in 2 to 3 tablespoons (to taste) of pure vanilla extract after beating in the butter.

CHOCOLATE BUTTERCREAM

[CRÈME AU BEURRE AU CHOCOLAT]

For an 8-inch cake, add the whole Chocolate Sauce recipe (page 344) made with ¼ cup water. For a 9-inch cake, make the chocolate sauce with 5 ounces of chocolate and 5 tablespoons of water. Cool the sauce before adding to the buttercream.

COFFEE BUTTERCREAM

[CRÈME AU BEURRE AU CAFÉ]

Use 2 tablespoons Coffee Syrup (page 358) or Quick Coffee Syrup (page 358). Cool before adding to the buttercream.

LIQUEUR OR EAU-DE-VIE BUTTERCREAM

[CRÈME AU BEURRE À L'EAU-DE-VIE]

Add 2 to 3 tablespoons (to taste) of Grand Marnier, framboise, or any liqueur or eau-de-vie (fruit brandy) of your choice.

PRALINE BUTTERCREAM

[CRÈME AU BEURRE PRALINÉE]

Add 2 to 3 rounded tablespoons (to taste) of Praline Paste (page 356).

ROYAL ICING

[GLACE ROYALE]

A ROYAL ICING is a quickly made sugar icing that can be used in place of fondant (a cooked sugar icing). It is made by stirring confectioners' sugar and egg white together and brightening it with a little lemon juice.

Royal icing is used in a thin consistency to frost small cakes and cream puffs. A thicker version is used in combination with Ganache (page 349) to decorate cakes (see "Decorating a Cake with Ganache and Royal Icing," page 238). To use for lettering on a cake, it is thickened to a point where it will hold its shape well when squeezed from a decorating cone.

Once made, the icing begins to dry or harden rapidly. If it is not going to be used immediately, it should be covered tightly with plastic wrap. Most often, I use royal icing for decoration and spoon it into a parchment or wax paper decorating cone. I often divide one recipe to make a variety of colors. When doing this, I use vegetable coloring sparingly to create pastel shades and fill individual cones with the different colors. **MAKES ENOUGH TO DECORATE ONE 8- OR 9-INCH CAKE**

About ⅔ cup confectioners' sugar
About 1 tablespoon egg white
About ¼ teaspoon lemon juice
Vegetable food colors (optional)

1. With a wooden spoon, mix the confectioners' sugar, egg white, and lemon juice together in a small bowl to form a thick, smooth paste that falls slowly from your spoon.

2. If the icing is too thick, add a few drops of water or a very small amount of additional egg white. If the icing is too thin, add a little more sugar.

3. If the icing is to be colored, stir in vegetable coloring, one drop at a time, until the desired color is reached.

4. If not used immediately, cover the surface of the icing with plastic wrap or store in airtight decorating cones (see "Making and Using a Decorating Cone," facing page) and refrigerate. Royal icing will keep, if airtight, for a week or so.

IN ADDITION

You can make an even less complicated icing simply with confectioners' sugar and water called *sucre glace*. A similar coffee icing can be made using Coffee Essence (page 358) in place of the water. Another version is *glace à la liqueur,* made with confectioners' sugar and a small amount of any liqueur or alcohol you choose. These icings are not as smooth or strong as royal icing, and since royal icing is so easy to make, I seldom use the others.

Making and Using a Decorating Cone

To write "Happy Birthday" or to make a simple decoration on a cake, it is necessary to have either a small pastry bag fitted with a small decorating tube, or a decorating cone. It is extremely difficult to explain in words how to make a cone from a triangular-shaped piece of paper, but it should be easy for you to follow the drawings.

Start with a square piece of parchment or waxed paper and fold it in half to form two triangles, cutting to separate them.

The triangle in front of you should have a point facing up. Bring one of the corners up to the top of the point, twisting it gently so that the two points meet, forming a cone. Holding the two points together with one hand, wrap the second corner up and around the cone so that it joins the other two points from behind. If the point of the cone is not tightly closed, adjust the ends to close it. Use a stapler to fasten the three points together or fold over to secure them. Fill the cone half to three-quarters full with royal icing and fold the top of the cone over several times to securely enclose it. Again, use a stapler to fasten the folds shut.

The icing is now secured in an airtight paper cone and can be refrigerated until you are ready to use it. When ready to use the icing, snip off enough of the point with a pair of scissors to allow the icing to be squeezed out. The amount of the tip that is snipped off will determine the thickness of your lettering.

Before decorating your cake, practice your decoration on a plate or a piece of waxed paper.

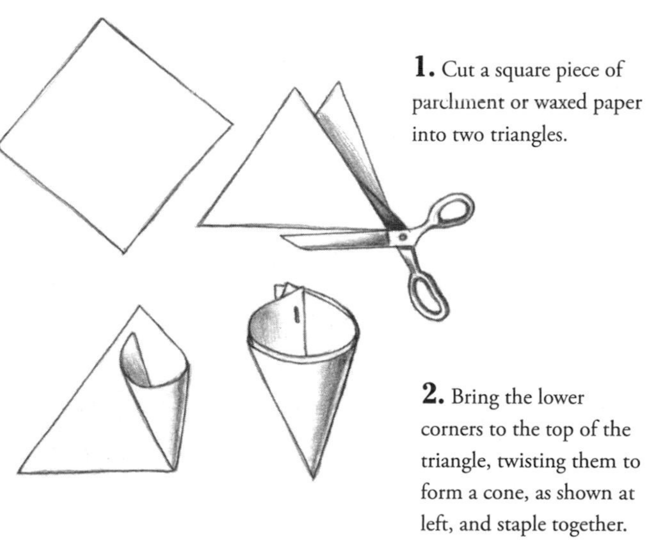

1. Cut a square piece of parchment or waxed paper into two triangles.

2. Bring the lower corners to the top of the triangle, twisting them to form a cone, as shown at left, and staple together.

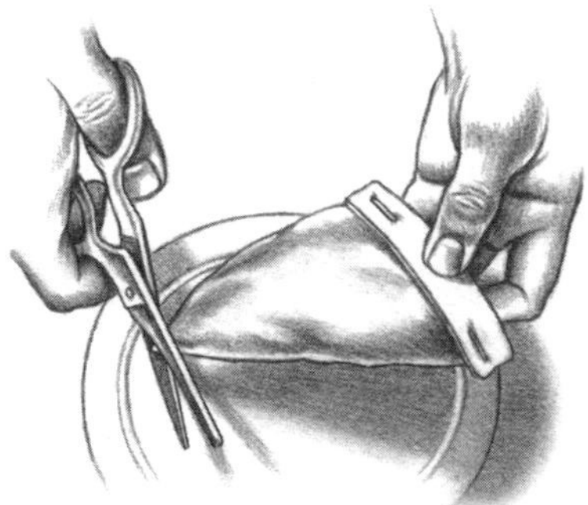

3. Snip off the tip of the filled and sealed cone to form the desired size opening.

APRICOT OR CURRANT JELLY GLAZE

[GLAÇAGE À L'ABRICOT, GLAÇAGE À LA GELLÉE DE GROSEILLE]

TARTS HAVE TRADITIONALLY been glazed with either strained apricot jam or red currant jelly. The apricot is used for light-colored fruits, and the currant jelly for darker ones. However, in the past 25 years or so, in striving for "purity," many chefs have been glazing tarts with jelly made from the fruit that is in the tart itself. Classically, an apple tart would be glazed with apricot jam; today, chefs might glaze it with apple jelly. I have always found a tart's flavor more interesting and complex when the classic glazes are used.

Most glaze recipes call for the jam or jelly to be melted over heat with a tablespoon or two of water. Since jams and jellies vary in consistency from one manufacturer to another, the amount of water you will need will vary.

Both apricot and currant glazes can be thinned further with water or liqueur to make colorful and flavorful sauces. For example, an apricot glaze thinned with a little water and rum or Cognac makes a delicious sauce for Rum-Flavored Banana Fritters (page 223), poached fruit, or pound cake. **MAKES ABOUT 1 CUP**

1 jar (10 ounces) apricot jam or red currant jelly (see Note)
Water

APPLYING A GLAZE

Glazes are used to both decorate and sweeten fruit tarts and other desserts. Use the glaze while it is still hot, and apply it with a pastry brush. Do not make strokes across the fruit with the end of the brush as you would with a paintbrush. Instead, dip the pastry brush into the glaze and then dab it onto the tart with the brush. This is a softer motion than an ordinary brush stroke; it doesn't disturb the delicate fruit, and allows the glaze to be applied gently.

1. In a small saucepan, melt the jam or jelly slowly over low heat.

2. If you are making apricot glaze, it is usually strained at this point. Most of the time I find this an unnecessary step since the pastry brush used to apply the glaze picks up the liquefied jam but leaves the heavier fruit in the pan. However, if you need a perfectly smooth jam for glazing a cake, strain it. If necessary, thin the jam with a little water to make it flow more easily through the strainer.

3. For either glaze, once melted, dip a spoon (or a piece of the fruit for the tart to be glazed) into the hot glaze. If the spoon or fruit comes out nicely coated, then it is not necessary to add water. On the other hand, if the glaze runs off the fruit or spoon, increase the heat and boil the jam or jelly until it thickens sufficiently to coat. If the coating seems very thick, add enough water to thin it and make sure to boil it and recheck its consistency before using. If not using right away, store in the refrigerator.

NOTE: If you can only find jams and jellies in 12-ounce jars, don't worry. The extra 2 ounces will make no difference to the recipes in this book. In most cases, you will have a small amount of glaze left over, which can be kept, refrigerated, for future use.

RASPBERRY JAM

[CONFITURE DE FRAMBOISES]

JAM IS MADE by cooking fruit and sugar together to the point where the moisture in the fruit evaporates and the sugar and fruit thicken. Most jams in France are made with either equal weights of fruit and sugar, or four parts fruit to three parts sugar (i.e., 1 pound fruit to ¾ pound sugar). I find that these proportions are too sweet for my taste, and therefore use two parts fruit to no more than one part sugar. Using less sugar results in less jam, but a greater intensity of flavor is achieved. The results are expensive but worthwhile, and a little goes a long way.

Although almost any fruit can be used, my three favorites are raspberry, apricot, and strawberry. Both raspberry and apricot work very well with the 2:1 ratio of fruit to sugar, but I find strawberry jam made with this ratio a little sweet. To adjust the sweetness, I either add a little lemon juice, or start by using a ratio of 3:1 to 4:1, which produces a marvelous jam.

Jam cooks in two distinct stages. During the first stage, the moisture of the fruit evaporates, and during the second the fruit and sugar thicken. In the thickening stage, the fruit and sugar can easily stick to the bottom of your pan and burn if they are not stirred frequently.

The recipe and variations that follow are for relatively small quantities of jam. They cook rapidly and are easily prepared. Larger amounts take considerably more time to cook, and should not be tried until you master the process with the smaller quantities. I keep the small quantities of jam in my refrigerator or freezer. **MAKES 3½ CUPS**

2 pounds fresh or unsweetened frozen raspberries
2 cups (1 pound) sugar

1. In a large, good heat-conducting saucepan, combine the fruit and sugar and bring to a boil over high heat. Stir frequently with a wooden spoon.

2. Allow the jam to boil rapidly for about 10 minutes, but adjust the heat, if necessary, to prevent it from boiling over. Skim off the pale pink foam that rises to the surface into a glass or small bowl. Stir the jam each time after skimming. As the foam collects in the bowl, you will notice clear jam settling under the foam. Discard the foam and return the clear jam to the saucepan.

3. After about 15 minutes you will begin to feel and hear the jam sticking to the bottom of your saucepan as you stir. This is an indication that the jam is thickening and will be finished in about 5 minutes. Lower the heat to medium-high and continue cooking, stirring frequently to prevent burning. The jam is done when the liquid thickens to coat a spoon with some of the seeds or small pieces of fruit sticking to it.

4. Pour the jam into clean heavy glass or porcelain jam jars. Cover the surface with a layer of plastic wrap. Refrigerate or freeze for up to 6 months.

IN ADDITION

In France, a large, unlined copper pan was traditionally used for making jam. Many cooks still use them today. Although good heat-conducting pans help when cooking jam, any pan can be used if care is taken.

VARIATIONS

Strawberry Jam

[CONFITURE DE FRAISES]

In place of the raspberries, use 3 pounds fresh or unsweetened frozen strawberries.

Apricot Jam

[CONFITURE D'ABRICOTS]

In place of the raspberries, use 2½ pounds fresh apricots, halved (or quartered if large) and pitted to yield 2 pounds. In step 1, add ½ cup water along with the fruit and sugar. Apricots are not as juicy as berries, so water is needed to dissolve the sugar and to prevent it from caramelizing or burning.

PRALINE PASTE

[PÂTE DE PRALIN]

PRALINE PASTE, found in supermarkets in France, is used for making candies or flavoring ice cream, pastry creams, and Bavarian creams. It is a characteristically French flavor, and many Americans do not appreciate it at first. Given time, however, I have never met anyone who has not learned to like it in one form or another.

Finding blanched hazelnuts in the market is easy in France, but not as easy in the United States. They are, however, available online and in many specialty food markets.

MAKES 1 POUND

¼ pound (¾ cup) whole blanched almonds
¼ pound (½ plus ⅓ cup) whole blanched hazelnuts
½ pound (1 cup) sugar
½ cup water

1. Preheat the oven to 400°F.

2. Roast the almonds and hazelnuts on ungreased baking sheets until the nuts are beige and shiny, 5 to 7 minutes. Do not let the nuts burn.

3. Lightly oil a marble surface or uncoated baking sheet (if you have only nonstick baking sheets, oil the back of one as the hot caramel is too hot for the nonstick coating and will damage it).

4. In a small saucepan, bring the sugar and water to a boil over medium-high heat. Boil the mixture without stirring until it turns to a medium caramel color, about 5 minutes.

5. Remove the saucepan from the heat and stir in the nuts so they become coated with the caramel. Immediately pour the mixture onto the lightly oiled baking sheet or marble surface and allow to cool.

6. Break the caramelized nuts into small pieces and place in a food processor or blender. If a blender is used, blend in small quantities. Process for several minutes until a smooth paste is formed. This paste can be stored in the refrigerator or freezer for several months.

IN ADDITION

Although New Orleans praline is made with pecans and brown sugar, in France *pralin* was originally made with almonds and caramelized sugar. Quite a few years ago hazelnuts were mixed with the almonds and it is this combination that is used commercially today.

VARIATIONS

Granulated Praline

[PRALIN GRANULÉ]

In step 6, process for only a few seconds. Praline in this form can be sieved for uniformity and used for decorating pastries and desserts by sprinkling or pressing onto a buttercream pastry.

Praline Powder

[PRALIN EN POUDRE]

In step 6, process for several seconds beyond the granulated praline stage. Praline powder can be used in baking cakes and cookies by using it in place of a portion of the flour, for example, half flour and half praline powder.

COFFEE SYRUP

[SIROP DE CAFÉ]

IF YOU FIND the Coffee Essence (below) too bitter as a flavoring, make this coffee syrup and use it instead. **MAKES ½ CUP**

Coffee Essence (below)
Sugar or Heavy Sugar Syrup (facing page), to taste

Mix the coffee essence with sugar or heavy sugar syrup to taste. If you sweeten the coffee essence with granulated sugar, add it while the coffee essence is still hot.

VARIATION

QUICK COFFEE SYRUP

[SIROP DE CAFÉ RAPIDE]

Dissolve one part instant coffee granules and one part sugar in one part boiling water.

COFFEE ESSENCE

[ESSENCE DE CAFÉ]

COFFEE ESSENCE is a concentrated, strongly brewed coffee for flavoring desserts. It can be stored in a small bottle and used like vanilla extract to flavor ice cream, pastry cream, soufflés, candies, cookies, cakes, sauces, and milk shakes. It is used in concentrated form, as are other flavoring extracts, to not upset recipes by adding excess liquid. You may need to add more sugar to some of your recipes, since the essence is unsweetened. If you find that you always add sugar when using it, make a Coffee Syrup (above).

The best way to get full coffee flavor out of coffee grounds without extracting bitter oils is to use as little liquid as possible. The only good way to brew a lot of coffee grounds with a small amount of liquid is to force it through the coffee grounds under pressure—like espresso. To get around the problem, this two-part brewing method uses a small amount of liquid to brew a small amount of coffee. Then the same liquid is used to brew the second small amount of coffee. **MAKES ½ CUP**

1 cup water
1 cup ground coffee (see Note)

1. In a small saucepan, bring the water to a boil.

Stir half the coffee into it. Allow to infuse for 10 to 15 minutes. Strain the mixture through a coffee filter.

2. Place the remaining ground coffee in another filter. Bring the strained coffee to a boil and pour it over the ground coffee.

3. Store in the refrigerator in a small jar or bottle and keep tightly closed.

NOTE: Use your favorite coffee to make the essence. I prefer dark roasted French-, Italian-, or Viennese-style coffees, and often use a decaffeinated variety. Once on hand, you will find many uses for this wonderful flavoring. It is easy to double or triple the recipe, if necessary.

VARIATION

QUICK COFFEE ESSENCE

[ESSENCE DE CAFÉ RAPIDE]

I make this quick essence as I need it. Dissolve two parts instant coffee granules in one part boiling water.

SUGAR SYRUP

[SIROP DE SUCRE]

THE CLASSIC FRENCH sugar syrup is what we know as a "simple syrup." It is used to sweeten drinks, poach fruit, moisten cakes, and make sorbets. I find this syrup, which is made with equal parts of sugar and water, too sweet for just about everything except lemonade. When making sorbets I find it too thin. For this reason I make an extremely light syrup to use generally, and a very heavy one for a few special uses, such as the making of sorbets and flavoring syrups.

The proportions for the two syrups are given in the following recipe, enabling you to make whichever one suits your purpose. I usually make double the quantity shown, keeping any leftover covered in the refrigerator. It will keep for months, and you will find many uses for it if you have it on hand.

MAKES 1 CUP LIGHT SYRUP

1 cup water
¼ cup sugar

MAKES 2 CUPS HEAVY SYRUP

1 cup water
2 cups sugar

1. In a saucepan, bring the water and sugar to a boil over medium-high heat. Boil for 30 to 45 seconds until the syrup is perfectly clear. Stir to make sure all the sugar has dissolved, and remove from the heat.

2. Allow the syrup to cool and pour it into a glass or plastic container. Store in the refrigerator.

APPENDIX A

THE METRIC SYSTEM IN COOKING AND PASTRY MAKING

Cooking is more an art than a science, and as such gives the individual a considerable amount of freedom. Pastry making, on the other hand, is a science and requires precision and accuracy for consistently successful results.

For years, Europeans have had the advantage of the metric system in the kitchen. When correctly used, this system of weights and measurements not only preserves the freedom inherent in the "art" of cooking, but also ensures accuracy in the "science" of pastry making. The key advantage of the metric system lies in the principle of weighing solids and measuring the volume of liquids, as opposed to our system of measuring the volume of both.

Ideally, recipes should list ingredients as we find them or buy them at the market—e.g., 1 eggplant, 1 pound (500g), diced. This describes the size and weight of the eggplant to buy and what to do with it once you get it home. Many American recipes list ingredients by volume measurement—e.g., 3 cups diced eggplant; ½ cup chopped onion; 6 cups sliced apple; a slightly rounded cup of grated cheese. This is impractical.

A "slightly rounded" cup of grated cheese always puzzled me until one day when I was writing a recipe for a cheese sauce. In making the sauce, I took a piece of cheese (100g) out of my refrigerator, cut it into a few pieces, and melted it in the liquid in my saucepan.

Simple enough. But, in writing the recipe for a nonscale-using audience, I found that I had to describe the amount of cheese in cups. I grated the same weight of cheese and then sprinkled it into a cup. Finding it was slightly more than 1 cup, I described it as a slightly rounded cup of grated cheese. I could have easily pressed it gently and then called it a "lightly packed" cup of grated cheese. In both cases, the grating and measuring are time-consuming procedures. They were not needed when I made my sauce. They were needed only because the average reader doesn't have a small, inexpensive kitchen scale (see "Buying a Scale," facing page).

Although the scale is merely helpful in making most cooking easier, in the science of pastry making it is *indispensable*. Most problems in baking come from the inaccurate measurement of flour.

Back in the '30s, when the first Betty Crocker cookbook was written, readers were told to sift flour onto a piece of wax paper and then spoon it into their liquid measuring cups. (Dry measuring cups had not come onto the market yet.) Since the book was so popular, this form of measuring flour became the norm until Julia Child appeared on the scene. In her first book, she measured flour by sifting it directly into a dry measuring cup and leveling it off. In her subsequent books, her flour has been measured by dipping the cups into the flour and leveling them off.

How do *you* measure flour? How do your friends, who give you recipes, measure their flour? And, most important, how do the authors of your cookbooks measure flour?

To illustrate the problem, let me show you

the different results you can get depending on the measuring method used.

METHOD A

1 cup (sifted and spooned into a liquid measuring cup) = 130g

METHOD B

1 cup (sifted into a dry measure and leveled) = 105g

METHOD C

1 cup (dipped with a dry measure and leveled) = 140g

If the author of a book measures with Method B and you use Method C, you have a failure. If you use Method A and the author Method C, your results are different. But if you both use a scale, you can have the same results.

Why, then, don't we weigh? Because most of us don't have scales in our kitchens. And why don't we have scales? Because most writers and publishers don't want to use both weight and volume measurements in their recipes.

If recipes had weights, we would have scales. It is as simple as that!

BUYING A SCALE

There are a variety of gram/ounce kitchen scales available in stores and online today. A scale must be easily readable to be useful. Perhaps the best scales are the digital ones.

Look for one that can read in 1- to 5-gram increments and will weigh up to at least 5 pounds. Such scales are excellent for weighing flour, eggs, sugar, butter, nuts, cheese, etc. When it comes to weighing larger items like meat, fruit, and vegetables in quantity, use the scales at the market.

With a scale in the kitchen, we can use recipes from around the world, as well as endless variations of them. Without a scale, however, we are limited to those recipes that conveniently fit into cups. Once in the kitchen, the scale and the metric system will become so useful that you will wonder how you ever got along without them.

APPENDIX B

HIGH-ALTITUDE COOKING

I taught classes in Denver, the "mile-high city," for many years. A number of my students lived in the mountains near Denver at considerably higher altitudes. Although all the recipes in the book have been tested at sea level, they have also been successfully prepared at altitudes of one mile or more.

Certain things happen at high altitudes that necessitate some changes in sea-level recipes. Understanding the effects of high altitudes will help you prepare these recipes successfully at whatever altitude you may happen to be.

Atmospheric pressure decreases at high altitudes; consequently, water boils at a lower temperature, and it evaporates more quickly. As a result, you will find that ingredients cooked in boiling water will take longer to cook. Normally I will tell you how to judge when something is properly cooked, and you will look for those signs rather than using the cooking times.

Since the moisture evaporates more rapidly, you may find that your sauces are too thick at the end of the cooking time. To remedy this, add a little more water to thin the sauce to the desired consistency. When a recipe calls for a tight-fitting lid, its purpose is to retain moisture in the cooking utensil. At high altitudes, this is more important than at sea level.

While boiling usually takes longer at high altitudes, baking and some roasting take less time. If a pastry recipe calls for baking 25 to 30 minutes, you should check for doneness at 20 minutes.

Similarly, because of the dryness generally found at high altitudes, recipes for tart dough (*pâte brisée*), noodle dough (*pâtes fraîches*), and similar recipes will require small amounts of additional water or moisture, since the flour is much drier at high altitudes than at sea level.

The rising time for yeast doughs is decreased at high altitudes. Because there is less atmospheric pressure, expansion is more rapid. For a similar reason, the baking time of cakes and bread is usually shortened by 5 to 10 minutes.

The proper rising of a génoise at high altitudes can be guaranteed by reducing the butter called for in the recipe by half. Here's why this works: At high altitudes, the air bubbles in a cake expand more and can't support the weight of the butter, causing the cake to collapse. Reducing the amount of butter solves the problem. (Some chefs increase that amount of flour to keep the air from expanding so much, but this produces a heavier cake.)

Books on high-altitude cooking often instruct the reader to increase the oven temperature when baking or roasting. Since the French use considerably higher temperature in their ovens than Americans do, I have not found it necessary to alter the temperature of recipes when cooking at high altitudes.

CONVERSION TABLES

LIQUID CONVERSIONS

U.S.	IMPERIAL	METRIC
2 tbs	1 fl oz	30 ml
3 tbs	1½ fl oz	45 ml
¼ cup	2 fl oz	60 ml
⅓ cup	2½ fl oz	75 ml
⅓ cup + 1 tbs.	3 fl oz	90 ml
⅓ cup + 2 tbs.	3½ fl oz	100 ml
½ cup	4 fl oz	125 ml
⅔ cup	5 fl oz	150 ml
¾ cup	6 fl oz	175 ml
¾ cup + 2 tbs	7 fl oz	200 ml
1 cup	8 fl oz	250 ml
1 cup + 2 tbs	9 fl oz	275 ml
1¼ cups	10 fl oz	300 ml
1⅓ cups	11 fl oz	325 ml
1½ cups	12 fl oz	350 ml
1⅔ cups	13 fl oz	375 ml
1¾ cups	14 fl oz	400 ml
1¾ cups + 2 tbs	15 fl oz	450 ml
2 cups (1 pint)	16 fl oz	500 ml
2½ cups	20 fl oz (1 pint)	600 ml
3¾ cups	1½ pints	900 ml
4 cups	1¾ pints	1 liter

WEIGHT CONVERSIONS

US/UK	METRIC	US/UK	METRIC
½ oz	15 g	7 oz	200 g
1 oz	30 g	8 oz	250 g
1½ oz	45 g	9 oz	275 g
2 oz	60 g	10 oz	300 g
2½ oz	75 g	11 oz	325 g
3 oz	90 g	12 oz	350 g
3½ oz	100 g	13 oz	375 g
4 oz	125 g	14 oz	400 g
5 oz	150 g	15 oz	450 g
6 oz	175 g	1 lb	500 g

OVEN TEMPERATURES

FAHRENHEIT	GAS MARK	CELSIUS
250	½	120
275	1	140
300	2	150
325	3	160
350	4	180
375	5	190
400	6	200
425	7	220
450	8	230
475	9	240
500	10	260

NOTE: Reduce the temperature by 20°C (68°F) for fan-assisted ovens.

APPROXIMATE EQUIVALENTS

1 stick butter = 8 tbs = 4 oz = ½ cup = 115 g

1 cup all-purpose presifted flour = 4.7 oz

1 cup granulated sugar = 8 oz = 220 g

1 cup (firmly packed) brown sugar = 6 oz = 220g to 230 g

1 cup confectioners' sugar = 4½ oz = 115 g

1 cup honey or syrup = 12 oz

1 cup grated cheese = 4 oz

1 cup dried beans = 6 oz

1 large egg = about 2 oz or about 3 tbs

1 egg yolk = about 1 tbs

1 egg white = about 2 tbs

Please note that all conversions are approximate but close enough to be useful when converting from one system to another.

INDEX

A

B

C

D

J

K

L

M

N

O

P

Q

R

S

T

V

W

Z